Feminism and the Politics of Childhood

'This ground-breaking work straddles the divide between theory, practice, and activism. By reflecting on the mother-child relationship and analyzing care work in capitalist and patriarchal societies, this book provides a powerful counter-narrative to the pervasive individualistic social ontology that permeates Western academia. The authors' approaches are sensitive to the legacy of colonialism and the divides between feminism/s. The ideas and problems explored in this book are both inspiring and provocative.'

Rachelle Bascara,
Filipino Domestic Workers Association, UK

'Insightful, provocative and evocative, *Feminism and the Politics of Childhood: Friends or Foes?* challenges readers to grapple with the uneasy ideological and political tensions arising whenever those positioned as children and as women commingle. Rosen and Twamley, together with a strong array of contributors, invite active and sometimes messy engagement with varieties of feminisms and childhoods so as to enable public, connected and relational ways of knowing, telling and doing. A must-read for scholars and activists alike.'

Daniel Thomas Cook,
Rutgers University—Camden, USA

'This book is genuinely ground-breaking. It spans disciplinary boundaries to foreground fundamental issues of care, relationality and justice, forging fresh and exciting new directions in conceptual theory and political action. The dialogical style and collaborative ethos underpinning its production is original and uplifting, making it an expansive, ambitious and exhilarating read.'

Val Gillies,
University of Westminster, UK

'Traveling the fraught borderlands between women and children, women's studies and childhood studies, *Feminism and the Politics of Childhood: Friends or Foes?* asks an impossible question, and then casts prismatic light on all the corners of its impossibility – illuminating the temporalities and spatialities of the vexed and beautiful relational politics around love and labour, power and violence, care and antagonism, empire and liberation, social movements and interdependence. With contributions from a truly international group of authors in formats including photo essays, interviews, narratives and scholarly articles, these pages are filled with beautiful, provocative, important conversations about the fluid and differentiated relations among and between women and children, worldmaking in their effects and possibilities.'

Cindi Katz,
City University of New York Graduate Center, USA

'This provocative and stimulating publication comes not a day too soon. Exploring the profound complexities embedded in the woman and child relationship, it challenges the reductive instrumentalisation of women as simply a means of realising children's rights, and makes a powerful case for recognition that the perpetuation of a hierarchy of rights impedes justice and dignity for both women and children.'

Gerison Lansdown,
Chair, Child to Child, UK

'A smart, innovative, and provocative book, *Feminism and the Politics of Childhood* explores the confluences and disjunctures between feminist studies and childhood studies by disaggregating the "woman and children/womanandchild" dyad. It breaks new ground theoretically and methodologically by foregrounding the political economy of the unequal distribution of need and vulnerability in struggles for social justice for women and for children in diverse geopolitical landscapes.'

Chandra Talpade Mohanty,
Distinguished Professor of Women's and Gender Studies
Syracuse University, USA

'It is a rare book that can be said to inaugurate a new field of study. *Feminism and the Politics of Childhood: Friends or Foes?* raises and addresses issues so pressing that it is surprising they are not already at the heart of scholarship on feminisms and the politics of childhood. It draws on an impressive range of empirical, theoretical and practice material from different perspectives, disciplines and everyday practices. In doing so, it enables potentially antagonistic positions to be aired and refuses to reduce women and children to equivalences or to flatten differences between women and between children. Together, the chapters make a cutting-edge, critical intervention that readers will enjoy dipping into, but that will repay close and repeated reading.'

Ann Phoenix,
Thomas Coram Research Unit – UCL, UK
The Jane and Aatos Erkko Professor at the Helsinki University
Collegium for Advanced Studies from 2016–2018, Finland

'This stimulating book explores the relations between women and children in a contextualised way that is conceptually challenging and methodologically innovative. The product of a subtle and rich intellectual debate, the book fully embodies its driving inspiration: to foster a "generous encounter" of mutual learning between feminism and childhood studies, and between academia and the world of political and social activism.'

Ana Vergara Del Solar,
Universidad Diego Portales, Chile

Feminism and the Politics of Childhood

Friends or Foes?

Edited by Rachel Rosen and Katherine Twamley

First published in 2018 by
UCL Press
University College London
Gower Street
London WC1E 6BT

Available to download free: www.ucl.ac.uk/ucl-press

Text © Contributors, 2018
Images © Contributors and copyright holders named in the captions, 2018

The authors have asserted their rights under the Copyright, Designs and Patents Act 1988 to be identified as the authors of this work.

A CIP catalogue record for this book is available from The British Library.

This book is published under a Creative Commons 4.0 International license (CC BY 4.0). This license allows you to share, copy, distribute and transmit the work; to adapt the work and to make commercial use of the work providing attribution is made to the authors (but not in any way that suggests that they endorse you or your use of the work). Attribution should include the following information:

Rosen R. and Twamley K. (eds.). 2018. *Feminism and the Politics of Childhood: Friends or Foes?* London: UCL Press. DOI: https://doi.org/10.14324/111.9781787350632

Further details about Creative Commons licenses are available at http://creativecommons.org/licenses/

ISBN: 978–1–78735–064–9 (Hbk.)
ISBN: 978–1–78735–065–6 (Pbk.)
ISBN: 978–1–78735–063–2 (PDF)
ISBN: 978–1–78735–062–5 (epub)
ISBN: 978–1–78735–061–8 (mobi)
ISBN: 978–1–78735–060–1 (html)
DOI: https://doi.org/10.14324/111.9781787350632

For women and children everywhere,
in our struggles for social and economic justice.

Foreword

We are very pleased to welcome the publication of this book, which investigates an important (but neglected) field for study: how and how far feminism can take account of children and of childhood, and simultaneously what childhood studies and activism aimed at improving children's status can learn from feminism. The 18 papers result from a collaborative process of learning and refining. Starting with a two-day symposium at which some of the chapters in this volume were presented and discussed, the editors and contributors have reviewed the papers and so ensured thorough, valuable and nuanced discussions of the intersections between gender and generation. This book makes an important contribution to improving understandings of interrelations between women's studies and childhood studies, and their related social movements.

The re-emergence of feminism from the 1960s onwards was matched by a new interest in childhood viewed as a social phenomenon. Both movements have been concerned with social and political status and have fought for the recognition of rights. Furthermore, whilst women have sought to problematise social assumptions about their relations with children, childhood studies have sought to extract children, theoretically, from 'the family' and to site them as a social group with their own interests, and to attend to their specific interrelations with macro forces.[1]

Our contribution here is to provide a viewpoint drawing on the history of the women's movement and its work with and for children. This fascinating (but largely forgotten) social history predates, contributes to and in some ways challenges modern discussions of feminism and childhood.

A key theorist for this viewpoint was Charlotte Perkins Gilman. In her novel *Herland*, first published in 1915, three young men find themselves in a society where there are no men. This is a society run by wise, active, competent women, who plan an ordered community, self-sufficient in all necessary resources, and who do all the work needed to maintain it. Children are central to the design and workings of society.

After the first months of breastfeeding, they grow up with the best of professional care, in joyous, active groups, learning by doing, according to the latest educational ideas. Nuclear families have been abandoned, since they stunt and distort children's concept of themselves and waste female resources. During the course of the three men's stay in this utopian land, they are forced to learn important lessons about gender and generation (although only after considerable displays of misogyny).[2]

Some of these lessons were spelt out in Gilman's non-fictional *Concerning Children,* published 15 years before *Herland*, which argued forcefully for more thought to be given to the status of childhood. 'We should bear in mind in studying children', says Gilman, 'that we have before us a permanent class, larger than the adult population ...As members of society, we find they have received almost no attention. They are ...not recognised as belonging to society.'[3] Yet children were newly visible to adults, as they took their place in the public world of education.

Gilman was one of many women thinkers and reformers in Europe and the USA who, in the last decades of the nineteenth and early decades of the twentieth century, drew public attention to children as a social minority group. Most of these reformers were more concerned with changing laws and social policy to enhance children's status and rights than they were with theoretical debates about relations between feminism and childhood. They spearheaded many social policy reforms spanning the fields of health, welfare and education, and were members of a transnational network that campaigned for civil rights, especially for women, children and exploited industrial workers. Many of these women reformers were driven by radical visions, such as that outlined in *Herland*, of a society organised for adults and children alike around the core values of justice, equality and non-aggression. It is no coincidence that in Britain the advent of women's suffrage (granted on limited terms in 1918) and the establishment of the Save the Children Fund (1919) and of children's rights (1924) by one of these women reformers, Eglantyne Jebb, happened at about the same time. In the USA, recognition of children as a social group led to many reforms of the Progressive Era. A key organisation was the federal Children's Bureau, founded in 1912, and directed by the sociologist Julia Lathrop, one of the women reformers associated with the renowned Chicago settlement house, Hull-House. The Children's Bureau promoted the interests of children and designed welfare and health services for them.[4]

Both of us (independently) have been working recently on this social history,[5] drawing on the lives and work of some remarkable women pioneers. The papers in this book update our modern understandings of the ways in which advancing the interests of women and children may or may not be linked at practical and theoretical levels. They provide a range of explorations of the complex interrelations of women's and children's lives. Critical to this is the conceptualisation of gender and generational relations that arrived with the women's movement of the 1970s and 1980s. Since then, reconceptualisation of children as a social group who contribute to the socio-economic welfare of families and communities has highlighted how childhood may be understood as a relational status wherein the child, though a bearer of human rights, is also subordinate to the older generation. Many of the chapters in this volume point to new directions for exploring how intergenerational relations across the life-course persist, but are also challenged and modified, not least in the light of social, political and economic macro and micro forces.

At the same time we should stress, as the editors do, the overriding importance of achieving social justice for women and children everywhere, since they continue to share the fate of being more likely than men to live in a condition of poverty and economic dependence, to lack basic rights, and to experience the violence of men and nation-states. Scholarship such as this book offers on the complex intersections of feminism and childhood will help to address these urgent and unsolved issues of public policy.

Berry Mayall and Ann Oakley

NOTES

1 In this respect, it is interesting to note the rise of academic work focusing on children who live outside families and who are workers rather than objects of schooling. These points are developed in various chapters in this book.
2 Charlotte Perkins Gilman, *Herland* (New York: Pantheon Books, 1979, first published 1915).
3 Charlotte Perkins Gilman, *Concerning Children* (Walnut Creek, CA: AltaMira Press, 2003, first published 1900): 45.
4 Robyn Muncy, *Creating a Female Dominion in American Reform 1890-1935* (New York: Oxford University Press, 1991).
5 Ann Oakley, *Women, Peace and Welfare: A suppressed history of social reform, 1880-1920* (Bristol: Policy Press, 2018). Berry Mayall, *Visionary Women and Visible Children, England 1900-1920: Childhood and the Women's Movement* (London: Palgrave Macmillan, 2017).

Acknowledgements

This book would not have been possible without the engaged contributions of participants at our 2015 symposium *Feminism and the politics of childhood* and the dedication of volume authors to a sustained process of discussion and debate. Their commitment is what has allowed us to bring together such a stimulating and dialogic set of contributions.

We would like to thank Kristin Liabo, Berry Mayall and Ann Varley for their support in formulating the original project and hosting the 2015 symposium. A small grant from UCL Grand Challenges was also crucial to the symposium's success.

Our appreciation goes to Ann Oakley, Ann Phoenix, Virginia Caputo, Ohad Zehavi, Nara Milanich and Valeria Llobet for taking the time to read and comment on our draft introduction. All gaps and insufficiencies are our own.

Finally, our thanks go to the anonymous reviewers of our proposal and draft manuscript for their perceptive feedback, and Chris Penfold for his flexibility and guidance on all editorial matters.

Contents

List of figures	xviii
List of contributors	xx

Introduction
The woman–child question: A dialogue in the borderlands 1
    Rachel Rosen and Katherine Twamley

Section 1   Tense Encounters: Gender and Generation 21

1. A necessary struggle-in-relation? 23
   Erica Burman

2. Working-class women and children in Grassroots Women 40
   Merryn Edwards

3. When the rights of children prevail over the rights of their caretakers: A case study in the community homes of Bogotá, Colombia 50
   Susana Borda Carulla

4. Thinking through childhood and maternal studies: A feminist encounter 66
   Rachel Thomson and Lisa Baraitser

5. Notes on unlearning: Our feminisms, their childhoods 83
   Debolina Dutta and Oishik Sircar

6. Ideal women, invisible girls? The challenges of/to feminist solidarity in the Sahrawi Refugee Camps 91
   Elena Fiddian-Qasmiyeh

7. A 'sort of sanctuary' 109
   An interview with Liz Clegg by Rachel Rosen

Section 2   Life's Work 115

8. Love, labour and temporality: Reconceptualising social reproduction with women and children in the frame 117
   Rachel Rosen and Jan Newberry

9. Caring labour as the basis for movement building 134
   An interview with Selma James by Rachel Rosen

10. Care labour as temporal vulnerability in woman–child relations 139
    Gina Crivello and Patricia Espinoza-Revollo

11. International commercial surrogacy: Beyond feminist conundrums and the child as product 155
    Kristen E. Cheney

12. Stratified maternity in the barrio: Mothers and children in Argentine social programs 172
    Valeria Llobet and Nara Milanich

13. Decolonising childrearing and challenging the patriarchal nuclear family through Indigenous knowledges: An Opokaa'sin project 191
    Tanya Pace-Crosschild

Section 3   Political Projects and Movement Building 199

14. 'Too Young to Wed': Envisioning a 'generous encounter' between feminism and the politics of childhood 201
    Virginia Caputo

15. Feminists' strategic role in early childhood education 218
    Sri Marpinjun, Nindyah Rengganis, Yudha Andri Riyanto and Fransisca Yuni Dhamayanti

16. 'Gimme shelter'? Complicating responses to family violence 225
    Sevasti-Melissa Nolas, Erin Sanders-McDonagh and Lucy Neville

17. Becoming-woman, becoming-child: A joint political programme 241
    Ohad Zehavi

18. Feminist intuitions in Peru's Movement of Working Children 257
    A dialogue between Alejandro Cussianovich Villaran and Jessica Taft

Bibliography 261
Index 279

List of figures

Fig. 2.1	Mother's Day march and rally, 2004	41
Fig. 2.2	Women's and children's conference poster	42
Fig. 2.3	Grassroots Women press conference	43
Fig. 2.4	Labour Committee mural	44
Fig. 2.5	Postcard campaign for childcare	45
Fig. 2.6	Storytelling for children, Mother's Day rally, 2008	46
Fig. 2.7	Children at the microphone, Mothers' Day rally, 2008	46
Fig. 2.8	Laundry line art and resistance, Mothers' Day rally, 2008	48
Fig. 2.9	Laundry line art and resistance, Mothers' Day rally, 2008	48
Fig. 5.1	At the Amra Padatik rally, Kolkata, on International Sex Workers' Rights Day, 3 March, 2009	85
Fig. 5.2	Film poster artwork by Anirban Ghosh depicting the five protagonists	87
Fig. 5.3	Debolina with Gobinda at his residence, during the filming of WAFS	88
Fig. 10.1	Time allocation by girls and boys on different activities on a typical day (in minutes)	147
Fig. 13.1	Blackfoot girl playing by the Old Man River that borders the Blood Indian Reserve and city of Lethbridge (Photograph by her father, Bill Healy)	193
Fig. 13.2	Grandparents talking with their new grandson (Photograph by mother, Jessica Goodrider-Loewen)	194
Fig. 13.3	Blackfoot cousins playing (Photograph by mother, Chantilly Prairie Chicken)	195
Fig. 13.4	Father connecting with his son (Photograph by mother, Alison Crop Eared Wolf)	196
Fig. 15.1	Early Childhood Care and Development Resource Centre (Yogyakarta, Indonesia)	219

Fig. 15.2	Teachers reflect upon what it means to be men and women	221
Fig. 15.3	Girls and boys have equal access to learning materials	221
Fig. 15.4	Children learn to work together and respect others	222
Fig. 15.5	Mapping parents' and teachers' experiences of violence	223
Fig. 15.6	Involving fathers and mothers in an outing	223

List of contributors

Lisa Baraitser is Reader in Psychosocial Studies at Birkbeck, University of London, and a psychotherapist in independent practice. She is author of the award-winning monograph *Maternal Encounters: The Ethics of Interruption* (2009), which explores the intersections between maternal subjectivity and ethics, and a forthcoming monograph with Bloomsbury, *Enduring Time* (2017), on temporality, care and gender. She is co-founder, with Sigal Spigel, of the research network MaMSIE (Mapping Maternal Subjectivities, Identities and Ethics) and the journal *Studies in the Maternal* (Open Library of the Humanities).

Susana Borda Carulla holds a PhD in Ethnology from Université Paris Descartes (France) and presently works as an independent international consultant. As External Scientific Collaborator at the Centre for Children's Rights Studies of the University of Geneva, she has teaching and research responsibilities. Drawing mainly on social regulation theory and on the notion of translation of rights, her research explores the tensions inherent to the implementation of children's rights in the framework of a major public childcare programme in Colombia. She is the president and founder of SieNi, a Swiss-based NGO for educating Colombian children about water conservation.

Erica Burman is Professor of Education, Manchester Institute of Education (MIE), University of Manchester, and a United Kingdom Council of Psychotherapists-registered Group Analyst. She is well known as a critical developmental psychologist and methodologist specialising in innovative and activist qualitative research. She is author of *Deconstructing Developmental Psychology* (Routledge, 3rd edition, 2017), *Developments: Child, Image, Nation* (Routledge, 2008), and *Fanon, Education, Action: Child as Method* (Routledge, 2018). She currently leads the Knowledge, Power and Identity research strand at MIE. She is a past Chair of the Psychology of Women Section of the British Psychological Society, and in 2016 she was awarded an Honorary Lifetime Fellowship of the Society.

Virginia Caputo is an Associate Professor in the Department of Anthropology at Carleton University in Ottawa, Canada, where she also serves as Director of the Landon Pearson Centre for the Study of Childhood and Children's Rights and former Director of the Pauline Jewett Institute of Women's and Gender Studies. Virginia's expertise lies in studies of girlhoods, gendered childhoods and the changing contours of young people's globalised lives. Her recent publications appear in the *International Journal of Human Rights and Childhood*, a journal of global child research. She is managing editor of the *Canadian Journal of Children's Rights*.

Kristen E. Cheney is Senior Lecturer in Children and Youth Studies at the International Institute of Social Studies in The Hague, Netherlands. Her research examines the political economy of childhood, including how the global 'orphan industrial complex' – orphan tourism, childcare institutions, and intercountry adoption – affects child protection in developing countries. She is author of *Crying for Our Elders: African Orphanhood in the Age of HIV and AIDS* (The University of Chicago Press). She is also concerned with various aspects of sexual and reproductive health, including international commercial surrogacy. In 2014, she organised and hosted the International Forum on Intercountry Adoption and Global Surrogacy.

Liz Clegg is the founder of the Unofficial Women's and Children's Centre in Calais, France, where she spent 18 months as a volunteer working with displaced people living in the unofficial refugee camp. She currently lives in Birmingham, UK, and is involved in setting up a project with children and women migrants who continue their migration journeys to and in the UK. Meena (which means 'love' in Pashto) provides safe spaces, activities and education for migrants about achieving asylum and their rights in the UK, as well providing training for social workers and foster carers, offering insights into working with asylum-seeking children.

Gina Crivello has a PhD in Anthropology and is a Senior Research Officer with Young Lives based in the Department of International Development, University of Oxford. Her research explores the life trajectories of girls and boys who grow up in poverty, with a particular interest in the gender and generational dynamics of mobility and migration; early marital life and parenting; and the interaction between productive and reproductive work in transitions to adulthood. In Young Lives, she is PI on a comparative study of child marriage and parenthood, and leads a qualitative longitudinal study of childhood poverty in Ethiopia, India, Peru and Vietnam.

Alejandro Cussianovich Villaran is a Peruvian educator and Catholic priest. He teaches courses on Social Policy and Childhood and Educational Psychology at the Universidad Nacional Mayor de San Marcos. Since 1964 he has worked with the Juventud Obrera Cristiana and was involved in the formation of the Movimiento de Adolescentes y Niños Trabajadores Hijos de Obreros Cristianos (MANTHOC) in 1976. His writings include *Llamados a Ser Libres* (1974); "El Protagonismo como Interés Superior de Niño" (2000), A*prender la Condición Humana: Ensayo Sobre Pedagogía de la Ternura* (2007), and many other influential texts on childhood and children's work.

Fransisca Yuni Dhamayanti graduated with a BSc from Gadjah Mada University, Yogyakarta, Indonesia, and gained her Masters in Education from Yogyakarta State University, Indonesia, in 2014. An opportunity to volunteer as a senior high school teacher at Kolese Le Cocq D'Armandville, the Jesuit College in Nabire, Papua, Indonesia, opened her mind and heart to the importance of early childhood education. She joined the Early Childhood Care and Development Resource Centre (ECCD RC) in June 2010. Currently, she is the principal of Rumah Citta Labschool at ECCD RC, Yogyakarta.

Debolina Dutta is a doctoral researcher at the Institute for International Law and the Humanities, Melbourne Law School. She is currently putting together an illustrated book of stories called *The Rule of Laughter*, which looks at how sex workers in India use humour to challenge the criminalisation of their lives. She has previously worked as a sexual rights activist at the UN Human Rights Council as well as with local human rights organisations in India. She co-directed (with Oishik Sircar) *We Are Foot Soldiers*, a documentary film on the collectivisation of children of sex workers in Sonagachi, Kolkata, which received the third prize at the Jeevika: Asia Livelihood Documentary Festival (2012).

Merryn Edwards was active with Grassroots Women, an anti-imperialist women's group based in East Vancouver, Canada, from 2002 to 2010. She now lives with her partner and two young daughters in Edmonton, Canada, where she continues to be an active community organiser building grassroots, collective resistance in defence of women's rights and the rights of all. She has worked in the labour movement since 2007, first as a union organiser with the Justice for Janitors campaign and currently as a communications officer with the Alberta Union of Provincial Employees.

Patricia Espinoza-Revollo holds a DPhil in International Development and is a Quantitative Research Officer in Young Lives at the University of

Oxford. Her research agenda focuses on inequality, social stratification and mobility, emerging middle classes, and child and youth development with a focus on gender inequalities. She coordinates Young Lives panel survey design and implementation in four developing countries.

Elena Fiddian-Qasmiyeh is a Reader in Human Geography and Co-Director of the Migration Research Unit at UCL, where she is also the coordinator of the Refuge in a Moving World Research Network. Her research focuses on the intersections between gender, generation and religion in experiences of and responses to conflict-induced displacement and statelessness, with a focus on the Middle East and North Africa. Her recent publications include *The Ideal Refugees: Gender, Islam and the Sahrawi Politics of Survival* (Syracuse University Press, 2014), *The Oxford Handbook of Refugee and Forced Migration Studies* (co-editor, Oxford University Press, 2014), and *South-South Educational Migration, Humanitarianism and Development* (Routledge, 2015).

Selma James co-founded the International Wages for Housework Campaign in 1972, which demanded social and financial recognition for the work of reproducing the human race. The Global Women's Strike, which she now coordinates, grew out of this campaign. It is an active grassroots network of organisations which share the perspective 'Invest in caring not killing!' She is co-author of *The Power of Women and the Subversion of the Community* (with Mariarosa Dalla Costa) and the author of *Sex, Race and Class: The Perspective of Winning, a selection of writings 1952–2011*.

Valeria Llobet is Professor of Human Rights, Escuela de Humanidades, Universidad Nacional de San Martín, and Researcher at CONICET. Her research areas include childhood, gender, social policies and human rights. She received her PhD in Psychology from Universidad de Buenos Aires and has published in journals such as *Desarrollo Económico*, *Revista Latinoamericana de Ciencias Sociales*, *Niñez y Juventud*, *Fractal*, *Frontera Norte*, and *Revista de Psicología de la U de Chile*. Her most recent books are *Pensar la Infancia desde América Latina. Un estado de la cuestión* (CLACSO, 2014), *Infancias: políticas y saberes en Argentina y Brasil (siglos XIX y XX)* (Teseo, 2011), and *¿Fábricas de niños? Instituciones y políticas para la infancia en la era de los derechos* (Noveduc, 2010).

Sri Marpinjun has a BA in cultural anthropology and has been working in women and children's rights for 30 years. She was a co-founder of two Yogyakarta-based organisations dedicated to women and children in Indonesia: the Institute for Women and Children's Studies and Development (1991) and the Early Childhood Care and Development

Resource Centre (2002). From 2008–12, she was a co-chair of the qualitative methods learning group Una, an international network for researchers, practitioners and policy makers concerned with children and ethnic diversity. Currently, she is active in the Institute for Women's Empowerment, a regional organisation for feminist leadership in Asia.

Nara Milanich is Associate Professor of Latin American History, Barnard College, Columbia University. Her research areas include comparative history of family and kinship, childhood, reproduction, gender and law. Her book *Children of Fate: Childhood, Class, and the State in Chile, 1850–1930* (Duke University Press, 2009) received the Grace Abbott Prize from the Society of Childhood and Youth History. She is currently writing a global history of paternity testing, *The Birth of Uncertainty: Testing Paternity in the Twentieth Century* (Harvard University Press, 2018). She is also interested in refugee issues and has worked with Central American mothers incarcerated in immigrant detention centres on the US–Mexico border.

Lucy Neville is a Senior Lecturer in Criminology at Middlesex University. She is a feminist and activist, and one of the founding members of the FemGenSex network of feminist scholars interested in investigating areas around women, gender and sexuality. Her research interests relate to understanding women's engagement with pornography, sex and sex work; sex work policy in the UK and internationally; violence towards women; domestic violence; violent crime; and the impacts of austerity on responses to violent crime.

Jan Newberry is an anthropologist and the Co-Director of the Institute for Child and Youth Studies (I-CYS) at the University of Lethbridge, Canada. She has conducted ethnographic fieldwork in central Java, Indonesia since 1992. Her original work considered domestic labour in lower class urban communities. Her recent research examines the introduction of early childhood care and development (ECCD) programmes in Indonesia as a form of globalisation that challenges local meanings of childhood and childrearing. She is also director of Raising Spirit, a collaborative, transmedia project on ethnographic methods and childrearing values conducted along with Blackfoot people, young and old.

Sevasti-Melissa Nolas is a Senior Lecturer in Social Work at the University of Sussex. She has an interdisciplinary background in the social sciences. She works on three distinct but overlapping research areas: (1) the dynamics of participation in professional and community responses to social issues, (2) the intersections of activism, the life course and everyday life, and (3) methodological approaches for growing publics. She is currently the Principal Investigator of the ERC-funded comparative and longitudinal ethnographic Connectors Study, which explores the relationships between childhood and public life: https://connectorsstudy.wordpress.com.

Tanya Pace-Crosschild, Naatoyitspa'pawaakaaki (Holy Walks Across Woman), is a member of the Kainai Nation of the Blackfoot Confederacy. A long-standing advocate of Indigenous children and families, she is currently the Director for Opokaa'sin, an Indigenous child and family centre in Lethbridge, Alberta, Canada. Opokaa'sin, which means 'children' in Blackfoot, is a strength-based service agency that incorporates Indigenous approaches to programme service delivery. Tanya is currently working on the Raising Spirit research project, which examines Blackfoot childrearing values and practices.

Nindyah Rengganis is a graduate of the Psychology Faculty, Gadjah Mada University, Yogyakarta. Her passion for gender and children's voices started when she began working as a junior researcher for the Institute for Women's and Children's Studies and Development. She was an educator in the Warna-warni Education and Care Centre, which incorporated gender equity and multiculturalism into its programme, and a junior contributor to *Cultural Psychology of Coping with Disaster: The Case of an Earthquake in Java, Indonesia* (Springer). Since 2014, she has been Executive Director of the Early Childhood Care and Development Resource Centre in Yogyakarta.

Yudha Andri Riyanto is an educator at the Early Childhood Care and Development Resource Centre (ECCD RC), Yogyakarta, where he has been working since 2011. He is also a student in the Faculty of Psychology at Proklamasi 45 University, Yogyakarta. His interest in child development led him to become active in organising a discussion forum on inclusive and multicultural early childhood education for students at the university and a group discussion on inclusive education on Facebook.

Rachel Rosen is a Senior Lecturer in Childhood at the UCL Institute of Education. Her scholarship is situated at the intersection of materialist feminism and the sociology of childhood, and focuses on unequal childhoods; migration, social reproduction and care; and the commonalities and conflicts between women and children. Recently, she has been researching separated child migrants' experiences of care, and caring for others, as they navigate the complexities of the asylum–welfare nexus in the UK. She is co-author of *Negotiating Adult-Child Relationships in Early*

Childhood Research (Routledge, 2014) and co-editor of *Reimagining Childhood Studies* (forthcoming, Bloomsbury).

Erin Sanders-McDonagh is a Lecturer in Criminology at the University of Kent. She is a feminist public scholar with a commitment to radical and engaged pedagogic practices. Her research explores inequality in different forms, and she has worked with a range of marginalised groups in recent research projects. She has a strong commitment to working with scholars from across disciplinary boundaries and to moving research findings into the public arena.

Oishik Sircar is an assistant professor at the Jindal Global Law School, O.P. Jindal Global University, and doctoral scholar at the Institute for International Law and the Humanities, Melbourne Law School. Oishik is co-director (with Debolina Dutta) of the documentary film *We Are Foot Soldiers*, on the activism of children of sex workers in Kolkata's Sonagachi red light district. The film won the third prize at the Jeevika: Asia Livelihood Documentary Festival in 2012. Oishik's writings have appeared in *Unbound*, *No Foundations*, *Economic & Political Weekly*, *Childhood*, *Himal Southasian*, *Feminist Studies* and the *Osgoode Hall Law Journal*. Oishik has recently co-edited *New Intimacies, Old Desires: Law, Culture and Queer Politics in Neoliberal Times* (Zubaan, 2017).

Jessica Taft is Associate Professor of Latin American and Latino Studies at the University of California – Santa Cruz. Her research focuses on the political lives of children and youth in North and South America. She is the author of *Rebel Girls: Youth Activism and Social Change Across the Americas* (NYU Press, 2011) as well as numerous articles on young people's politics, including discussions of girls' organisations and the public sphere, youth activists' critiques of youth councils, and peer-driven political socialisation processes. She is currently working on a book manuscript on the dynamics of age and intergenerational collaboration in the Peruvian working children's movements.

Rachel Thomson is Professor of Childhood & Youth Studies at the University of Sussex and a director of the Sussex Humanities Lab. She is a sociologist with interests in gender, the life course and the interplay of personal and historical change. Her published works include *Inventing Adulthoods: A Biographical Approach to Youth Transitions* (Sage, 2007), *Unfolding Lives: Youth, Gender, Change* (Policy Press, 2009), *Researching Social Change: Qualitative Approaches* (Sage, 2009), and *Making Modern Mothers* (Policy Press, 2011). She is currently finalising a new book with Liam Berriman and Sara Bragg titled *Researching Everyday*

Childhoods: Time, Technology and Documentation, which will be published in 2018 by Bloomsbury.

Katherine Twamley is a Leverhulme Trust Early Career Fellow in the Department of Social Sciences, UCL. She is a sociologist specialising in gender, love and intimacy, feminist practice, and family, with a particular interest in India and the Indian diaspora. In addition to co-editing this volume she is author of *Love, Marriage and Intimacy Among Gujarati Indians: A Suitable Match* (Palgrave Macmillan, 2014) and co-editor of *Sociologists' Tales: Contemporary Narratives on Sociological Thought and Practice* (Policy Press, 2015).

Ohad Zehavi received his PhD from the School of Philosophy at Tel Aviv University in 2013. In his dissertation he studied the role of child figures in Gilles Deleuze's philosophy. He has an MFA in Fine Art Media from the Slade School of Fine Art, UCL (2004). He teaches at Tel Aviv University, at Bezalel Academy of Arts and Design and at Shenkar College of Engineering, Design and Art. He lectures and writes on various issues in visual culture, on Deleuze and Guattari's 'schizoanalysis' and on the philosophy of children.

Introduction
The woman–child question
A dialogue in the borderlands

Rachel Rosen and Katherine Twamley

Do children and women inevitably have shared concerns and experiences of oppression that are best addressed together? Or are there fundamental conflicts between children's interests and women's interests?

As Erica Burman points out,[1] formulations of relations between women and children typically fall into one of two un-nuanced polarities: 'womenandchildren', to use Cynthia Enloe's evocative term,[2] or 'women versus children', the 'foes' to whom the title of this book refers. At the womenandchildren pole, we have ubiquitous portrayals of woman and child, which appear across geographical and historical periods: a child cradled in a woman's arms, an infant swaddled to her chest or back, or a woman and child walking hand in hand. Such representations reflect the durable binding of the lives and fates of women and of children in public imaginaries. This is also made apparent by considering another dyad – men and children – a couplet which is no less possible, but which tends to evoke very different imaginaries. While the lives of women and children are deeply entangled – because children are, to varying degrees, positioned as primarily dependent and women take the greatest responsibility for their care – the bundling of women and children has been comprehensively critiqued. Feminist and childhood academics and activists point out that the imposition of seemingly coherent and given categories of 'woman' and 'child' are grounded in, and ground, asymmetrical power relations. They have also questioned, for example, constructions of the family as a singular unit and 'private' institution, highlighting the ways this obscures gendered and generational inequities both within and beyond families.[3]

However, in challenging the womenandchildren elision, feminists and those concerned with challenging the oppression of children have often ended up in antagonistic oppositions. For instance, the growing importance attributed to the first 1,000 days of a child's life has increased the global focus on early education, which is viewed as fundamental to children's present and future well-being. However, feminists have pointed out that this provision often relies on voluntary or low-paid women's labour.[4] Efforts to achieve publicly funded childcare are likewise critiqued, but by those primarily concerned with children's struggles. They argue that these efforts largely reduce children to objects of care, with the provision of care assumed both empirically and normatively to be the purview of adults, and ignore the way in which children's concerns within and about childcare may conflict with women's.[5]

Despite the far-reaching social, political and intellectual consequences of the ways in which we conceptualise connections between women and children, they have received only scant attention in academic, activist and policy fields.[6] This is not simply a benign omission: it is a reflection of the difficult and, at times, fiercely territorial relationship between feminists and those concerned with children's struggles.[7] In some cases, such conflicts have manifested in the outright rejection of efforts to bring together concerns with women's lives and children's lives. Stepping into this difficult terrain, *Feminism and the Politics of Childhood: Friends or Foes?* aims to stimulate, and serve as a space of, dialogue and debate about perceived commonalities and conflicts between women and children and, more broadly, intersections and antagonisms between various forms of feminism and the politics of childhood. Bringing together 18 chapters from academics and activists, this edited collection offers unique responses to the following questions: How might a conversation between feminism(s) and the politics of childhood speak to the everyday and conceptual affinities and tensions between women and children? What are the consequences of theorising women and children together? How do we strive for social and economic justice for children and women, particularly in contexts where their interests may (appear to) be in conflict?

Staging a dialogue

Our aim in bringing this book together has been to stage a dialogue that might provide alternative approaches to the recurring dead ends of elision or antagonism, offering new responses and possibilities for action along the way. In doing so, we sought to foster three 'boundary crossings' which we felt were most relevant and likely to produce new insights: between the fields of childhood and women's studies;[8] across academic scholarship and the 'publics', notably social/political movements; and across varying global contexts. The analogy of 'generous encounters' from Sara Ahmed,[9] which Virginia Caputo evokes in Chapter 14, encapsulates our vision. In generous encounter, Ahmed attempts to move beyond dialogue premised on finding similarities or equivalences in experience and position. She accepts that there may be fundamentally incommensurate perspectives, such as between some forms of feminism and the politics of childhood. But she does not dismiss the possibility of learning through their encounter, and even because of their contradictions. In this way, one perspective does not need to triumph over the other: instead such encounters can be understood as dialogues across varying perspectives. Below, we go through the three boundary crossings that, with 'generous encounters' in mind, we conceive of as dialogues in the borderlands.[10]

Childhood studies and women's studies

The first of these borderlands lies between childhood studies and women's studies, which through their synchronicities and at times fractious relations we felt could together provide a fruitful space of encounter. There are many parallels between the social position of children and women, who have been similarly constituted and subjected to treatment as vulnerable victims, or valorised as angelic innocents of home and hearth, and the subject through which hopes for national development flow. Erica Burman, however, cautions against reducing these to equivalences in the positioning of women and children.[11] She points out that while there are linkages, generation cannot simply be superimposed on gender, not least because this could conceal very real antagonisms and power relations between women and children. To do so would also negate advances in feminist scholarship which point to the intersectional character of identities and social relations where gender and generation, as well as class and 'race', operate simultaneously.

Nonetheless, we contend that there are synergies between these two fields of studies indicating that a productive dialogue is possible. For instance, understandings of the position of children as a social group and efforts to address their subordination, which are central to childhood studies, owe a great deal to feminist political and intellectual efforts. Feminism has opened the 'private' sphere, reproductive labour and intimate relations to extended consideration and critique.[12] More recently, feminist perspectives have been mobilised in the study of children and childhood, to highlight the limits of liberal individualism with its adherence to competence, independence and rationality, as well as the importance of intersectional perspectives for understanding the trope of the child and gendered subjectivities of girlhood and boyhood.[13] Insights into the processes whereby gender is 'made' and 'done' have inspired similar theorisations in childhood studies around the notion of generation.[14]

Arguably, less consideration has been given to the ways that feminists can learn from childhood studies. Despite astute critiques of essentialist treatments of sex and gender, which have made significant inroads in shifting academic scholarship and common-sense ideas, much feminist scholarship operates with a surprisingly unexamined view of children and childhood. 'The child' is often taken-for-granted, understood through externally ascribed attributes such as universalist notions of ages and stages as biological unfolding. Yet, childhood studies' relentless questioning of 'the child' demonstrates the very situated ways in which certain humans are made into children and others into adults. As a result, childhood theorists have commented that feminism is an 'adultist' enterprise, rendering children largely absent from the social world and sociological consideration except as objects of socialisation.[15] Combined with a growing body of empirical studies on children's lives in contexts where middle-class Euro-American, or 'Minority World', idealisations of childhood have not gained hegemonic status, childhood studies scholarship prompts reconsideration of work, care and political activism in the lives of children and adults, and the ways these intersect.

Despite our description of these two academic fields as two separate entities, they are not as bifurcated as the above description suggests. Many would consider themselves to be committed to both feminism and childism (to borrow from John Wall),[16] including those who have contributed to this book. What is notable, however, is that despite germinal texts which identified commonalities and conflicts between those positioned as women and children,[17] little attention has been given in either women's studies or childhood studies to the ways that these relations are understood, (re)produced and conceptualised.[18] This is an absence, and a challenge, taken up in this volume.

Academia and 'publics'

In the borderland encounter between academia and 'publics'[19] we have been inspired by Michael Burawoy's proposal for a 'public sociology'. Posing the questions of 'knowledge for whom' and 'knowledge for what',

Burawoy argues for the importance of scholarship that extends beyond the academy to 'strike up a dialogic relation between sociologist and public in which the agenda of each is brought to the table, in which each adjusts to the other'.[20] There is a 'double conversation' involved here, as 'the public' is not a monolithic entity but is internally divided, involved in intense debates across multiple groupings which shape understandings of social issues and responses, at the same time as being brought into conversation with academics.[21] Nor do most academics stay confined within the 'hallowed halls' of the ivory tower. We can learn from feminism about the inadequacy of such sharp dichotomies, and resist the decoupling of academic lives and 'private' lives where scholars live, love and engage in social and political struggles as members of 'the publics'.

Over the course of this project we have aimed to bring together various ways of knowing, including experiential, empirical and philosophical knowledge, as well as knowledge forged through political struggle. We have solicited contributions from those who identify with, and write from, varying academic and advocacy positions. Further, several contributors are explicit about their own engagement in remaking the borders between academics and publics. For instance, Debolina Dutta and Oishik Sircar, in analysing their participatory research and film production with Amra Padatik – a collective of children of sex workers in Kolkata – reflect on constraints surrounding such encounters in fields of extreme inequality. They stress the importance of 'unlearning to make way for learning anew' (Chapter 5). For them, working the borderlands between academia and publics included challenging the concentration of research outputs in expensive, English-language academic journals, with little benefit for research participants.

Some of the contributions to this book were first brought together via an international symposium involving thirty academics and activists held in November 2015.[22] The format of the symposium, where pre-circulated papers were discussed in one large circle of participants, was chosen to encourage dialogue and learning between and across authors and participants.[23] This ethic has continued in the process of creating the book, wherein all contributors were invited to read, comment and draw on other chapters as they developed their own. Our aim was to involve both academics and activists in a collaborative learning process, going beyond the standard process of formal review.[24]

Such co-construction as a way to challenge hierarchies of knowledge production is central to Burawoy's public sociology. He also wishes to reclaim approaches which do not just describe or 'conserve' the status quo, but which take as their primary purpose the generation of world-changing knowledge.[25] His passionate calls have importance in the context of the questions animating this book, given their social and political consequences for the lives of marginalised social groups. The volume is organised so that the varied contributions are given analogous status, in a manner that lends credence to diverse forms of knowledge production. This leads to a complexity across the volume as authors mobilise different forms of evidence and rhetoric, some more compelling in their ethical or emotive polemic and others in their systematic and logical construction. We specifically invited contributors to experiment with the format of their contributions, to engage with the affective and multi-sensorial registers of embodied social being and to recognise 'the value of other ways of telling' beyond the traditional academic text.[26] We also asked authors to take into consideration a varied readership, aiming to maximise the accessibility of the book both through publishing with an open access press and by avoiding jargon-laden language. Contributors took up the challenge in fascinating ways, including through photo essays and conversations staged across academic disciplines and academic-publics. No doubt reflecting the conventions and pressures under which academics work, it was our activist contributors who were the more innovative, while some contributors writing from academic perspectives (including ourselves!) struggled to write in more accessible ways. Nonetheless, it is our hope that by bringing concepts and research data alive through multiple modes, the book will make visible the vitality of the questions we are asking, thereby provoking ongoing public scrutiny and critical reflection on woman–child relations.

It is worth noting that despite these goals, stratified relations of knowledge production are evident in the generational status of contributors. Although 'children' are interlocutors in many of the chapters, we did not succeed in directly facilitating children's responses to the volume's questions. Even those children's movements which have contributed are represented here by adults. As much as we have tried to work from a perspective of generational solidarity in curating this volume, we nevertheless recognise this as a significant absence.

Global contexts

A final way in which this collection operates in the borderlands relates to discussion across diverse global contexts. As Gurminder Bhambra points out, much social theory is impoverished because it is premised on Eurocentric assumptions.[27] We have been mindful of her call for 'connected sociologies', a reconstitution of the very ground on which conceptualisations of the social world are built. Such an approach allows for social theory to be opened up to new ways of thinking and understanding, through epistemic contributions that are cognisant of histories of dispossession, enslavement, appropriation and lives in neo/post-colonies. For instance, in Chapter 13, Tanya Pace-Crosschild highlights the impact of Canadian settler colonialism on Indigenous communities. She points to the need to decolonise approaches to childrearing, which include the violent and punitive imposition of patriarchal woman–child relations.

Contributions to this volume cover research, advocacy and movement-building in five world continents, although we would have liked to include more from contributors based in the 'Majority World'. This is a prescient reminder that even politically committed projects operate on a playing field constrained by neo-colonial relations of knowledge production. As Burman's probing questions – 'which children?' and 'which women?' – suggest, neither women nor children are homogenous groups,[28] and we must struggle against a flattening of in-group differences as we strive for more rigorous conceptualisations and potent political projects.

In this regard, we are inspired by Cindi Katz's notion of 'countertopography', which provides an approach to understanding the transnational connections which ground people's localised and everyday experiences. Katz argues that:

> Not all places affected by capital's global ambition are affected the same way, and not all issues matter equally everywhere. By constructing precise topographies at a range of scales from the local to the regional and beyond, we can analyze a particular issue – say deskilling – in and across place, mapping sites connected along this contour line.[29]

This is a 'noninnocent' topography which attends to the centrality of mapping and border-making. Such 'countertopographical' knowledge helps to illuminate the processes whereby certain practices, social positions or social relations come to be made, as well as the gaps in available conceptualisations. Such insights are made apparent in Valeria Llobet and Nara Milanich's treatment of Conditional Cash Transfers (CCTs) in Argentina (Chapter 12). By carefully attending to the situated ways in which CCTs are enacted and lived, they point out that there are more affinities between women and children than between variously positioned women in the Argentine barrio. This is in contradistinction to dominant feminist readings that argue CCTs are fundamentally productive of antagonisms between women's rights and children's rights.

For this reason, as well as their potential for highlighting the fissures in seemingly intractable unequal social relations and the fragility of capital accumulation, countertopographies are not only epistemologically but also politically generative. As a number of the chapters in this collection make clear, without understandings of the political economy of (neo)colonialism, efforts at solidarity with women, children or women and children will likely involve the imposition of normative ideas or an imperialist politics of pity. For example, in her detailed examination of life in the Sahrawi refugee camp in Algeria, Elena Fiddian-Qasmiyeh shows how benefactors' idealisations of the empowered feminist refugee camp recipient, render solidarity highly conditional and produce serious contradictions on the ground between women and girls.

The process of collectively curating this book has also generated a countertopography of sorts. In reading across the contributions, we can see how the issue of 'woman–child' relations shift across space, place, political orientation and varying class, 'race' and gendered positions. To offer one such example, Sri Marpinjun, Nindyah Rengganis, Yudha Andri Riyanto and Fransisca Yuni Dhamayanti draw on their activism in Indonesia to make the case that, in a context of deeply embedded patriarchal norms, providing anti-sexist early childhood education has been a crucial feminist practice amongst their largely university-educated members. In contrast, in the Colombian context that Susana Borda Carulla describes, impoverished women's provision of childcare and early education, albeit not explicitly anti-sexist, is naturalised by the state through maternalist discourses and effectively produces the conditions whereby women's rights are violated. That is, it is not the practice itself (i.e. early childhood care and education) that is either the problem or the panacea, but the conditions of its emergence and operation, as well as how it relates to pre-existing inequities.

In sum, then, by engaging in generous encounters in these borderlands, this collection provides a rich account of multiple and dynamic relations between women and children. This dialogue calls up taken-for-granted assumptions, foci and absences for scrutiny and provides explanations for these by bringing varying conceptual formulations and empirical realities into conversation. Together, the texts highlight alternatives to the womenandchildren and women versus children quagmire, and offer insights into the conditions necessary for realising social and economic justice for children *and* women. The 18 chapters from academics and activists have been collated under three headings that signpost the main topics the authors deal with in responding to our questions. In the first section, 'Tense Encounters: Gender and Generation', authors address the often simultaneously fraught and reciprocal relations between and across women and children. These authors tackle most explicitly the question posed in our subtitle 'Friends or foes?', discussing how, when and why animosities or complicities are created and enacted. In the second section, 'Life's Work', authors consider the kinds of labouring that take place between and by women and children, unpacking how conceptions of these labour relations can extend and/or rupture the binding of women and children's interests. In the final section, 'Political projects and movement building', authors focus on assessing the challenges and suggesting alternative paths to advance equality for women *and* children. Together, the generous encounters between these contributors bring deep insights into the questions which began this book, and it is to these cross-cutting themes that we now turn.

Beyond 'friends or foes?'

The provocative subtitle of our volume, which asks whether feminism and the politics of childhood are 'friends or foes', generated discomfort for contributors, given its binary formulation. In their contributions, most authors push back against the idea that either 'friends' or 'foes' accurately describes the complex relationship between the two, while recognising the way it 'topicalises'[30] the tensions. Posing the question in this way did, however, stimulate debate and various proposals for other ways to think with feminism(s) *and* the politics of childhood when considering the everyday and conceptual affinities and tensions between women and children. Here we highlight three key themes that emerge across the volume: the necessity of a relational lens; shifting vantage points for rethinking woman–child relations; and the need for new concept-metaphors to support such efforts.

A relational lens

A common theme across contributions was the rejection of (neo)liberal individualism and the autonomous, independent subject as ways for thinking about either women or children. Many of the authors issue calls for 'relationality' as an alternative. Broadly speaking, relationality can be understood as calling attention to the profoundly interactive and transactional character of human life. Relationality is not mobilised in the chapters as an evaluative term – as in good relationships or bad, or relations as a solution to antagonisms. Instead, it is present in the chapters as a way to grapple with the book's problematic by dismantling artificially imposed boundaries between women and children, and to engage in the complexity of social relationships and relations which can be simultaneously ones of love, reciprocity, oppression, struggle and exploitation.

As Sasha Roseneil and Kaisa Ketokivi point out, an emphasis on relationality has 'found widespread favour' as part of the 'relational turn' within the social sciences.[31] However, it is under-theorised and is mobilised in varying ways which can lead to confusion. As such, it is worth dwelling on some of the distinctive ways relationality has been taken up by the contributors. In some chapters, there is a relatively 'weak usage' of the concept, where it references the relationships people have with each other.[32] For instance, Selma James speaks about the caring relationships between women and children, stressing the potential of these relationships for mutuality and shared concern, and arguing that caring relationships can serve as the basis for anti-capitalist ways of being which subvert market-based logics of profit. Invoking relationality in this sense draws attention to the everyday processes and associations whereby people make lives together through their interactions with each other. This offers an important corrective to the autonomous liberal self, acting and responsible alone for his or her own life trajectory.

A 'stronger' formulation of relationality is taken up by several other contributors to make sense of the processes whereby the self is produced and interpellated, and the way that inequitable social relations are reproduced, challenged, resisted and transformed. These contributions point to the ways in which the positions of 'woman' and 'child' are often dialectically constituted, where one cannot exist without the other. Ascribed characteristics often shape their linkage and differentiation. For instance, vulnerability and victimhood are often treated as foundational and all-encompassing characteristics for both women and children in relation to men. Nevertheless, as a number of chapters point out, 'the child' is increasingly viewed as the ultimate vulnerable and dependent subject, deserving of every care and attention, often to the detriment of women to whom responsibility often falls. The status of victim is problematic; this reduces the complexity of any human being as well as individualises social problems, including the political production of vulnerability, by rooting them in essentialist notions of the self. While the contributions to this volume maintain such a critique, we can also witness a return to these concepts in an effort to recognise the existential needs and vulnerability of being human and the political precarity produced in contexts of injustice. There is an effort to attend to the relationally produced and unequal distribution of need and vulnerability as part of political projects for social justice.

The emphasis in these stronger approaches to relationality is on the socio-political (Burman), patriarchal (Zehavi), neo-colonial (Fiddian-Quasmiyeh) and capitalist (Rosen and Newberry) practices and interactions which ground the social positions of 'woman' and 'child', as well as the relations between them. Emboldened by the overarching counter-topographical dialogue of the book, this move away from substantialism draws attention to the historically and geographically shifting processes which make women, children and woman–child relations. As many of the contributors point out, this requires attention to diversities amongst women, and amongst children; to men, the state and the political economy. These texts call on us to attend to the dynamism at the heart of woman–child relations, rather than starting out with what we think we already know.

The risk here is that such an emphasis can turn into a form of unrelenting presentism, missing the historicity of such relations, not to mention the reasons for their 'grinding stability and exploitative continuity',[33] a challenge which the chapters herein address with various degrees of success. Erica Burman, for example, draws on psychoanalytic theory to address such questions, giving affect significant explanatory power (Chapter 1). Rachel Rosen and Jan Newberry stress the globally and sectorally differentiated ways that capital attempts to reduce its labour costs, and how this rewrites relations of care, concern and provisioning, grafting on to existing inequalities and thereby often increasing stratifications (Chapter 8).

Without outright rejecting this stronger usage of relationality, Ohad Zehavi provokes interesting questions in Chapter 17. He points out that once we accept the impossibility of an independent self, the notion of separate or separable beings (e.g. woman *and* child) is also open to contestation. Linking to Rachel Thompson and Lisa Baraitser's discussion of 'fleshy continuities' (Chapter 4) of mother and feotus/infant, he argues that conceptualisations which move away from a model of the atomised liberal self could help to invoke other, more subtle manifestations of the 'undifferentiated, shared entit[ies]' in which we participate (Chapter 4). This takes us down a different path than relationality, to the extent that it asks us to consider the conditions under which separate subjects, which are required in relational understandings, become possible or desirable.

Similarly, the notion of entanglements which we invoke at various points in this chapter is part of our effort of refusing any simple binaries, separations or antagonisms as founding woman–child relations.

Shifting vantage points

The preceding discussion of relationality already hints at some of the distinctive approaches taken when pushing against the friends-or-foes binary. Here we outline five vantage points which contributors take to rethink woman–child relations: looking in; looking out; looking back; widening the frame; and breaking away. No single chapter takes only one vantage point, even if we highlight particular exemplars here. These vantage points bring varying questions, conceptualisations and possible responses to the fore.

One approach involves *looking in* to the woman–child relation, considering the ways in which these dyads are made, sustained and broken. For instance, Gina Crivello and Patricia Espinoza Revollo argue for a revisiting of concepts of care relations between women and children, taking into account 'temporal vulnerabilities', and therefore varying care relations between them over the life course. In arguing that vulnerability is central to human experience, including agency,[34] they suggest that there is a necessity to caring relations between women and children. But by problematising the boundaries between childhood and adulthood, and questioning the feminisation of care, they make the case that all human relations involve both giving and receiving care. Over all, *looking in* offers deep insights into conflicts, tensions and reciprocities as they are lived and enacted by women and children.

A second vantage point involves *looking out*. Here the focus is on the politically, economically and spatially specific ways in which relations between different women and different children, and their antagonisms, emerge and are sustained. *Looking out* is premised on the notion that while antagonisms and elisions may be experienced in everyday life as being between women and children, to explain their persistence and dynamism we must look elsewhere. Erica Burman, for instance, uses intersectional, disability and psychoanalytic theories to interrogate the 'sociopolitical, structurally elaborated positions that constitute and constrain relations between women and children' (Chapter 1). In their chapter, Rosen and Newberry also engage in a practice of *looking out*, but their focus is on understanding why particular socio-political norms and positions persist. They point out that in the context of late capitalism and austerity, the ways in which communities provide for their needs is increasingly refamilised, at the same time as compulsory schooling and early years education are increasingly mandated on a global scale. This often positions women and children at odds in relation to social reproductive labour, which they may have previously carried out together.

Closely related is *looking back*,[35] a focus on the history of the present. Caputo, for instance, in her chapter on 'Too Young to Wed', a photo exhibit on early and forced child marriage, considers the historical precedence for the depiction of girls as vulnerable victims, noting the marked similarities to images of women in the past (and present). By tracing the historical roots, deeply embedded in colonial relations, that situate the exhibit as it moves around the globe, she is able to 'contemplate the resemblances between the lives of children and women without hierarchy' (Chapter 14) to develop what she calls a feminist childhood studies lens. In sum, *looking out* and *looking back* provide ways to avoid individualising antagonisms, encouraging rich contextualisation of the woman–child question within a wider sphere of social relations, as well as historical, political-economic and structural explanations.

A fourth approach offers a different vantage point by *widening the frame*. This offers the promise of prising open the singular womanand-child entity, bringing in other social actors including men and other women and children. For example, Sevasti-Melissa Nolas, Erin Sanders-McDonagh and Lucy Neville highlight the ways in which essentialist ideas about domestic violence position men as violent perpetrators, women as vulnerable victims and children as witnesses and occasional victims. They point out that this can place women and children in competition for support and that it obscures the complexities of maternal care, particularly in contexts of violence. By bringing into the frame men, the practices of women's refuges and the state, they work to complicate and enhance approaches to domestic violence. In her chapter on the Sahrawi refugee camps, Fiddian-Qasmiyeh brings members of solidarity movements into the frame, demonstrating that conflicts between women and girls in the camp resulted from the limits of liberal forms of solidarity, which paid little attention to local norms or understandings of emancipation, care and responsibility to the other.

Contributors working from the four preceding vantage points seem to accept Caputo's assertion of the impossibility of moving 'beyond' the woman–child binary. The tensions exist, at least at the present conjuncture, and they explore the possibilities of moving 'across, through and around' (Chapter 14) this complex terrain. A final vantage point makes a different case. This anti-categorical position, which we have called *breaking away*, suggests instead the possibility of becoming otherwise in ways which dismantle not only the binary but subject positions and power relations altogether. This position is exemplified in Ohad Zehavi's chapter. He argues that the production of distinctions based on gender and generation serves as the basis of 'oppressive social regimes'(Chapter 17). As a result, he argues there is a need to jettison both femininity and childhood as well as their dualisms: masculinity and adulthood. He seeks to accomplish this move via Deleuze and Guattari's minoritarian politics of becoming, to do away with historically sedimented categories and their differential privileges. 'Becoming-girl' features centrally for Zehavi, given that 'the girl' sits as the founding location of both patriarchal and adultist repression. Becoming in this sense is the job of those positioned as privileged (e.g. men, adults), for whom there is a 'relinquish[ing]' of 'fabricated authority' and a rejecting of a priori positions (Chapter 17). Contributors who offer a vantage point of *breaking away* provide us with a reminder that relations of inequality are always also micro-political in nature and offer a sense of hope that things can be otherwise.

New concept-metaphors

The third cross-cutting theme we wish to highlight is that of 'concept-metaphors', which contributors developed in their response to the book's questions. A 'concept-metaphor' is a phrase which encapsulates a conceptualisation and its relation to the world in an imaginative and productively ambiguous way. Concept-metaphors occupy a space somewhere between universal abstractions and unique, situated experiences. By evoking imagery which can stimulate new bases for dialogue, concept-metaphors 'open up spaces for future thinking' and 'practical action'.[36]

Many of the authors, in attempting to walk a careful line – on the one side recognising the affective, material, practical and ideological connections between women and children in their lived experiences; on the other challenging the problematic elisions and antagonisms that emerge as a result – highlight the need for new concept-metaphors to support such efforts. The metaphors of 'conceptual autonomy' and 'strategic essentialism', as well as liberal versions of solidarity and competing or complementary rights, which have animated much preceding feminist and childhood thought, are treated with some suspicion by contributors to this volume. They are found wanting in the effort to understand diverse processes, interconnections and spatial-temporal contexts. In their place, new concept-metaphors to deal with relationality and the shifting vantage points discussed above are offered. These include 'struggle-in-relation' (Burman), 'weaning' (Thomson and Baraitser), 'temporal lag' (Rosen and Newberry), and 'becoming-girl' (Zehavi).

The chapter by Thomson and Baraitser, for example, focuses on the interconnections between mothers and their children. They seek to read exemplars by bracketing mothers and children in a way that does not collapse them into one. As an answer to the impasse created by notions of 'conceptual autonomy', they proffer the concept of 'weaning', to 're-conceptualize the push and pull between mothers' and children's needs, and between motherhood and childhood studies' (Chapter 4). Weaning, as they describe it, brings forth an image of temporal and gradual separation, without ever cutting off the relational link. The temporal aspect of relationality can also be witnessed in Rosen and Newberry's chapter, in which they propose the concept-metaphor of 'temporal lag'. This points to temporal differentiations in the appropriation of surplus value to illuminate how women and children, and the relations between them, are constituted through their uneven and situated profitability for capital, in ways that ground their subordinated status. The development of new concept-metaphors in this book is an indication of the challenging and original work which these borderland dialogues have provoked.

Achieving justice for women *and* children

As the chapters in this volume make clear, the connections and complications between women and children are not simply about difference or affinity but are deeply tied to political questions of power and injustice. Contributors point to the varying ways in which women and children are oppressed and exploited given their intersectional positions and 'minority' social status.[37] These relations of subordination pervade any effort to consider woman–child relations, particularly as they often shape the nature of the connection. For instance, children are used rhetorically to control the sexuality and reproductive capacities of impoverished women, as Kristen E. Cheney makes clear in her chapter on surrogacy, or to ensure the voluntary labour of women in various forms of childcare. Women use ascriptions of vulnerability and dependence to control the mobility and participation of children, or they (inadvertently) objectify children in their efforts to achieve status and recognition for their maternal competence or to engage in community-based organising.

As a result, understanding woman–child relations is central to any project concerned with challenging the injustices faced by either group. How we might do this, and whether this necessarily involves taking up

Shulamith Firestone's powerful invocation that 'we must include the oppression of children in any program for feminist revolution',[38] are open questions which lie at the heart of this collection. Here we wish to highlight three themes in contributors' responses to these unabashedly political questions.

First, despite efforts in most chapters to think with both feminism and childism, and an acknowledgement of the productivity of doing so, these are generally depicted as being very separate political projects, with contradictory attributions of the relative 'success' of each. For instance, Zehavi argues that – unlike for feminism – the time for childism is still to come. Here he is comparing feminism as a revolutionary political project with a '"childism" [that] is still awaiting its *first* wave' (Chapter 17). In contrast, Thomson and Baraitser argue that childhood studies has been far more successful than women's studies in terms of 'field building', with a wide variety of journals, graduate and post-graduate programmes of study and impact on policy and practice. They point to the 'dissolution' of many women's studies departments and programmes as the field shifted towards gender studies (Chapter 4). Whether this does indeed represent a dissolution rather than a positive development is the subject of another paper.[39]

Here, we point out that in some ways, the differing responses reflect the uneasy relationship between academia and activism as well as the basis upon which 'success' is measured (e.g. number of programmes of study, shifts in public imaginaries, etc.). It is worth noting the different histories of women's and childhood studies. As Ann Oakley notes, women's studies emerged out of the women's movement, a prolonged struggle to challenge the autonomous Man that lay unremarked in much traditional theory. Women, understood as both its subjects and agents, were central to the project. Childhood studies is populated by many who seek to challenge the minoritised social status of children, but not typically children themselves. Children's political movements certainly exist but their membership has not made the same inroads into the academy, nor has an understanding of children's activism been mainstreamed in the same way as women's activism and feminism.[40]

Contradictory readings of the relative success of childism and feminism across chapters highlight the difficulty in thinking relationally about achievements in a context where the two have been increasingly depicted, and experienced, in oppositional terms. For instance, the dialogue between Alejandro Cussianovich Villaran and Jessica Taft highlights the limited explicit linkages between the Peruvian Working Children's Movement and feminist groups who either reflect elite interests or struggle to reconcile themselves to the type of childhood espoused by the movement. Cussianovich poses some intriguing questions about how explicit consideration of synergies might transform both movements. His reflections again point us towards relational thinking about feminist movements and children's struggles, as does Merryn Edwards's reflexive photo essay about community-based organising with Grassroots Women in Canada. She argues that the organisation missed opportunities to better understand the exploitation and oppression of women through interrogation of the experiences of others – including children – with whom they live their lives. Relational thinking about political projects reinforces the point that political gains are not 'wins' if they are achieved on the backs of marginalised Others. The only way to eliminate one injustice is to eliminate all forms of oppression: this call to action, issued by Firestone, is strengthened through recent intersectional theorising.

Second, contributors discuss, to differing degrees, whether and how an emphasis on women and children might be problematic. We have been preoccupied with this problem since we began this project, concerned that our focus, while ostensibly aiming to challenge their elision, might simply end up reproducing the womanandchild bundle. Our use of terminology – e.g. 'positioned as a woman or child' – was aimed directly at these concerns, as was our inclusion of questions about the role of the state, capital and men.

We continue to worry away at this problem and it is similarly evident in a number of the chapters. Kristen E. Cheney, for example, is at pains to describe and explain the ways that discussions and practices around international surrogacy can be said to both denaturalise and reinforce the mother–child dyad, and the potential consequences of this. In contrast, a number of the chapters coming more explicitly from activist contributors signal the problems of reification primarily by noting the problematics of everyday entanglements of women and children, but turn their attention to other concerns. For instance, in talking about the Unofficial Women and Children's Centre in the Calais refugee camp, Liz Clegg comments on the unfair burden of care responsibility placed on women, and – by extension – the exclusion of women and children from broader efforts to run and organise in the camp. However, her primary emphasis is on the challenges of providing space and support for women and children in the context of politically precarious migration journeys, rather than challenging the conflation of women and children.

In taking up Clegg's points, we could read our worries over reification as examples of academic concerns over precise conceptualisations problematically trumping the pressing injustices and grinding realities of daily life. But we suggest a more charitable interpretation: the academic–publics dialogue offers a process of de-centring. It helps to illuminate which topics become the foci for differently positioned actors and why, allowing consideration of what is lost or gained with different approaches. In relation to the question of reification, the dialogue makes clear that this can neither become the sole focus nor be swept aside, in any effort towards social and economic justice.

Finally, the chapters do not offer explicit or unequivocal suggestions as to whether childism should be a central tenet of feminism and vice versa. Overall, they suggest that the everyday entanglements of women and children necessarily connect such struggles and that both could add to the other's understandings of the dynamic processes whereby inequities are made, replicated and challenged. As Cheney puts it, feminism and childism can offer new lenses to see through the 'dead ends' of each other's internal debates. In tackling this question, we indicate the necessity of disaggregating the people and social groups who are the subjects, nay agents, of such movements from their intellectual foundations and political analysis. In the case of the former, we contend that organisations do not necessarily need to be cross-sectoral in constitution. Given the problematic conflations of women and children to which this volume speaks and which it seeks to redress or address differently, this would likely mean that women in particular are held responsible for the emancipation of children. To the extent that children are viewed as political actors, the reverse would be true for them. In the case of the latter, we would suggest that the cause of feminism and the cause of childism should be foundational tenets of all critical intellectual endeavours and political movements, regardless of the constitution of their membership or the causes that they pursue.

NOTES

1 Erica Burman, 'Beyond "Women Vs. Children" or "Womenandchildren": Engendering Childhood and Reformulating Motherhood,' *The International Journal of Children's Rights* 16, no. 2 (2008).
2 Cynthia Enloe, 'Womenandchildren: Propaganda Tools of Patriarchy,' in *Mobilizing Democracy: Changing the U.S. Role in the Middle East*, ed. Greg Bates (Monroe, ME: Common Courage Press, 1991).
3 Jane Ribbens McCarthy, Carol-Ann Hooper and Val Gillies, eds., *Family Troubles: Exploring Changes and Challenges in the Family Lives of Children and Young People* (Bristol: Policy Press, 2013).
4 Maxine Molyneux, 'Mothers at the Service of the New Poverty Agenda: Progresa/Oportunidades Mexico's Conditional Transfer Programme,' *Social Policy & Administration* 40, no. 4 (2006).
5 Berry Mayall, *Towards a Sociology for Childhood: Thinking from Children's Lives* (Buckingham: Open University Press, 2002).

6. Katherine Twamley, Rachel Rosen and Berry Mayall, 'The (Im)Possibilities of Dialogue across Feminism and Childhood Scholarship and Activism,' *Children's Geographies* 15, no. 2 (2017).
7. Thanks to Virginia Caputo for challenging our reticence to address these tensions head-on.
8. We use the term 'women's studies' here in reference to coherent programmes of study and scholarship which take an explicitly feminist position, but recognise that in many higher education institutions 'gender studies' may be more commonly used and feminist studies/scholarship is likely to be found across many disciplines.
9. Sara Ahmed, *Strange Encounters: Embodied Others in Post-Coloniality* (London: Routledge, 2000).
10. Our use of borderlands to indicate the transformative potentials of encounters of emancipatory and non-hegemonic knowledges within liminal spaces takes inspiration from an important history of post-colonial feminist scholarship, notably Gloria E. Anzaldúa, *Borderlands/ La Frontera: The New Mestiza* (San Franscisco: Aunt Lute Books, 1987).
11. Burman, 'Beyond "Women vs. Children"'.
12. Jane Helleiner, 'Toward a Feminist Anthropology of Childhood,' *Atlantis* 24, no. 1 (1999).
13. See special issues of the *Australian Feminist Studies*, edited by Baird (2008), and *Feminist Theory* edited by Erica Burman and Jackie Stacey (2010).
14. Leena Alanen, 'Generational Order,' in *The Palgrave Handbook of Childhood Studies*, ed. J. Qvortrup, William Corsaro and Michael-Sebastian Honig (Basingstoke: Palgrave MacMillan, 2011).
15. Mayall, *Towards a Sociology for Childhood*.
16. Wall uses this term as a parallel to other social movements for 'minorities', which aim to radically transform normative values, power relations and historical modes of social ordering. John Wall, 'Childism: The Challenge of Childhood to Ethics and the Humanities,' in *The Children's Table: Childhood Studies and the New Humanities*, ed. Anna Mae Duane (Athens, GA: University of Georgia Press, 2013).
17. Leena Alanen, 'Gender and Generation: Feminism and the "Child Question",' in *Childhood Matters*, ed. Jens Qvortrup et al. (Aldershot: Avebury, 1994). Ann Oakley, 'Women and Children First and Last: Parallels and Differences between Children's and Women's Studies,' in *Children's Childhoods: Observed and Experienced*, ed. Berry Mayall (London: Falmer Press, 1994).
18. Although see Burman, 'Beyond "Women vs. Children"'.
19. There is significant debate about what or who constitutes 'the publics'; here this term refers broadly to those outside of academia.
20. Michael Burawoy, 'For Public Sociology,' *American Sociological Review* 70 (2005): 9.
21. Ibid., 7.
22. We are grateful to our colleagues Kristin Liabo, Berry Mayall and Ann Varley, who were involved with us in coordinating earlier aspects of this project, and to UCL Grand Challenges for financial support.
23. Identification of both omissions and emerging themes in symposium papers guided our call for book chapters and our commissioning of others. We specifically solicited contributions from activists in recognition that it was primarily academics who were responding to our early calls, a reflection of the project's framing within academic debates, conventions and outputs. See Twamley, Rosen and Mayall, 'The (Im)possibilities of Dialogue'.
24. The realities of community organising and social movement-building meant that those without academic posts had less time for this part of the process and perhaps less motivation, given other pressing concerns.
25. Burawoy, 'For Public Sociology,' 5.
26. Nirmal Puwar and Sanjay Sharma, 'Curating Sociology,' *The Sociological Review* 60, no. 1 suppl (2012): 44.
27. Gurminder K. Bhambra, *Connected Sociologies* (London: Bloomsbury, 2014).
28. Burman, 'Beyond "Women vs. Children"'.
29. Cindi Katz, 'On the Grounds of Globalization: A Topography for Feminist Political Engagement,' *Signs: Journal of Women in Culture and Society* 26, no. 4 (2001): 1229–30.
30. See Burman, this volume.
31. Sasha Roseneil and Kaisa Ketokivi, 'Relational Persons and Relational Processes: Developing the Notion of Relationality for the Sociology of Personal Life,' *Sociology* 50, no. 1 (2016): 143–4.
32. Roseneil and Ketokivi, 'Relational Persons and Relational Processes,' 145. Their use of 'weak' and 'strong' in a descriptive sense is somewhat unfortunate given the evaluative connotations of these terms.

33 Lisa Blackman et al., 'Creating Subjectivities,' *Subjectivity* 22, no. 1 (2008): 19.
34 See also Phillip Mizen and Yaw Ofosu-Kusi, 'Agency as Vulnerability: Accounting for Children's Movement to the Streets of Accra,' *The Sociological Review* 61, no. 2 (2013).
35 Thanks to Virginia Caputo for suggesting this helpful elaboration of our vantage point metaphor.
36 Henrietta L. Moore, 'Global Anxieties: Concept-Metaphors and Pre-Theoretical Commitments in Anthropology,' *Anthropological Theory* 4, no. 1 (2004): 74.
37 See Mayall, *Towards a Sociology for Childhood*; Wall, 'Childism'.
38 Shulamith Firestone, *The Dialectic of Sex: The Case for Feminist Revolution* (London: Jonathan Cape, 1971), 118.
39 We note critiques of the reified 'woman' at the heart of women's studies and the impact of mainstreaming on women's studies' more radical impulses.
40 Kirsi Pauliina Kallio and Jouni Häkli, 'Are There Politics in Childhood?,' *Space and Polity* 15, no. 1 (2011).

Section 1
Tense Encounters: Gender and Generation

1
A necessary struggle-in-relation?

Erica Burman

Introduction

It is now nearly 30 years since Barrie Thorne put the question of feminism and the politics of childhood on the agenda, in the very first issue of *Gender & Society*.[1] While the early twenty-first century has at last seen this grow as a topic of interest, until recently this engagement or concern seemed to be emerging from within feminist analyses rather than childhood studies.[2] Reasons for this may include the different positioning of feminisms within the distribution of childhood studies across the world. This ranged from outright hostility (as I sometimes encountered at early conferences) to presumed alignment (especially in policies and practices in the global south). The presumed, and presumed common, marginalised position of women and children is more open to question these days. This has come about not only via the 'international child rights regime' that Vanessa Pupavac proposed as reflecting and warranting a diminished political subjectivity,[3] but also because of the increasing recruitment of women – and even some forms of feminisms – in the financialisation (and further feminisation) of the poor.[4]

While this volume topicalises the theme of the politics of feminisms and childhoods, I am not sure about setting up their relationship as 'friends or foes'. Nevertheless, what this title highlights are the longstanding tensions between, and efforts to ward off, reductionisms in either direction (that is, in favour of either feminisms or childhoods).[5] Rather this brings into focus the various complications and inevitable mutualities between feminisms and childhoods, that also enter into questions of the relationships between *the politics of* feminisms and childhoods. Since we have all been children, and some children will grow up to be women, thus 'child' and 'woman'/'mother' carry mutual implications that both feminists and childhood researchers have struggled with and against.[6]

Reflecting this complexity and mutual configuration of positions, the analytical approach taken in this chapter is to read the positions of women and children as they are presented within several frameworks. The rationale for doing this is so that we might better understand the contribution and limitations of each – what each one topicalises, or alternatively occludes – in their construction of the relations between feminisms and childhoods. I therefore consider here three current frameworks: intersectionality theory, psychosocial analyses and critical disability studies. Clearly these are not the only, or perhaps the 'best', frames or lenses through which to explore such considerations. Rather I engage these as indicative and increasingly influential contemporary theoretical resources. Further these three frameworks share a common rationale, as each emerged as a response to the limits of prevailing rights-based and humanist models. As such, they also share some limitations. Whether these help or hinder consideration of the (political) relations between feminisms and childhoods is a matter I will return to at the end.

I will argue that while intersectionality theory, psychosocial analyses and radical disability studies approaches may indeed invite interesting and useful navigations of the boundary and binary between feminisms and childhoods nevertheless, useful as these may be, remaining tensions may be irresolvable. I frame this conceptual analysis around an example from a recent research project I have conducted on the educational impacts of the 'bedroom tax' – a recent welfare reform that cuts rent subsidies for families. I will suggest that the answer does not lie within the configuration of the binary but outside it – in the sociopolitical, structurally elaborated positions that constitute and constrain relations between women and children.

Like other chapters in this book (Borda Carulla's and Llobet and Milanich's), I address the complexities of these questions through attention to a specific context and example. Like these other chapters, my analysis is generated in relation to a specific child-focused welfare measure – although my focus here is less on the measure than what we can learn from analysis of a key informant's comment about it. There are some methodological continuities between these chapters, since they also address what happened over the lifecourse of these measures. Like mine here, they highlight the instrumentalisation of women's rights and women's labour and how the social investment state literally capitalises on and from these, but claim that this is not all that is effected in this transaction. However, the specific example around which I will frame my discussion is a statement made by an individual (rather than focusing, as other chapters do, on policies in general).

This example was encountered (as emerging rather than deliberately generated) in a recent local research project I co-directed, exploring the educational impacts of the 'bedroom tax'.[7] I say 'encountered' because such a reaction or response was unintended, a small and arguably minor fragment emerging amid the mass of other material generated for this project.[8] Yet 'minor' themes emerging from an analysis can be at least as interesting as 'major' themes.[9] Indeed, perhaps precisely because of this, they may be among their most 'telling' features; that is, speaking outside the expected methodological or topicalised frames of the study, to bring into focus less explicit presumptions structuring research interactions.

First I will briefly summarise the three frameworks, and then explore how well each fares in explicating the example.

Intersectionality theory

While intersectionality, which aims to theorise the interplay between complex social identities and the production of inequalities, has been hailed as feminist theory's key and unique contribution, albeit based on black feminist activisms and legal interventions,[10] it has also been taken up in childhood studies. An indicative example is the increasing identification and targeting of the gendered ('girled') child as the object of international development policy,[11] which was anticipated by Nieuwenhuys[12] (albeit within a Marxist framework) in terms of the 'global womb' or superexploitation of women's and children's labour. Given the intensity and fruitfulness of the debates on intersectionality for feminist analyses, an interesting question arises as to whether these translate to childhood studies. Debate has focused on whether intersectionality recapitulates or, alternatively, renegotiates the pitfalls of the earlier identity politics informing such feminisms, which treated identities as separate from each other and so ushered in vistas of hierarchies of oppression as well as giving rise to a solipsistic politics whereby each woman's combination of identities was so specific that none other shared her experiences and so position. Such questions are also relevant since a feminist politics, like a politics of childhood, is committed to attending to identities rather than only structural positioning.[13]

The limits and dangers identified in relation to intersectionality within feminist analyses can be seen as relevant to its uptake in childhood studies, including the charge of 'washing away' differences that are also power relations until they appear as mere complexity;[14] of reiterating rather than transforming categories, whereby 'ultimately [these assertions] romanticise and idealize positions of social subordination and reinstall conceptions that black women's bodies are sites of "strength" and "transcendence" rather than complex spaces of multiple meanings'.[15] Alternatively, critics claim intersectionality merely reproduces the focus on the 'big two' traditional sociological preoccupations of class and 'race'/gender (or all 'three'), rather than more deeply exploring tensions, connections and mutual constitutions. A further problem discussed concerns that of the (temporal as well as experiential and cultural) reification of categories[16] and in particular threatens a spurious universalisation that thereby precisely reproduces the dynamics of normalisation and pathologisation that intersectionality theory was formulated to address.[17] Perhaps a most obvious connection with childhood studies and the politics of childhood is the focus on ethical dilemmas in representational practices – with claims of reproducing othering and reinscribing identity politics.

As applied to childhood, such arguments have parallels in debates about where and how the category of childhood functions, in terms of *which* children appear as prototypical children (usually those from the global north) and which ones appear to deviate from these norms. The question of the relationship between the domains of the experiential and structural also arises within childhood studies, in terms of arguments about the status of 'voice' and what is involved in generating and documenting accounts of children's perspectives.[18] A further parallel to intersectionality is whether and how children experience themselves as 'children', and how that experience is structured by prevailing discourses and practices. While this foregrounds the contexts in which representations of children are produced, it also highlights the ethics, politics and structural positioning of the viewer, importing a necessary reflexive and affective dimension. Hence this brings the concerns of psychosocial studies into the picture.

Psychosocial studies

This new discipline mobilises a range of resources – from psychoanalysis to other varieties of posthuman theories – to attend to the role of fantasy, the irrational or affective, the unconscious; to address the body, embodiment and the ways this messes with and complexifies prevailing binaries between inside and outside, as well as self and other.[19] An interesting metatheoretical question to consider is why psychoanalytic versions of psychosocial studies have been more focused on maternal subjectivities (e.g. MaMSIE,[20] and see Baraitser and Thompson, this volume) while its other resources (e.g. Deleuze; Haraway) have been applied more extensively to childhood studies – although recent discussions of interembodiment[21] that address the complex and messy inter-relations between interactants may be changing this. Traditional constructions of childhood have been deconstructed to expose the cultural masculinism and colonial assumptions structured by their origins in the humanist and enlightenment theories of the European eighteenth century onwards. Or (to use more intersectional and posthuman terminology) these constructions have been reconfigured through Haraway's feminist radical ecological posthumanism to focus on commonworlds and contact zones among children, between children and adults, and between children and their environments.[22] Similarly, Deleuzian notions of liminality and immanence have been deployed by childhood and youth researchers precisely because they are not tied to a notion of (normative) ideal form, but rather attempt to focus on such key features as *processes* of becoming (rather than static and deficit understandings of childhood; see also Zehavi, this volume), and on the ecology of material bodies engaged in collective projects. Rather than seeking closure and certainty they celebrate indeterminacy. Not only do such frameworks not privilege reason over sensation, they claim to document and support histories of struggle and contestation.[23]

My reading of the example discussed below takes 'psychosocial studies' as importing a combination of psychoanalysis and Foucault – that is, to interrogate practices of subject-formation and subjectification.[24] However, contrary to the reputation of posthumanism/psychosocial studies for being unnecessarily complex, it should be acknowledged that the intertwining of generational and other institutional power relations need not call for very sophisticated theorising to address the complexities of interiorised identities and subjectivities. An example of this less complicated approach is found in Alasuutari's recent work identifying how children's views are discounted within childcare contexts in favour of confirming the institutional positions and authorities of mothers and teachers.[25] Clearly this process of discounting relies upon a set of mutually negotiated and attributed anxieties and insecurities that are not only institutional (so confirming the proper role of the parent or the teacher and the practices of the childcare organisation) but also psychically invested.

Critical disability studies

The social model of disability separated impairment from its stigmatising and dis-abling consequences. Questions of socio-political responsibility for and construction of disabling social and material environments were foregrounded. Further critical work emerging from disability studies resists the conventional normalisation of development and the pathologised positions offered for those who do not 'fit', reframing notions of deficit to focus on being *differently* abled. In relation to childhood studies, such perspectives support critiques of models of child development. Beyond this, a focus on interdependence (rather than dependence) emerges as positive and necessary, rather than a limitation to the presumed cultural ideal of autonomous independence.

More recent work has shifted away from demarcating a clear binary between the social and the individual, most recently forging fruitful connections (through the 'affective turn') with queer theory.[26] Not only does the emphasis on provisionality and shifts of (dis)able-bodiedness critique the defensive, rational, autonomous model of cultural masculinity, and so put into question the anxieties and partialities underlying prevailing understandings of 'competence', but these considerations paradigmatically reformulate notions of relatedness, dependence and interdependence.[27]

Recent examples connecting with and extending links between childhood and disability studies include Lupton on infancy, 'interembodiment' ('skinship'), leaky bodies and competing imperatives for contemporary parents;[28] Rosen on soundscapes of children's screams in institutional settings, mobilising a Bakhtinian understanding of 'answerability';[29] while Åmot and Ytterhus topicalise young children's use of the body in negotiations between adults and children in early education settings.[30] Lesnik-Oberstein's collection heralds disability studies as a key resource for challenging essentialisms, including those residual essentialist assumptions lurking within otherwise radical resources.[31] At the broadest level, what disability and queer theory bring to childhood studies is a further set of resources to challenge normative modes and models of development, whether in terms of critiquing its presumed directionality and so championing the plurality and non-teleology of growing 'sideways', rather than 'growing up',[32] or of the mutating or compliant body.[33]

Thus equipped with these three analytical frames, we can now move to read my example.

'Tell your professor we are good mothers'

The example I want to discuss occurred in an interview with a parent affected by cuts in welfare benefits. The interview was conducted for a small, local pilot study exploring educational impacts of the 'bedroom tax'.[34] The 'bedroom tax', more officially called the 'removal of the spare room subsidy' but widely known by the former description, was introduced by the UK Parliament in April 2013. It reduces housing benefits (rent subsidy) for working-age social housing tenants judged to be under-occupying their homes (i.e. having 'spare bedrooms'). Families subject to this measure receive 14 per cent less housing benefit if they have one 'spare' bedroom, and 25 per cent less for two or more 'spare' bedrooms. While the policy is supposed to reduce the housing benefit bill, make better use of the housing stock, and incentivise tenants to raise their income by getting into or increasing their paid employment and so to depend less on state welfare, it is widely regarded as 'failing' in its own and other terms.[35] This specific context is noteworthy since, although our study recruited participants with school-age children, we were not investigating or explicitly asking questions about (the adequacy of) parenting but rather generating accounts of the consequences of having to limit resources. In this interview with one such mother, her appeal 'tell your professor we are good mothers...' arose as a culmination of stories she narrated about women's struggles to be supported, and not stigmatised or judged according to middle-class professional criteria and without trying 'to understand where you're coming from and how your family is'.

While certainly not typical of the accounts we generated, this appeal is clearly worthy of attention. This is the case beyond the methodological claims I make above: in this case, the participant was explicitly adopting a representative position of 'speaking for' others, and so claiming to offer a generalizable analysis in her own right.

Here is the extract, together with some of the text that followed it:

P. We are good mothers (.) tell your professor we are good mothers (.) we are poor we live in council houses we have life skills (.) uff because we have suffered not because we are dummy not because we don't want to study <u>life</u> keep us there I'm a postgraduate

I. Yes my professor knows that it's other you know it's other people the government that needs to hear that isn't it

P. Yes a postgraduate but <u>life</u> puts you my son's not well life puts you in that situation and you don't get a breather you're

> not getting an opportunity to rest your brain and decide what [you] want to do with your career you're constantly battling they will reduce this they send this they will stop this eviction letters this and that bills coming left right centre.

This example is also preceded by a more general claim about women, mothering and how the experience and activity of being a mother is framed by state and service practices: '… these council houses women they are the most loving to their families it is the external environment which is causing because they want to <u>change</u> the family dynamic…' (underlining indicates emphasis).

Here 'council houses women' acts as code for poor women in receipt of socially subsidised housing. Key discursive entities distinguished are 'council houses women' as mothers; their relationship with their 'families', which she characterises as being 'loving' (with 'loving' later qualified or reframed in more technical (and hence debatable) terms as a 'family dynamic'). This is contrasted with the 'external environment' that 'wants to change the family dynamic'. Notwithstanding the clarity, cogency and passion of her claims, her efforts to be diplomatic should be noted; indeed the narrator starts to make a claim about 'external' pressures on women 'causing' the change of family dynamic but reformulates it into a more indirect 'want' or desire.

Significantly, her demand to 'tell your professor' carries no hint of uncertainty about being a good mother, or deference to the received status of the 'professor' (and by implication the researcher and research) to confirm her claim of being 'good mothers'. This is indicated by the priority accorded the claim 'we are good mothers', asserted before and then repeated (for emphasis) after 'tell your professor'. This statement ('we are good mothers') stands, literally, irrespective of the 'professor' in the sense that it is structured as a separate clause. We could also reflect on the unmarked gendered position of the 'professor', and how or whether this sits as antithetical to or potentially overlapping with 'mother'….).[36]

Now I will read this comment in relation to the three frameworks I introduced earlier: intersectionality, psychosocial studies and disability studies. Rather than being separate, I see these as cumulative in building and enriching the analysis.

Reading the example

In relation to intersectionality, 'tell your professor we are good mothers' clearly speaks to the relational constitution of positions, within research practices as well as in wider social practices, and around mothering, families and the state. Moreover, while of course all accounts are produced or generated in relation to others, here the speaker not only comments on the situated character of what is said, but is also communicating and negotiating her understanding of what this interview is for, as a means of accessing and influencing practices of knowledge generation and circulation. Underlying this claim, 'tell your professor we are good mothers', is a presumed, commonly recognised discourse of mutual configuration of woman-as-mother and child(ren) relations. This discourse speaks precisely to the tension between feminisms and the politics of childhood arising from the asymmetry of their positionings. The dominant discourse of innocent childhood pits worthy children against, or at best in relation to, mothers who are themselves then qualified as being more or less worthy.[37] What this comment topicalises, therefore, is the invidious position/regulation of mothers, as a consequence of state (physical, mental – behaviour, attainment) scrutiny and evaluation of their children.[38]

The relevance of a psychosocial studies perspective is highlighted by the fact that, in addition to the overt state regulation and (threat of) intervention in families, this link between women-as-mothers and children could not exercise its traction without the emotional investment of women in being seen as 'good mothers'. Longstanding and perhaps obvious though this theme is, it is worth spelling out; moreover there are specific new twists and turns in the dilemmas facing parents. Recently Geinger *et al.* have discussed how the trope of autonomy in expert (including 'professorial' or academic?) discourse creates an impossible position for parents within a neoliberal context of increasingly individualising responsibility.[39] Both parents and experts value the promotion of autonomous children, and childcare advice claims to support parental autonomy from expert intervention. Yet there is pressure against parents authorising themselves as being autonomous, in the sense of being insensitive to external evaluation, since the very mandatory subject position of the good parent demands that they perform relational anxiety. Parents therefore are positioned in a double bind: they cannot (claim to) be confident or assertive about their own parenting skills; but are rather obliged to be uncertain and confess anxieties: 'It is clear that utterances of doubts are recognized by other parents as characteristics of the good parent…'[40]

Unlike the parent users of social media discussed by Geinger *et al.*, however, it seems that the parent of 'tell your professor we are good mothers' is under such pressure to 'prove' good motherhood that she transgresses the current norms (of what has been called intensive mothering)[41] that mandate such expressions of doubt and uncertainty.[42]

In this case, the fact that her son has been diagnosed with disabilities (see later) intensifies those anxieties, but acknowledging this also can be read as offering an arena for performing appropriate maternal care and relationality. What this also illustrates is the individual 'costs' for autonomous projects of (economic) development for relational commitments, indicating the deeper paradox that Geinger et al. note at work in current discourses of autonomy. They work to undermine both parental and child autonomy: the passive parent reproducing expert advice and the passive child recipient.[43]

So what a psychosocial frame brings to this example is, first, an attention to the socioculturally determined investment of women-as-mothers in being perceived as 'good'. Taking this further, this identity is portrayed as binary – good vs. not good/bad. This reflection invites a further key question: where is the 'good enough' mother, the figure of mothering that the psychoanalyst and radio broadcaster Donald Winnicott popularised from 1953 onwards by reassuring women that it was possible to be 'good enough'?[44] While even though the 'good enough' mother' discourse can of course still exercise coercion, Winnicott's formulation aimed to support women dealing with escalating societal prescriptions around children's psychological and emotional development. But now this discourse has disappeared and instead it seems that zero sum absolutism prevails in current state and welfare discourses, with high stakes in the assessment of parenting as well as children.

Clearly, second, there are fantasies of the others that lie behind the researcher at play – including 'the professor' but beyond her. This attention to other imagined addressees or audiences also connects with analyses of how current austerity policies target poor communities psychically as well as financially. There is widespread documentation of a sense of shame in disclosing poverty[45] and this has been seen to contribute to what Shildrick and MacDonald have called 'scroungerophobia',[46] as well as the wider debates on intensification of mothering – sometimes called entrepreneurial mothering – with imperatives for compulsory freedom and enjoyment mandated by the childcare advice literature as noted above. Relevant also here is the extra (and usually gendered) emotional labour of managing within reduced resources, as well as the physical labour (shopping more often; at particular times of day to find 'reduced' price items, walking instead of paying for transport etc., as well as having to justify increasingly strict limits on consumption and activities to children). Across our study of the 'bedroom tax', perhaps the most commonly recurrent theme from all our participants, spanning parents and school and community organisation staff, was food deprivation – how parents are cutting down on shopping, compromising on food quality, only eating on some days so that children can eat, such that as one parent put it 'fresh food is out of the question'. It is in this context that recent government proposals for a 'sugar tax' should be regarded as yet another attack on the coping strategies of the poor. And as a comment on the resources informing psychosocial analyses, it is worth noting how (not) feeding is typically discoursed within psychoanalysis in metaphorical terms, a feature which perhaps also reflects its own specific economic presumptions (of privilege).[47]

Thirdly, the many material examples documented in our study of necessary relationality and co-dependence also highlight tensions – not only between adults and children but also between siblings, perhaps not surprisingly when domestic space is being contracted. So this parent complained of difficulties for her teenage daughter, doing 'A' levels while sharing a room with a toddler; just as parents with non-custodial childcare commitments were reduced to sofa surfing when their children come to stay.[48]

But perhaps what is most startling about 'tell your professor..', as read from a psychosocial perspective, is that it is a good example of maternal resistance – of talking back, of assuming a collective voice, rather than being interpellated into the reflexive, self-regulating, individual confessional subject incited by the evaluation of mothering. This collective voice, moreover, is active and critical as well as asserting class and gender solidarity; it accuses/critiques dominant discourses. In terms of psychosocial discussions, we could perhaps see this as making the shift from subjectification, in the sense of being subjected to the regulatory gaze of the other/the state, to what might be called subjectivity or even some situated agentic engagement.[49]

As discussed earlier, discourses of disability can be linked to challenges to competence (in this case of not being a 'good mother'). They are also structured into notions of adult–child relations around (good) parenting; that is, in relation to dependency and interdependency. It is relevant to note the over-representation in our family sample both of children with diagnosed disabilities and of parents with mental health difficulties.[50] This is not surprising since poverty brings fewer resources and opportunities for entertainment and socialising with others, and fosters much greater isolation. Moreover the connection with questions of disability therefore brings to the fore a site of contestation and connection not only between women and children, but also between disability and mental health activisms.[51] Significantly, the speaker of 'Tell your professor' was a mother of three children, one of whom has disabilities. This puts her comment 'I'm not dummy' in an interesting light, in relation to the classing of received notions of cleverness, as well as generational and gendered notions of competence. There are also further mutual determinations between poverty and disability that need to be acknowledged: disability is related to poverty in terms of reduced quality of life and life expectancy. Being poor increases the chances of having a congenital or acquired impairment, and being disabled increases the chances of being poor. In relation to the recent welfare cuts it has been calculated that people in poverty will lose on average five times more than the general population as the result of cuts, whereas disabled people will lose nine times more.[52] Beyond this, parents of disabled children encounter increasing surveillance.[53]

This mother's statement 'my son's not well life puts you in that situation' highlights the role of relational commitments, and how these constrain individual projects of self-realisation. This speaks to the ways responsibilities limit women's capacities to become the agentic, enterprising, planning, ideal-typical subjects of neoliberalism. The interdependent character of disability was also highlighted by the examples we documented of using a child's Disability Living Allowance to support the whole family, just as also the Pupil Premium (money allocated to schools to support disadvantaged children) is currently being used to support all children.

Preliminary conclusions

To end this treatment of the relations between feminisms and the politics of childhood, I will attempt to go beyond applying and exemplifying the three frameworks I have been considering to offer some final reflections on emerging connections and tensions between these.

Like Cheney's chapter (this volume), this discussion has focused more on general theoretical tensions and dilemmas, but this is in the service of evaluating and formulating political agendas. Perhaps one key challenge for/by intersectionality theory is that childhood is a temporary/unstable 'condition', albeit constituted as a generational relationship.[54] Disability studies, however, addresses this question, by highlighting how the able-bodied are only temporarily so, just as levels of disability shift according to time and conditions. The temporary status of childhood poses several interpretive challenges. Does this exemplify (the strengths and need for) intersectionality, or does it undermine it? Does intersectionality theory presume that the axes or positions that intersect, while shifting salience according to particular conditions, are otherwise stable?

Returning to my example, the 'bedroom tax' can be understood as both fixing identities and unfixing their places.[55] This is because families become more or less subject to the 'bedroom tax' according to the changing ages of their children while, arguably, the government policy takes a strikingly unpsychosocial understanding of families, employing (as indicated above) a chronological rather than biographical/generational definition of adults and children. The increased salience of age and gender, and their transitional meanings according to particular age thresholds, becomes a site for strategic planning and management, with some families paying the 'bedroom tax' because one of their children is about to transition to an age when they would qualify to not have to share a bedroom[56] and others worrying about becoming subject to the 'bedroom tax' because of children leaving home to go to college. Through such policy structures, therefore, particular trajectories or traversals of the age/gender intersection have acquired sociopolitical salience. What this does is to fix and essentialise (and normalise) those positions, whilst covertly also simultaneously *underlining* their provisionality and relationality (relative age of siblings, and their gendered positionings). Adult co-habiting couples are, of course, expected to share a bedroom, though this expectation is often an undue presumption. Alongside this, there is an undermining or unsettling of place or positioning, a destabilisation of fixed abode/presumed inhabited position and a discourse of mobility that is part of the much discussed 'agility' and 'flexibility' of neoliberal policies.[57] This includes how adult children no longer have rights to a bedroom in their parents' house – which not only enforces a restricted model of family, but also constrains/prevents relationships of support and care.

All this works to strip families and communities from their networks of mutual support and threatens their sense of stability and entitlement to a home. As this participant pointedly asserted later in the same interview: a home is not just a house ('you put your love into it'). Returning to a psychosocial frame, it is important to acknowledge that the meanings of that home are not only bounded by the physical walls of the building but extend across neighbourhoods and interpersonal networks. Here notions of 'psychological homelessness' (a term sometimes used figuratively in the psychotherapeutic literature to refer to psychic consequences of inadequate histories of attachment)[58] become materialised in the threat of physical loss or leaving of home, even homelessness.[59] Significantly, the loss of attachment at stake here seems to be that of the state's commitment to its own citizens, whose claim to home and community – and even capacities of self-definition in relation to the allocation and distribution of the 'inner space' of home – is being undermined. Since all three frames destabilise the unity and separability of the entities under investigation, by highlighting mutual configurations (intersectionality), traversals of identification and emotional investment (psychosocial studies), and destabilisations of what counts as dis/ability (disability studies), there remains the question of how to choose the unit of analysis – where does the emotional 'buck' stop and, indeed, start?

Returning to the key question posed in and by this volume, from this analysis I suggest that the answer to the 'friends or foes?' relation between the politics of feminisms and childhoods does not lie within the configuration of the binary between women and children, nor between feminisms and childhoods. Rather the answer lies outside it, in the socio-political, structurally elaborated positions that constitute and constrain relations between women and children. I have attempted to tease out from this example how the constitution of the binary, and correspondingly its deconstruction, lie in historically sedimented, but also continuously reproduced, sociopolitical practices.

The 'bedroom tax' interview highlights the complex relationalities and mutualities between the participant's mental and physical states and those of her children. The mother said: 'you don't get a breather' and 'you're not getting an opportunity to rest your brain and decide what [you] want to do with your career' and said of her children 'life puts you my son's not well life puts you in that situation'. This is a demand to be recognised as having knowledge and desires that are both forged and constrained by childcare commitments and poverty; constraints that are clearly attributed to conditions of perception and reception as well as material conditions ('you're constantly battling they will reduce this they send this they will stop this eviction letters this and that bills coming left right centre'). But most significantly there is a refusal to be interpellated as possessing or 'owning' these as individual 'problems'. So in this sense this mother can be read as articulating a feminist identification that engages in a relational politics of childhood, moreover one that counters current claims of the demise of working class solidarity inculcated by and as 'scroungerophobia'.[60] Given the ethical-political issues at stake, foregrounded both by the analytical frameworks I have used and by this example, perhaps what we need most to address, following this participant, are the roles and responsibilities of politically engaged academics, and how the frameworks we use to engage with research participants and interpret what they say are fostering conditions to resist the responsibilisation of the poor and to document, promote or even help to reinstate a collective 'we'.[61] That is, at the level of political action, to consider how best 'we' can deliver on the rightful demands made of us when we do research.

NOTES

1. Barrie Thorne, 'Re-envisioning Women and Social Change: Where Are the Children?' *Gender & Society* 1, no. 1 (1987): 85–109.
2. Barbara Baird, 'Child Politics, Feminist Analyses,' *Australian Feminist Studies* 23, no. 57 (2008): 291–305; Erica Burman and Jackie Stacey, 'The Child and Childhood in Feminist Theory,' *Feminist Theory* 11, no. 3 (2010): 227–40.
3. Vanessa Pupavac, 'Punishing Childhoods: Contradictions in Children's Rights and Global Governance,' *Journal of Intervention and Statebuilding* 5, no. 3 (2011): 285–312.
4. Adrienne Roberts, 'Gender, Financial Deepening and the Production of Embodied Finance: Towards a Critical Feminist Analysis,' *Global Society* 29, no. 1 (2015): 107–27.
5. Christine Sylvester, 'Homeless in International Relations? Women's Place in Canonical Texts and Feminist Re-imaginings,' in *Feminism & Politics,* ed. Anne Phillips (Oxford & New York: Oxford University Press, 1998): 67–92.
6. Erica Burman, 'Beyond "Women vs. Children" or "Womenandchildren": Engendering Childhood and Reformulating Motherhood,' *International Journal of Children's Rights* 16, no. 2 (2008): 177–94; Erica Burman, 'Conceptual Resources for Questioning Child as Educator', *Studies in Philosophy and Education* 32, no. 3 (2013): 229–43.
7. Joanna Bragg et al., *The Impacts of the 'Bedroom Tax' on Children and Their Education: A Study in the City of Manchester* (Manchester: Manchester Institute of Education, University of Manchester), http://www.seed.manchester.ac.uk/research/poverty-and-social-justice/bedroom-tax/
8. See also Anat Greenstein et al., 'Construction and Deconstruction of "Family" by the "Bedroom Tax"', *British Politics* 11, no. 4 (2016): 508–25; Erica Burman et al., 'Subjects of, or Subject to, Policy Reform? A Foucauldian Discourse Analysis of Regulation and Resistance in UK Narratives of Educational Impacts of Welfare Cuts – The Case of The "Bedroom Tax"', *Education Policy Analysis Archives* (in press); Laura Winter et al., 'Education, Welfare Reform and Psychological Well-being: A Critical Psychology Perspective,' *British Journal of Educational Studies* (2016). DOI: 10.1080/00071005.2016.1171823.
9. Cindi Katz, 'Towards Minor Theory', *Environment and Planning D: Society and Space* 14 (1996): 487–99.
10. Kimberlé Williams Crenshaw, 'Mapping the Margins: Intersectionality, Identity Politics, and Violence Against Women of Color,' *Stanford Law Review* (1991): 1241–99.
11. Ofra Koffman and Ros Gill, '"The Revolution Will Be Led by a 12-year-old Girl": Girl Power and Global Biopolitics', *Feminist Review* 105, no. 1 (2013): 83–102; Heather Switzer, '(Post) Feminist Development Fables: The Girl Effect and the Production of Sexual Subjects,' *Feminist Theory* 14, no. 3 (2013): 345–60.
12. Olga Nieuwenhuys, 'Embedding the Global Womb: Global Child Labour and the New Policy Agenda,' *Children's Geographies* 5, no. 1–2 (2007): 149–63.
13. Jennifer C. Nash, 'Re-thinking Intersectionality,' *Feminist Review* 89, no. 1 (2008): 1–15; Sumi Cho, Kimberlé Williams Crenshaw and Leslie McCall, 'Toward a Field of Intersectionality Studies: Theory, Applications, and Praxis,' *Signs: Journal of Women in Culture and Society* 38, no. 4 (2013): 785–810.
14. Umut Erel et al., 'On the Depoliticisation of Intersectionality Talk: Conceptualising Multiple Oppressions in Critical Sexuality Studies,' in *Theorizing Intersectionality and Sexuality,* eds. Yvette Taylor, Sally Hines and Mark E. Casey (Basingstoke: Palgrave Macmillan, 2010), 56–77.
15. Nash, 'Re-thinking Intersectionality'.
16. As in Lykke's (2011) critique of the presumed orientation around 'race' (Nina Lykke, 'Intersectional Analysis: Black Box or Useful Critical Feminist Thinking Technology?' in *Framing Intersectionality: Debates on a Multi-faceted Concept in Gender Studies*, ed. Helma Lutz, Maria Teresa Herrera Vivar and Linda Supik, (Farnham: Ashgate, 2011): 207–20, and Nash's 2008 claims (Nash, 'Re-thinking Intersectionality') that this homogenizes and ignores differences among black women.
17. Maria Carbin and Sara Edenheim, 'The Intersectional Turn in Feminist Theory: A Dream of a Common Language?' *European Journal of Women's Studies* 20, no. 3 (2013): 233–48.
18. Pam Alldred and Val Gillies, 'Eliciting Research Accounts: Re/producing Modern Subjects,' in *Ethics in Qualitative Research*, ed. Tina Miller et al. (London: Sage, 2002): 146–65.

19 Stephen Frosh and Lisa Baraitser, 'Psychoanalysis and Psychosocial Studies,' *Psychoanalysis, Culture & Society* 13, no. 4 (2008): 346–65.
20 MaMSIE is an online journal produced by the Psychosocial Studies department of Birkbeck University. It is devoted to the theme of maternal subjectivity.
21 See, for example, Deborah Lupton, 'Infant Embodiment and Interembodiment: A Review of Sociocultural Perspectives', *Childhood* 20, no. 1 (2013): 37–50.
22 Affrica Taylor, *Reconfiguring the Natures of Childhood* (London: Routledge, 2013).
23 Hans Skott-Myhre, Veronica Pacini-Ketchabaw and Kathleen Skott-Myhre, eds. *Youth Work, Early Education, and Psychology: Liminal Encounters* (Basingstoke: Palgrave Macmillan, 2015).
24 Michel Foucault, 'The Political Technology of Individuals', in *Technologies of the Self: A Seminar with Michel Foucault,* eds. Luther H. Martin, Huck Gutman and Patrick H. Hutton (London: Tavistock, 1988), 145–62.
25 Maarit Alasuutari, 'Voicing the Child? A Case Study in Finnish Early Childhood Education,' *Childhood* 21, no. 2 (2014): 242–59.
26 Jasbir K. Puar, '"I Would Rather Be a Cyborg Than a Goddess": Becoming-Intersectional in Assemblage Theory,' *PhiloSOPHIA* 2, no. 1 (2012): 49–66.
27 Anat Greenstein, *Radical Inclusive Education: Disability, Teaching and Struggles for Liberation* (Hove: Routledge, 2016).
28 Lupton, 'Infant embodiment'.
29 Rachel Rosen, '"The Scream": Meanings and Excesses in Early Childhood Settings,' *Childhood* 22, no. 1 (2015): 39–52.
30 Ingvild Åmot and Borgunn Ytterhus, '"Talking Bodies": Power and Counter-power Between Children and Adults in Day Care,' *Childhood* 21, no. 2 (2014): 260–73.
31 Karin Lesnik-Oberstein, ed. *Rethinking Disability Theory and Practice: Challenging Essentialism* (Basingstoke: Palgrave Macmillan, 2015).
32 Kathryn Bond Stockton, *The Queer Child, or Growing Sideways in the Twentieth Century* (Durham: Duke University Press, 2009).
33 Helen Meekosha and Russell Shuttleworth, 'What's So "Critical" About Critical Disability Studies?' *Australian Journal of Human Rights* 15, no. 1 (2009): 47–75.
34 Bragg et al., *Impacts of the 'Bedroom Tax'*.
35 Kenneth Gibb, 'The Multiple Policy Failures of the UK Bedroom Tax,' *International Journal of Housing Policy* 15, no. 2 (2015): 148–66; Steve Wilcox, *Housing Benefit Size Criteria: Impacts for Social Sector Tenants and Options for Reform* (York: Joseph Rowntree Foundation, 2014).
36 Thanks to my (professorial) colleague on this project, Ruth Lupton, for alerting me to the implied but not directly posed question of the gendered positioning of the 'professor'!
37 While questions of class are foregrounded in her account, extra-textual information – also reflected elsewhere in the interview – concerns the more familiar territory of intersectionality theory in the relation between class and racialised positioning – in which it may be relevant to note that neither the interviewer nor interviewee were native English speakers and both are migrants to the UK, although the interviewer is white and the interviewee of African background.
38 See Valerie Walkerdine and Helen Lucey, *Democracy in the Kitchen: Regulating Mothers and Socialising Daughters* (London: Virago, 1989); Rosalind Edwards, Val Gillies and Nicola Horsley, 'Brain Science and Early Years Policy: Hopeful Ethos or "Cruel Optimism"?' *Critical Social Policy* 35, no. 2 (2015): 167–87.
39 Freya Geinger, Michel Vandenbroeck and Griet Roets. 'Parenting as a Performance: Parents as Consumers and (De)constructors of Mythic Parenting and Childhood Ideals,' *Childhood* 21, no. 4 (2014): 488–501.
40 Geinger et al., 'Parenting as a Performance', 498.
41 Davi Johnson Thornton, 'Neuroscience, Affect, and the Entrepreneurialization of Motherhood,' *Communication and Critical/Cultural Studies* 8, no. 4 (2011): 399–424.
42 Although it should also be noted that the mandate to perform expressions of doubt and certainty may be more pronounced in peer-to-peer communication (on the parenting websites that Geinger et al. discuss, for example) than in more 'official' accounting contexts, such as interviews with state or para-state (such as academics) representatives.
43 Geinger et al., 'Parenting as a Performance'.

44 Donald Woods Winnicott, 'The Theory of the Parenting Relationship,' in *The Maturational Processes and The Facilitating Environment: Studies in the Theory of Emotional Development*. (London: Hogarth Press, 1965), 37–55.
45 Elaine Chase and Robert Walker, 'The Co-construction of Shame in the Context of Poverty: Beyond a Threat to the Social Bond,' *Sociology* 47, no. 4 (2013): 739–54.
46 Tracy Shildrick and Robert MacDonald, 'Poverty Talk: How People Experiencing Poverty Deny Their Poverty and Why They Blame "the Poor",' *The Sociological Review* 61, no. 2 (2013): 285–303.
47 Manasi Kumar, 'The Poverty in Psychoanalysis: "Poverty" of Psychoanalysis?' *Psychology & Developing Societies* 24, no. 1 (2012): 1–34.
48 Interestingly, we interviewed several fathers who shared custody of their children with their now separated spouse and were affected by the 'bedroom tax'. The pressures this put on their efforts to deliver on their childcare responsibilities highlight the hypocrisy of conservative discourses promoting involved fatherhood.
49 See also our analysis of this in Burman et al., 'Subjects of, or Subjects to, Policy Reform', and Erica Burman 'From Subjectification to Subjectivity in Educational Policy Research Relationships', in *Discursive Perspectives on Education Policy and Implementation*, ed. Jessica Lester et al. (New York: Palgrave, in press).
50 See Bragg, *Impacts of the 'Bedroom Tax'*.
51 See Mick McKeown, Fiona Jones and Helen Spandler, 'Challenging Austerity Policies: Democratic Alliances Between Survivor Groups and Trade Unions,' *Mental Health Nursing* 33, no. 6 (2013): 26–9.
52 http://www.centreforwelfarereform.org/uploads/attachment/354/a-fair-society.pdf (accessed 14 February 2017).
53 Sara Ryan and Katherine Runswick-Cole, 'Repositioning Mothers: Mothers, Disabled Children and Disability Studies,' *Disability & Society* 23, no. 3 (2008): 199–210.
54 Leena Alanen, 'Explorations in Generational Analysis', In *Conceptualizing Child-Adult Relations*, ed. Leena Alanen and Berry Mayall (London: RoutledgeFalmer, 2001): 11–22.
55 Greenstein et al., 'Construction and Deconstruction'.
56 Under the 'bedroom tax' conditions, adult couples, pairs of children aged 10 and under, and pairs of children of the same sex aged 16 and under are expected to share bedrooms.
57 David Gillies, 'Agile Bodies: A New Imperative in Neoliberal Governance,' *Journal of Education Policy* 26, no. 2 (2011): 207–23.
58 Iain Dresser, 'Psychological Homelessness: A Clinical Example,' *Journal of Social Work Practice* 1, no. 4 (1985): 67–76.
59 See Lisa A. Goodman, Leonard Saxe and Mary Harvey. 'Homelessness as Psychological Trauma: Broadening Perspectives,' *American Psychologist* 46, no. 11 (1991): 1219.
60 Shildrick and MacDonald, 'Poverty Talk'.
61 See also Mark Cresswell and Helen Spandler, 'The Engaged Academic: Academic Intellectuals and the Psychiatric Survivor Movement', *Social Movement Studies* 12, no. 2 (2013): 138–54.

2
Working-class women and children in Grassroots Women

Photo essay by Merryn Edwards[1]

Grassroots Women (GW) was an anti-imperialist, feminist organisation in East Vancouver, Canada, first initiated by the Philippine Women Centre, which was at the forefront of community organising in Vancouver in the early 1990s. The group included single mothers, women on welfare, migrant and Indigenous women, childcare workers (including migrant domestic workers), health and service sector workers, lesbians/queer women and students. Participants in GW events collectively analysed their own lives and experiences, reflected on their childhoods and family histories, and examined the conditions in which they related to their own and other children.

Recognising that working-class women would not be able to participate unless their children were also welcomed and included, GW encouraged women to bring their children to organisational activities. As a result, children were almost always present. They played, slept or ate nearby, and sometimes they participated in GW activities. The absence of other children was also keenly felt, as in the case of migrant women participating in GW who had been forced to leave their families to take up domestic work through Canada's Live-In Caregiver Program. This photo essay looks at the dynamics between working-class women and children within the organisation over the 15 years it was active.

Universal childcare is a woman's right

Fig. 2.1 *Grassroots Women reclaimed the activist roots of Mother's Day, stemming from women's anti-war and anti-poverty organising, by hosting an annual Mother's Day march and rally as part of the group's 11-year childcare campaign 'Universal Childcare Is a Woman's Right'. Because GW saw universal childcare as an essential (but insufficient) condition for women's emancipation, its childcare campaign was not isolated from its other activities. For example, participants in GW's 2006 Mother's Day march denounced Canada's participation in the war on Afghanistan and the redirection of funding from childcare to the military by carrying a cardboard tank and calling for 'childcare not warfare'. (Source: Grassroots Women)*

A woman's place is in the struggle, a child's place is by her side

Fig. 2.2 *One of GW's early activities was a women's and children's conference to analyse and resist the harmful impacts of imperialist globalisation. The conference provided childcare in order to facilitate women's participation, but despite the name focused on the experiences and contributions of children only as adjunct to their mothers. (Source: Grassroots Women)*

Fig. 2.3 *Although GW focused on women, children influenced the culture of the organisation enormously. They were almost always present during GW's activities including at moments, such as a press conference pictured here, where their presence might have been unexpected without GW's commitment to welcoming children in order to facilitate their mothers' participation. The presence of children at GW activities was an example of the burdens women faced in confronting and working collectively to end their own exploitation, as well as an expression of their resistance to and defiance of that exploitation. (Source: Grassroots Women)*

A culture of resistance

Women in GW quickly identified the lack of childcare as a central concern impacting all areas of their lives: contributing to keeping them in low-wage, 'flexible', or part-time jobs; excluding them from educational or other opportunities; trapping them in abusive relationships; or exposing them to invasive and punitive state scrutiny. GW's consistent grounding in a conception of capitalism's dependence on unpaid or underpaid reproductive labour helped the organisation challenge understandings of childcare as solely a concern of childcare workers and parents, claiming it as a critical collective responsibility. GW's work demonstrates the clarity and strength that comes from moving beyond simply documenting experience to an engagement with an anti-imperialist, materialist and feminist tradition of understanding the world in order to change it.

Fig. 2.4 *GW's Labour Committee created a mural to depict the challenges working-class women face as workers and their determination to resist. (Photograph by Martha Roberts)*

This engagement is evident in the wide variety of cultural expressions that emerged from GW activities, including visual art, music, theatre and creative writing. It was in the cultural arena that GW most consciously engaged children's participation. Children made artwork used in campaign materials, painted a mural at the 2004 Mother's Day March and Rally, and contributed music and poetry at an open mic session in 2008. Although children's participation in GW did not take place within the same careful process of collective social investigation that GW applied to analyzing women's experiences, the cultural contributions of children were not presented as fundamentally different from those of adults. They often shared a similar do-it-yourself aesthetic and communicated a common desire to see past often harsh lived realities to more liberatory social relations based on dignity, co-operation and reciprocity.

Fig. 2.5 *GW used children's artwork for a postcard campaign directed at the federal government, which was supported by over ten thousand people. (Drawing by Andrew Sayo)*

The limits and possibilities of children's participation

Figs. 2.6 and 2.7 *Activities for children at GW meetings and events ranged from simply keeping them occupied so their mothers could participate to more fully engaging children as the intended audience or as contributors, such as at the Mother's Day activities pictured here. (Photographs by Britt Permien)*

Although GW at times welcomed children's contributions, the organisation stoppped short of an in-depth analysis of children's experiences. This omission was in part a reaction to calls for childcare and other social policies framed around the elimination of child poverty which obscured how the impoverishment of children was inseparable from the poverty of the adults in their lives. Many GW members and participants had learned to be wary of ideas about the 'deserving' or 'undeserving' poor or the ways in which 'the child' became a powerful symbol used to justify coercive state intervention into and control over the lives of working-class mothers.

Certainly, GW had many good reasons not to centre the call for childcare or other campaigns around children's experiences, and any insistence on doing so would have risked alienating some women or reinforcing notions that 'good' women put children's interests ahead of their own. Nevertheless, in a campaign focused on a critical aspect of children's as well as women's lives, there was a missed opportunity for GW to undertake a more considered analysis of the interests of children in its efforts to win universal childcare and its wider attempts to build an anti-imperialist movement that included a conception of children as political allies capable of their own collective resistance.

The women (and children) united will never be defeated

In its final years, GW became increasingly interested in creating a childcare centre aimed at supporting women's political organising, with a nascent vision of the radical possibilities of early childhood education. However, this vision would not come to fruition and a number of circumstances led to the decision to close the office and put the organisation on hiatus in 2010, in the hopes that an anti-imperialist feminist organisation could one day be revived in Vancouver.

Childcare continues to be an urgent need and a strategic site for organising in the current austerity context. GW's 15-year history is a powerful example of working-class women's collective action: to question the very basis of the neoliberal state and the capitalist organisation of childcare and reproductive labour, and to resist the exploitation and oppression of working-class women and children.

The inclusion of children in GW in order to facilitate working-class women's participation was fundamental to the organisation's success. Future social movements can also learn from GW's untapped potential

Figs. 2.8 and 2.9 *The overlapping connections between the oppression and exploitation of working-class women and children are evident in this 'laundry line' displayed as part of GW's Mother's Day activities. It speaks of conditions caused by a lack of accessible, affordable, high-quality childcare, including children's un- or underpaid labour caring for other children; stress and insufficient resources for families to survive and thrive; the redirection of resources away from childcare and other social services toward warfare; and a denial of childcare as a collective responsibility and a concurrent devaluing of women's role in caring for children. (Photographs by Britt Permien)*

for a deepened conception of the reproductive labour of both working-class women and children and the unexplored possibilities of working politically with children, especially when taking up issues directly relevant to children's lives. In progressing forward, we can continue to learn from such grassroots struggles and build a movement to acknowledge childcare as a collective responsibility and contribute to more just ways of being, living and caring.

NOTE

1 This photo essay is based on ideas developed in Rachel Rosen, Suzanne Baustad and Merryn Edwards, 'The Crisis of Social Reproduction under Global Capitalism: Working Class Women and Children in the Struggle for Universal Childcare,' in *Caring for Children: Social Movements and Public Policy in Canada*, ed. Rachel Langford, Susan Prentice and Patrizia Albanese (Vancouver: UBC Press, 2017).

3
When the rights of children prevail over the rights of their caretakers
A case study in the community homes of Bogotá, Colombia[1]

Susana Borda Carulla

Introduction

Children's and women's lives are deeply entwined and interdependent. As Rosen and Newberry suggest in this volume: 'Women and children are linked through species-being, a labour relation that anchors socially necessary labour.' Women take the greatest responsibility for children's care both in formal and informal settings, and in many societies bearing and raising children is seen as an essential component of womanhood.[2]

Despite their interdependency, children's and women's issues are two dissociated chapters of international law and policy, particularly since the adoption of the Convention on the Rights of the Child by the UN General Assembly in 1989. Not only are children's and women's issues addressed separately, but a clear hierarchy has been established by international organisations through promoting the idea that protecting children's rights is a lever for the social and thus the economic development of a nation.[3] As UNICEF put it in its 1995 report on the *State of the World's Children*: 'It is UNICEF's belief that the time has now come to put the needs and the rights of children at the very centre of development strategy. (...) The world will not solve its major problems until it learns to do a better job of protecting and investing in the physical, mental and emotional development of its children.'[4] The idea of prioritising children's issues is an 'active concept'[5] in the sense that it is a true motor of social change in contemporary societies.

What are the social consequences, for children and for women, of putting children first?

In this chapter, I will combine a study of the legal corpus which regulates the Colombian government's childcare programme (community homes, operated by female caretakers known as community mothers) with an ethnographic study of its implementation in an underprivileged neighbourhood on the southern periphery of Bogotá. I will expose the enduring tensions between the Colombian government – which advocates the dominance of children's rights over the rights of others – and the community mothers – whose labour rights are systematically violated by the state, prompting them to take action. Shedding light on how these tensions came to be will lead me to argue that if women's rights are not protected, there is a strong chance that the rights of the children they care for will not be protected either.

I will first discuss the history of the community homes programme: the legal situation and the ideological stance of the two social actors involved in the dispute (the Colombian state and the community mothers). I will then go on to analyse scenarios from daily life in the community homes, where community mothers break programme regulations. This will allow me to discuss the negative consequences of dissociating, in public policy terms, the rights of children from those of women.

State policy: 'children first'

The community homes are social childcare centres co-managed by the Colombian state and communities. They have been in operation since the 1980s in vulnerable neighbourhoods of large Colombian cities. Under this scheme, to become a community mother, a woman can offer to provide childcare services in her own home, to approximately 15 children aged from birth to six. The state provides resources to support the operation costs of the community homes, which are managed by associations comprising parents of the children and the community mothers from around twenty community homes. Programme implementation is the responsibility of the ICBF (*Instituto Colombiano de Bienestar Familiar* – Colombian Institute for the Wellbeing of Families), the public body responsible for child protection.

Since its inception in 1986, this childcare programme has grown exponentially and remained, until recently, the Colombian state's main child protection initiative. González and Durán estimate that in 2011, the programme involved 77,377 community mothers caring for 1,219,098 children, aged from birth to six, in 70,825 community homes based within the country's most vulnerable populations, both in urban and densely populated rural zones.[6] According to the same authors, in 2011 the programme covered 13 per cent of the total Colombian population aged from birth to six. In the context of Latin America, this is exceptional coverage for a public childcare programme.

Responding to a national crisis

Until 1979, the concept of child protection in Colombian legislation covered only judiciary protection and nutritional care.[7] It was the state's obligation to ensure that each Colombian child had a recognised father, even if he/she was born outside of marriage, and to ensure that all children received sufficient nutrition. In 1979, the notion of child protection was redefined within Colombian domestic law[8] as 'integral protection': [9] this included the right to a name and a nationality, education, nutrition, special care for disabled children, as well as the right to medical assistance, culture, leisure, family and home. In the same year, the provision of pre-school education and nutrition for all children also became an obligation for the state.

Enforcing the new child protection laws proved particularly challenging as Colombia was going through a profound social crisis. Between 1970 and 1980, the annual population growth rate was around 3 per cent. Internal migration rapidly transformed a rural country into an urban one: in only two generations, the urban population grew from 40 per cent to 74 per cent of the country's total.[10] As cities grew, the gap between the poor and the rich became more pronounced, leading to the development of segregated, concentrated zones of poverty, uncontrolled by the state. In this context, enforcing the new child protection laws also meant expanding provision to these new, rapidly growing and often very poor urban populations.

The community homes programme was born in response to this critical situation. During the 1970s, in the poor neighbourhoods of the large Colombian cities where the state was absent, there existed a multiplicity of autonomous community childcare initiatives. UNICEF showed interest in them and in 1977 began supporting the Colombian state, technically and financially, to identify, analyse and support the individual initiatives. The study produced positive results, leading to recognition of the use of autonomous community childcare initiatives as a model of intervention.[11]

The social crisis of the 1980s went hand in hand with a profound political crisis in Colombia. After 20 years of generalised political violence (1945–65), the country found itself in the midst of an internal armed conflict involving left-wing guerrillas, right-wing paramilitaries and the military. Drug trafficking was at its peak and the first extradition agreements signed between the Colombian government and the United States provoked a number of terrorist attacks in public spaces. The legitimacy of the state was called into question by a large part of the Colombian population.[12]

In 1985, at the very peak of the political crisis, President Virgilio Barco from the Liberal Party was elected. Social policy as a means of pursuing peace and reconciliation occupied a central place in his political agenda, with community homes playing a key role in the strategy. By 1988 – only two years after the pilot programme was launched – the government had created 100,000 community homes, mainly in the poorest parts of the country, to accommodate 1.5 million children aged from two to six. After only five years of operation, the programme covered 83 per cent of Colombian children living in poverty.[13] For the World Bank and the Inter-American Development Bank, the community homes were a 'model of social development' at this time.[14]

Child protection as the key to national integration

In testimony published in 1995, Jaime Benítez Tobón, one of the main ideologists behind the programme and a key figure in Barco's government, describes the place of the community homes within Barco's political agenda as follows:

> One of the keys towards the national integration we longed for was the child. Children would guide the general interest and would be the centre, the articulation of actions, the supra-value that would assemble citizens, providing them with common interests and objectives. Children would trigger the discovery of values of solidarity that would arise around them: friendship, neighbourly relations, work, joint effort, the interest in the common good. (...) In that manner, the State would act directly in favour of its citizens, (...) starting from the child; improving the life conditions of Colombian children would help to improve the Colombian State; by acting on the children, we would achieve the wellbeing

of families and, at the same time, family integration; and family integration would necessarily provoke national integration, which would necessarily result in the well-being of the State and the reality of the Nation.[15]

For the Barco government, child protection was the starting point, the rationale and the motor of a national integration movement. Barco's political desire was to articulate around child protection several processes: community-building within groups of forced migrants, who often had no shared cultural heritage; fruitful dialogue between the state and civil society that would progressively repair the legitimacy of the state; child protection education for the poorest populations; and modernisation of public institutions. In a society devastated by structural violence affecting family cohesion and the legitimacy of public institutions, child protection would be a vehicle for constructing a new national identity. Child protection was erected as a pillar of moral value, which could be shared by all across social and political divides.

The birth of the predominance principle

Interestingly, a few years later, 'children first' transitioned from a political ideal to a juridical principle and was enshrined in the Constitution. In 1991, following the surrender of arms by certain guerrilla groups followed by their reintegration into civil life, a plebiscite called for the rewriting of the Colombian political constitution. Jaime Benítez Tobón was elected as a member of the Constitutional Assembly. He was the author of Article 44 of the 1991 Constitution, which states, among other things, that 'children's rights prevail over the rights of others'. This idea is often referred to as the 'predominance principle'.

Juridical principles are not only basic rights but also rules of procedure and hermeneutical statements.[16] The 'predominance principle' thus has a particularly powerful juridical status: it is 1) a specific norm that contains obligations; 2) a general norm, applicable in many cases and in all domains of law; and 3) a norm that helps juridical operators take decisions in extreme cases. Through the drafting of the 'predominance principle', Benítez Tobón transformed the ideological basis of the community homes – child protection as a moral super-value – into the cardinal rule of the entire Colombian child protection system.[17]

As previously mentioned, the idea of the predominance of the rights of children over the rights of others is not uncommon in international children's rights advocacy. Nevertheless, from a human rights perspective, it is deeply problematic because it runs counter to human rights ideals. As Nigel Cantwell points out, children's rights are part of the human rights system, within which all rights are universal, interdependent and deeply linked to each other.[18] States are thus expected to protect and promote all human rights and fundamental liberties on an equal basis.

The community mothers' ongoing struggle for their labour rights

As Linda Gordon points out, 'The child-centred imperative has sometimes pitted children's "interests" against those of parents, especially mothers'.[19] This was certainly the case in Colombia: I will now argue that the Colombian predominance principle has had extremely negative effects on the community mothers' well-being: it has legitimised an open violation of their labour rights.

The legal situation

An exceptional administrative contract, the 'contribution contract' (*contrato de aportes*), links the community mothers to the ICBF. The contribution contract was created in 1979 specifically to ensure the operation of community homes: the law stipulates that the contract cannot be established and enforced by any other Colombian public institution.[20] Only the ICBF, because of the 'special nature of its service' – i.e. child protection – can enact this type of contract.[21]

The contribution contract stipulates that the ICBF should provide each association of community homes with the resources necessary for their operation. The community mothers themselves are defined in the contract as volunteers and, as such, are not employed by the state or the association. Through their association, the community mothers receive financial aid to support the operation of their community homes; a monthly 'grant' (less than the national minimum wage) to cover daily food provisions and some educational material for the children, plus funds to cover the public service expenses incurred by the community home. The community mothers may also benefit from financial contributions from the parents of the children they care for (up to 37.5 per cent of the minimum wage), of which 34 per cent must be invested in activities for the children. However, there is no obligation on parents to pay this contribution and a child cannot be removed from the community home if the parents do not pay. The community mothers thus face permanent financial insecurity and, despite recent legal changes (discussed below), they do not benefit from basic labour rights (e.g. social security or a retirement pension).

The social movements

As a social group, the community mothers soon realised that the contribution contract was not to their benefit. In 1988 – only two years after the inauguration of the community homes – they began to take action, seeking recognition of their labour rights. AMCOLOMBIA, the Colombian Association of Community Mothers and Fathers for a Better Colombia, was established in 1991. Created under the initiative of a group of community mothers from Bogotá who called upon their colleagues from all over the country to unite in the face of their shared challenges, AMCOLOMBIA has two missions: to defend the collective interests of the community mothers and demand protection of their rights by the Colombian State; and to influence public policy concerning childhood and families. Many NGOs focused on women's rights advocacy also support the cause of the community mothers. Currently, AMCOLOMBIA encompasses 20 municipal and regional associations of community mothers.

During the 1990s, other community mothers' organisations were created across the country, operating at the local, regional and national levels. Among the most powerful are SINTRACIHOBI (National Syndicate of Workers for the Protection of Childhood in the Community Homes), ADDHIP (Association for the Defence of the Rights of the Sons of the People), and USTRABIN (Union of Workers of the Community Homes). In the last decade of the twentieth century, these groups regularly organised demonstrations, public assemblies and occupations of public space, and held negotiations with the ICBF. All of these organisations fought for the same causes: 1) the effective inclusion of the community mothers and of their nuclear families in the national social security system; 2) the right for community mothers to have pensions; 3) community mothers' access to professional training in early childhood care; 4) designation of the status of public servant, and not volunteer, for community mothers; and 5) a minimum wage for those working as community mothers.

The judicial quagmire

During the 1990s, the community mothers brought their case to the Constitutional Court three times.[22] Each time, the court ruled on an

Action of Tutela (*Acción de Tutela*)[23] raised by a community mother on labour rights grounds, following the shutdown of her community home for reasons she deemed unfair. Each time, the court concluded that there was an absence of any labour relationship between the community mother and the state, or between the community mother and their association. For the Court, there was no legal basis on which to rule in favour of the community mother.

That being said, the three judgements of the Constitutional Court during the 1990s created strong disagreement among the Supreme Court judges. In 1998, three judges published their objections to the court's original judgement, coming out on the side of the community mothers.[24] They argued that the court had only conducted a formal analysis of the situation and omitted to take into account a number of social realities: 1) the existence of a relationship of subordination and dependence of the community mothers vis-à-vis the ICBF; 2) the existence of obligations for the community mothers defined by the ICBF; and 3) the fact that the community mothers' pay was inferior to the minimum legal wage. The judges argued that, had these elements been taken into consideration by the court, the conclusion would have been that 'what's at stake is the work of an important number of Colombian women, who are clearly discriminated in comparison to other employees, and whose only income, which allows only for minimum subsistence, is compromised'.[25]

The United Nations Committee on Economic, Social and Cultural Rights, ratified by Colombia in 1969, also pronounced itself twice in favour of the community mothers' labour rights. Among its recommendations, the committee asked the Colombian state to 'improve the training of the "community mothers" and regularize their work situation, treating them for all purposes as workers in the employ of a third party'.[26]

Slowly but surely, under the pressure of social movements, women's rights advocacy organisations, and the international community, community mothers' social rights have evolved. In 1990, they were included in the social security system; in 2008, they acquired the right to earn a pension and their allowance was raised to 70 per cent of the legal minimum wage. Finally, in 2012, the community mothers' labour rights were fully recognised: confronted with a new Action of Tutela brought by a community mother following the shutdown of her community home, the court ordered the ICBF to install a process allowing the community mothers to progressively, but rapidly, earn the equivalent of a minimum wage.[27] The judgement demanded that all community mothers who work full time must earn, throughout the year 2013, a minimum wage: by

2014, a work contract subject to domestic labour law had to be established between each community mother and the ICBF.

However, to date, implementation of this judgement is far from being realised. Community mothers still do not earn a minimum wage, nor do they have a proper work contract. Indeed, the fiscal impact of the court's judgement is such that it endangers the very existence of the ICBF. The Colombian president has recently rejected a new bill covering implementation of the law, thus blocking its submission to Congress. According to the president, the bill jeopardises children's rights because its implementation would inevitably result in the dissolution of the public institution entrusted with their protection. On these grounds, the president argues, the bill is unconstitutional.

Breaking programme regulations

Policies that put women's labour into the service of the state in the name of children's well-being, and mobilise it through spuriously gendered altruism, are a common liberal strategy (see Llobet and Milanich; Rosen and Newberry, this volume). I will now go on to discuss ethnographic data showcasing daily interactions between community mothers and the children they care for, in order to highlight the contradictions and tensions produced on the ground by such policy. I will argue that the predominance principle does not achieve the purpose of ensuring children's well-being and the protection of their rights, but rather exacerbates the problem by creating a legislative framework for violating women's rights.

Ethnographic data was generated between 2011 and 2013 in Ciudad Bolívar, a southern suburb of Bogotá. Ciudad Bolívar is one of the poorest areas of the city: its population has been growing steadily since the 1980s due to the regular arrival of rural migrants, among whom many are internally displaced persons fleeing the armed conflict in their hometowns.[28] Ciudad Bolívar was one of the areas chosen by the Colombian state for piloting the community homes programme in 1986 because it was judged a true 'governance challenge' by Latin American leaders at the time.[29] Compared to other areas where the programme was implemented, in Ciudad Bolívar community homes developed rapidly and intensively.[30] Not coincidentally, Ciudad Bolívar is also the birthplace of the community mothers' social movement.[31]

The scenes described in the following pages all have one thing in common: they showcase community mothers breaking programme regulations. As a result, the children they care for are not fed as they ought to be; children's care is often delegated to non-qualified persons[32] (most often, minors); and much of the community mothers' energy is diverted from childcare tasks to the challenges of running a family enterprise.

Feeding the children

Making sure that children are properly fed is a key dimension of the community homes programme. Children who attend community homes are given a snack upon arrival in the morning, then lunch at noon, and another snack in the afternoon. These meals are supposed to cover between 65 per cent and 70 per cent of the calorie input recommended for the age group. Menus are prepared each week by nutritionists at the local office of the ICBF and the community mothers are expected to adhere to them. Every month, the ICBF transfers to the associations the money needed to buy the ingredients for meal preparation.

In the context of the poor communities involved, the provision of food in the community homes is a vital component of their offer. According to the community mothers interviewed, many parents whose children benefit from the programme rely almost entirely on community homes for provision of their child's daily nutrition. For unemployed young mothers, their key motivation for sending their children to the childcare centre is that the children will be well fed. For a family of three or four living on only one minimum wage, having their child fed is of significant importance.

Claudia, a young community mother, discovered after only one year of being involved in the programme that within her association the prescribed menus were not respected by the other community mothers, who used the associated funds for other purposes:

> *I struggle so that they* [the other community mothers from the association] *give me my groceries, because they have to give me what's written there, what Bienestar* [the ICBF] *writes on the menus. They give us money to do what's written you understand? But I'm often told that we don't have enough. (...) I struggle because I see there is so much corruption with the money for the children's food. (...) I often fight with them* [the other community mothers from the association] *because of the food. I have a child under my care who eats only the cheese I give him, I know it's the only one he'll eat during the week because I give it to him, because his mother has other things to do or maybe has no money, (...) so I tell myself that if I have the possibility of giving the child a yoghurt,*

then I should give it to him. And I struggle for my yoghurt! If it's written that you have to give them pasta and cheese, well then give me the cheese: if you have the money to buy the cheese, why don't you give it to me? They [the other community mothers] *are not used to these kind of remarks, if they don't have the cheese they don't stress (...). They tell me I'm a beggar, but I demand it, they must give me what's written because many children only eat what I give them.*

Claudia is implying that some of the community mothers in her association are keeping for themselves a part of the funds intended to buy food for the children. Thus, Claudia cannot always buy all the products required for the ICBF menu, and so the children she cares for are not fed as they ought to be. Unlike most other community mothers, Claudia does not rely on the food she buys for the children in order to feed her own family; her husband has relatively good employment, and as a couple, they reside at her in-laws' family home.

Numerous examples of corruption in the use of public funds intended to buy food for the children were revealed during field work. The ICBF is well aware of this, and supervises closely the beneficiary children's nutritional status: each month, the community mothers must submit the weight curves of the children they care for and special utensils for measuring the exact quantity of food that must be given to each child are provided. When officials pay their surprise visits to the community homes for programme evaluation purposes, adherence to menus is a major component of their assessment.

Choosing an assistant

Caring for the children during the day is not the only activity expected of community mothers engaged in the programme. Systematic observation conducted in five community homes revealed that the community mothers spent most of their work time away from the children under their care. A certain number of obligations require them to regularly leave the direct supervision of the children: cooking three meals each day for the children, attending the numerous compulsory training sessions offered by the ICBF and attending to administrative tasks linked to the operation of the community home. Leaving the children without supervision is a big risk for any community mother. The law is clear that temporary abandonment of the children or even lack of attention are sufficient reasons to close a community home.[33] Engaging an assistant to run the community home is thus a necessity for most community mothers.

Accordingly, since 1989, the law states that in order to run her community home, each community mother must have the help of an assistant, who can be the mother or another relative of a child she cares for.[34] According to the law, the assistant should help the community mother in carrying out activities with the children, but should not be regarded as a substitute. Indeed, delegation of the children's care to a third person is a justifiable cause for immediate closure of a community home.[35] No money is transferred to the association in order to pay these assistants and, per a law passed in 2011 to regulate food rations within the community home,[36] no ration is allocated to the assistant (the community mother's ration is included in the count).

Counting on the children's parents to assist them, as the law suggests, is unrealistic, since most of them work full-time and far from their homes. Under these conditions, meeting these legal requirements seems like an impossible task. How do the community mothers deal with this legal quagmire? Many community mothers, like Carolina,[37] rely on their own daughters:

> *I have three daughters: one is 17, the other is 15 and the other is 11 years old. They are my right hand. In the evening, they help me out a lot. (...) For example, today it was Leidy – they alternate. In the evening, she woke the children from their nap, she gave them their snack and she brushed their hair and cleaned their face and teeth before sending them back home.*

Having teenage daughters is certainly an advantage. But sometimes, even small children have to contribute to running the community home:

Susana (ethnographer): *So, someone helps you out with all these children?*
María (community mother): *Mmm... no, not always.*
Susana: *Not always? So sometimes, yes?*
María: *Well when I really need it I look for someone to help me out, because to tell you the truth, I like to work alone.*
Susana: *In spite of everything you have to do?*
María: *Yes, in spite of that, I try to handle everything myself.*
Susana: *And when you need someone, what do you do?*
María: *Well we help each other out, among family members or with the daughters of other community mothers. Actually, only recently did I start to work alone, because my children used to help me out a lot, even when they were little.*
Susana: *How did they help you?*

María: *Well by playing with them... also my daughter, when she was eight, had to stay alone with them one time. It was a risk, but I really didn't have a choice because the lady who told me she'd come finally didn't show up, and I left convinced that she would come later! (...) Another time, it was the same story with my son – he was seven or eight: I had to go to training and the lady didn't show up, so he prepared the milk for the children himself!*

When the family network is missing, there are always alternative solutions. In these very poor neighbourhoods, it is not difficult to find a vulnerable person who agrees to help the community mother on a regular basis, in exchange for food only. I observed two examples of this approach. On one occasion, a young woman with a mental disability was helping one community mother on a regular basis; she was fed at noon but received no financial compensation. In another instance, the three daughters (15, 11, and 9 years old) of an internally displaced woman who had just arrived in the neighbourhood were helping out the community mother: 'I pity them,' she said. 'Their mother left to do some ironing and earn some money, so I take them in: they help me out with the children and I give them food in exchange.'

Although delegating the care of the children to a minor is, according to the law, a cause for immediate closure of a community home,[38] this practice is very common, certainly because it is difficult for the ICBF to detect it, and it thus is of less risk to the community mothers.

Small family enterprises

As Llobet and Milanich (this volume) point out, the position and the social status of 'mother' can be used strategically by women living in constrained circumstances. This is undoubtedly the case in the community homes, where women mobilise their good reputation within the community and the rich social networks created across the associations to set up and run small, often successful, family enterprises from their home.

María runs a tailoring business, specialising in repairing clothes and in producing cheap covers for the mattresses where the children take their naps. She sells them by the hundred to counterparts in her association, as well as those across other associations in the neighbourhood.

Ana also runs a tailoring business. With the help of her daughters and two mothers of children she cares for, she makes uniforms for children in the programme. She sells them in large quantities to other community mothers in the neighbourhood, who in turn rent them out to parents for 'graduation day'– when six-year-olds leave the community homes to go to school. Ana's sister Camila, who is also a community mother in the same association, creates personalised diplomas for each child, which parents enthusiastically purchase. Needless to say, the graduation day is the community mothers' invention.

Carolina's husband is retired. He bought a bus and set up a small group-transport enterprise. His wife likes to promote the fact that she is the only community mother in the association who often takes her children out for 'educational excursions'. Her husband takes care of the transport, and parents are willing to pay for excursions promoted by the ICBF.

Marta's daughter, who is 16 years old, takes full advantage of her mother's community home to offer her own childcare services. According to regulations, among the 14 children who can be cared for in any given community home only two can be under two years of age. In the neighbourhood, the childcare offer for children under two is therefore more limited than it is for children between two and six, and young mothers often struggle to find a place for babies within the community homes. Marta's daughter, who still lives with her parents, offers childcare services to children under two, in parallel to her mother's community home.[39]

The ICBF is conscious of this reality as well; in 1996, a law was issued indicating that offering childcare services for financial compensation is cause for immediate closure of the community home. Nevertheless, this too seems to be a law that is readily circumvented.

Conclusion: The paradox of the predominance principle

Through this case study I have shown how, on a daily basis, community mothers utilise both individual and collective strategies in order to make their daily childcare activities financially sustainable. These strategies involve breaking programme regulations regarding the children's nutrition, their supervision and their early education. I have also shown that the driving force behind these strategies are the social injustices faced by the community mothers, namely the flagrant, long-running violation of their labour rights by the Colombian state for almost 30 years.

I can now come back to the question raised in the introduction: What are the social consequences, for children and for women, of putting children first? This case study demonstrates that if women's rights are violated, children's rights will most probably be violated as well. The predominance principle enshrined in Article 44 of the Colombian Constitution intends to give absolute priority to the protection of children's rights but paradoxically, by legitimating the subordination of the women's labour rights to those of the children, the children's own well-being is negatively affected, and they are neither being fed nor cared for as they ought to be from a children's rights perspective.

This is yet another example of 'what is wrong with putting children first', as Linda Gordon would put it.[40] Achieving social justice for both women and children requires working beyond liberal, individualist understandings of rights, towards a recognition of children's and women's social interdependency.

NOTES

1. Research leading to the writing of this contribution was undertaken in the framework of the authors' doctoral studies at Université Paris Descartes, Ceped. The author wishes to thank the CEF (Corporation of Studies in France of the French Embassy in Colombia), ICANH (Colombian Institute of Anthropology and History), COLFUTURO (Foundation for the Future of Colombia), and COLCIENCIAS (Administrative Department of Science, Technology and Innovation of the Colombian government) for their financial support in the process. Special thanks to the editors for their patient and thorough review of this text, and to Heather Purdie for English proofreading.
2. Katherine Twamley et al., 'The (Im)possibilities of Dialogue across Feminism and Childhood Scholarship and Activism,' *Children's Geographies* 15, no. 2 (2017): 249–55.
3. Susana Borda Carulla, 'L'enfant comme levier du développement: régulation sociale par les politiques sur l'enfance en Colombie,' *Autrepart* 4, no. 72 (2015): 23–40.
4. UNICEF, *State of the World's Children Report* (1995).
5. James Ferguson, *The Anti-Politics Machine: Development, Depoliticization and Bureaucratic Power in Lesotho* (Cambridge: Cambridge University Press, 1990).
6. José-Luis González Ramírez and Iván Mauricio Durán, "Evaluar para mejorar: el caso del programa Hogares Comunitarios de Bienestar del ICBF," *Desarrollo y Sociedad*, no. 69 (2012): 187–234.
7. Florentino Malaver and Jorge Serrano, 'El Instituto Colombiano de Bienestar Familiar, ICBF: un caso de gestión pública. Las paradojas de una evolución incomprendida,' *Revista Innovar Journal*, no. 7 (1996): 27–49.
8. Law 7 of 1979.
9. This evolution within Colombian domestic law parallels the evolution of the international paradigm on child protection. In 1978, Poland submitted to the United Nations its project for a convention on the rights of the child. This initiative would evolve, 11 years later, into the adoption of the Convention on the Rights of the Child by the UN General Assembly. In order to encourage States to act in favour of the protection of the rights of the child, the UN declared 1979 the 'International Year of the Child'. During this period, the concept of children's rights took form and became a series of consensuses on the international level. Indeed, before this date, the concept of children's rights was much more limited in terms of diversity of rights and international consensus existed only concerning issues such as health and education. The International Year of the Child was the occasion to quantify, for the first time, issues such as children's imprisonment, sexual exploitation and work.
10. Marco Palacios, *Entre la legitimidad y la violencia. Colombia, 1875–1994* (Bogotá: Grupo Editorial Norma, 2003).
11. Jaime Benítez-Tobón, *Por los niños de Colombia* (Medellín: Martín Vieco, 1995).

12 Palacios, *Entre la legitimidad y la violencia*.
13 Carlos Castillo-Cardona et al., *Los hogares comunitarios de bienestar y los derechos del niño: el caso colombiano*. Innocenti Occasional Papers, Child Rights Series 3 (Florence: Unicef, 1993).
14 Presidencia de la República de Colombia, *Por nuestros niños. Programas para su protección y desarrollo en Colombia* (Bogotá: Benjamín Villegas, 1990): 94.
15 Benítez-Tobón, *Por los niños*, 97–9. The English translation is the authors'.
16 Manuel Fernando Quinche-Ramírez, *Derecho constitucional colombiano. De la Carta de 1991 y sus reformas* (Bogotá: Ediciones Doctrina y Ley Lta., 2010).
17 It is worth noting that although the 1991 Constitution also gives other population groups (mothers, the elderly, internally displaced persons) the right to special protection, only in the children's case is a predominance principle pronounced. See Quinche Ramírez, *Derecho constitucional colombiano*.
18 Nigel Cantwell, 'Are Children's Rights Still Human?' in *The Human Rights of Children: From Visions to Implementation*, ed. Jane Williams and Antonella Invernizzi (Farnham: Ashgate, 2011): 37–61.
19 Linda Gordon, 'The Perils of Innocence, or What's Wrong with Putting Children First,' *The Journal of the History of Childhood and Youth* 1, no. 3 (2008): 331.
20 Cf. Law 7 of 1979 and related Decree 2388 of 1979 (Article 127).
21 Law 7 of 1979 and related Decree 2388 of 1979 (Article 127).
22 Judgement T-14-92 of 1992; Judgement T-269 of 1995; and Judgement SU-224 of 1998.
23 The *Action of Tutela* is a mechanism installed by Article 86 of the Colombian Constitution which aims to protect the fundamental constitutional rights of individuals when they are menaced by the action or omission of a public authority and when there is no other means for the victim to enforce them. The court has the obligation to treat *Tutela* cases within ten days of their filing and they have priority over all other judicial actions.
24 This reserve is exposed within Judgement SU-224 of 1998.
25 The English translation is the author's. (Judgement SU-224 of 1998).
26 Committee on Economic, Social and Cultural Rights. Consideration of reports submitted by states parties under Article 16 and 17 of the Covenant: Concluding observations of the Committee on Economic, Social and Cultural Rights: Colombia. E/C.12/115/12, 1995.
27 Constitutional Court Judgement T-628 of 2012.
28 María Victoria Angulo-González and Mike Núñez Lozano, *Diagnóstico, políticas y acciones en relación con el desplazamiento forzado hacia Bogotá* (Bogotá: Secretaría de Hacienda Distrital, 2004).
29 Benítez Tobón, *Por los niños*, 97–9.
30 Ángel Libardo Herreño-Hernández, *No hay derecho...Las madres comunitarias y jardineras frente al derecho laboral* (Bogotá: ILSA, 1999).
31 Claudia Patricia Sierra-Pardo, *La organización gremial de las madres comunitarias: un proceso de participación y movilización popular* (Bogotá: Universidad Nacional de Colombia, 1992).
32 In the late 1990s, as a result of negative programme evaluation in terms of the quality of the attention provided to the children, the government set up a compulsory training programme for the community mothers. Women who joined the programme during the 1990s were given the opportunity to complete the training if they did not want to quit, but this was often problematic because many of them had not completed high school, which made learning in formalised settings a slow and often daunting process. Women who have joined the programme since the turn of the century must take intensive training during their first year acting as community mother. The intention of the government is to gradually professionalise the community mothers.
33 ICBF, *Acuerdo 50 de 1996*, Article 3, section h.
34 ICBF, *Acuerdo 21 de 1989*, Article 11.
35 ICBF, *Acuerdo 50 de 1996*, Article 2, section f.
36 ICBF, *Resolución 776 de 2011*. Title V, section 5.1, paragraph ii).
37 All names have been changed in order to protect the identity of the interviewees.
38 ICBF, *Acuerdo 50 de 1996*, Article 3, section h.
39 ICBF, *Acuerdo 50 de 1996*. Article 2, section m.
40 Gordon, *Perils of Innocence*.

4
Thinking through childhood and maternal studies
A feminist encounter

Rachel Thomson and Lisa Baraitser

Conceptualising 'child' and 'mother'

Our starting point for this paper is the relation between two fields of study – 'childhood' and 'maternal' studies. Although it might have been simpler to start with the relation between the terms 'child' and 'mother', or 'childhood' and 'motherhood', we want to focus on the collective efforts that have been made, to make sense of these terms. Neither 'child' nor 'mother' are static, ahistorical concepts, and the ongoing investigation of what it might mean to be a child and a mother, as particular, embodied, and socially and historically constrained experiences, has its own genealogy. Our approach is to put childhood studies and maternal studies into dialogue to see what each can learn from the other.

We should say from the outset that we do not think that if you add together the insights from these fields, an overall picture of mother–child relations emerges. In fact, part of our argument is that mother and child remain opaque to one another, two adjacent positions of experience that simply cannot 'know' one another. This incommensurability inflects the ways that maternal and childhood studies also remain opaque to one another. However, this does not mean that we cannot think about the relations between the fields, perhaps precisely at the point where occlusions in their capacities to inter-relate become manifest. In fact, we want to ask whether one field can be thought about without the other at all. What is the child for maternal studies, the mother for childhood studies, and how do these concepts anchor each field through processes of engagement and othering?

Interdisciplinary childhood studies can be understood as a 'compensatory' project, working against the notion of the child as a developing subject, on the way to adulthood, or as an always-already vulnerable subject attached to adult figures. What founds the field is an attempt to move away from both development and attachment, and understand the child autonomously, yet as relationally defined by generational positions and practices.[1] Approaching the child as a discrete yet situated subject has been called 'conceptual autonomy' by Barrie Thorne, and is partly underpinned in the field of childhood studies by a shift in focus away from dependency on the figure of the mother.[2] Maternal studies has had a similar struggle. The question for maternal studies has revolved around how we conceptualise the maternal subject as a subject position that is not synonymous with 'woman', nor the subject who puts her needs and desires aside for the sake of the always-more-vulnerable child. In order for the child or mother to emerge as the main focus of each field, it appears that both must 'bracket' the other, even when empirically children can be mothers, and mothers, children. The question then is what it means when these two fields that have been bound up in the struggle for their own conceptual autonomy come together. Put another way, what is the anxiety about getting together, and in what ways does this getting together make 'feminist' trouble?

This brings us to our second consideration: the function of 'feminism' as a third term in the dialogue between childhood and maternal studies. The dialogue we wish to engage inevitably takes in histories of feminist thought, as the study of childhood and maternity is entangled with both terms. Indeed, one strand of second-wave feminism showed how 'woman', 'mother' and 'child' have been written into one another, through the social and political analysis of the potential reproductive capacity of women's bodies, and through forms of regulation of both children and women which reiterate and displace this connection. Feminist legal work in the 1990s on the Victorian period, for instance, elucidated how late-nineteenth-century legislation produced the very categories of womanhood, motherhood and childhood that eclipsed and fixed classed ideals of dependency and interdependency.[3] Further feminist work revealed both the relations between the regulation of motherhood and childhood, and how such forms play a crucial role in securing class privilege and empire.[4] Here feminist and post-colonial scholars have examined how women, children and racialised or enslaved others are also inextricably linked in a colonial imaginary of 'primitivism', revealing how these subject positions are mutually associated with 'pre-maturity' in relation to the masculine, autonomous, white, self-sufficient adult subject, who does not bear or care for children. If one impulse of feminism in thinking through maternal–child relations was to turn to history, then another was to pay attention to differences in geopolitical location and social position, and the aftermath of empire.

More recently feminism and queer studies have begun to appreciate time as productive of patterns of social belonging which have particular implications for childhood and maternal studies.[5] Elizabeth Freeman, for instance, shows how the narratives of linear timelines – such as birth, development, maturation, reproduction, the accumulation of wealth, its passing on to dependents, and death – come to function as a temporal 'norm', rendering lives that do not unfold along these lines as 'deviant' and 'immature'. Lee Edelman has famously argued that the figure of the Child (and we would say, by association, the mother) plays a crucial role in suturing the social and national imaginary, such that the future of the nation and of the social bond is figured through heterosexual reproduction that subsumes all other forms of futurity. The child, in this temporal narrative, is the figure for the 'yet-to-come' and so occupies the temporality of anticipation, rather than temporalities that may be specific to childhood, such as those of immediacy or the situated present. Alongside this, we have seen analyses of maternal temporalities that depart from classical accounts of 'women's time', which has been described as both cyclical and bound up with the monumental time of the regeneration of the species.[6] A focus on the temporalities of waiting, duration and interruption has emerged, one that elucidates how care work in the global north continues to be the domain of women,[7] a situation that brings with it complex negotiations of time (see also Rosen and Newberry, this volume).[8] Scholars have therefore sought to uncouple both motherhood and childhood from the normativity of 'development' and have proposed both mother and child as figures that are 'for the future' without needing to be used as figures for 'futurity' per se.[9]

Finally, in feminist theory, the relationality of the terms 'woman', 'mother' and 'child' has emerged as a central preoccupation, implicit in much early radical feminism that identified a reproductive capacity as the 'grounds' of oppression.[10] What is striking is the way 'mother' and 'child' as categories of analysis have been both pushed and pulled in and out of focus in this feminist work. At certain points the child gets pushed to the margins of feminism so as to make room for the agentic, autonomous notion of 'woman'. And the 'mother' becomes equally suspect for feminism, with intensive debates on that term reaching their height in the 1980s and subsiding into an uncomfortable agreement that a 'strategic essentialism'[11] may be the best way of dealing with the troubling issues of reproductive bodies, dependent others, the ethics of care and the messy borders between self and other, biology and sociality. Yet motherhood was always a central issue for feminism[12] and, as Angela McRobbie elucidates, women raised on a diet of liberal feminism in the period after feminism's second wave find that equality is attainable only so long as they are child free.[13] Nevertheless, the work of granting mother and child conceptual autonomy is ongoing. For example, Claudia Castañeda observes how the figure of the unfinished and mutable child is central to much contemporary social theory that privileges 'becoming', while also occupying a space within psychoanalytically informed feminist theories where adult subjectivity incorporates the child within.[14] She notices that just as the child appears to emerge as an ontological category that is not dependent for its coherence on a relation with another, the child is drawn on to bolster accounts of decentred or unfolding subjectivities.[15] The adult–child relation therefore continues to challenge our capacity to fashion theories that are relational whilst also allowing subjects conceptual autonomy. In Castañeda's terms, it pushes us to articulate a politics in which 'mother' or 'child' can remain privileged terms, without producing an abstract Other (whether Mother or Child) through which this privilege is secured.

In a similar way, the deconstruction of the autonomous, rights-bearing subject has been central to feminist care ethics, and by extension to maternal studies. The philosopher Christine Battersby has suggested that feminist philosophy could do well to start from the question of what would have to change in order to take seriously the notion that a 'person' could, at least potentially, become two. 'Could we retain a notion of self-identity,' she asks, 'if we did not privilege that which is self-contained and self-directed?'[16] The potentiality to become two, in other words, could be a starting point for understanding identity, along with a conception of the self as always already relational, embodied and fleshy. This view theorises relationships with dependent others as constitutive of the self, such that inequalities and power-dependencies are basic and fundamental.

These features of maternity can be applied as much to childhood as to motherhood. We can think of 'the child' as potentially multiple, interdependent, a 'fleshy continuity' emergent at the intersection of self and other, shifting the rights-based, autonomous, agentic child-subject closer towards the emergent co-dependency of subjectivity per se, a subjectivity that is shared with the messy co-dependence of the mother. As Thorne argued, if we reconfigure notions of self in terms of relationality, even while acknowledging hierarchies of difference, then this changes the ways we understand the social matrix as constituted through relations, and this in turn changes the ways in which we theorise both mothers and children.[17] Perhaps what is now important is that we acknowledge that both analytic categories of mother and child can do the work of destabilising theories of agentic subjectivity, rather than each field trying to claim this work as unique, whilst simultaneously being at the expense of the other.

Fields and journeys through them

There is a now well-worn story about how the 'new' childhood studies emerged in the late 1980s. This included a move by sociology and anthropology to intervene in a field dominated by psychology, and the desire to extend the practices of social construction to reveal the child as agentic, specific and rights-bearing – a move linked in policy terms to the UNCRC (1989).[18] In retrospect we can admire this as an effective instance of field-building that could be compared to the more precarious history of 'women's studies', which, through mainstreaming, largely dissolved as a distinct academic field of research, being replaced by gender studies in many parts of the globe. Childhood studies has involved a timely embrace of interdisciplinarity, whilst retaining several crucial components: a power base within the social sciences; clear links to policy and practice via the articulation of children's rights within education and social work training; and methodological innovation, as researchers have sought to realise the promise to articulate children's standpoints. Twenty years on there are specialist journals, international research centres and thriving degree and postgraduate programmes that attest to the resilience of the project and its responsiveness to developments within and beyond the academy. What is important, perhaps, in giving this account is that childhood studies emerged at a specific theoretical juncture, when researchers had become frustrated with the resources available to them. This sense that something is not quite right in the way a concept or experience is being articulated or understood is perhaps the most valuable affect of them all. However, we might ask why it is that childhood studies may need the mother or the maternal in order to enrich its thinking. Can it do its work of studying childhood without reference to the mother at all?

Maternal studies, on the other hand, is a more diffuse field. There are no departments of 'maternal studies' worldwide, no degree programmes that take that name in the UK, and just a handful of dedicated journals and informal, largely unfunded networks, that attempt to address motherhood as distinct from studies of parenting and the family.[19] Whilst it has become an intensely interdisciplinary domain, maternal studies retains the affect of embarrassment within the academy, through its continued desire to study and understand parenting 'in the feminine'. In insisting on gendering the field, maternal studies in effect feminises it in a way that may no longer be tenable elsewhere. Although 'maternal studies' might well include the role of men in engendering and rearing children, and of queer and trans mothering practices, in its attempt to honour the ongoing reality that it is women who perform the majority of childrearing and domestic labour maternal studies brings with it anxieties and unease. This includes concern over whether this deliberate focus on the mother returns us to 'maternalist' sensibilities, essentialist debates, 'difference' feminism and its failures to embrace multiple differences beyond the gender binary; to bodies, even if they are now spread across multiple material, affective, and subjective sites.

Perhaps what remains most difficult about maternal studies is the assertion that the 'quality' of relations still matters. By refusing to attend to what is specific about the relationship between women and children, we leave the space between them open to oppressive discourses of intensive parenting, or discourses of blame, ridicule and the depoliticising of motherhood. Yet to work in this space entails dealing with discomfort, or revulsion, or even the unbearable. There is an element of the mother–child relation that we want to push away from, even when that pushing is also self-destructive. It is interesting, therefore, to see a return, through maternal studies, to psychoanalytic theories drawn from the work of Donald Winnicott, Wilfred Bion and Bracha Ettinger, theories of interconnectivity, or of what Ettinger has termed 'transsubjectivity', that put the child back without naturalising this relation.[20] Conceptual autonomy as a project, we would argue, therefore becomes simply impossible. In this sense maternal studies refuses *not* to deal with the unfinished and unfinishable business of feminism.

During initial discussions that led to this paper, we explored the question of what maternal studies could learn from childhood studies and vice versa. For maternal studies we discussed how a focus on the diverse, concrete present, which has been a focus of childhood studies, could help identify what it means to mother at particular historical junctures; how an engagement with the ways in which the category is mediated by material culture could enhance similar interests in motherhood and material culture; and how an attentiveness to futurity that has characterised childhood studies could be used to help think through the kinds of futuricity embedded in motherhood as a state of being. For childhood studies we identified that it could take from maternal studies a politics of inter-subjectivity or inter-connectedness that does not end in a collapse of one set of needs in the face of the other, and a focus on the non-linear temporal realities of inter-generation. As we came to write, we realised that these were the lessons *we* had learned; that is, they reflected the ways in which we had hit particular impasses in thinking. They involved a desire to understand the mother and the child more relationally even when the desire was also to shore up the boundary between the two.

Thinking through relational entities

What might it look like, then, to think differently of the push and pull between the needs of the child and those of the mother? If we accept that conceptual autonomy is a fantasy that has structured both childhood and motherhood studies, we might be able to think about the push and pull in the practice of being and theorising mother and child. Pushing and pulling, in other words, happens for theorists as much as for all of us in our everyday lives. What happens if we stop trying to resolve it, but instead make the uncomfortable move of reconceptualising it as a form of 'weaning'? Instead of either pulling away or collapsing into one another theoretically, perhaps processes of separation between mothers and children leads to the establishment of relational entities and chains of mother and child, understood through small moments of substitution, mediation and scaffolding that can be traced across time and space.

Child and mother are constantly remade. Working historically and empirically, you begin to learn something about what this remaking looks like, its consequences and implications. In Rachel Thomson's research this involves working qualitatively and longitudinally with women who also become mothers, and moving with relational convoys over time, understanding biographies as dynamic and indexical and 'mother' and 'child' as co-existent, contested and emergent, yet profoundly patterned and governed. In Lisa Baraitser's work it involves working conceptually through the quotidian, everyday, overlooked and mundane scenes of motherhood, whether described anecdotally, or 'found' in the myriad of places that maternal stories emerge, mining the 'incidental' for its theoretical import, in order that theory is never anything other than an attempt to make sense of experience.

We would like, therefore, to use the second half of this chapter to examine a fragment of case material drawn from Rachel's study *Making Modern Mothers,* using 'weaning' as a way to conceptualise the push and pull between mother's and children's needs, and between motherhood and childhood studies. If, as we have been arguing, the fantasy of conceptual autonomy needs to be disrupted by a willingness to bracket mothers and children *together* (without collapsing one into the other), then we may learn something about the relation between mothers and children, and between maternal studies and childhood studies, by working through the case study together.

David and Anastasia

The *Making Modern Mothers* study is an empirical research project that captures and characterises the experience of a diverse group of British women becoming mothers for the first time in 2005.[21] The study is a collective endeavour involving four researchers: Rachel Thomson, Mary Jane Kehily, Sue Sharpe and Lucy Hadfield. Starting in 2005 with 60 participants, it narrowed from 2009 to focus on six, whom researchers followed from pregnancy into the second year of the children's life and most recently met with again in 2013 when the children were eight years old. The research uses a range of methods in order to capture aspects of the women's experiences, including interviews, photographs and observation. This includes a 'day in a life' experiment that involves participants allowing researchers to spend an 'ordinary' day with them, producing 'micro-ethnographies' composed of photographs and reflective field notes written by the researcher soon after the observation. The method enables researchers to include children within the project in a new way. This material has been curated on an interactive digital website through further collaboration with the filmmaker Susi Arnott and the photographer Crispin Hughes.

Rachel writes: The research began as a study of new motherhood. Children were not yet born. Over the study we witnessed the ways in which the arrival of a separate yet dependent being acted as an interruption and provocation to the lives of the women and those around them. A longitudinal extension of the original study forced us to refocus our attention when experiencing a 'day in the life' of the mothers – finding our gaze grasped by toddlers, intent on being part of the action, drawing us into communication and interactions around food and control. Further funding opportunities allowed us to focus explicitly on the children, at which point mothers seemed to fade into the background, operating as a kind of 'necessary context' for access and interpretation. The documents that we made together increasingly operated as memorialising opportunities for fast flowing family cultures – too mundane to be celebrated formally and yet part of a nexus of everyday practices that scaffold interdependent projects of selves.

From the outset we noticed the material culture of mothering – documenting the buggy and bag; the toys that had been passed down or along, and where it seemed right to start afresh. We were interested in how the objects gathered around a new baby were like a firmament, with each star representing a valued place or person who it was hoped would accompany the child as time passed. We noticed when particular objects 'failed' and were given away or simply gathered dust. Bedrooms became full and were emptied as new beginnings were initiated. The research itself was an important part of the 'firmament' surrounding the child and mother, travelling together, explicitly reminding both of earlier conversations, decisions, hopes. We periodically asked mothers to reflect on time passing using our own documentation as provocation. We extended these conversations to involve children who were asked to understand and consent to a process that had begun before they were born.

How we think about the child is then shaped by both theory and research design – where we draw the boundary of what is included in view. In this study we drew lines in gendered terms around mothers and grandmothers. Fathers could be included if invited in by mothers, but so could a friend, a sister, a neighbour. Child siblings were not included, though they inserted themselves insistently. Neighbourhoods and homes were the sites of interviews, and observations. Most recently school became part of what was seen and incorporated into view. Theoretically we were motivated by an existentialist interest in self-making and a materialist notion that such projects involve situated practice. We were suspicious of outcome-oriented developmentalism but excited by more open-ended notions of becoming.

We present here a fragment of fieldwork notes from a research encounter with David, aged eight, and his mother Anastasia, which captures the moment that they look at the multi-media document created through the research, showcasing David's bedroom and his account of his 'favourite things' (see 'Favourite things': http://modernmothers.org/favs/d/david.html). The fieldnote is followed by our reflections, capturing some of the productive tensions between childhood and maternal studies outlined earlier. To appreciate the discussion we encourage readers to first look at the multimedia document by following the link above. David is an only child, living with mum (Anastasia) and dad (Richie) in a flat in North London. Dad works shifts and mum has been developing a kitchen-table business since his birth in 2005, making and selling things on eBay. Sue, the researcher, has become friends with the family since first interviewing Anastasia in 2005 when she was eight months pregnant; each research visit is an opportunity to 'catch up'.

4.45pm: The meal is on the table, and I eat with them. Anastasia has put out some nice warmed Greek bread and salad and hummus, and the boys dive into the bread. It's pasta and meatballs for Anastasia and me, and pasta and frankfurter sausages for the boys. The boys have eaten so much bread that they don't have much appetite left for the pasta and leave a lot. They head off back to the Xbox and I take the opportunity to give thank you vouchers to Anastasia. She's delighted, but saying we didn't have to give her anything for doing this.

I wanted to show Anastasia the Favourites website with David on it so she put the laptop on to warm up because it is so old and slow now. She had asked to see it on her phone but I said it wouldn't really show properly in my view.

In the meantime she wanted to have a cigarette on the balcony, and I went outside with her and we chatted. She has a little business going making super hot chilli sauce. She had offered me some with the pasta and I had a tiny bit – it is certainly a very hot one. She's trying to earn money because she has to pay a lot of money for doing her NVQ course, since she already has a degree they charge her more.

We put the website on and she watched it, both laughing and covering her face at some of it, especially where David talks about shooting 'Dad's fat belly and mum's fat bum'. She enjoyed it and said she thought it was great, but also felt that it wasn't really her family. She couldn't believe it was her son speaking so confidently to me, she was thinking how different he is when she's not around. She didn't worry about the things I thought she might, like the belly and bums bit, or where he talks about them being busy because they have to pay the gas bill etc., and said she 'can't wait to show it to my friend'. I told her that it wasn't 'out' yet and we were still working on it so it wasn't public. She called David in to watch it, and J came as well. David thought it was OK, but tended to get a bit bored with it after a few minutes and was chatting over bits of himself talking, after he'd got used to what it was about. When Barnaby, his soft toy dog, came up in focus he said that sometimes he didn't sleep with him (in response to his voice on the website saying he did). He didn't seem bothered about listening to his own voice. Anastasia teased him about her 'fat bum' and asked him if she really had one and he said 'So-so'; she threatened to take something away so he said 'No she wasn't fat' and we all laughed.

Anastasia said she couldn't think why he hadn't included his Lego in his favourites and showed me his Lego models and I took a couple of photos. But when I asked David if he still played with them he said no. In fact, Anastasia had told me earlier that he didn't really play with anything except the Xbox since he'd got it. (I had thought of doing a panoramic shot of his bedroom, but it was now rather different and some toys had been cleared away and the hanging basket previously full of soft toys was completely empty, so I didn't.)

Thinking together

The first question of any case study must be – a case of what? If this were a childhood studies project this might be the 'case of David', itself speaking to a wide range of categories, including eight-year-old boys, only children or urban childhoods, for instance. For maternal studies we might be thinking in terms of Anastasia: a case of migrant mothering? But our approach endeavours to think about a mother and a child together and over time – a case of relationship in context, that asks what we might understand if we just keep looking. This is an approach to 'caseness' which in Andrew Abbott's words 'has to do with endurance and thingness; appearance, disappearance, combination and transformation'.[22] It is impossible to think of Anastasia without David and vice versa, and neither would be available to us without Sue's presence as a trusted researcher. From the outset of the project Anastasia welcomed the research into her world. Sue's field notes always included details of hospitality and warmth. As migrants from two different continents Anastasia and her partner had met and settled in London and were careful about gathering and cultivating resources. Relatives could be a source of threat as well as security, and 'making do' in a long-hours, low-wage economy demanded an entrepreneurial collective strategy. The research and Sue herself were seen as something good, to be welcomed into the tight-knit trio. So, already, the 'caseness' of this case study involves the relatedness of David, Anastasia, her partner and Sue, as they appear, disappear, combine and transform over time.

When Anastasia was pregnant with David she emphasised her strong identity as a worker, and through the research she expressed frustration in the difficulty she experienced in regaining her pre-birth identity and body. Sue records that work plans are always being hatched. The documentation of David's favourite things and a day in his life, made several months apart in his ninth year, capture a dynamic and contingent moment in the life of the family. David himself is on the cusp of something: orienting towards friends in a new way, discovering the virtual space of the internet for himself, beginning to let go of the soft toys of his early childhood. Seeing David at school is strange for the researcher. He seems like a different boy. We have a taste of how Anastasia might struggle to recognise the grownup-sounding boy, recorded narrating his toys. Anastasia is busily involved in self-making: studying for new qualifications, producing and selling her own chilli sauce. We get a feeling of how this purposeful activity appears to David by noticing his remark that 'this family is too busy, making money to pay bills'... to host playdates or sleepovers? But we also know that this is about to be unsettled. It is no surprise when just a month later his room has been redecorated in a more grownup style and David is installed with a friend at the new Playstation.

The longitudinal method allows access to moments in the flow of a family's life; making 'scenes' from what is experienced as the everyday. Our interest in the connected maternal and child subjects mean that the scenes reveal, literally, how we are made out of each other, spurred on and enabled by the presence, absence, actions, reactions and anticipations of each other (amongst others). With the passage of time and the accumulation of new scenes this relationality turns into the stuff of life. It becomes possible to see how this case of Anastasia and David has *become what it is*. The way that we narrate these changes depends on our frame, and need not be determined by notions of linear development that fix subjects into well-worn trajectories. Indeed, we may be better served by tropes of dialogue, entanglement, echo and repetition which chime with the choreographies of lived experience. Our interpretations are shaped by preoccupations and methods that conceal and reveal, and which themselves become part of the lives that they document. At the time of writing this paper we learned from Sue that Anastasia is now working as a teaching assistant at David's school, pleased to be in a job with prospects but also baffled by seeing the school from inside in ways that are prefigured in Sue's observation of David's day.

From a maternal studies perspective, our first thought is about the shifting location of the 'subject' of the case study, and how we might locate mum, dad, David and Sue in this account. There is Anastasia, David's mum, but there is also Sue, the researcher, who enables a conversation with David about mum and dad, and a conversation with mum about David and dad. There is the mum and dad of David's private talk with Sue, and there is the mum, Anastasia, in the field note, who has her own work, her future aspirations, her past in another country, and her own relation with Sue, dad and David, the mum who listens in to the conversation between Sue and David with pride, and some amazement. There is also the mum and dad of David's fantasy world – not just the dad with the 'fat belly' and the mum with the 'fat bums', who are unable to play pool because they are working to pay for the electric and gas bills – but the mum, for example, whom David associates with the soft cuddly toys of his childhood, and whom he is both drawn towards and repudiates, reminding those assembled that he doesn't always need Barnaby to go to sleep. Perhaps 'mother' is a term, then, that attempts to tie together an embodied subject who delights in the otherness of the child (Anastasia), as well as a form of mediation (Sue's practice as a researcher), and a mental and emotional image (David's relation to an internalised version of 'mum'). This tying together is loose, and the maternal subject is always on the move.

The conversations between Sue and David are linked, on the website, to objects in David's room. The material culture of David's world includes toys that allow some form of regression and comfort, such as Barnaby, and the tiger-cat, and those that seem to be about managing aggression, fear and competition, such as guns, a Darth Maul mask, the Dalek, car games, pool and chess. Barnaby is held onto in a supermarket and mum responds to David's immediate need for its softness by tearing off the label and allowing him to hold it even while she pays. She refuses to separate David from Barnaby. Yet later the cuddly toys are put away by mum, as if *she* has grown out of, or become embarrassed by, David's early attachments. The guitar is a 'substitute' or fake, but David is also proud of his 'real' phone, the pool table, the Dalek that speaks, and the wooden games set. Anastasia is surprised he hasn't chosen the Lego, noting how much time David used to spend with this before the Xbox stole his attention. The materiality of both motherhood and childhood means negotiations about money, and endless attempts at working the line between trying to get what you want and getting what others deem good for you, or what you are convinced is good for others. It makes visible the struggle to identify whose needs are whose, and the relative urgency of those needs. There is a trace of these negotiations in all the objects David plays with, in his room, and how it is configured, and in how it changes over time.

There is also profound identity work going on in David's talk: 'I win'; 'you'd better watch out for me and my guns'. There is his identification as a rock guitarist, and the invitation by a friend to come and see his band: these seem to be bids for a separate and powerful identity, as someone who can kill off his opponents with a bang. The question 'who am I' and 'who am I to you' are also questions of 'who am I without you' and 'what can you do to me', and they apply to mother and researcher too. Mum is trying to get ahead, or maybe just keep afloat, and does and doesn't want to be pulled into an engagement with David. The cigarette on the balcony seems to signify time out, connecting Anastasia to her own needs and desires, recalling a time when she may have been separating from her own mother through marking out her body and desires as her own. It is also a shared moment between women. We are told that Sue and Anastasia have become friends, and that Sue comes round to 'catch up'. What goes on between the two of them? And what does the researcher want?

Posing the same question but changing the subject helps to see multiple perspectives that are relationally premised. Reading together allows us to see the push and pull between Anastasia and David that is both a bid for separation and an expression of their ongoing relation to one another. Separation, here, is not simply a push away, but also the movement towards inhabiting the position of the other, in order to understand something, that allows further separation. 'Weaning', understood broadly as a process of separation, from this perspective, is mutual, gradual and recursive. In order to shed his earlier childhood identity, David needs to return to the question of his relation to others. His questions may be aimed at Anastasia, but in the case material they are mediated through a third figure, Sue. In psychoanalytic theory this third position that facilitates separation is usually characterised as a 'paternal' function that enables separation between mother and child. However, where feminism and psychoanalysis have fruitfully engaged, it has been precisely around this issue of the gendering of thirdness (with its connotations of the symbolic world beyond the milky dyad). Anastasia continually welcomes the other in, and yet is surprised by the developmental shift that David has taken, which is manifest in the adult-sounding recording of his conversation with Sue. Her own self-making is not a process of simply pursuing her course, her kitchen-table business, or her project of survival, but is enabled through her ongoing relation to her separating and returning son.

By bracketing mother and child together, rather than separately from one another, we can allow the conceptual entanglement of 'mother' and 'child' to be tolerated and sustained in a way that enriches both childhood and maternal studies. Reading together involves an engagement between sociology and psychoanalysis, noticing the relational practices of 'childing' and 'adulting' through which social categories are created,[23] and how these flesh out the mother for the child and the child for the mother. In becoming objects for each other it becomes possible to do the work of separation and, leading from this, to become subjects through whom relationality becomes possible.[24] We can understand the encounter between mother and child, and between childhood and maternal studies, as a 'growing sideways' that is relational, dynamic and generative.[25] Thinking *through* in this way involves at least two projects of self in relationship, as precipitated by one other but also by the material and temporal properties of the environment in its concrete and abstract manifestations.

Maintaining a focus over time enables us to see the fluid character of this relationality, but also the obstacles and inflexibilities which may structure the pathways of least resistance. The temporalities involved are complicated. There are practices of waiting (to get back to your 'old life', to being 'old enough'). Things move slowly and suddenly very fast as we realise that something may have happened outside of view (our child has become someone else). Technologies become sluggish and eventually obsolete, and an upgrade or a new toy can feel like time travel into the future. The child and the mother – if thought together – express a tension between together and apart, acting as the 'other' to one another. They are each other's audience, whether they like it or not, though they may only come to realise it through the mediation of a third. When we hold them in mind within a research frame it becomes possible to notice and think about the qualities of this relationship, and to offer a different kind of audience or sense of the 'public' from which to see them.

In conclusion, we have taken up the challenge of using feminism as a space of encounter for connecting childhood and maternal studies, allowing us to think about how we conceptualise the relationship between mother and child. Our approach has tracked how notions of conceptual autonomy and relationality have become important in both fields, reappearing in successive waves of theorising. We have also explored why they may be so difficult to maintain, in the face of the pull and push of conceptual collapse and separation. Our aim has been to show how it might be possible to think mother and child together in such a way that escapes the temptations of abstraction, maintaining a connection to situatedness, contingency and intersubjectivity. By using the terminology of 'weaning' we may have provoked some of the uncomfortable associations of maternalism, while asking our readers to follow through an expanded reading of relationality enriched by this affective charge. Feminism is the unmarked yet prime mover that shapes our conviction that it is possible to generate new knowledge by engaging seriously with the ordinary business of living as mother and child. For us the feminist encounter involves the acknowledgement of a political dimension to our investigations, and this feminist encounter has prompted us to think about what might be unthinkable for childhood and material studies.

NOTES

1. Leena Alanen and Berry Mayall (eds), *Conceptualizing Child-Adult Relations* (London and New York: Routledge Falmer, 2001).
2. Barrie Thorne, 'Re-Visioning Women and Social Change: Where are the Children?' *Gender and Society* 1, no. 1 (1987): 85–109.
3. Carol Smart, *Regulating Womanhood: Historical Essays on Marriage, Motherhood and Sexuality* (London: Routledge, 1992).
4. Denise Riley, *War in the Nursery: Theories of the Child and Mother* (London: Virago, 1983); Valerie Walkerdine and Helen Lucey, *Democracy in the Kitchen: Regulating Mothers and Socializing Daughters* (London: Virago, 1989); Nira Yuval-Davis, *Gender and Nation* (London: Sage, 1997); Erica Burman, (2008) *Developments: Child, Image, Nation* (London: Routledge, 2008).
5. Elizabeth Freeman, *Time Binds: Queer Temporalities, Queer Histories* (Durham and London: Duke University Press, 2010); Lee Edelman, *No Future: Queer Theory and the Death Drive* (Duke University Press: Durham and London, 2004).
6. Julia Kristeva, 'Women's Time,' *Signs* 7, no. 1 (1981): 13–35.
7. Michael Bittman and Judy Wajcman, 'The Rush Hour: The Character of Leisure Time and Gender Equity,' *Social Forces* 79, no. 1 (2000): 165–89; Jonathan Gershuny, *Changing Times: Work and Leisure in Postindustrial Society* (Oxford: Oxford University Press, 2000); Jerry A. Jacobs and Kathleen Gerson, *The Time Divide: Work, Family, and Gender Inequality* (Cambridge, MA: Harvard University Press, 2004); Majella Kilkey and Diane Perrons, 'Gendered Divisions in Domestic-Work Time. The Rise of the (Migrant) Handyman Phenomenon', *Time and Society* 19, no. 2 (2010): 239–64; Sullivan, O., 'The division of domestic labour: Twenty years of change?' *Sociology* 34 no. 3 (2000): 437–456; Oriel Sullivan, 'Changing Gender Relations Within the Household: A Theoretical Perspective,' *Gender & Society* 18, no. 2 (2000): 207–23.
8. Christine Everingham, 'Engendering Time: Gender Equity and Discourses of Workplace Flexibility,' *Time & Society* 11, no. 2/3 (2002): 335–51; Judy Wajcman, 'Life in the Fast Lane? Towards a Sociology of Technology and Time', *British Journal of Sociology* 50, no. 1 (2008): 59–77.
9. See Edelman, *No Future*; Lisa Baraitser, 'Maternal Publics: Time, Relationality and the Public Sphere,' in *Critical Explorations through Psychoanalysis*, ed. Ayden Gulerce (Basingstoke: Palgrave, 2011): 221–40. Reprinted in *Mothering and Psychoanalysis*, Demeter Press, 2014.
10. e.g. Shulamith Firestone, *The Dialectic of Sex: The Case for Feminist Revolution* (London: Jonathan Cape, 1971); Adrienne Rich, *Of Woman Born: Motherhood as Experience and Institution* (New York: Norton, 1976).
11. A term coined by Gayatri Chakravorty Spivak to describe how and why marginalised groups present themselves through apparently shared characteristics such as nation, 'race', sexual identity, etc., while also recognising the constructedness and contingency of these characteristics.
12. Lynne Segal, *Making Trouble: Life and Politics* (London: Serpent's Tail, 2007).
13. Angela McRobbie, 'Top Girls: Young Women and the Post-feminist Sexual Contract,' *Journal of Cultural Studies* 41, no. 4–5 (2007): 718–37.
14. Claudia Castañeda, 'The Child as a Feminist Figuration: The Case for a Politics of Privilege,' *Feminist Theory* 2, no. 1 (2010): 29–53; Erica Burman and Jackie Stacey, 'The Child and Childhood in Feminist Theory,' *Feminist Theory* 11, no. 3 (2010): 227–40.
15. See Ohad Zehavi, this volume.
16. Christine Battersby, *The Phenomenal Woman: Feminist Metaphysics and the Patterns of Identity* (London: Polity Press, 1998).
17. Thorne, 'Re-visioning Women'.
18. See for example the successive prefaces to Allison James and Alan Prout, *Constructing and Reconstructing Childhood* (Routledge, 1990, 1997, 2015).
19. For example, MaMSIE (Mapping Maternal Subjectivities, Identities and Ethics) at http://www.mamsie.org.
20. Bracha L. Ettinger, *The Matrixial Borderspace* (Minneapolis and London: University of Minnesota Press, 2006).

21 The MoMM study was funded by the Economic and Social Research Council RES-148-25-0057. For project findings see Rachel Thomson et al., *Making Modern Mothers* (Bristol: Polity Press, 2011); for interactive multimedia website see http://modernmothers.org/; follow-up study of children see Rachel Thomson, Liam Berriman and Sara Bragg, *Researching Everyday Childhoods: Time, Technology and Documentation* (London: Bloomsbury, 2018); and website http://blogs.sussex.ac.uk/everydaychildhoods/.
22 Andrew Abbott, 'What Do Cases Do?' in *Time Matters: On Theory and Method* (Chicago: University of Chicago Press, 1992): 63–4.
23 Alanen and Mayall, *Conceptualizing Child-Adult Relations*; Samantha Punch, 'The Generationing of Power: A Comparison of Child-parent and Sibling Relationships in Scotland', *Sociological Studies in Childhood and Youth*, 10, ed. Loretta Bass (2005): 169–88.
24 See for instance Jessica Benjamin, *Like Subjects, Love Objects* (Princeton: Yale University Press, 1998).
25 Kathryn Bond Stockton, *The Queer Child, Or Growing Sideways in the Twentieth Century* (Durham and London: Duke University Press, 2010).

5
Notes on unlearning
Our feminisms, their childhoods

Debolina Dutta and Oishik Sircar

When we first watched the documentary film *Born into Brothels* (*BiB*) in 2008,[1] little did we know that a couple of years later we would be urged by a group of children of sex workers,[2] not unlike those in *BiB*, to make a film to counter its narrative. As feminist human rights lawyers, our first impulse on watching *BiB* was an amazement at the film's omission of any references to a vibrant sex workers' collective right next door to where the film had been shot in the Sonagachi red-light district in Kolkata.[3] The Durbar Mahila Samanwaya Committee (DMSC), a sex worker-led organisation with more than 65,000 female, male and transgender sex worker members, has been active there since 1997. However, *BiB* chose to make no mention of them. For us, such active exclusion was of grave consequence because we believed it only added to and strengthened a dominant narrative that worked to create an image of the sex worker as helpless, incapable and in need of rescue. Such narratives also lend legitimacy to a global saviour impulse that is put into practice by a whole host of state and non-state actors, even when sex workers refute the asserted need for external interventions in their lives.[4]

The DMSC protested against the film's voyeuristic and denigrating portrayal of the lives of sex workers and their children.[5] But the directors' portrayal of their own struggle to rescue children of sex workers in Kolkata from their suffering had won hearts – and also the Oscar for best documentary in 2005. The film had become famous for the distanced publics of global compassion that it mobilised.[6] The filmmakers were celebrated for their display of courage in the face of indigenous patriarchy, an underdeveloped and corrupt state and the incompetent, immoral parents of the children. If it was not for their intervention, the film suggested in no uncertain terms, the children would have had to remain captive within the hellish brothels, a location that was their home. The removal of the children from their homes, from their mothers, was the valiant mission that the filmmakers were undertaking. The directors were the protagonists of the film; it was their story about their triumph over Third World miseries.

When we first watched *BiB* we had already been associated with the DMSC as feminist allies for many years. We supported their struggles for the right to sex work, and the rights of sex workers. We had been part of their rallies and written about their activism. As human rights lawyers we had held legal awareness workshops with their members. In the course of our interactions with sex worker activists we had learnt a key lesson in feminist politics, which was conveyed to us through a well-known slogan of the global sex workers' rights movement: 'nothing about us without us'. We learnt that the communities of people with whom a feminist engages and works must be regarded as active subjects capable of knowing, evaluating and deciding on what is best for their lives; that the feminist self who claims to be an ally in the struggles of marginalised people must not also claim superiority of knowledge and being.

Over the years, during our visits to the DMSC's offices in north Kolkata, we would meet many of the children of the sex workers milling about and participating in the DMSC's work. We would join with them to raise slogans at protests. Yet until we had watched *BiB* it did not occur to us with full clarity that children of sex workers are a group exploited by abolitionist feminists to trump arguments in favour of the right to sex work. *BiB* was, in many ways, an extension of such a feminist position, and reinforced an image similar to that of the Third World sex worker without agency, as was deployed in the 1996 Emmy Award-winning documentary *The Selling of Innocents*.[7] These films have portrayed children born to sex workers as being trafficked at birth. By marshalling specific filmmaking techniques – the use of grainy, red-filtered, shaky images and haunting background scores – the films pursued a pedagogical mission: to train their viewers to believe that children of sex workers would naturally grow up to be prostitutes if they were girls and pimps if they were boys. Their fates were sealed – unless the abolitionist feminists intervened.

Strangely enough, as pro-sex-work feminists, we had seldom thought of the children of sex workers from the DMSC as fully agential subjects. Our focus was almost solely on the rights of sex workers and their right to sex work. This included their right to the custody of their children, but not necessarily the children's right not to be forcibly removed from their mothers. However, the fact that the children had stakes in their mothers' struggles, that they too were political actors who were an integral part of the sex workers' rights movement, didn't dawn on us until we attended a DMSC protest rally led by Amra Padatik (AP), a collective of children of sex workers formed under the aegis of the DMSC.

On the evening of 3 March 2009 – International Sex Worker Rights Day – over 3,000 children of sex workers (aged between 6 and 25 years), all from Kolkata's Sonagachi and surrounding red light districts, marched through College Street. They held placards and shouted slogans demanding their rights as children to be free from stigma and discrimination. They also demanded their mothers' rights to perform sex work. The rally was organised and led by AP.

Fig. 5.1 At the Amra Padatik Rally, Kolkata, on International Sex Workers' Rights Day, 3 March 2009. (Photograph by Oishik Sircar)

One of the marchers' most popular slogans targetted India's then Minister for Women and Child Development: *'Renuka Chaudhary'r Kalo Hath Guriye Dao, Guriye Dao'* (Smash Renuka Chaudhary's Black Hand). In using this slogan the children in the march were alluding to an amendment that the ministry had been seeking to make to the Immoral Traffic (Prevention) Act, 1956, to criminalise clients of sex workers. This move would have pushed sex work underground and exposed the children's mothers to additional violence and extortion. Along with this, they were also protesting against a provision in the same law that would allow the state to remove children attaining the age of majority from their mothers if they were defined as living off their mothers' earnings (in other words, living with them).

It was at this rally that we conceived the idea of a project on the collectivisation of children of sex workers, and their activism as political actors.[8] We felt that it was necessary for the human rights world, of which we were a part by profession, to hear this story that we were learning about. In the light of a film like *BiB*, we aimed to foreground the experiences of these children from Sonagachi to challenge the singularity of focus on suffering that their ostensible plight has attracted. We did not mean to dismiss it, but to bring to light the multiple and overlapping realities of coercion, celebration, negotiation and determination that marked their lives. It was also an attempt at exposing how a singular focus on suffering worked to erase the complexity of their lived experiences – in turn, denying these children an opportunity to be recognised as citizens who have the capacity and vision to give meaning to how their lives are to be perceived or lived. While children of sex workers are on the receiving end of multiple forms of disadvantage they are also active agents in resisting disadvantage and formulating daily negotiation strategies which constitute an exemplary show of resilience.[9] When they are minors, age not only leads to the violation of the rights of these children: it also becomes the reason why compassionate interventions do not consider them as citizens whose voices matter.

As feminists whose politics were strongly informed by a postcolonial sensibility,[10] we assumed that our idea already carried an ethical heft. As part of our participatory methodology, we discussed our idea with a group of members from AP to get their feedback. While the group, which comprised AP's office-holders Pinky, Gobinda, Ratan, Mithu and Chaitali, were happy about a project of this nature, they raised doubts about its transformative capacity. They were concerned that we would end up publishing the outcome in English, in an academic journal, which would be of no use to them: it would benefit only us. The suggestion came from one of them that we make a film that could both offer a counter-story to that of *BiB* and that AP could use as a part of their own advocacy work. Both Pinky and Gobinda had watched *BiB*, and they were troubled by how a film that demeans them and their mothers could find such widespread appeal, not only globally but also in India.

Fig. 5.2 Film poster artwork by Anirban Ghosh depicting the five protagonists. (Source: Anirban Ghosh)

In 2011, we completed the documentary film *We Are Foot Soldiers*,[11] which featured as protagonists the five members of AP mentioned above. We also published an article that accompanied the film.[12] While writing the article was a rehearsal of activist-academic conventions in feminism and jurisprudence, making the film was a provocation to unlearn a lot of these very conventions. It was not our inexperience in the technique of filmmaking that was the cause for this provocation. That challenge, although pertinent, we had overcome by bringing on board like-minded friends who had the requisite technical knowledge.[13] Rather, it was the challenge of thinking about a form of storytelling that was able to bring our pro-sex-work feminism into conversation with the politics of AP. The risk in such a conversation was of letting our feminist interpretive lens become a totalising explanatory framework for AP's narratives of childhoods. How do we tell a story which is both ours and theirs? How do we tell a story in which the aesthetics will not overwhelm the politics and vice versa?

The film was a collaborative exercise and yet not. It appeared to us that the children were, through active participation in the filming, assuming ownership of the film which was seeking to tell their stories. But as directors we exercised creative control and authority. At the time

Fig. 5.3 Debolina with Gobinda, at his residence, during the filming of WAFS. (Photograph by Anindya Shankar Das)

of filming, we decided never to enter the frame of the camera during interviews. Yet, from over 12 hours of footage, the decision of which frames to retain into the final 26-minute cut was ours.[14]

Of course, these are standard dilemmas regarding the ethics of documentary filmmaking, especially when there is a clear differential in power between the filmmakers and the human subjects of the film. But for us, negotiating these dilemmas was more than a practice of professional ethics. These negotiations enabled us to witness a material encounter between our feminisms and a politics of their childhoods. Within pro-sex-work feminist discourses, children of sex workers often appear either as an apology or a justification for their mothers' choice of occupation. Through the conversations with our protagonists we realised that we needed to walk a fine line between foregrounding a pro-sex-work politics and at the same time not making that politics the sole foundational peg for the film. How could the film foreground an account by one of our protagonists who, while supporting the right to sex work, did not like identifying as the child of a sex worker all the time? How were we to present disagreements between children and their mothers without being predisposed to either position? If the children were to occupy centre stage in a narrative about their lives, the film had to make space for accounts that were not entirely in alignment with our pro-sex-work feminism. This necessitated that both we and the sex workers remain entirely out of the frames; thus, we decided to not interview any sex-working mothers.

The encounter between feminisms and childhoods that we saw was not one of rivalry, but unfolded as a dialogue in which we had to confront the fact that feminism, even in its best-intentioned and most self-reflexive versions, must recognise its limitations. For us, this recognition hasn't been a paralyzing force. The encounter has shown us the merits of unlearning to make way for learning anew.

NOTES

1 *Born into Brothels*, directed by Zana Brisky and Ross Kaufman (2004; New York: THINKFilm).
2 Our use of the term 'children' does not denote minors: it refers to those born to sex workers, or those whose mothers sell sexual services for a living. The protagonists in our film, mostly adults, referred to themselves as 'children of sex workers' and used it as an identity category.
3 Sonagachi has been a zoned red-light district in Kolkata since the days of colonial occupation. Its proximity to the Calcutta port enabled easy access for sailors and officers of the East India Company to the prostitutes. In those days the red-light district was marked out, for the purposes of quarantine and surveillance, by the Contagious Diseases Act, which sought to protect English soldiers. For a detailed historical insight into Sonagachi, see Sumanta Banerjee, *Dangerous Outcaste: The Prostitute in Nineteenth Century Bengal* (Kolkata: Seagull Books, 2000).

4 Jo Doezema, *Sex Slaves and Discourse Masters: The Construction of Trafficking* (London: Zed Books, 2010).
5 Swapna Gayen, 'Nightmares on Celluloid,' *The Telegraph*, 15 March 2005. Available at: https://www.telegraphindia.com/1050315/asp/opinion/story_4491793.asp.
6 Birgitta Höijer, 'The Discourse of Global Compassion: The Audience and Media Reporting of Human Suffering,' *Media Culture and Society* 26, no. 4 (2004): 513–31.
7 *Selling of Innocents*, directed by Ruchira Gupta (1996; Toronto: Associated Producers Ltd.).
8 The initial funding for this project came from the National Child Rights Fellowship, which we had received from Child Rights and You (CRY) in 2009 to write a research paper on Amra Padatik's activism.
9 We want to note that the lives of children of sex workers aren't homogeneous. There are many different forms of sex work – brothel-based, home-based, street-based etc. – which means that the lives of the children take varied forms. While children of sex workers living in brothels become easily identifiable, and therefore more vulnerable on certain counts, it also means that they are likely to have a community of people, including other sex workers' children, around them that is not available to others.
10 Ratna Kapur, *Erotic Justice: Law and the New Politics of Postcolonialism* (Ranikhet: Permanent Black, 2005); Sarada Balagopalan, *Inhabiting 'Childhood': Children, Labour and Schooling in Postcolonial India* (London: Palgrave Macmillan, 2014).
11 *We Are Foot Soldiers*, directed by Debolina Dutta and Oishik Sircar (2011; New Delhi: Public Service Broadcasting Trust). Available at: https://www.youtube.com/watch?v=Bfm06qBo4c4
12 Oishik Sircar and Debolina Dutta, 'Beyond Compassion: Children of Sex Workers in Kolkata's Sonagachi,' *Childhood* 18, no. 3 (2011): 333–49.
13 Our team comprised Anindya Shankar Das, Prachi Tulshan, Anirban Ghosh and Sakyadeb Chowdhury. We would like to acknowledge the inspiration drawn from Shohini Ghosh's important documentary film on the DMSC. See *Tales of the Night Fairies*, directed by Shohini Ghosh (2002; New Delhi: Mediastorm Collective). See also Shohini Ghosh, 'Sex Workers and Video Activism: Tales of the Night Fairies: A Filmmaker's Journey,' *Inter-Asia Cultural Studies* 7, no. 2 (2006): 341–43.
14 The decision to keep the film to exactly 26 minutes wasn't entirely ours. All PSBT-funded films are broadcast on national television, and thus must satisfy particular timings.

6
Ideal women, invisible girls?
The challenges of/to feminist solidarity in the Sahrawi refugee camps

Elena Fiddian-Qasmiyeh

Introduction

Since their establishment in the mid-1970s, the Sahrawi refugee camps in South West Algeria have become internationally recognised – and constituted – as ideal spaces in which gender has been successfully mainstreamed and female empowerment has been achieved. Such a gynocentric[1] representation has been projected, repeated and consolidated by the Sahrawi refugees' political leaders and a wide range of international actors – ranging from UN agencies to Western academics, journalists, and NGOs – as an essential part of the Sahrawis' politics of survival, to secure humanitarian and political support for this enduring refugee community. However, this idealised depiction of the camps has simultaneously been characterised by a homogenisation of an idealised image of 'the Sahrawi woman', and by rendering invisible and unaddressed both 'non-ideal' Sahrawi women and girl-children, and their respective, diverse and at times competing rights, needs and concerns. This occurs on multiple levels and scales: local, national and international alike.[2]

How can we understand the hypervisibility of 'Sahrawi refugee women' in representations of, and responses to, these protracted camps, while girls remain largely invisible? How and with what effect can feminist solidarity for 'refugee women' be implicated in processes of marginalisation on the basis of, inter alia, gender and generation? This chapter addresses these questions through a case study of the Sahrawi refugee camps, which appear to be a success story[3] in that Sahrawi refugee women have long been identified not as 'generic' refugee women (read passive, subjugated, violated), but as 'ideal' refugees in 'ideal camps': active and empowered agents who effectively run gender-equal camps which are free from violence against women. This chapter examines both empirical instances of the apparent disjuncture between the roles played by – and given to – women and girls in these camps, and the *representational* (and thus constitutive) processes that centralise particular figures in this refugee situation whilst marginalising others. The aim of the chapter is not to offer an absolute account of Sahrawi refugees' lived experiences in the camps, but, rather, to highlight the paradoxical nature, and implications, of mainstream representations of women and girls in this refugee situation.

The following reflections are based on my ethnographic research. This had two focuses: on the one hand the roles of gender and Islam in everyday sociopolitical dynamics in the Sahrawi camps, and on the other the significance of gender and religion in Sahrawi refugees' interactions with diverse international audiences, including providers of humanitarian aid and political support.[4] In particular, my research has examined the ways in which the Sahrawi's political representatives – the Polisario Front – have presented an idealised depiction of equal gender relations and the empowerment of women in the camps as part of a broader representational strategy designed to attract and maintain international humanitarian and political support for the camp's inhabitants and the Sahrawis' quest for the right to self-determination. As such, my research into the roles of gender and religion in supporting the Sahrawi 'politics of survival'[5] has not explicitly aimed to explore the *relative* position of girls and women in the Sahrawi camps or across the transnational networks that provide different forms of assistance and support to Sahrawi children, youth and adults. Nonetheless, the differential position given to 'women' and 'girls' by diverse international state and non-state actors repeatedly emerged as a key theme throughout my multi-sited research in Algeria, Cuba, Syria and Spain.

Since 2001, this research has involved a total of over 100 interviews with Sahrawi refugee adults, children and youth residing in the refugee camps in Algeria; with Sahrawi refugee youth participating in a transnational education programme in Cuba and Syria; and with Sahrawi youth and adults studying and living in Spain, in addition to interviews with more than 50 European aid providers and pro-Sahrawi solidarity activists across these and other spaces.[6] My fieldwork has also included participant observation of diverse encounters between Sahrawi refugees and various aid and solidarity providers. Such encounters included high-profile political meetings between female Sahrawi political representatives and

European solidarity activists in the camps, local-level encounters between 'aid providers' and various 'beneficiaries' of humanitarian programmes (such as the children's activity camp discussed below), and diverse representational encounters between Sahrawi refugees and external readers and observers, through media and NGO reports published in the international arena and via the parades that the Polisario regularly organise when non-Sahrawi visitors travel to the camps.

The chapter is structured as follows. I firstly provide a brief history of the Sahrawi refugee situation – noting an early commitment to gender equality stated by the Polisario. I then outline the now-hegemonic depiction of the Sahrawi camps as 'ideal', gender-equal and democratic spaces – a depiction which I refer to as 'gynocentric' in nature. I then set out the relationship between this discursive representation and international support for the camps and their inhabitants. With the gynocentric foundations of Western humanitarian and political support for the Sahrawi in mind, I then analyse firstly the position (or absence) of girl-children in accounts of the camps, and secondly the ways in which Sahrawi refugees and members of a Spanish solidarity-based aid programme responded to a group of refugee mothers' reluctance to allow their daughters to participate in an overnight camping activity outside of the 27 February refugee camp. While the activity camp could be seen as a welcome attempt to redress the longstanding invisibility of refugee children in aid programmes in the Sahrawi camps, this case study ultimately highlights not only the difficulties that refugee girls may face in accessing projects in these idealised 'gender-equal' camps, and the tensions that might exist between different groups of girls and women in the camps, but also the paradoxical ways in which feminist rhetoric is invoked by Spanish NGO leaders during their interactions with Sahrawi women and children. Ultimately, the camps emerge as microcosms that exemplify the potential for feminist discourse and claims of solidarity to be used against, rather than to support, 'real' beneficiaries of international aid programmes, women and children alike.

Setting the scene

The inhabitants of the North African territory now known as the Western Sahara were historically members of nomadic tribes with mixed ethnic origins (including Arab and Berber), who spoke Hassaniya Arabic, shared a series of cultural practices and followed the Maliki school of Islam.[7] While the term 'Sahrawi' in Arabic refers to any inhabitant of the desert (*sahra'*), this identifier is now most frequently used to refer to the people who traditionally lived in and moved throughout the Western Saharan territory. This usage of the term Sahrawi is relatively recent, emerging as a key identifier in the anti-colonial movements which developed in the 1960s and 1970s, towards the end of the Spanish colonial occupation of what was then referred to as the Spanish Sahara.

In 1964, the territory was placed on the UN Decolonisation Committee's agenda and, after the birth and suppression of a number of anti-colonial movements, the Popular Front for the Liberation of Saguiat El-Hamra y Río de Oro (known by its Spanish acronym Frente POLISARIO, henceforth Polisario) was established in 1973. Polisario gained popular support as it resisted first Spanish colonialism and later Moroccan and Mauritanian claims over the territory. Although Spain conducted a census of the population in December 1974 to prepare for a referendum on self-determination, Spain subsequently withdrew from its colony without holding a referendum in late 1975, and the territory was then occupied by Morocco and Mauritania, which claimed historic rights over this area. Following the Spanish dictator Franco's death in November 1975 the conflict between Morocco, Mauritania and Polisario intensified, with a mass exodus of Sahrawis being displaced first to other parts of the territory and later to the nascent Algerian-based refugee camps near these countries' common border.[8]

Mauritania withdrew from the conflict soon after, while Morocco and the Polisario continued to engage in armed conflict until 1991, when a ceasefire was brokered by the African Union. Today the Western Sahara remains on the UN's list of non-self-governing territories pending decolonisation, and the camps continue to be home to both Sahrawi refugees and the Polisario.

Before turning to the camps themselves, given this chapter's focus on the centrality of gender equality in accounts of the camps a brief reflection is necessary vis-à-vis the Polisario leadership's official position on gender equality. In essence, the Polisario's leaders were primarily male activists who, as a result of their educational experiences, brought to the movement a range of anti-colonial, socialist and non-aligned theories and frameworks which permeated the region at the time.[9] Amongst the implications of these approaches is the extent to which external analysts documented Polisario's 'strong commitment to the principle of women's emancipation' in the 1970s (echoing a central concern across socialist and non-aligned movements at the time).[10] Amongst its priorities in the 1970s, the Polisario officially aimed to establish equality both between the men of different tribes, and also between men and women. Solidifying the notion of the pre-colonial freedom of nomadic women in the territory,[11] the Polisario asserted that Spain's colonial occupation had imposed artificial restrictions on Sahrawi women, and, in its 1975 Programme of Action, declared that it would struggle 'to *reestablish* the political and social rights of the woman and open up all perspectives to her'.[12]

In addition to the ideological commitment to 'reestablishing' the rights of women and promoting equality and unity between all men and women, these moves were pragmatic in nature since they automatically increased the movement's potential membership base, as evidenced in the following extract from the Polisario's official journal published in 1974:

> It has become necessary for our struggle...that the Sahrawi woman bears all responsibilities and undertakes her duty in the national struggle by participating actively in the armed revolution like her sisters in the Palestinian, Algerian and Guinea-Bissau revolutions.[13]

As I argue below, the centrality given to 'Sahrawi women' has continued to be a central motif of the Polisario's struggle for self-determination, and has also become central to accounts of social dynamics in the camps. For instance, following her visit to the camps in 1981, Harrell-Bond reported that the Polisario had built 'a twentieth-century democratic nation, women's equality being one of the strongest features of their social organization',[14] and Oxfam's desk officer in the mid-1980s wrote that 'Perhaps the most impressive thing about Sahrawi society is that it is the most fundamentally balanced society I have ever come across in terms of the relationships between men and women'.[15]

Although the movement's early political commitment to women's emancipation may indeed have been related to its ideological position in the 1970s, I argue that it is important to also consider the significance of *pragmatics* when we consider the Polisario's modes of politically and discursively mobilising Sahrawi women through what I denominate the Sahrawis' gynocentric politics of survival.[16]

Women's position in the Sahrawi refugee camps

Since the mid-1970s, Polisario has governed and administered the Sahrawi refugee camps and its refugee population via the 'state in exile' (the Sahrawi Arab Democratic Republic, SADR) which it constituted on the 27 February 1976, one day after Spain officially withdrew from its colony. The Polisario and its SADR state has developed its own constitution, camp-based police force (and prisons), army, and parallel state and religious legal systems.

Although the camps are almost totally dependent upon externally provided aid, since the 1980s they have been heralded as 'unique' and even 'ideal' due to the Sahrawis' self-management and administrative, bureaucratic and professional self-sufficiency,[17] with analysts identifying the camps as 'models of efficient local government' and even 'the best run refugee camps in the world'.[18]

Importantly, between the mid-1970s and the 1991 ceasefire, the camps were effectively run and managed by Sahrawi women. This was, on a pragmatic level, necessary as the majority of male refugees were either at the military front or representing the political struggle abroad.[19] In the words of a woman who arrived in the camps in March 1976 and who was 74 years old at the time of her interview:[20]

> We [the women] took care of the organisation of life in the refugee camps, while the army took care of the war of resistance. We started building our schools and tents. Children went to Algeria, Cuba and Libya for schooling. The other tents were used as classrooms. Literacy campaigns were launched, and women were the basis of this construction, and despite the suffering of families since 1976 until now, women have been contributing to the state and their families.[21]

During this time, women played a key role in all aspects of life in the camps: distributing aid and being officially recognised as heads of household, playing active roles as builders, teachers, doctors and as active members of the camp-based National Union of Sahrawi Women and of parts of the SADR.

Given the minimal presence of men in the camps throughout the first decades of the conflict, Sahrawi refugees have publically celebrated the determination and resourcefulness of Sahrawi women as they managed the harsh camp conditions despite suffering as mothers, wives, sisters and daughters:

> One could not see men around here, maybe you would find one man in each [camp district]. The men were fighting at the battlefronts, and women did not know whether they would be called to

be told that a husband or brother was martyred. Despite all this, women worked with enthusiasm and conviction.[22]

Further reflecting the transgenerational nature of these female-centred accounts of the camps, a 14-year-old girl born and raised in the camps also indicated that 'the Sahrawi woman':

> is the most important [in the camps]. She built the tents, and provides the food, organises the [camps'] municipalities, and in all the refugee camps, they are active. During the war, the men were not in the camps, otherwise they would have helped.[23]

Echoing these narratives, in academic accounts[24] as well as in solidarity events designed for Western visitors to the camps, Sahrawi refugee women are primordial and almost omnipresent,[25] not as victims but rather as empowered, liberated and active agents, who, to a large extent, appear to overshadow their male compatriots in the camps.

The idealisation – and mobilisation – of Sahrawi refugee women

In 2001, the UNHCR's Refugee Women and Gender Equality Unit not only declared that the case of Sahrawi refugee women's empowerment is 'unique' but explicitly presented the camp-based National Union of Sahrawi Women as an example of 'good practice on gender mainstreaming'.[26] In turn, in its overview of camp conditions in 2002, the World Food Programme stated that Sahrawi women 'are known to be assertive and to participate in all aspects of camp life',[27] indicating that between 2000–04 Sahrawi women comprised 80 per cent of the health workers in 29 health centres in the camps and 60 per cent of both medical and paramedical staff and camp teachers.[28] The organisation's description of Sahrawi women's participation in the camps was substantially magnified in 2004, when the organisation claimed – with no reflection on the meaning of the terms invoked – that 'Saharan society is primarily *matriarchal* and the women are *totally empowered*'.[29]

It is clear that Sahrawi women have played a key role in establishing and running the camps, and yet a key question which arises for the purposes of this chapter is why and with what effect women's roles have been mobilised on the international stage through gynocentric accounts which have been projected both to and by international observers. Indeed, the longevity of this idealised depiction of women's roles in the camps is particularly notable when we acknowledge that the common understanding of the camps as 'feminised' and female-run spaces is largely based on a continued acceptance of war-time demographics, in spite of increasing numbers of Sahrawi men having 'returned' to the camps since the 1991 ceasefire and the WFP estimating that by 2000–02, 40 per cent of the camp population was male.[30]

On an empirical level, depictions of the camps as female-dominated and female-run spaces simultaneously elide the heterogeneity of the female camp population and the extent to which women's spheres of action and access to resources have historically depended on age, tribal background, education and marital status (amongst other factors); equally, they fail to acknowledge the presence or activities of different groups of men in the camps, or, indeed, the extent to which the camps' political structures have consistently been managed by elite males since the 1970s. With only one woman (Senia Ahmed Marhba) ever having acted as a camp governor, since the 1970s men have held the most powerful positions in the political administration of the individual camps, districts and neighbourhoods, and have also systematically controlled Rabouni, the camps' male-dominated 'capital' and structural core.[31]

Nonetheless, in spite of the clear demographic shifts which have taken place since 1991, and elite men's long-standing and ongoing monopoly over key spaces and politico-administrative positions, discourses which represent the camps as feminised spaces inhabited by active women continue to prevail, with diverse effects.

Whether 'real' or not, I argue that representations of active and empowered Sahrawi women are particularly powerful – and attractive – precisely because they are unexpected when compared with the standardised and generic images which have become the norm when discussing refugee camps.[32] Indeed, mainstream accounts of refugee settings habitually reproduce the image of women as helpless victims of war and forced displacement,[33] re/creating 'the refugee' as a generic and essentialised figure, either Madonna-like[34] or as weakened, dependent and victimised 'womenandchildren'.[35] The centrality of this essentialised figure leads Malkki to suggest that refugee women's and refugee children's symbolic power may be derived from their 'embody[ing] a special kind of powerlessness' or being the embodiment of 'pure humanity' and simultaneously of 'a pure victim'.[36] Importantly, Malkki also suggests that the extent to which the repetition of such conceptualisations of 'normal' or 'generic' refugees potentially provides a framework against which other refugees can be compared.[37] In effect, the tendency to compare refugee groups and evaluate them accordingly is confirmed by mainstream accounts of the Sahrawi camps, including a report by the Norwegian

Refugee Council, which explicitly indicates that the Sahrawi camps are 'unique' by virtue of their difference from 'other' camps.[38] The Sahrawi camps are said to be an 'exception' to 'what has become the norm',[39] and Sahrawi women are, precisely, a 'positive example' when compared with the 'usual' position of generic refugee women in generic refugee camps.[40]

As such, the Sahrawi camps, as portrayed by Polisario/SADR and Western observers alike, are in essence the antithesis of what refugee camps are 'meant to look like':[41] they are democratic, empowering spaces that are safe for active and empowered women. In this context, we could argue that the symbolic power of Sahrawi refugee women arises precisely because they are *not* passive, powerless, 'pure victims', but because they embody an *idealised* form of female agency.

This uniqueness, and the centrality of Sahrawi women in the camps, is also central in sustaining the transnational networks which provide humanitarian and political support for the Sahrawi people and their quest for self-determination. Importantly, in addition to general support for Sahrawi refugees from across a range of transnational civil society networks, many Western observers directly relate their support for the Sahrawi to the 'special' nature of Sahrawi women in the camps, with an International Platform of Solidarity with Saharawi Women having been created in 1998. Indeed, one of the primary aims granted by the SADR Constitution to Sahrawi mass organizations and unions, such as the camp-based National Union of Sahrawi Women (NUSW), is precisely to '*help widen the field of solidarity* with the Sahrawi people and to draw attention to its national cause'.[42] The NUSW – which is based in the 27 February Refugee Camp (also known as the 'Women's Camp') – states that one of its international objectives is to 'enlarge the solidarity and support base for our people's struggle for self-determination and independence',[43] and

> calls for all women across the world to express their moral and political solidarity with the legitimate struggle of the Sahrawi people...We consider that solidarity between all women...is highly important because that solidarity constitutes an essential pillar in the interwoven relations of cooperation, solidarity and friendship and exchange of experiences and thus constitutes an essential factor in the search for solutions for the innumerable problems which women encounter in their struggle for the freedom and dignity of women.[44]

In many ways, the distinctive content of the gynocentric representation of life in the Sahrawi camps, and the NUSW's call for international audiences to act in 'cooperation, solidarity and friendship' with Sahrawi women as active agents and equal partners, could appear to be diametrically opposed to the universalising representational practice apropos refugee women identified by Malkki.[45] However, while providing an important counter-narrative to the tendency of viewing refugee women as passive and vulnerable recipients of aid, in the following section I examine the extent to which girls are simultaneously rendered invisible in such accounts, and consider the tensions that have emerged when Spanish 'solidarity' organisations have developed and implemented programmes in the camps.

'Where are the girls?'

As I have argued elsewhere,[46] one element of the official discourse's representation of ideal Sahrawi women has been its failure to account for changes and differences in positions, responsibilities and needs throughout different stages of women's lifecycles in the camps. The static and eternalised image of women re/presented in the mainstream discourse neither defines the term 'Sahrawi women' (thereby eliding the heterogeneity of the term) nor reflects on the processes by which one becomes a woman (following de Beauvoir)[47] or, indeed, how one becomes a girl in the camps. While I have elsewhere explored girls' experiences of growing up in the camps and participating in transnational education and fostering programmes in Cuba, Libya and Spain – including by noting the extent to which opportunities for mobility and transnational education have been limited by parents' and relatives' fears vis-à-vis puberty and nascent 'womanhood'[48] – here I argue that Sahrawi girls are in effect invisible in the official discourse projected to and by Western audiences and, concurrently, in projects designed for and implemented in the camps.

With reference to the broad corpus of representations of displaced and conflict-affected peoples, Nordstrom documents and denounces the tendency for such representations to 'focus almost entirely on adults' whilst failing to ask 'where are the girls?'[49] Indeed, prevailing accounts of, and projects for, conflict-affected 'children' have long been criticised for systematically failing to ask whether the term 'children' 'really [means] girls and boys, or just boys?', and girls are therefore frequently rendered invisible or muted.[50] In the Sahrawi context, few academic studies or NGO projects have focused on documenting or addressing girl-children's experiences of growing up in the camps or in the *Vacaciones en Paz* programme through which circa 10,000 children leave the Sahrawi camps to be hosted by Spanish families every summer.[51] On an operational level, while there are numerous projects 'for children' in the Sahrawi camps and beyond, none of the projects established or run in 27 February Camp at the time of my research (2001–09) were gender-sensitive, with a 'gender-blind' approach to Sahrawi childhood meaning that initiatives were designed by external actors for (ideal-typical) boy-children.

One result is that, although women are (hyper)visible throughout the camp[52] and a number of 'women's' spaces exist in the camp (including the 27 February Camp itself *as* 'The Women's Camp'), and boys and young men have access to a wide range of 'public areas' (including a space by the entrance to the 27 February Camp's administrative core – an archway known as the *gaws* – where they regularly play football), there is a distinct absence of facilities, services or spaces for girls outside of their tents.[53] For instance, a 17-year-old girl stressed that

> Life is very difficult in the camps, and girls have very limited places to meet or play. We meet with each other in our homes, in my room for example, and discuss school, the future, and politics.[54]

Further, a 54-year-old woman indicated that the humanitarian system has failed to address the specific needs of girls, stating that 'we need programmes that provide skills for girls and enable them to remain near their families'.[55]

These quotes, which echo sentiments arising in a broader series of interviews and my ethnographic research in the camps, highlight that many girls and women are longing for spaces where girls will be able to participate in different activities. Yet the second quotation also highlights that another dimension of 'space' – girls' *proximity* to their families – is also central to understanding which kinds of activities and spaces are considered to be desirable or undesirable for different groups of girls, according to different groups of camp residents and, indeed, external observers.

The feminist politics of supporting girls

Against this backdrop – on the one hand the discursive idealisation and hypervisibility of active Sahrawi women, and on the other the invisibility of 'girls' both in mainstream accounts of the camps and in the camp's public spaces – I now explore the tensions that underpin and arise from a Spanish NGO's activity camp recruitment drive in spring 2007. The drive sought Sahrawi children to participate in a three-day trip (*rihla*) for an 'activity camp' to be held in the sand dunes located between the refugee camps. A brief examination of how the trip was designed and how children were 'recruited' simultaneously reveals the difficulties which girls may face in accessing projects, and the extent to which the priorities of different groups of women and girls may be positioned at loggerheads in the camps.

Having arranged to take a group of boys and girls to the nearby sand-dunes for three days, the members of a Spanish NGO expressed surprise and anger when the children's mothers allowed their sons to spend a few days away from home 'having fun,' but refused to allow their daughters to do the same. Inter alia, the mothers wanted to know where the girls would sleep, what sort of contact they would have with the boys, who would be responsible for them (i.e. Spanish or Sahrawi, female or male instructors), and when they would return home. Given social, cultural and religious norms in the camps underpinning (adult) perceptions of un/acceptable behaviour and activities for girls and boys, I suggested to the Spanish organisers that they ask female, rather than male, Sahrawi instructors to speak with the mothers about the project and to explain the sleeping and supervisory arrangements that would be in place. The Spanish organisers replied that the mothers were simply 'ignorant' ('*son unas ignorantes*') not to allow their daughters to 'have fun' in the dunes.

The Spanish organisers – longtime supporters of the Sahrawi people – indicated that they were particularly disappointed to encounter such resistance in the 27 February Camp since it is the home of the National Women's School and the Headquarters of the NUSW. One of the organisers angrily stated:

> I can't believe this is happening here. We've been running projects around the camps for five years and we've never encountered such ignorance. And this is meant to be 'The Women's Camp'? They are just ignorant.

The NGO representatives stringently declared that unless the girls were allowed to participate, they would never run a project in that camp again. They demanded that a group of girls be ready for collection in the morning outside of the *gaws* and sent home all the children who were ready.

The designation of the mothers as 'ignorant', in contrast with the NGO workers' emphasis on the 27 February Camp as a supposedly female-centered and female-powered camp, is notable. It directly reflects the Spanish women's preference and identification with the now-hegemonic gynocentric representation of the camp, and their rejection of the 'ignorant' mothers' perspectives. In essence, Sahrawi women, in these

Spaniards' imagination, should have unequivocally accepted the project because 'educated' and empowered women *should* hold the same views as them; they should not have questioned its organisers or demanded information about supervisory arrangements, and should, instead, have resolutely encouraged their daughters to participate in the 'fun' outing. Any understanding of why these Sahrawi mothers might have expressed concerns regarding their daughters' contact with unrelated Sahrawi boys and men without proper supervision, especially when their daughters were approaching puberty, was absent. In effect, if Sahrawi women's 'spaces' in the camps are directly associated with their (hyper)visibility in certain locations, the *rihla* had the potential to make these girls temporarily 'disappear' from the spaces which their parents considered to be appropriate and acceptable: near their families.[56]

Several girls did eventually go to the dunes, meaning that both boy and girl children took up the opportunity to participate in this activity. However, it was clear that not only gender, but also birth order and age affect girls' opportunities for movement in the camps. In the case of one family which I visited almost daily over the course of two months' fieldwork in the camps in 2007, the mother rapidly granted permission for one of her younger daughters (aged eight) to go on the *rihla* once a responsible female guardian had been identified, but she prohibited her eldest daughter, aged 13, from doing so.

The mother invited me to act as an intermediary between herself and the female Spanish NGO representative, asking me to explain to the Spanish woman that:

> I am alone with the children and I need to take my baby to the hospital. She [pointing to her eldest daughter] has to help me with the other children. Ask *her* [the Spanish woman] where the girls will sleep...Will she be in the *khayma* [tent] with the girls? She will? *Tayeb* [ok]. Tell her that I will let my [younger] daughter go with her. Tell her that. [Pointing at the Spanish woman emphatically] With her.[57]

The NGO workers were so happy to have 'gotten another girl' that they made no attempt to understand the reasons why the mother had blocked her eldest daughter from participating in the trip. Any possibility of this, or future, projects meaningfully listening to and addressing Sahrawi girls' and women's preferences and needs was also curtailed early on as a result. In this sense, even when some girls' participation was 'successfully' secured, 'Sahrawi girls' were literally rendered invisible in the *rihla* because *certain* girls were blocked from participation. They simultaneously figuratively disappeared, as attempts to implement the project erased any possibility of understanding the position of different groups of girls and diverse approaches to girlhood within the camp's socio-cultural and religious normative frameworks.

Importantly, the ultimate outcome of this encounter (in which the youngest daughter was able to participate while the eldest daughter could not) must be situated within the context of eldest daughters in the camps typically being expected to help their mothers with younger siblings, household tasks, and looking after infirm relatives.[58] Equally importantly, this trend is conceptualised, justified or resisted differently by different girls and young women. For instance, one eldest daughter in her early twenties informed me that she had voluntarily decided to leave school elsewhere in Algeria to return to her home camp during her mother's last pregnancy, and had eventually been able to pursue further education classes at the vocationally focused 27 February National Women's School.[59] While she explained this as having been a choice that she did not regret, as she had been able to combine supporting her mother with subsequently completing her studies, another eldest daughter was highly resentful that she had been withdrawn from school at 11 years old to help her mother with her younger siblings, and wanted desperately to leave the camps to return to her studies in northern Algeria.

This girl – aged 13 at the time of our discussions – explained that she understood that her withdrawal from school had been particularly urgent because her father had left the camps for life-saving medical treatment in Spain; however, she repeatedly asserted – often in her mother's presence – that she was not happy having to help her mother with the new baby at the expense of her education.[60] It was, precisely, this eldest daughter who had been unable to participate in the activity trip examined above. She vocally expressed her distress at the injustice of being prevented from accompanying her friends and younger sister to the activity camp, with this girl's experiences clearly exemplifying the extent to which mothers and daughters on the one hand, and different groups of women (Sahrawi and non-Sahrawi) on the other, may have seemingly irreconcilable desires, priorities and preferences.

Where the 13-year-old girl was shocked at the injustice of being prevented from participating in the activity due to her imposed responsibilities as an eldest daughter, the Spanish organisers were shocked that their ideals and aims were neither shared nor upheld by Sahrawi mothers (who, as such, clearly were not the 'ideal' women they had previously assumed inhabited the camps); in turn, many mothers were shocked that their concerns regarding girls being 'away from home' at night and their own need for support at home were ignored both by their daughters and by the Spanish organisers.

In this instance, just as the Polisario/SADR and NUSW has developed an alternative to the normative 'dependent-victim-refugee' script by demonstrating its self-sufficiency and independence to non-Sahrawi observers through (amongst other things) the mobilisation of the representational figure of the 'ideal' Sahrawi woman, many mothers were also determined to negotiate the terms of engagement with the NGO on the basis of their own social, cultural and religious norms and priorities regarding gendered and generational roles and responsibilities. In many ways, this particular mother felt that she had 'won' an uneven battle in which 'other' women were trying to take her daughter away from her against her will and in contravention of diverse norms prevalent in the camps. At the same time, this and other mothers' refusal to allow the Spanish women to simply 'take' their daughters threatened to exacerbate the vulnerability of the relationship between Sahrawi refugees and 'their' aid providers, who assert that they are motivated to support the Sahrawi by the intersecting principles of feminism and solidarity. Simultaneously, the battle over the girls' participation in the *rihla* fought by these groups of Spanish and Sahrawi women continued to render certain girls invisible, and demonstrated the extent to which different groups of women's and girls' desires and rights may be in conflict in the camps, as elsewhere.[61] The challenge of developing and maintaining a meaningful and respectful encounter between these different groups of citizen and refugee women on the one hand, and between different groups of women and refugee girls on the other, remains.

Conclusion

This chapter has explored the relationship between the hypervisibility of an 'idealised' agentic and empowered 'Sahrawi woman' and the apparent marginalisation of Sahrawi girl-children's needs, rights and desires. I have argued that the international projection of the camps as ideal spaces characterised by gender equality and female empowerment must be understood on both pragmatic and ideological levels. This is because this representation is intimately related to a rhetoric of political solidarity and humanitarian impulse which is conditional upon refugees fulfilling what Kandiyoti refers to as 'the trinity of democratisation, good governance and women's rights'.[62] When 'real' refugees do not embody and enact the 'idealised' position assigned to them both locally and internationally, the fragility of the conditional systems of aid and solidarity comes to the fore, with external actors threatening to withdraw assistance and support for the 'real' inhabitants of these longstanding refugee camps.[63] While the *rihla* case study explored above demonstrates that 'real' Sahrawi refugee women may actively challenge what they perceive to be neo-colonial interventions which undermine social, cultural and religious norms vis-à-vis appropriate gendered and generational responsibilities and behaviour in the camps, such acts of resistance and agency may nonetheless take place in ways which reassert the marginalisation of different groups of girls in the camps. Although the Spanish women and Sahrawi women referred to above ultimately felt they had each 'won' (respectively by securing and preventing *some* girls' participation in the activity), a space for girl-children's voices and desires to be heard not only failed to emerge but was never even considered to be a necessity from these adults' perspectives.

With the National Union of Sahrawi Women soliciting political and humanitarian support from non-Sahrawi women 'motivated to support the Sahrawi by the intersecting principles of feminism and solidarity', the question which remains is whether, and if so how, Sahrawi *and* non-Sahrawi representational, political and pragmatic responses to protracted displacement can be developed in such a way that they challenge, rather than re-inscribe, forms of gendered and generational inequities that marginalise diverse groups of 'real' women *and* girls in the camps.

NOTES

1 I use the term 'gynocentric' to refer to the central position given to 'Sahrawi women' and to specific representations of female experience and agency, in contrast to the normative 'androcentric' framing of refugee studies and refugee law more broadly. See Elena Fiddian-Qasmiyeh, 'Gender and Forced Migration,' in *The Oxford Handbook of Refugee and Forced Migration Studies*, ed. Elena Fiddian-Qasmiyeh, Gil Loescher, Katy Long and Nando Sigona (Oxford: Oxford University Press, 2014).

2 Thanks and acknowledgements are due to Lisa Baraitser, Gina Crivello, Patricia Espinoza, Rachel Rosen and Jan Newberry, who reviewed an earlier iteration of this chapter and provided helpful suggestions to further develop and refine the argument.

3 Eftihia Voutira and Barbara E. Harrell-Bond, '"Successful" Refugee Settlement: Are Past Examples Relevant?' in *Risks and Reconstruction: Experiences of Resettlers and Refugees*, ed. Michael M. Cernea and C. McDowell (Washington, DC: World Bank, 2000): 56–76; Barbara E. Harrell-Bond, *Imposing Aid: Emergency Assistance to Refugees* (Oxford: Oxford University Press, 1986).

4 Elena Fiddian-Qasmiyeh, *The Ideal Refugees: Gender, Islam and the Sahrawi Politics of Survival* (New York: Syracuse University Press, 2014).

5. Fiddian-Qasmiyeh, *Ideal Refugees*.
6. Fiddian-Qasmiyeh, *Ideal Refugees*.
7. Tony Hodges, *Western Sahara: The Roots of a Desert War* (Westport: Lawrence Hill, 1983), 8–9; Fiddian-Qasmiyeh, *Ideal Refugees*.
8. For a history of the conflict, see Fiddian-Qasmiyeh, *Ideal Refugees*.
9. On Sahrawi women's roles in the Polisario during the colonial era, see Fiddian-Qasmiyeh, E. 'Histories of Displacement: Intersections between Ethnicity, Gender and Class,' *Journal of North African Studies* 16, no. 1 (2011): 31–48; and Fiddian-Qasmiyeh, *Ideal Refugees*.
10. Hodges, Tony. *The Western Saharans*. (London: Minority Rights Group, 1984), 164.
11. Fiddian-Qasmiyeh, *Ideal Refugees*.
12. Quoted in Hodges, *Western Saharans*, 164; emphasis added.
13. Quoted in Hodges, *Western Saharans*, 164.
14. Barbara E. Harrell-Bond, 'The Experience of Refugees as Recipients of Aid'. In *Refugees: Perspectives on the Experience of Forced Migration*, ed. Alastair Ager, (London: Pinter, 1999), 156.
15. Chris Mowles, *Desk Officer's Report on Trip to the Sahrawi Refugee Camps near Tindouf, Southern Algeria, June 16-21, 1986* (Oxfam, 1986): 9.
16. Fiddian-Qasmiyeh, *Ideal Refugees*.
17. See e.g. Barbara E. Harrell-Bond, *The Struggle for the Western Sahara* (Hanover: American Universities Field Staff, 1981): 1–4; Mowles, *Desk Officer's Report*, 8–9.
18. Chris Brazier, 'War and Peace in Western Sahara,' *The New Internationalist*, no. 297 (1997): 14.
19. Whilst beyond this chapter's scope, it is worth noting the parallel with the roles played by nomadic women living in and across Saguiat el Hamra y Río de Oro during the pre-colonial and colonial periods alike, as women were responsible for managing nomadic encampments when men and older boys were away from the camp engaging in diverse mobile livelihood strategies – see Fiddian-Qasmiyeh, *Ideal Refugees*; Fiddian-Qasmiyeh, *Histories of Displacement*.
20. This and subsequent interviews quoted in this sub-section were conducted by local researchers in the Sahrawi refugee camps as part of the University of Oxford project, led by Dawn Chatty, entitled 'Children and Adolescents in Sahrawi and Afghan Refugee Households: Living with the Effects of Prolonged Armed Conflict and Forced Migration' (funded by the Andrew Mellon Foundation between 2002 and 2005). These interviews have previously been cited in Fiddian-Qasmiyeh, *Ideal Refugees*.
21. Cited in Fiddian-Qasmiyeh, *Ideal Refugees*.
22. 38-year-old woman cited in Fiddian-Qasmiyeh, *Ideal Refugees*; emphasis added.
23. Cited in Fiddian-Qasmiyeh, *Ideal Refugees*.
24. Including Anne Lippert, 'The Saharawi Refugees: Origins and Organization, 1975–1985,' in *War and Refugees: The Western Sahara Conflict*, ed. Richard Lawless and Laila Monahan (London: Pinter, 1987); Christiane Perregaux, *Femmes sahraouies, femmes du désert* (Paris: L'Harmattan, 1990).
25. D. Vidal, 'Apre, doux, suave,' *Révolution*, 22 March 1986.
26. UNHCR Refugee Women and Gender Equality Unit, *A Practical Guide to Empowerment: UNHCR Good Practices on Gender Equality Mainstreaming* (Geneva: UNHCR, 2001).
27. WFP, *Protracted Relief and Recovery Operation – Algeria 10172.0*. (WFP, 2002).
28. WFP, *Protracted Relief and Recovery Operation – Algeria 6234.00*. (WFP, 2000); WFP, *Protracted Relief and Recovery Operation – Algeria 10172.1*. (WFP, 2004).
29. WFP, *PRRO – Algeria 10172.1*: 8; my emphasis.
30. WFP, *PRRO – Algeria 6234.00; PRRO – Algeria 10172.1*.
31. Fiddian-Qasmiyeh, *Ideal Refugees*.
32. Robert Fisk, 'Remaining Issues', *London Review of Books* (23 February 1995): 15, cited in Seteney Shami, 'Transnationalism and Refugee Studies', *Journal of Refugee Studies* 9, no. 1 (1996): 9. See Fiddian-Qasmiyeh, *Ideal Refugees*.
33. Liisa Malkki, *Purity and Exile* (London: University of Chicago Press, 1995a); Lisa Malkki, 'Refugees and Exile: From "Refugee Studies" to the National Order of Things,' *Annual Review of Anthropology*, 24 (1995b): 495–523.
34. Liisa Malkki, 'National Geographic: The Rooting of Peoples and the Territorialization of National Identity among Scholars and Refugees,' *Cultural Anthropology* 7, no. 1 (1992): 33; Liisa Malkki, 'Speechless Emissaries: Refugees, Humanitarianism, and Dehistoricization,' *Cultural Anthropology* 11, no. 3 (1996): 389.
35. Cynthia H. Enloe, '"Womenandchildren": Propaganda Tools of Patriarchy,' in *Mobilizing Democracy: Changing the US Role in the Middle East*, ed. Greg Bates (Monroe: Common Courage Press, 1991).

36 Malkki, *Purity and Exile*, 11–12.
37 See Shami, 'Transnationalism and Refugee Studies,' 6.
38 Norwegian Refugee Council. *NRC Reports: Western Sahara. Occupied Country, Displaced People* (NRC, 2008): 7.
39 Voutira and Harrell-Bond, '"Successful" Refugee Settlement,' 68.
40 On refugee women's exclusion in the Calais 'Jungle' camp, see Clegg, this volume.
41 This was an exclamation of surprise made by a visitor to a Tanzanian refugee camp (quoted in Malkki, *Purity and Exile*, 40).
42 My translation and emphasis; also stressed by Mohamed-Fadel Es-Sweyih, *El Primer Estado del Sahara Occidental*, trans. Nathanaël Raballand and Carmen Astiaso (Tindouf: Sahrawi Arab Democratic Republic, 2001): 62.
43 NUSW pamphlet on file with the author; my translation.
44 NUSW statement at http://www.arso.org/UNMS-1.htm (accessed on 31 December 2008; my translation.
45 Malkki, *National Geographic*.
46 Fiddian-Qasmiyeh, *Ideal Refugees*.
47 Simone de Beauvoir, *The Second Sex*, trans. H. M. Parshley (Harmondsworth: Penguin, 1972): 267.
48 Elena Fiddian-Qasmiyeh, 'Representing Sahrawi Refugees' "Educational Displacement" to Cuba: Self-sufficient Agents or Manipulated Victims in Conflict?' *Journal of Refugee Studies* 22, no. 3 (2009): 323–50; *Ideal Refugees*; *South-South Educational Migration, Humanitarianism and Development: Views from the Caribbean, North Africa and the Middle East* (Oxford: Routledge, 2015).
49 Nordstrom, Carolyn. 'Girls and War Zones: Troubling Questions,' in *Engendering Forced Migration: Theory and Practice*, ed. Doreen Indra (New York: Berghahn Books, 1999): 63–82.
50 Nordstrom, 'Girls and War Zones,' 75.
51 For exceptions see Fiddian-Qasmiyeh, 'Representing Sahrawi Refugees'; *Ideal Refugees*; Gina Crivello and Elena Fiddian-Qasmiyeh, 'The Ties that Bind: Sahrawi Children and the Mediation of Aid in Exile,' in *Deterritorialized Youth: Sahrawi and Afghan Refugees at the Margins of the Middle East*, ed. Dawn Chatty (Oxford: Berghahn Books, 2010): 85–118.
52 Sahrawi women move around the camps freely, visiting friends and relatives, attending school, participating in NGO projects or local committees, going to work or to complete household-related tasks. Nonetheless, on restrictions on women's – and girls' – freedom of movement, see Fiddian-Qasmiyeh, *Ideal Refugees*.
53 As I have noted elsewhere, girls and younger women have often been excluded from accessing many 'women's spaces' and even participating in the Women's Union, as these have long been dominated and even monopolised by older generations of women – see Fiddian-Qasmiyeh, *Ideal Refugees*.
54 Cited in Fiddian-Qasmiyeh, *Ideal Refugees*.
55 Cited in Fiddian-Qasmiyeh, *Ideal Refugees*.
56 On the invocation of cultural and religious 'proximity' in justifying girls' participation in specific transnational educational opportunities outside of the camps, see Fiddian-Qasmiyeh, *South-South Educational Migration*.
57 My translation and emphasis.
58 Fiddian-Qasmiyeh, *Ideal Refugees*; on eldest daughters' responsibilities in the camps, see Crivello and Fiddian-Qasmiyeh, *The Ties that Bind*; on children's and youths' perspectives on domestic responsibilities according to age, class and gender elsewhere, also see Crivello and Espinoza in this volume.
59 Interview in 27 February Refugee Camp, Spring 2007.
60 On tensions between different women, and different children, in relation to changes in social reproduction tasks, see Rosen and Newberry, this volume.
61 See Borda Carulla, and Rosen and Newberry, both in this volume.
62 Deniz Kandiyoti, 'Political Fiction Meets Gender Myth: Post-conflict Reconstruction, 'Democratisation' and Women's Rights,' *IDS Bulletin* 35, no. 4 (2004): 134.
63 Also see Elena Fiddian-Qasmiyeh, 'Transnational Abductions and Transnational Jurisdictions? The Politics of "Protecting" Female Muslim Refugees in Spain,' *Gender, Place and Culture* 21, no. 2 (2014): 174–94.

7
A 'sort of sanctuary'

An interview with Liz Clegg by Rachel Rosen

The past few years have borne witness to the largest global movement of people on record, with 65.3 million people forcibly displaced by war, conflict, persecution, dispossession and environmental devastation as of the end of 2015.[1] An increasing number of these migrants are women, children and young people.[2]

Within Europe, the ongoing effects of the 'global economic slump'[3] and a politics of austerity have fostered a particularly vitriolic form of right-wing nationalism across the continent.[4] From 2014–16, this new wave of anti-migrant rhetoric in the UK turned the spotlight on 'the Jungle', an unofficial refugee camp in Calais, France. The camp is situated in a key location at the edge of the Channel Tunnel between France and the UK, where many migrants hope to settle and gain asylum. At the time of its demolition in autumn 2016, estimates put the population of the camp at 9,106 people, 865 of whom were under 18 years old.[5]

Liz Clegg has achieved considerable recognition as the founder of the Unofficial Women and Children's Centre (UWCC) in the unofficial Calais camp. Located in a donated double-decker bus, the UWCC provided food and basic amenities for women and children, offered classes and other support and ran an early learning area. I was interested to interview Liz to hear more about the challenges, and successes, that come from working with both women and children. It also seemed that this grassroots effort could offer insights into the crisis of conviviality and solidarity we have witnessed in many contemporary responses to global migration.

Rachel: Could you start by talking about why you decided to start the UWCC?

Liz: I was working at Glastonbury festival clearing up thousands of tents, sleeping bags, cooking equipment, etc. And of course, Calais is so close, it seemed ridiculous not to take it. I discovered there were about six people on site distributing and they were completely overwhelmed. It was like a bottleneck of foreign aid. So I started distributing out of the back of a truck and managed to find various random volunteers to help me.

After a few weeks, I started to realise there were women and children in the camp and everything to distribute was for men. I spoke to some of the Eritrean refugees that had made community style structures. They were wonderful and said that I could use their space for women's distribution. Because it's very undignified, queuing to be handed something that may or may not fit you... we were able to work with the refugees and make a space for distributing to women and children in a better way where people could have some choice in what they were taking. Treating people with respect, and taking a little bit of the desperation away, brings back a bit of dignity.

The women living in the 'Jungle', depending on their social background or where they'd come from, were certainly not used to mixing with huge amounts of unknown males. There's alcohol on the site and there's people from different cultures that behave in ways that would be unacceptable to these women. Women being isolated was a huge problem. So we secured the UWCC space and we made it quite clear that this is women only. We had some Irish architects arrive, and they built us an amazing space and we were able to secure a perimeter. We had a playground, we had a women-only toilet, and we managed to get a shower in there.

Rachel: So, an unplanned shift from distributing supplies to the slightly more formalised UWCC space... If you were to describe the UWCC, what would you say are your goals and activities now?

Liz: The whole idea was to make this space women-only: to gather, to get information, to distribute from. I think because we were living in 'the Jungle' we had a better connection with the women, because they saw that we were living in the thick of it. So, we built up this kind of trust. We tried to be the bridge between the refugees and the French services. We got Doctors Without Borders to come and start doing their surgery [clinics] out of our space.

We asked the women what they'd like to use the space for, because obviously it was for them. One of the things they asked for was beauty day. It makes an incredible difference to their psychological well-being and of course this is reflected in the kids' well-being. If we can support mothers then we're supporting their children.

The stuff it brings up when a woman is allowed to relax and be pampered and cared for: huge amounts of tears; huge amounts of outpourings; disclosures, lots of disclosures... Suddenly it comes out that they lost a couple of kids on the way. There was a woman not long ago who was being massaged and she just came out and said she'd been really badly raped and it had caused a lot of damage to her. She hadn't told anybody because she was so ashamed. And there were some other girls who'd had similar experiences, and they were able to go, 'It's all right'. We can provide the space and we can provide hair oil and this, that, and the other, but it's that extra bit where suddenly they end up laughing and joking about problems and supporting each other with finding ways through it.

Rachel: You mentioned that the UWCC is a 'women only' space, but of course there are both male and female children there. Can you say a bit more about why you decided to start a centre for women *and* children, not just women *or* children.

Liz: We targeted the most vulnerable in our eyes: the women and children. I became aware that women weren't coming out of their tents and basically there was nowhere for them to go. There was no place that recognised their cultural or religious needs for security. Of course, there's been sexual assaults on the camp. I mean the camp is chaos. Distress levels are massive and it's very difficult for women to survive in that environment, especially as the majority of women have got younger children. And well, obviously, women with their children is a package. Looking after children is the norm... it's very difficult for them to get involved in anything outside that. It's the same story though, isn't it, across the world?

They have community meetings but no women go to these meetings. So, we've started to set up meetings where the agencies could come and talk to the women. Of course, the littlies were there. And the people who were running the meeting were getting quite stressy: 'Could you do something with that child?' This is the reality of women's lives and by default they're excluded from community meetings and decisions for the camp.

In our environment, women feel empowered with their children. The parent who feels isolated because her eight-year-old son's a nightmare, she can come and feel welcome with her child. It's really important because lack of childcare severely isolates women.

Rachel: Have you faced any particular challenges because the centre is for both women and children?

Liz: It's an absolute madhouse, but that's on some days. There are severe challenges to working with a lot of children, particularly the younger ones that are unaccompanied. Huge behavioural problems. Huge lack of boundaries. But we never excluded these children. A lot of the women also recognised that we couldn't abandon these children.

Rachel: You seem to be describing a kind of solidarity between women and children who use, but also are active in shaping, the centre, and a solidarity with those of you who volunteer at the UWCC.

Liz: It's a very tricky dynamic, isn't it, between those of us who provide the space and people who are receiving the aid and what have you. We have access to stuff and a lot of the refugees think we're government organisations. They think we're all paid and we've got access to an endless amount of everything. Of course, we don't. So, it's an interesting dynamic to have incredibly close relationships with people and yet it is 'them' and 'us' and we are never going to be equal. You can't resolve it. I tell all my volunteers: 'Never forget: even though we'll never be equal we are all human. Never, ever forget this is not about you. This is about supporting people in crisis. And be careful that it doesn't switch to being about you because you can lose what you're doing.' But having said that, of course it's about you, of course it's about your experience and of course it's about being conscious of being unequal... Quite tricky dynamics isn't it?

Rachel: You've talked a lot about the injustices in the camp and the horrific conditions of migration journeys. What needs to change, from your perspective?

Liz: Well I guess we could stop bombing Syria right now, couldn't we? We have the means and Europe needs to...We as human beings need to declare it a humanitarian crisis. And, it's not just about making sure the camps are safe and appropriate. But once refugees have come here, we need to make sure that our system is doing what it says it should be doing, particularly with women and children. We need to uphold their rights and give them quality support for their future.

NOTES

1. Adrian Edwards, 'Global Forced Displacement Hits Record High,' UNHCR News and Stories, 20 June 2016. http://www.unhcr.org/uk/news/latest/2016/6/5763b65a4/global-forced-displacement-hits-record-high.html
2. UNHCR Operational Portal, 'Refugee Situations. Mediterranean Situation,' http://data.unhcr.org/mediterranean/country.php?id=83
3. David McNally, *Global Slump: The Economics and Politics of Crisis and Resistance* (Oakland, CA: PM Press/Spectre, 2010).
4. Bridget Anderson, 'Against Fantasy Citizenship: The Politics of Migration and Austerity,' *Renewal: a Journal of Labour Politics* 24, no. 1 (2016): 53–62.
5. September 2016 data from the unofficial census conducted by the charities Help Refugees and L'Auberge des Migrants. Help Refugees, 'Latest Calais Census,' 24 August 2016. http://www.helprefugees.org.uk/2016/08/24/latest-calais-census/

Section 2
Life's Work

8
Love, labour and temporality
Reconceptualising social reproduction with women and children in the frame

Rachel Rosen and Jan Newberry

A research conversation over dinner

We first met at one of the many conferences organized in recent years around the issues of childhood and youth. This conference was hosted by the University of Sheffield's Centre for the Study of Childhood and Youth in 2014. Here, we recreate the conversation that led to this chapter.

Jan: So, my new research is on the early childhood education and care (ECEC) programmes appearing in Indonesia. That's where I did my original work on how the state had used the 'volunteered' labour of lower-class women to deliver social services to local neighbourhoods. I've been surprised during this new project because even after democratization these same women are being asked to deliver local early childhood programmes. It was as if all this global interest in the child has pushed the interests of women to the side.

Rachel: In my own community-based research with mothers, as well as childcare and domestic workers, in Vancouver it was stark how mothers felt trapped and scrutinised by the state because of the expectations that were placed on them in contexts of impoverishment and retrenchment. We called our project 'Between a rock and a hard place' because of the sorts of impossible choices facing mothers – like leaving young children at home alone to work to pay for food and heating when there was no childcare available. The sorts of 'voluntary' work expected wasn't around ECEC programs but 'investing in' their own children through extra-curricular activities, home reading, and so on.

Jan: So, I've argued two things about this kind of labour. First, the Indonesian state benefits tremendously from this unwaged support for low-cost social reproduction. Basically, women's community work keeps wages very low to support a surplus-labour economy. But I've also argued that locals do this because of the strong value put on women's community work to support their local neighbourhoods. The Indonesian state has been remarkably successful in mobilizing this ideology to its own ends. Because most of these programmes are being run in their own neighbourhoods, young women may be doing this for their own children. But many of these 'volunteers' are retired teachers and older women whose children are grown. Their motivations are tied up with this ethos of community welfare and social support. Very little of it looks to be about women's needs for childcare.

Rachel: In Canada, our research also found that childcare workers and domestic workers were working well beyond the hours they were paid for, staying at the setting if carers were late, developing learning materials, cleaning and more. Migrant domestic workers were effectively on-call 24 hours a day because the immigration system required that they both work and live in their employer's home. In my research in England, educators have described staying up until late at night completing copious assessment and paperwork requirements. We argued that because caring work pivots on responsibility to others, this emotionally, ethically and institutionally impels 'voluntary' work. This happens often in ECEC where ideas about the maternal easily slip into work relations and where conceptions of childhood vulnerability and innocence dominate.

Jan: But here we are at a child studies conference and as usual I'm talking about women's labour. I always feel a little guilty that I'm not really engaged in child studies. I mean what I saw was that the global push for early childhood programming was coming at the expense of women. What about young people here?

Rachel: It seems to me that there is a difference between the interests of children and the global interest in 'the child'. In my research, educators and parents have been heavily preoccupied with child development. This is often well intentioned, but underpinned by all sorts of ideas about controlling the future: the idea that teaching children to verbally express emotions or sit in a circle will have predictable results such as self-regulation, 'school ready' bodies, and improved school achievement – as though these were unproblematic measures of well-being and social justice. And, this is all potentially very different than the interests of children themselves. Children employ all sorts of embodied responses to such interventions: for example, through screams, silences, hiding and more.

There is also something about the way this sort of framing ends up positioning children, or attention to the well-being of children, as the cause of women's subordination. This turns attention away from questions of 'who is benefitting?' from the increasing focus on the child. I suspect the answer is neither marginalised women nor children.

Jan: I've been trying to sort through the different motivations for these ECEC programs and the effects for women and children. There is the clear influence from World Bank-funded programming aimed at human capital development but there is also the influence from OECD approaches that include supporting women's ability to work. These desires meet in the small, almost accidental spaces in neighbourhoods and rural hamlets where local Indonesians are attempting to meet the demand for these programmes driven not just by global mandates but also the Indonesian state. And it's far from clear who sees the benefit of all this programming.

Rachel: There is another question about the way that labour gets framed in these discussions about ECEC: where does children's activity fit? When I think about my own research, children were involved in all sorts of 'labour' in ECEC settings: cleaning, food preparation, caring for others, and labouring on themselves. Yet this was referred to as 'developing/learning to…' rather than 'contributions to…'

* * *

Between dinner and dessert, our conversation shifted to the tensions which ECEC surfaced between women and children. Women, in our own work and that of others, noted the importance of loving relationships with children and the simultaneous pressure that entailed, with some even feeling exploited for their 'motherly love' in home or work settings.[1] Children also experienced conflicts: finding joy and support in their relationships with women, but occasionally feeling scared, aggrieved or disrespected by women's actions. We noted the tendency towards two dichotomous poles: either a conflation of 'women's interests' and 'children's interests' or an assumption of antagonism, where the needs of one group are viewed as trumping the other's or advances for one group were seen to be won to the detriment of the other.[2] We began to wonder: could we think through our experience with ECEC in different contexts to theorize women–children relations while keeping both in the frame of analysis?[3] The following is our response.

Revisiting social reproduction

We first spoke together not long after the 2007/8 global financial crisis. As regimes of austerity and retrenchment deepened globally, we saw the potential of 'social reproduction' as a way to address our questions. 'Social reproduction,' writes Katz, 'is the fleshy, messy, and indeterminate stuff of everyday life.'[4] Understood in its more specific form as socially necessary labour or the reproduction of labour power, social reproduction has been used by Marxist and other feminists to understand the labour involved in ensuring daily existence and generational survival and to explain the oppression and exploitation of women. The concept has experienced a certain revival in the context of decreasing state social welfare provision, the global movement of domestic workers, and neoliberal restructuring that has released capital from the need to ensure that social reproduction is accomplished in a particular place due to its largely unhampered mobility.[5] Feminists point out that the shifting organisation of social reproduction is creating new forms of subordination as it is simultaneously re-familialised, with women primarily held responsible for providing this necessary labour as with the 'voluntary' labour of Indonesian women, and marketised, via quasi-familial migrant domestic work and privatised ECEC programmes. Much of this prior and contemporary feminist analysis, however, figures children primarily as little more than the *objects* of social reproduction, those beings who need to be fed, clothed, cared for, educated and socialised for their *futurity* as waged workers.

Despite this critique, childhood scholars have productively taken up the notion of social reproduction to consider the place of children in the division of labour, both within and beyond the market-based economy. Research in the 'global South' has employed the concept to analyse children's contributions to household economies, including care labour in familial settings and paid domestic work. This research has included attention to the reproductive labour of the very young (see Crivello and Espinosa, this volume, for a detailed discussion). In the 'global North', however, the concept of social reproduction has had less purchase in explaining children's activity. Investigations of 'young carers', for example, focus on 'non-normative' childhoods rather than social reproduction.[6] Even so, moves to foreground children's socially necessary labour, however important, run the risk of bypassing – and by corollary not being able to account for – the gendered division of social reproductive labour.

In revisiting the concept to keep both women and children in frame, we propose that social reproduction can be understood as both a useful analytic tool and an unfinished political and theoretical project. We begin first by suggesting that women and children are linked through species-being, a labour relation that anchors socially necessary labour. We move on to consider how women and children's interests can become differentiated and stratified, arguing that temporality is central to these processes,[7] thereby putting the concepts to a new use to answer lingering questions about the implications of social reproduction for women and children and the relations between them.

Species-being as labour and love

Here, we begin by returning to species-being, Marx's sketch of a concept, to firmly anchor labour at the centre of the shared work that makes us human while questioning the limits of any *necessary* relation between women and children. Taking up species-being again is timely given that the boundaries of the human are under discussion, but here we do so to remind ourselves of Marx's prescient use of the concept to foreground relationality and contingency in the making of humans and social value.

Marx's species-being describes human nature as neither fixed nor given but rather as made through practical activity and relations of labour that are historically specific and contingent. As the definitive form of human productive activity, species-being is 'the medium through which we recognize both others and ourselves'.[8] It is this recognition of an active material process, and its historical specificity, that we emphasize. If species-being is 'life-engendering life' as Marx himself said, it is also the ground for our relationships to self and other mediated through our activity in the world. These arguments, which point to the limits of the self-contained liberal subject, share much with other chapters here (e.g. Baraitser and Thomson; Burman). Without dismissing the psychosocial aspects which they foreground, relationality in our account is strongly embedded in the social relations of labour. This allows us to pay heed to labour's world-making possibilities and to question why particular relationships come to be seen as normal and desirable.

We are proposing a rescue of labour from those who would most closely tie it to Marx's critique of industrialization and the extraction of surplus value. Rather, we situate it in its human-making potential: how we make ourselves and are made as humans is a labour process. This positions labour as neither before nor after capitalism. Here too, we re-appropriate appropriation. That is, we understand appropriation first as a 'process in which bodies interact with and are affected by sensuous engagement with the world'.[9] Children, for example, appropriate the lap of caregivers, using what is available to meet their species-being needs. We are, each of us, an affordance for others; a potentiality. By seeing labour and appropriation as requiring others we underline its relational character and its connection to affect, care and love. Our research highlights the highly emotive decisions women have to make when leaving their own children in the care of others in order to send remittances from domestic work abroad or the struggles over ECEC closure times, when workers have to forfeit time attending to their own needs or time with their own children to stay with those in their care until a guardian arrives.[10] Children, too, experience the affective and power-laden dimensions of such activity; for example, children who act as language brokers may deeply desire to help out their parents in these interactions but feel anxious about finding appropriate terms or translating comments that may be considered rude.

These examples demonstrate that 'the evident and implied passions of the participants do not disqualify their efforts as "labour" but, on the contrary, are *part* of the work'.[11] By understanding this species-being activity as both love *and* labour it becomes possible to consider how such energy, time and effort is divided and valued.

Species-being needs

In species-being, humans become aware of themselves and others in a process that shapes our experience and our stance in the world as well as the world itself. Because our species-being is fundamentally wrapped up with others, Marx understood it to be the basis for human freedom, creativity and love. That is: 'human freedom is actually intertwined with others'.[12] As evaluative and vulnerable beings we act – at least in part – because things matter to us. In pointing to the politicised precarity of human life, Sayer gives us pause to open up the concept of species-being to consideration not only as a labour relation but as embodied needs.[13] 'Need' has become a dirty word in childhood studies, with a seminal paper arguing that a framework of 'children's needs' should be jettisoned because it is 'a powerful rhetorical device' which entrenches protectionist relations between adults and children and advances idealised middle-class and Western childhoods and forms of care as universal prescriptions.[14] Yet, as Hennessy points out: 'Needs are corporeal – because they involve keeping the body alive – but they are not "natural", because meeting these corporeal needs always takes place through social relationships.'[15] And here the mutual interdependence at the centre of species-being elucidates how corporeality, care and need are part of that labour relation. As such, need can be understood as a fundamentally human condition linked to our existential precarity, and simultaneously as historically located, spatially situated and fundamentally social in production, interpretation and satisfaction. While there is likely widespread 'thin' agreement about human needs (e.g. for nourishment, shelter, relationships), any 'thicker' investigation will reveal that needs – their interpretation and satisfaction – are not the same across time and place, making them subject to extensive contestation.[16]

We are connected via our species-being needs and the ways these are satisfied (or not), yet our needs are *differentiated* in ways which have corporeal and social dimensions. Young human beings have needs particular to the limits and possibilities of their bodies: put bluntly, infants would die without the species-being labour of another. Despite important critiques of 'children's needs', a neglect of differentiated needs can foreclose attention to the embodied experience of being a young human being and the needs produced by being positioned as a child in particular time-space. Similarly, some needs can be linked to being positioned as a woman, such as those related to the possibility of menstruation, giving birth, or increased vulnerability to rape and male violence.

Globalisation compounds differentiated needs based on the desire for and possibility of mobility, affected by physical capabilities, legal regulations, normative views of the 'proper' place of childhood and adulthood, as well as class relations and access to resources. Being a newcomer to a social world produces different needs, but being a newcomer is not coterminous with childhood. Those positioned as children can have far more experience in a particular field than an adult and being a newcomer is not only about time, but also about space – someone can be a newcomer in a new locale regardless of the length of their life.

Attending to both shared and differentiated needs prompts questions as to who interprets needs and their satisfaction. How is the labour required to satisfy species-being needs distributed across time and space, and what changes are wrought to the interpretation and satisfaction of needs in late capitalism?

The outlawing of needs

Socially necessary labour, or the ways in which communities organise provisioning and survival, and the meeting of species-being needs takes a particular form in capitalist economies. Following Marx, Vogel identifies a 'social component' of necessary labour, that portion of the day where workers produce value equivalent to the commodities they need for their own (and their dependents') subsistence.[17] Marx's contribution was to highlight that the working day extends beyond this time, and that the appropriation of this surplus labour is what allows for capitalist accumulation. What Vogel and other feminist scholars have argued is that only part of what people require for their subsistence is covered by the wage form. Our species-being means that we get dirty, hungry, tired and grumpy and have needs for love and relationships, intimacy, learning and leisure, and it is a political question as to how a line gets drawn between which of these needs are viewed as requiring compensation and which are not included in a wage calculus.

It is here that the concept of 'outlawed needs' proposed by Kelsh is particularly helpful as a way of considering how this line gets drawn, argued over and reproduced.[18] In neoliberal capitalism, many needs that are outlawed, or excluded from legitimation, are those associated with people's daily maintenance and generational reproduction. The concept of outlawed needs helps to account for those human relationships and sensuous interactions in the world which are outlawed because they contradict hegemonic forms of familial structures: these include same-sex families, single motherhood and so on. The labour to meet outlawed needs is still socially necessary, but it is hived off (spatially, legally and discursively) from the recognised component covered by wages and is more frequently referred to as 'social reproduction'. Outlawed needs are a 'monstrous necessity' for capital. They are 'necessary' to ensure workers for capital. But they are 'monstrous' because they are a site of contestation, including whether they are recognised as being an object for political satisfaction by capital and/or the state at the cost of surplus value.

ECEC is a case in point. It has become recognised as a 'need' through changes in capital's demand for specific workers, such as the increasing numbers of women workers in growing service-oriented economies, and contestation over which institutions and actors are responsible for social reproduction. In Canada, in 1970s and 80s activism to bring the care of children out of the family and into the public realm, calls for childcare were linked to women's emancipation and the need for more collective responsibility for the care of young children. These demands were sidelined in the neoconservative climate of the 1990s: the 'need' for ECEC was increasingly reframed as a matter of social investment (e.g. of economic benefits outweighing the costs) in the developmental 'needs' of children, in the context of rising global interest in the 'first 1,000 days', without reference to women's needs for support. These new interpretations of needs shifted the way in which workforce and mainstream childcare organisations articulated their demands, as well as the ways in which the state rationalised and organised its ECEC funding and provision.[19] A similar phenomenon is apparent in the community mothers' programme in Columbia (see Borda Carulla, this volume).

While needs interpretation and satisfaction is an ongoing political struggle, in the meantime people must find ways to meet their outlawed needs, and it is in this process that differentiation and stratification occur.

Linkages and differentiation

Capital's drive to reduce the cost of socially necessary labour, including by outlawing needs, appears in historically and spatially distinct forms, and here we consider the way this both links women and children and differentiates them.[20]

To begin, we pick up McDowell's attempts to unweave the tasks subsumed under the umbrella of social reproduction to see how naturalization obscures the possibility for their satisfaction through other means.[21] Of all the aspects of this labour, McDowell argues it is only the generational replacement of workers that 'depends on a gender division of labour'. Recent changes in reproductive technology and our understanding of diversity in human sex and sexuality have challenged even this assertion, but here, we accept that species-being labour intimately links biological mothers with foetuses or newborns for some time at least, even if no longer than gestation and birth. McDowell's analysis identifies the tendency to over-extend the relations of giving birth in two ways. First, the very specific labour of child bearing often becomes conflated with other social reproduction tasks including cooking, cleaning, shopping, feeding, caring and more, tasks that can be completed by men as well. Second, the necessary link between biological mother and foetus/newborn is often generalised to the social position of all women, regardless of whether individuals have the potential or desire to give birth. By corollary, this is also stretched to the position of 'child', beyond the specific relationships individual children may have with individual women.

To this we would add another form of over-extension that multiplies the linkages between women and children. Young humans are reliant on others for their very survival, accounting for the only necessary division of social reproduction on generational lines. However, this early dependency has been increasingly taken to describe the institution of childhood, in its entirety, overwriting children's potential capabilities with social ascriptions of vulnerability, need and dependency. This achieved concrete expression in the twentieth-century growth of 'child protection institutions',[22] including ECEC programmes, nurseries and other 'specialised' sites of childhood.

That is, the responsibility for satisfying children's (ascribed and outlawed) needs tends to be placed with women – based on maternalist assumptions. It links children to such labour, based on their conflation with women. Indeed, historical and contemporary work in Childhood and Youth Studies has revealed both the level and variety of children's involvement in social reproductive tasks, making clear that the idealisation of a childhood sequestered into a realm of play, innocence and freedom from responsibility is a normative position with rather dubious effects, rather than a natural necessity. In the Indonesian case, for example, the idea of play as therapy and intervention represents a new way to understand the child and the child within the family.[23]

The point here, following McDowell, is that it is possible to acknowledge the socially necessary labour of species-being at the same time as noting that there is no natural necessity to the gendered division of this labour. Similarly, there is no necessary division of labour shaped by a generational order that ascribes the social quality of 'childness' and the status of 'child' to render young humans as the constitutive outside of labour.[24]

Temporality and the production of antagonisms

That much of the labour of social reproduction has fallen to women and children is indicative of its 'advantages [to class societies] – contested and constantly renegotiated – over the alternatives'.[25] While the dynamic of capital means there is a tendency for dominant classes to try to decrease the amount of socially necessary labour covered by wages, how this happens varies tremendously. The question becomes at what point does the process of appropriation at the heart of social reproduction become one of stratification, exploitation and accumulation? In this section, we argue that it is in this variation, particularly in the tempo of surplus value extraction, that we can begin to see how antagonisms among women, among children, and between women and children manifest.

The varied effects of capital's efforts to reduce its labour costs are, in part, a reflection of divergent interests among dominant classes. For example, corporate farming companies may urge the lowering of the working age so that they can employ the 'cheaper' labour of children. Others may support the extension of the compulsory school age, both upwards and downwards, and the linking of schooling to employers' 'needs' to try to meet their demands for workers with particular skills. But variations can also be understood in relation to tensions between capital's short- and long-term interests. Childbearing, and its generalisation to other tasks of social reproduction, limits the time available for wage labour. The *temporal lag* identified here leads to a potential contradiction for capital, between 'its immediate need to appropriate surplus labor and its long-term requirement for a class to perform it'.[26]

The demand for children to contribute their labour towards surplus value in the form of wage labour as quickly as possible can be in tension with the use of their labour to supplement or replace family members whose labour is demanded outside of a household. It also conflicts with children's potential involvement in their own (and others') development as generational replacements, an increasing amount of which is accomplished in non-familial ECEC and other educational settings. Indeed, Rikowski puts forward a powerful set of arguments suggesting that educational institutions are a key site for the 'quality enhancement' of labour power – a central strategy for increasing relative surplus value in contemporary capitalism.[27]

Rikowski focuses on the labour of teachers, educators and trainers (many of whom are women) in schooling. Similarly, the conceptualisation of generational replacement in much of the domestic labour debate is about 'raising' or 'socialising' children, which takes a more contemporaneous form in the notion of 'investing in children' where 'the [privileged] child as commodity is niche-marketed to secure success in the insecure future'.[28] This, however, implies that children are little more than objects of investment and others' labour. With Hood-Williams, we concur that this 'ignores the extent to which children...are actively engaged in the work of "reproducing" themselves'.[29]

We view the daily and generational replacement activities of social reproduction as a shared endeavour of species-being labour; in other words, an activity in which children are necessarily engaged.[30] This can range from the labour to develop particular skills and knowledge – for instance the literacy and numeracy skills that are central to many (post-)industrial jobs, whether in the service industry or export processing zones – and the labour involved in making the self and social relations. Take, for example, the ways in which children are actively involved in negotiating capitalist social relations via engagement in imaginative play involving commodity consumption.[31] Children also engage in caring labour in ECEC settings, inducting others into setting life, supporting and consoling those who are upset, and providing a sense of satisfaction and purpose for the adults. Rosen, for example, notes the way children in a London ECEC setting would 'humour' adult educators, accepting their interventions into and scholarisation of imaginative play, only to return to other themes when the educators left.[32]

Attending to variations in the tempo of appropriation and the sites where reproductive labour is accomplished allows us to see how children and women may be linked through social reproduction, but in ways which may put their interests at odds. Newberry documents how for Indonesian mothers the growing importance attributed to the early years of a child's life has occasioned an increase in domestic responsibilities and a hiving off of children's work away from contributing to the household and family reproduction.[33] In rural areas in central Java, women must now leave agricultural or factory labour to escort children to ECEC programmes, often offered at some distance from their homes (even though these programmes are quite limited in scope). Not only does this represent time away for women from their own immediate reproduction and waged labour, it represents a separation of children from the site of those activities, where typically they would be involved in various agricultural and household tasks. In urban settings, the innumerable small contributions of children, from sibling care to food preparation to help with informal industries, are necessarily limited by the time they must now spend in the classroom setting. In the Indonesian case, women's felt need to contribute to these community-based programmes comes at some cost to their own household-based reproduction, and it simultaneously introduces a differentiation in women's and children's contributions to that reproduction, both temporally and spatially. The household-based reproductive tasks that in many cases aligned the needs of women and children become outlawed, but in different ways: women must volunteer labour to offer local ECEC programmes, and children must attend. In the case of women, the surplus value of this volunteered labour is appropriated immediately while that of children is deferred through the longer-term enhancement of their labour power.

It is the tempo of the appropriation of surplus value, and the various attempts to 'fix' the contradictions between capital's short- and long-term interests, that is central to the differentiation of needs and to the outlawing of some. It is also a critical source of the tension between women and children in the meeting of these needs.

Stratification and the return of time

In this chapter we have argued that women and children are mutually implicated in one another through species-being labour, and this cannot be separated from love and concern for one another. This interdependence is world-making. In these labour relations, some needs may be satisfied in ways that align the interests of women and children; however, much is re-written under capitalism. The temporal contradiction between immediate surplus appropriation and long-term aspects of generational replacement are mediated by outlawing some needs and endorsing others, producing forms of differentiation and deepening stratification.[34]

Evidence of 'stratified social reproduction' has been identified for some time.[35] Theorisations of the international division of domestic labour or 'global care chains', for example, point to the devaluation of reproductive labour as it passes between people.[36] More privileged families in advanced capitalist countries, with the support of state policies, hire (im)migrant domestic workers who in turn hire internal migrants to care for their families, so that responsibility for reproductive labour is transferred to other family members. This labour is often transferred to girls in a gendered division of labour, although boys are also called upon in ways that are geo-spatially specific and limited by a lack of alternatives, as Crivello and Espinosa (this volume) point out.[37] At the same time, impoverished women and children within 'receiving' countries like Canada struggle to afford even basic ECEC services in an era of austerity and state retrenchment, 'making do' with a patchwork of kin-based, including sibling, care or leaving even the very young in their own care.[38] Alternatively, families enter into debt to ensure that their 'outlawed needs' can be met. It is not just a question of differentiation amongst those who engage in social reproductive labour: Kofman's analysis suggests that reproductive labour itself is being increasingly differentiated.[39] She argues that the 'dirty' aspects of daily maintenance and long-term reproduction have been pushed on to poorer women (and we add children), many of whom are migrants, freeing the more privileged to engage in esteemed work such as reading bedtime stories or engaging in prescribed adult–child bonding activities. Indeed, modes of differentiation and stratification in social reproduction seem to have exploded and intensified in the contemporary.

In concluding this chapter, we make a bold claim: by attending not only to uneven spatial flows but also to the *timing* of appropriation in terms of socially necessary labour, we can understand how the fates of women and children are both intertwined and at odds. The temporal aspects of social reproduction and appropriation underscore the subordination of those who engage in such labour, even as they introduce questions of aging and elder care that deserve further attention.

McDowell makes a distinction between those who provide subsistence via their wages and those who engage in reproductive labour during what we have referred to above as a 'temporal lag'.[40] She identifies the relationship of dependency which this creates, and its reinforcement by patriarchal state policies, as the grounds for women's subordination. To this we would add that this temporal lag, and the subordination it engenders, is unevenly distributed in the context of a racialised international division of labour and the increased rapidity with which surplus value is appropriated in the global South. This temporal lag is also central to accounting for children's subordinate social status. Children, particularly when very young, are often banned from working for wages and as a result end up working in unregulated sectors or not at all. When they do work for wages, children are often treated as a cheaper work force, paid lower wages for the same work as adults under the guise of euphemisms such as 'training wages'. Social benefits go to adults, not children. These features both ensure a cheaper source of labour for capital and also account for the socially constituted dependency of children on adults, as well as their generational subordination.

By returning to the example of global care chains, we can perhaps best see how subordination, grounded in the temporal lag, both links and differentiates women and children. As caring work gradually is transferred between various nodes of the care chain, girls in families with migrant mothers are placed in roles caring for younger siblings and other family members. The immediate appropriation of their labour in the wage sector, whether domestic or otherwise, can be delayed as they instead contribute to long-term reproduction. This effectively reinforces the dependency of children on their mother's foreign remittances. Migrant workers absorb the vagaries of the temporal lag for class-privileged women, via their low or unpaid domestic work. The stratification between children on various nodes of the 'care chain' is intensified through the stratification of reproductive tasks themselves, with more privileged children engaged in various forms of ECEC dedicated primarily to 'quality enhancement' of their own labour power and less privileged children in the chain responsible for replacement and replenishment activities far beyond themselves.

Perhaps, then, it is time to add time back in to our accounts of stratified social reproduction. Our discussion of global ECEC regimes in this chapter was an attempt to develop temporality as a lens for considering both elisions and antagonisms between women and children. We propose for further inquiry the question of the mechanisms that affect the timing of the appropriation of surplus value and the practical implications of these temporal differences. For instance, are the neoliberal debt-based economy and the marketisation of social reproduction speeding up the point at which appropriation takes place, at the same time as the extension of ECEC and compulsory schooling lengthen the temporal lag?

Conclusion

Our common interest in ECEC led us to discover another common interest in a Marxist feminist frame of analysis, one whose relevance is being marked again in renewed attention to social reproduction. We suggest that expanding the study of stratified social reproduction with a generational analysis can help account for the contradictions produced by the expansion of non-familial early years provision and its reliance on women's re-traditionalised, voluntary or low-paid labour, and the shifting imperatives for young children's social reproductive labour, such as the making of the self and caring responsibilities.

In so doing we have pointed to the ways that the interests of women and children can be aligned but also differentiated and made antagonistic as they engage in labour to satisfy outlawed needs. Rather than viewing these as inherent tensions between women and children, however, we have rehabilitated appropriation and added temporal differentiation to account for the ways these groups and the relations between them are constituted and their (uneven and situated) productivity for capital. Our contribution in this chapter has been an act of reimagining the importance of social reproduction for theorising woman–child relations, and underscoring its potential for emancipatory efforts which aim to keep both women and children in the frame.

NOTES

1. Helen Colley, 'Learning to Labour with Feeling: Class, Gender and Emotion in Childcare Education and Training,' *Contemporary Issues in Early Childhood* 7, no. 1 (2006).
2. See also Erica Burman, 'Beyond "Women Vs. Children" or "Womenandchildren": Engendering Childhood and Reformulating Motherhood,' *The International Journal of Children's Rights* 16, no. 2 (2008).
3. This is not merely an intellectual exercise, but a recognition of the impossibilities of granting even *conceptual* autonomy to women and children, as Baraitser and Thomson (this volume) point out. Men's contributions to reproductive labour have not received sufficient scholarly attention and certainly attention to species-being invites a fuller exploration. Here, however, our focus on the relations between women and children derives from our research in ECEC settings where women's care for children has been privileged. We bracket men's labour for the purposes of theorising the relations between women and children, just as these have been separated in practice under capitalism.
4. Cindi Katz, 'Vagabond Capitalism and the Necessity of Social Reproduction,' *Antipode* 33, no. 4 (2001): 711.
5. Katz, 'Vagabond Capitalism': 711.
6. See e.g. Sarah Crafter et al., 'Young Peoples' Representations of "Atypical" Work in English Society,' *Children & Society* 23, no. 3 (2009).
7. The so-called spatial turn of the 1990s was inspired by Foucault's analysis of space as neglected in relation to time. While not neglecting space here, we do suggest that time and temporality need to be reintroduced theoretically.
8. J. M. Held, 'Marx Via Feuerbach: Species-Being Revisited,' *Idealistic Studies* 39, no. 1/3 (2009): 146.
9. Gerda Roelvink, 'Rethinking Species-Being in the Anthropocene,' *Rethinking Marxism* 25, no. 1 (2013): 59.
10. Rachel Rosen, Suzanne Baustad and Merryn Edwards, 'The Crisis of Social Reproduction under Global Capitalism: Working Class Women and Children in the Struggle for Universal Childcare,' in *Caring for Children: Social Movements and Public Policy in Canada*, ed. Rachel Langford, Susan Prentice and Patrizia Albanese (Vancouver: UBC Press, 2017).
11. Sara Ruddick, 'Care as Labour and Relationship,' in *Norms and Values: Essays on the Work of Virginia Held*, ed. Joram G. Haber and Mark S. Halfon (Oxford: Rowman & Littlefield Publishers, 1998): 12, our italics.
12. Roelvink, 'Rethinking Species-Being': 60.
13. Andrew Sayer, *Why Things Matter to People: Social Science, Values and Ethical Life* (Cambridge: Cambridge University Press, 2011).
14. Martin Woodhead, 'Psychology and the Cultural Construction of Children's Needs,' in *Constructing and Reconstructing Childhood: Contemporary Issues in the Sociological Study of Childhood*, ed. Allison James and Alan Prout (London: Falmer, 1997): 77.
15. Rosemary Hennessy, *Profit and Pleasure: Sexual Identities in Late Capitalism* (New York: Routledge, 2000): 210.
16. Nancy Fraser, 'Struggle over Needs: Outline of a Socialist-Feminist Critical Theory of Late-Capitalist Political Culture,' in *Women, the State, and Welfare*, ed. Linda Gordon (Madison: University of Wisconsin Press, 1990).
17. Lise Vogel, 'Domestic Labor Revisited,' *Science & Society* 64, no. 2 (2000): 151–70.
18. Deborah P. Kelsh, 'The Pedagogy of Excess,' *Cultural Logic: Marxist Theory & Practice* (2013): 137–56.
19. Rosen, Baustad, and Edwards, 'Crisis of Social Reproduction'.
20. We are writing here about women and children from subordinated classes specifically. Reminding us that Marx's analysis is based on the reproduction of classes, Vogel explains that while reproduction takes place in any class, it is the total social reproduction of the working class that is the special interest of the capitalist.
21. Linda McDowell, 'Debates and Reports: Beyond Patriarchy: A Class Based Explanation of Women's Subordination,' *Antipode* 18, no. 3 (1986): 315.
22. John Gillis, 'Transitions to Modernity,' in *The Palgrave Handbook of Childhood Studies*, ed. Jens Qvortrup, William Corsaro, and Michael-Sebastian Honig (Basingstoke: Palgrave MacMillan, 2011): 118.

23 Jan Newberry, '"Anything Can Be Used to Stimulate Child Development": Early Childhood Education and Development in Indonesia as a Durable Assemblage,' *Journal of Asian Studies* (in press).
24 Leena Alanen, 'Generational Order,' in *The Palgrave Handbook of Childhood Studies*, ed. Jens Qvortrup, William Corsaro, and Michael-Sebastian Honig (Basingstoke: Palgrave MacMillan, 2011): 163.
25 Vogel, 'Domestic Labour Revisited': 5.
26 Lise Vogel, *Marxism and the Oppression of Women: Toward a Unitary Theory* (New Brunswick: Rutgers University Press, 1983): 145.
27 Glenn Rikowski, 'Alien Life: Marx and the Future of the Human,' *Historical Materialism* 11, no. 2 (2003).
28 Cindi Katz, 'Cultural Geographies Lecture: Childhood as Spectacle: Relays of Anxiety and the Reconfiguration of the Child,' *Cultural Geographies* 15, no. 1 (2008): 10.
29 John Hood-Williams, 'Patriarchy for Children: On the Stability of Power Relations in Children's Lives,' in *Childhood, Youth, and Social Change. A Comparative Perspective*, ed. Lynne Chisholm et al. (New York: The Falmer Press, 1990): 160.
30 Qvortrup develops an important argument that children's creative efforts and mental and physical energy expended in schools can be understood as a form of labour. He does so in order to stress the value of children's unrecognised economic contributions to the societies they live in. Here, however, we complicate his argument in two ways. First, we emphasise the contingency of school labour, suggesting that it is not always in the interest of capital for all children to move primarily into sites of compulsory education. Instead, we emphasise the geopolitical and gendered ways in which schooling and other forms of reproductive labour are distributed. Second, we emphasise the links between reproductive labour and capital accumulation. Jens Qvortrup, 'From Useful to Useful: The Historical Continuity of Children's Constructive Participation,' in *Sociological Studies of Children*, ed. Nancy Mandell and Anne-Marie Ambert (Greenwich, CT: JAI Press, 1995).
31 Rosen, Baustad, and Edwards, 'Crisis of Social Reproduction'.
32 Rachel Rosen, 'The Use of the Death Trope in Peer Culture Play: Grounds for Rethinking Children and Childhood?' *International Journal of Play* 4, no. 2 (2015).
33 Jan Newberry, 'Women against Children: Early Childhood Education and the Domestic Community in Post-Suharto Indonesia,' *TRaNS: Trans -Regional and -National Studies of Southeast Asia* 2 (2014).
34 There are parallels between our argument and others in this volume which, broadly speaking, make the case that affiliations and tensions between women and children lie not in some spuriously naturalised relationship but in the ways that these groups are socially constituted. Burman, for instance, points to the socio-political context via an intersectional lens and Fiddian-Qasmiyeh to neo-colonial micro-politics and the failures of liberal humanitarianism. These are not necessarily contradictory lines of analysis, but perhaps a difference of scale. This serves as an important reminder to keep the dynamics of capital, the state and micro-politics in view, even while the dictates of space may mean giving greater emphasis to one.
35 Shellee Colen, "Like a Mother to Them': Stratified Reproduction and West Indian Childcare Workers and Employers in New York,' in *Conceiving the New World Order: The Global Politics of Reproduction*, ed. Faye D. Ginsburg and Rayna Rapp (Berkeley: University of California Press, 1995).
36 Rhacel Salazar Parrenas, 'The Reproductive Labour of Migrant Workers,' *Global Networks* 12, no. 2 (2012).
37 This, of course, raises the important point that children are not a homogeneous group and attention needs to be given to gendering 'the child' in analysis much as it is in practice (see Fiddian-Qasmiyeh, this volume). Girl children are subject to adultism and misogyny, as both girls and incipient women (Zehavi, this volume). The relevance of unequal childhoods is not lost on us, although it is largely beyond the scope of this chapter.
38 Rosen, Baustad, and Edwards, 'Crisis of Social Reproduction'.
39 Eleonore Kofman, 'Gendered Migrations, Social Reproduction and the Household in Europe,' *Dialectical Anthropology* 38, no. 1 (2014).
40 McDowell, 'Debates and Reports'.

9
Caring labour as the basis for movement building

An interview with Selma James by Rachel Rosen

Rachel: You have a long history of commitment to social movements for women's emancipation. Could you begin by talking about how you got involved?

Selma: Well I started as an anti-capitalist, working-class child who was part of the movement of the 1930s. My community in Brooklyn, New York, was anti-capitalist and anti-racist in principle if not in practice. I was enormously interested in the relationships I saw and remember so many incidents that helped to shape my view of the world and particularly the relationships between women and men and children within the family.

I joined a socialist organisation when I was 15 because I was determined by then to be involved in changing the world. I always noticed what women were doing. I remember my close friend used to take five cents from her boyfriend so that she could put the money in the slot when she went on the underground. This was her statement of independence from him. (She had no money.) I was amused, but I wasn't too interested in such symbolism.

I had a child when I was 18 and I knew almost immediately that this was a profound shift in my life.

I joined women's liberation in 1970. I'd been reading Marx's *Capital* during the previous year and I was determined to find out where did we women fit in: what was women's relation to capital. I saw that Marx was speaking about labour power – that is the ability to work on which capitalist exploitation is based. And I thought all the Marxists must know that this basic capitalist commodity labour power is produced by women's unwaged work, and I didn't understand why they hadn't told me. Well they hadn't told me because they had never realised that women had anything to do with labour power. I met an Italian woman [Mariarosa Dalla Costa] and I told her that this is the basic relationship of power between women and capital, between women and men, and between children and adults. These are all power relations within the working class and within class society generally. She understood immediately. I convinced her that we had to have a movement of our own. She agreed and we wrote *The Power of Women and the Subversion of the Community* together.

Rachel: Your intellectual and political work makes the case that women's domestic labour in the home has gone unrecognised and unremunerated, yet capitalist economies are entirely reliant on it. The political solution you advocate is to demand that a moral, political and economic value is placed on women's caring labour. Can you expand on this a bit?

Selma: We said that the work we do is unacknowledged first of all financially, but in every way. Nobody knew how much work we did. Nobody even considered it work. And feminists were calling it a role. If you're an actress you stop at the end of the performance. This is not a role, this is a job.

We built an international Campaign for Wages for Housework.[1] We were regularly asked, but don't you think wages will institutionalise women in the home? It is lack of money and resources and recognition of the value of what we do unwaged that institutionalises us in the home and also now in the double day. Women are so taken for granted that what we accomplish is invisible: women are often the lifesavers during war and occupation, doing the justice work every day against every insult and indignity to those we care for. The question is not if you should be responsible for the well-being of others, but who else is responsible? The question is also whether society demeans you and impoverishes you for doing this work, or whether it backs you for doing it as well as for the many other things you may choose to do. Feminists spoke about men 'helping', but that's not good enough – for them or for us. They help, to be kind to us or because we would refuse to be in a relationship with them if they didn't help, but often, too often, we carry the responsibility alone. And being at the mercy of charitable feelings, or having to struggle to convince them that you deserve their help, in order to be 'liberated' is very dodgy indeed.

Over the years, it has become clearer to us that to make central the reproduction of the human race, and in fact the world, *is* the anti-capitalist perspective. Because the basis of capital is that the market, and producing for the market, must of necessity be the focus of society. We say: absolutely not. That is by its nature inhumane. Each individual no longer is who they might become, but is a cog in the wheel of production. How can we be for that? Why can't we start from the perspective of caring and the reproduction of the human race?

That's our perspective in the Global Women's Strike (GWS). The Wages for Housework Campaign has never died or been replaced, but has been updated in the GWS.

Rachel: One of the critiques that is sometimes raised about 'Wages for Housework' as the basis of the emancipation of women is that it turns children into objects of care, even a burden. How do you respond to those kinds of critiques?

Selma: The people who say that are missing the central quality of what caring is. Caring is a relationship. Only when caring is imposed on us does it cease to be a relationship or rather it is a relationship of repression, a power relation. That's not what we want caring to be committed to. We want to be concerned with the people we care for, and therefore establish with them a two-way relationship. If you think of children as the objects of care, you're not really caring. You're getting through the day. That contradicts our humanity. I mean caring is a very serious job of finding out what other people need, and that means that those you are caring for feel their needs and concerns are truly acknowledged. But the one thing that mothers are not supposed to do is to want anything for themselves. Well that's not on. If caring is society's starting point, then the carer and the needs and feelings of the carer also have to be central.

Rachel: Can you say a little bit more about where children figure in your work: both in terms of your intellectual contributions and your social movement organising?

Selma: One thing we are involved in is that children are being unjustly taken from their mothers by the state, and we try to prevent this or to get them back.[2] The most common reason that children are taken is that their mothers have been the subject of violence by partners and the mother is accused of and punished for not protecting the children from seeing or even experiencing this violence. In many cases, children are given to the very fathers who have been violent, and in some cases they and their mothers have been killed as a result of family court orders which force children into contact with their violent father. Mothers are accused of exaggeration and manipulation while fathers are believed. There is no acknowledgement that mothers are children's greatest protection in a very dangerous society. The justice work of protecting children from repression in schools, by police, by violent fathers, etc. is the most invisible part of women's caring work. I think that the fate of children is very dependent on how much power mothers have to protect them.

Mothers and their children are separated far too soon after birth because mum has to earn her living and the babe must forego the mother's milk of human kindness. Since reproducing humans is so little valued, the precious days and months of infants finding out if the world is a safe and nice place is short-circuited in favour of wage work which is often presented as liberation.

We also do a lot of work with women asylum seekers, most of whom are mothers. Many are escaping Western-promoted wars, destitution and rape, in Africa for example, and have had to leave their children behind. Both mothers and children endure years of separation, not knowing where they are or even if they are alive or dead. One struggle has been to reunite mothers and children. We sometimes succeed through hard and consistent collective work. Another struggle is to keep asylum seeking-mothers and their children out of detention centres – in reality prisons for the innocent who are often survivors of rape and other torture.

Rachel: Could you say a little bit about how you think we can achieve social and economic justice – particularly in situations where the interests of women and children seem to be in conflict (like that of 'child protection')?

Selma: The important thing about changing the world is that only a movement can do it. What began to happen in the 1960s is that people organised movements on the basis of their sector: women, lesbian, Black, immigrant, disabled, elderly, young, students, low-paid workers, sex workers...All of this has made the way for each of us to have a broader conception of who we can be with and how energising and truly empowering it is to bypass or destroy the boundaries that divide us. This is the key to changing the world, the basis of bringing our experience and power together to confront the powers that be. We are trying to work together against all the restrictions which surround and divide us.

We can consult each other and help each other to make sure that what we are demanding and organising for is not undermining other sectors but perhaps even enhancing and learning from what they teach us including about ourselves. That is movement work. That's what the Global Women's Strike is involved in doing every day and there's never an end to finding a better way and learning from each other.

Rachel: And do children form a sector, from your perspective?

Selma: Children absolutely form a sector. You know, my sister was a teacher of little ones, and she said when certain teachers came into the room all the children, the seven-year-olds, would put their heads on the desks. They registered their objection. They sometimes call children gangs because they don't want to give them the credibility of having formed an organisation and don't want to respect what the children are demanding or what they are able to create. Children have a lot to say about education. They can rip a school apart in a ten-minute conversation and let you know everything that's right or wrong with the education system, or at least a lot of it.

Rachel: And what has the Global Women's Strike learned from the children's sector?

Selma: Children perceive the world in ways that open our eyes to what is actually going on. They seem to understand the power relations between themselves and the adults they are dependent on even before they can talk. They are also capable of the greatest love for people, animals, things, places and connections. We respect their right to love, care and security, not to be used as pawns in other people's power struggles, and not to be pitted against each other in competition from the first day of school. They have a right to certainty that their society welcomes and protects them whoever they are and wherever they come from. That can only happen if their primary carer, usually the mother, is also respected and protected in the same way.

NOTE

1 Nina Lopez, *The Perspective of Caring: Why Mothers and All Carers Should Get a Living Wage for their Caring Work* (London: Global Women's Strike, 2016).
2 Anne Neale and Nina Lopez, 'Suffer the Little Children and Their Mothers: A Dossier on the Unjust Separation of Children from Their Mothers' (London: Legal Action for Women, Crossroads Books, 2017).

10
Care labour and temporal vulnerability in woman–child relations

Gina Crivello and Patricia Espinoza-Revollo

Introduction

In this chapter, we use 'care labour' as a lens to theorise relations between women and children, and to identify potential intersections and antagonisms between feminism and the politics of childhood. While care is widely recognised as a universal feature of human experience, and closely related to the concept of vulnerability, it remains a highly politicised topic in both research and policy. Indeed, the politics of feminism and the politics of childhood appear more likely to clash than they are to coalesce when it comes to 'care' on account of the perspectives of *either* women *or* children being advocated, and weak integration of gender and generational approaches.

Over the past four decades, feminism has inspired multiple, overlapping strands of academic research into care and unpaid work. A major contribution was to reject the view of care as a natural expression of (female) altruism located within the family and separate from individual self-interest and the marketplace.[1] Much of this research was developed through the points of view of women – as mothers, unpaid carers and underpaid service providers in places like the USA, UK and Europe. Feminists writing in the 1970s promoted a view of *care as burden* through their critique of housework and of women's socially-assigned duties for childcare.[2] Of chief concern was the sexual division of labour between men and women, with a particular interest in the relationship between women's reproductive roles and their oppression within the context of patriarchal capitalism.[3] The figure of the child has remained ever-present in feminist theorisations of care, yet somehow secondary, reflecting the tendency of feminist approaches to emphasise adult gender relations and women's identities and interests.

This chapter asks: is it possible to create a conceptual frame of care relations that takes both women and children into account, one that does not *de facto* hold one group's needs, views or rights above the other's? Our response is a call for greater attention to the temporal aspects of care and of vulnerability – in particular, to dimensions of the life course and to generational relations.[4] To this end, we use the concept of *temporal vulnerability* developed by the political philosopher Janna Thompson to describe the generational dependencies that exist between past, present and future generations.[5] In Thompson's view, humans are vulnerable as temporal beings 'subject to the changes that time brings'[6]; this includes the 'vulnerability that the very young possess in respect to older generations and the very old in respect to those who are younger'. Missing from Thompson's account, however, is due attention to the way 'time' (age/generation) intersects with other salient social differences, such as gender, class and location, to create vulnerability. We extend the notion of 'temporal vulnerability' to think through care relations and inequality across three temporal dimensions: childhood (as a socio-biological phase in the life course); care trajectories (biographical change); and generational relations. We do so by asking: How do care and vulnerability figure into the social construction of childhood? What affects children's experiences of care/caring across time? How is the management of care and vulnerability shared between the generations, and between women and children?

By infusing time, temporality and vulnerability into our theorisation of 'care' in woman–child relations, our aim in this chapter is twofold. First, we seek to challenge the implicit assumptions in both research and practice around childhood that children are essentially vulnerable and passive – in contrast to the active, protecting and responsible adults in relation to them.[7] Such understandings reflect an idealised vision of modern Western childhood, defined as a time of innocence free from responsibilities.[8] Child–adult relations in this view tend to 'exclude consideration of the cultural and social context in which vulnerability is constituted and to render children's own understandings of themselves and their bodily experiences as unimportant.'[9]

We demonstrate the diversity and complexity of care relations and children's roles by referring to evidence from *Young Lives*,[10] a longitudinal, multi-generational study of childhood poverty taking place in four low- and middle-income countries. The analysis illustrates the crushing effects of poverty on adults' capacities to care for the young and the need for intergenerational mutuality as a strategy for personal and collective survival. Girls and boys in many parts of the world contribute unpaid care labour to their families, yet their roles as social actors in care relations remain marginal within feminist care literature.

Second, we aim to decentre 'the child' in woman–child care relations, thereby opening the possibility of addressing the social and economic injustices faced by both women and children. For this, we consider inequalities and the wider structural factors that contribute to care disparities across the life course and between the generations. We are motivated by feminists who work in politically and ethically informed ways on questions of care and justice.[11] Rather than pitting 'women's rights' against 'children's rights', we urge a greater appreciation for how these are connected. Social and economic justice for the young and for the old requires a view of lives as linked,[12] both *in* time and *across* time, a view that is reflected in the all-embracing definition of care provided by Tronto and Fisher:

> a species activity that includes everything that we do to maintain, continue, and repair our 'world' so that we can live in it as well as possible. That world includes our bodies, ourselves, and our environment, all of which we seek to interweave in a complex life sustaining web.[13]

Our understanding of care as a necessary form of labour resonates with Rosen and Newberry's discussion of 'species-being' (Chapter 8) as 'the making of ourselves, others, and the world through our labour'. Our contribution to this literature is to complicate taken-for-granted assumptions that emphasise children as exemplars of vulnerability within care/labour processes. Temporal vulnerability, we contend, can fruitfully be applied to this task.

Feminist care ethics

Care ethics emerged as a distinct moral theory in the 1980s and represented a shift away from the casting of women as victims of oppression towards a positive framing celebrating women's 'difference' and maternal perspectives. Carol Gilligan's *In a Different Voice* (1982) was an early attempt to counter male bias in the field that perpetuated a view of women's inferior moral reasoning. Gilligan advanced the notion of an *ethic of care* – a distinct female capacity for empathy, compassion, sensitivity and contextual judgement, one motivated by relationships, responsibilities and the desire to care for those who are dependent and vulnerable. In contrast, 'masculine' moral reasoning represented an *ethic of justice* associated with rationality, the universal and the abstract, stressing rights and rules. However, feminists operating closer to the justice paradigm rejected the natural association drawn between care and women since this suggested that women *should* be in charge of care, thus providing political justification to inequities in the distribution of unpaid work.[14] Avoiding the accusation of female essentialism, a maternal perspective proposed 'mothering' and children as a paradigm for human relations *in general;* in this view, everyone, including men, has the capacity to become a 'mothering person'[15] (see Thomson and Baraitser, this volume). Others moved intentionally away from the language of 'mothers', as in Kittay's (1999) dependency paradigm that focused instead on 'dependency relations' and 'dependency workers' and the injustices suffered by them in society.

Our thinking in this chapter is influenced by feminist scholars who have sought to resolve the tensions between 'care' and 'justice' perspectives by reframing care as a political project.[16] The *political ethics of care* moved beyond gender and interpersonal relations and recast care as a fundamental human concern based in shared experiences of vulnerability. Unlike liberal notions of justice that assume individuals are independent and atomistic beings, the political ethics of care acknowledges that human relations are between unequal and interdependent persons. We are bound together by care since we are all at risk of being dependent on others for care at various points in our lives. According to Tronto, 'It is time we began to change our political and social institutions to reflect this truth'; the truth being that care requires 'time, financial and practical support and the recognition of choices'.[17] In essence, care is an essential ingredient of justice.[18]

Despite the widened definition of care, children's perspectives remained marginalised by a tendency to privilege the perspectives of those who *provide* care over the perspectives of those who *receive* it.[19] There is little recognition of children's agency within care relations and children are commonly included in the category of 'dependents', together with 'the elderly, the sick, and individuals with disabilities'.[20]

Next, we ask how an explicitly child-focused paradigm positions children with respect to care and to women, before exploring the potential of a stronger temporal framing of vulnerability to bring both children and women into the analytic frame of care.

Children, care and the politics of childhood

Over the past thirty years, the New Sociology of Childhood – which developed around the same time as feminist care ethics – has evolved into a rich blend of sociological, anthropological, geographical and educational approaches with an increasingly global reach. It emerged as a critique of the intellectual stronghold of developmental psychology in theorising child development as a series of universal sequential stages through which relatively passive children progress towards adulthood. The new sociological paradigm put emphasis on childhood as a social construction and on children's agency in their development and in their social worlds, placing children's perspectives at the centre of analysis.[21] Although the field has not produced a distinct set of care theories comparable to 'feminist care ethics', numerous individual studies provide insights into children's diverse care worlds and their unpaid labour.[22] Some studies emphasise children's care labour as an everyday part of learning responsibility, empathy and other pro-social skills, and of mitigating risks associated with poverty. Others echo feminist discourses of the 1970s and see children's care labour as a burden and a response to crisis. Indeed, much of the work that girls and boys undertake is hidden within the home and often not recognised as care or labour.[23] The everyday language of 'chores' and 'help' further undermines the value of their contributions.[24] A frequent assumption is that children prefer unpaid work for the family because it is safer and less prone to exploitation; however, children may also be exploited in their care roles, and they may prefer paid work for status and independence.[25]

The figure of the 'child carer' highlights complexities underpinning children's care relationships. Put simply, a child carer is a child who provides care, usually to 'a relative who has a condition, such as a disability, illness, mental health condition, or a drug or alcohol problem'.[26] This became a major topic for childhood research in the context of HIV and AIDS in Sub-Saharan Africa, where the effects of disease have had a substantial impact on generational care.[27] The label can signal problem childhoods and child caregiving as a source of vulnerability.[28] However, many studies show that care relationships are more complex. Evans and Thomas, for instance, drew on an *ethics of care* to understand the emotional dynamics of caring in families affected by HIV and AIDS in Namibia, Tanzania and the UK.[29] They found that caring relationships were fragile and subject to strain from a lack of adequate resources, physical and social isolation and the emotional demands of caring. A different study in South Africa concluded that despite considerable hardship, young carers did not see care as a burden or set of chores; they took on caring roles for a variety of reasons, including to increase intimacy with parents, gain self-esteem, enhance their status in the household, fulfil their roles as daughters and sons and to protect the entire domestic unit.[30] Such evidence demands a reconsideration of prevailing assumptions about family responsibilities and of the meaning of 'parenting' within the broader context of mutual support within and across the generations.[31]

Vulnerability across time: care relations in *Young Lives*

We turn to examples from *Young Lives*, a longitudinal study of childhood poverty that combines survey and qualitative approaches to trace the life trajectories of two age cohorts of children growing up in four countries: Ethiopia, India (in Andhra Pradesh and Telangana states), Peru and Vietnam.[32] We use data here from a cohort of children born in 1994, comprising three rounds of survey questionnaires and four rounds of qualitative interviews covering the period from age 12 to 20. The survey involves around 1,000 children in each country, plus caregivers and community members. The longitudinal design documents changes in children's lives and families, including in care arrangements, economic circumstances, time-use and in the distribution of responsibilities within the household. The survey collects detailed information on household circumstances, and asks children to report how they spend their time in a 'typical day', including the amount of time spent caring for others and on domestic chores.[33] The qualitative longitudinal research involves a sub-group of 50 children and their families, over a seven-year period.[34] Researchers use a suite of qualitative methods to engage participants, including repeat biographical interviews, group discussions, drawing and diaries.

The survey and qualitative analysis in this study is both cross-sectional (e.g. identifying gender-based differences amongst twelve-year-olds) and longitudinal (e.g. tracing gender inequalities across time). Combined with the multi-generational design, these characteristics offer considerable opportunities to reflect on temporal vulnerability in woman–child care relations.

Care in the time of childhood

Childhood is by definition a temporal and relational concept of the life course.[35] Yet there is considerable sociocultural variation in what it means to be a child, in perceptions of and responses to vulnerability and in children's roles in family care practices. Children everywhere value and expect love, support and care from others, even when poverty constrains others' capacities to deliver (see Rosen and Newberry, this volume). In this study, children consistently identified the presence of parents and harmonious family relations as top indicators of child well-being, whereas parental absence and family discord were signs of child ill-being.

Family strategies for addressing care needs vary, and some communities have longstanding traditions of circulating children through family networks to access services and to distribute financial burdens. In Ethiopia, where one in five of the children in our study had lost one or both parents by the age of twelve, household membership is fluid and children move homes, sometimes multiple times, as both recipients and providers of care.[36] In Peru, some girls from rural areas relocate to better-off families in the city with the expectation that they will provide childcare services in their new household in exchange for upkeep and access to school.[37] Boys also move, as in the case of Elmer from a rural village in Peru. When he was 12 his elder sister sent for him to join her in Lima (the capital) so that he could look after her children while she and her husband worked. In exchange, she paid for his upkeep and schooling. The previous year, Elmer's older brother (17 years old) had lived with her for the same reason, but he had since returned to his village to graduate. After one year, the brothers swapped again; Elmer returned to the village and his brother to Lima to continue studying and caregiving. Meanwhile, Elmer's parents moved to a different village (to farm) where schooling was not available so Elmer and his younger siblings rented a place near a school. When Elmer was 15, his mother travelled to Lima to take care of her daughter, who had fallen ill. Elmer found it difficult without his mother: 'I spent a year without her.' On weekends, Elmer and his siblings worked on their parents' farm. Elmer's family exemplifies why simplistic models of care relationships defined in dyadic 'caregiver/care-recipient' terms do not hold for much of the world, where responsibility for care is understood and structured in reciprocal terms and shared across the generations.

In reality, the majority of the world's children are active co-participants in the care, welfare and constructions of family life; childhood is seen as a time to contribute work to the household wherein children both give and receive care.[38] Children are drawn in to everyday work as 'a function of their roles as members of a household and family, and as part of their duty to their seniors as well as an opportunity to learn skills required in adulthood'.[39] Much of their work is unpaid, including collecting water and firewood, herding, farming, cleaning, food preparation and sibling caretaking. By age 12 in Ethiopia, many girls have acquired most of the essential skills necessary to substitute for female adults in the household: 'I can do all types of housework now... six months ago, I couldn't bake *injera* (flatbread) and now I can' (Mulu, age 12).

In this study, strong social norms dictate that girls, in particular, take on caring roles and unpaid work in the home. In India, 19-year-old Salman was keen to use his earnings as a driver to support his younger brother's education, yet he did not wish for his younger sister (a grade above the brother) to continue her studies: 'girls might study... but ultimately they have to come back to the house to wash utensils'.[40] However, impoverished families sometimes cannot afford to uphold society's gender rules, resulting in boys taking on 'girls' work' and vice versa, which can be shameful for them.[41] Twelve-year-old Seife, for instance, with no sisters at home, had many chores, such as cleaning the house and preparing *wot* (stew). He was ashamed because these were 'girls' tasks', and although he was keen to contribute to his family he did not want to transgress gendered norms of children's work.[42]

For girls, demonstrating competence to care for others can be a valuable personal asset and a way to manage reputational vulnerability. For example, Bhavana, age 16, in rural India, had left school in second grade. Her father had died and she lived with her mother, brother and sister-in-law, shouldering a disproportionate amount of housework which wore her down. She placed her hope in a good marriage that would help her escape the drudgery of hard work. Bhavana actively cultivated a reputation in her community for being modest, skillful and hardworking, attributes that are considered especially important once girls reach puberty and might impress her future in-laws. Her careful presentation of self was a personal asset in a situation where she was otherwise materially poor and relatively powerless. Viewed from the lens of temporal vulnerability, children like Bhavana embody both vulnerability and agency within their care relationships.

Care trajectories and the life course

Our second dimension of temporal vulnerability uses time-use data to look briefly at changes in care labour across childhood and in transitions from childhood to adulthood. We examine which children provide unpaid care in childhood and whether their contributions may affect their life chances. The survey records details on how girls and boys spent their time across seven activity categories on a 'typical day' between the ages of 12 and 19 in the four study countries (Figure 10.1).[43]

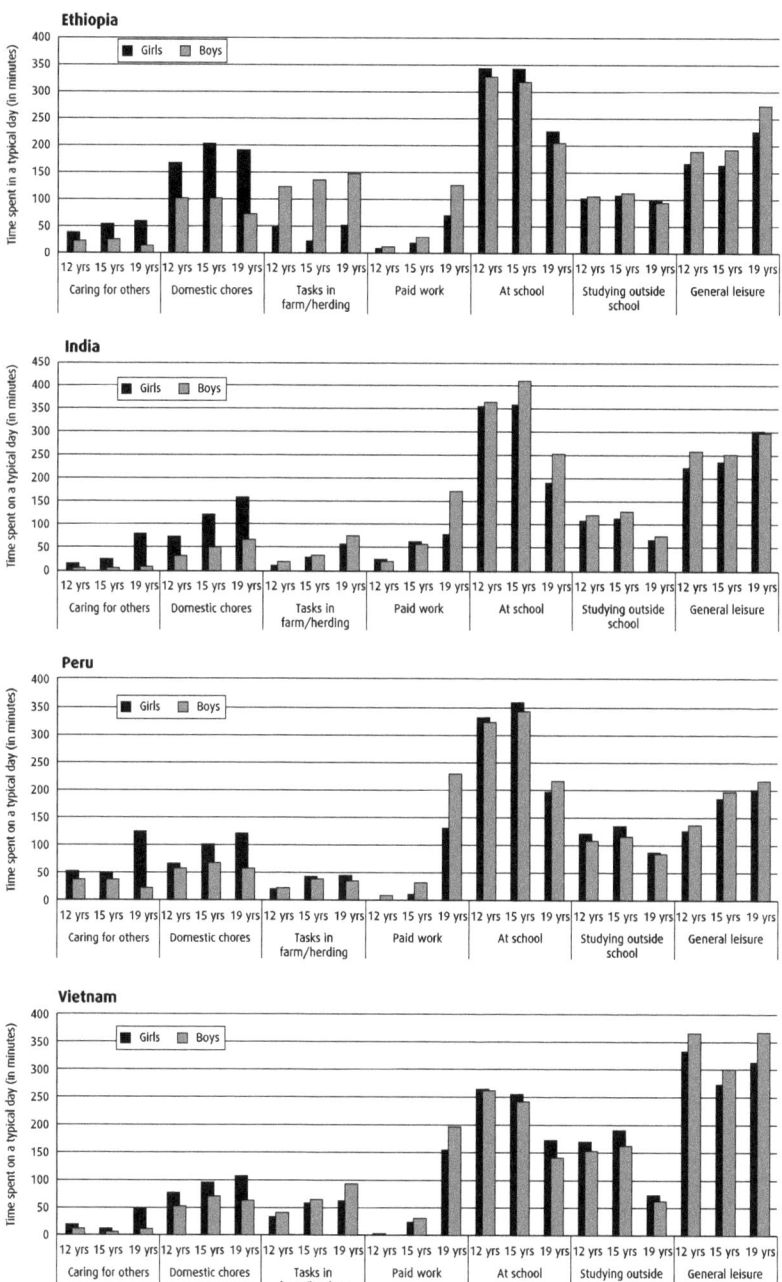

Fig. 10.1 Time allocation by girls and boys on different activities on a typical day (in minutes)

On account of limited space, we pull out a few highlights from the data, starting with gender differences.

Time spent on care labour differs significantly between girls and boys from age 12 in the four countries, and these differences widen at age 19 – a period coinciding for some with the transition to post-secondary schooling and, for many girls, the beginnings of marital life.[44] Care labour becomes increasingly 'feminised' across childhood. Girls' contributions to care begin earlier in childhood compared to boys, although there is considerable variation within and between countries.[45] In Ethiopia, 12-year-old girls spent around 3 hours and 25 minutes in unpaid care work, accounting for a difference of more than an hour and 20 minutes in relation to boys of the same age. In comparison, in Peru girls spent an average of 2 hours on care work, only 25 minutes more than boys. Gender differences widen during the second decade of childhood, especially between the ages of 15 and 19, in all the countries except for Ethiopia, where the greatest jump occurs earlier, between the ages of 12 and 15. By age 19, Ethiopian, Indian and Peruvian girls spend between 3 and 4 hours per day on care, which translates to a difference of more than 2 hours and 40 minutes with respect to boys of the same age.

Gender interacts with other factors to shape the distribution of care in childhood, such as wealth, location and the composition of children's households, as well as shocks and changing circumstances (e.g., parental divorce or illness).[46] Across all four countries, at age 12 the time spent on care by girls in poorer households, with less educated caregivers and in rural areas, is well above the country average. Further, girls living in households where there are children aged seven and younger report spending considerably more time caring for others compared to boys living in similar households. One of the main reasons why girls stop schooling is because they are needed at home for housework and to care for ill or aging family members.

By age 19, the impact of household composition becomes increasingly difficult to gauge since young people's living situations change. In India, many girls marry and relocate, and boys may be living away for higher education or for work. Indeed, the transition to adulthood entails many changes in young people's care worlds. Marriage has profound effects on girls' time-use, such that, on a typical day, girls who were married or living with a partner at age 19 were spending as much as 8 hours on unpaid care work in Peru and Ethiopia, 7 hours in India, and almost 6 hours in Vietnam. Such is the dynamic nature of vulnerability across the early life course. From a political ethics of care perspective, this signals a pivotal juncture when girls' and boys' trajectories diverge and when girls' caring responsibilities grow increasingly incompatible with education and employment opportunities, potentially affecting their economic exclusion in early adulthood and beyond, and deepening their vulnerability.

Care in generational relations – shared vulnerability

Our third dimension of temporal vulnerability locates care in the context of generational relations. Vulnerability in generational relations is frequently defined on the basis of chronological age, in the extremes of 'the very young' and of 'the very old', placing care responsibilities with the 'middle' generation (of women). However, our data indicate that an adult responsibility in one society may be children's responsibility in another. How then are we to understand care and vulnerability in the context of generational relations?

Some scholars use the concept of the 'intergenerational contract' to describe the direction and flow of care and support between the generations. In this 'contract', implicit bargains around care and dependency tie younger and older generations together in the understanding that parents look after their young children and in return expect to be looked after in old age by their children.[47] In reality, temporal vulnerability works differently in everyday family lives wherein the mutuality of care begins much earlier, and where care often flows *within* generations as well as between them. Siblings, for example, are a crucial source of material, emotional and practical support (see Elmer's case). In Peru, one boy's elder siblings who had left school encouraged their younger brother to stay in school and not to work, exclaiming, 'Dedicate yourself to your studies. We're working for your stomach!'

Whilst the underpinning sentiment of the 'intergenerational contract' – that children expect to reciprocate the care their parents gave them in childhood – rings true in our study, the rhythms of vulnerability are only partly influenced by chronological aging. Poverty adds another layer of vulnerability rendering families sensitive to household shocks and other changes, and adult 'caregivers' also experience vulnerability and may find themselves depending on their young. In this study, family illness is prevalent, but good quality health care, social protection and safety nets are lacking. Children frequently step in to fill the gaps: 'Since the death of my husband, I am dependent on my children's support' (Maregay's mother, Ethiopia).

Many children live in households with more than one physically or mentally impaired individual. In Vietnam, 16-year-old Long had until recently been living at home with her mother, who is ill, and her father and younger brother, both of whom are disabled. Long found it challenging to balance the demands of school with her domestic work. In 2007, her mother was diagnosed with a degenerative disease affecting her capacity to work. Two years later, Long failed her school exam, so she left school and began working in a nearby factory. Long considers herself the household's most capable worker: she works six days a week, returning home on Sundays to help her mother farm, and gives most of her earnings to her mother.

Children, like Long, are attentive to their families' changing needs and seek to assert their agency even as they are vulnerable. For example, some children avoid asking for things their parents cannot afford in a bid to protect their parents' feelings, avoid shame and safeguard their relationships.[48] Preserving their relationships is a chief concern for children of all ages, as in the case of 11-year-old Maralem in Ethiopia, who was acutely aware of her mother's vulnerability due to a chronic illness:

> My mother tries to do most of the [household] activities even though she has health problems. She does not force me to work. However, I don't want to complain about working because I don't want to see my mother work when she is sick...

Often, the adversities faced by families are long-term rather than short lived, though care strategies remain dynamic over time. Haymanot's case, in Ethiopia, is both complicated and revealing in what it shows about changes in intergenerational care and the varied ways in which care is expressed.[49] Haymanot was first interviewed aged 12, and most recently at age 20. She had enjoyed school and was a good student until her mother became gravely ill. At age 12 she left school (in fifth grade) to find work because drought and food insecurity affected her family. Her health declining, Haymanot's mother wanted to secure her daughter's future through marriage, but they couldn't afford a dowry and worried that 'no one looks to the poor for marriage'. Haymanot worked at a quarry where she met the man she would marry, aged 15, at her mother's insistence. She divorced and had a baby at age 17, returning home to her mother. She later remarried, explaining that this was 'because I didn't have any other options', but she was happier and stayed living close to her mother so that she could continue to look after her, along with her two children.

Clearly, many confounding factors shape the experiences of care between women and children, and generational dependencies themselves change over the life course. As the cases described above show, generational relations are both a source of, and a shared context for managing, vulnerability in and across time.

Conclusion

To conclude, we return to the core questions the chapter (and book) set out to answer: Is it possible to create a conceptual frame of care relations that takes both women and children into account? And with respect to care, how is the relationship between feminism and the politics of childhood best described – as one of friends or of foes?

One of our aims was to adapt the concept of temporal vulnerability to strengthen intersectional thinking about care in the context of the life course and in the way women and children relate through care, across time. Attention to temporal aspects of vulnerability brings women and children into the conceptual frame; that it retains a feminist focus on shared experiences of vulnerability is an additional point of appeal. Recognition that we are all vulnerable in our dependence, but not in the same way, nor at the same time, stimulates analysis of political concerns around ethics, inequality and justice. The data show that care labour is a site where multiple inequalities based on age, gender, physical ability and class are reproduced. Poverty, in particular, weakens the agency of adults to care for themselves and for the young, particularly in contexts lacking social protection and adequate services. Poverty deepens family vulnerability and requires children's active participation in providing essential care. In this scenario, vulnerability is not the opposite of agency; rather, vulnerability is the space wherein children cultivate their agency (however fragile) in the context of their caring relationships and labour.[50]

Whether attention to temporality brings us any closer to reconciling the relationship between feminism and the politics of childhood is less clear; each approach is compelled to foreground the views, standpoints and political interests of one group or the other, constricting the space for relational perspectives. The direction of cross-fertilisation is notable in that feminist approaches influence child-focused research, but the main concepts of childhood studies have not travelled so easily outside its core focus on childhood.

A framing around 'rights' promises political traction, but rights-based approaches individualise, so risk pitting women's rights against child rights, and they universalise, so are often in tension with local cultural understandings regarding childhood, risk and responsibilities for care. Indeed, the research evidence on young carers challenges universal discourses on care-free childhoods and implores us to re-think the nature of child–adult relations in care more globally.[51]

Part of the problem is the tendency to think in dichotomies, rather than in relationships and complexity. On reflection, we reinforce dichotomous thinking in this chapter, having separated out 'feminism' from 'childhood studies' in the interest of efficiency, although many scholars have critically engaged with the tensions and synergies between feminism/childhood studies, woman/child, women's rights/child rights, etc.[52] Our empirical evidence poses further challenges to such dichotomous thinking and points to the difficulties in drawing clear distinctions between childhood and adulthood, caregivers and care-receivers, work and care, dependence and independence, agency and vulnerability. Our hope is that developing stronger temporal frameworks reflecting life-course and generational concerns can go some way to promoting relational approaches, thereby integrating questions of care with concerns for justice for all.

NOTES

1 Seyla Benhabib, *Situating the Self* (Cambridge: Polity Press, 1992); Carol Gilligan, *In a Different Voice: Psychological Theory and Women's Development* (Cambridge, MA: Harvard University Press, 1982); Eva Feder Kittay, *Love's Labor: Essays on Women, Equality, and Dependency* (New York: Routledge, 1999); Joan Tronto, *Moral Boundaries. A Political Argument for an Ethic of Care* (New York, London: Routledge, 1993); Nancy Folbre, 'Who Cares? A Feminist Critique of the Care Economy' (New York: Rosa Luxemburg Stiftung, 2014); Shahra Razavi, 'The Political and Social Economy of Care in a Development Context. Conceptual Issues, Research Questions, and Policy Options,' *Gender and Development Programme* Paper Number 3 (Geneva: UNRISD, 2007).
2 Betty Friedan, *The Feminine Mystique* (New York: Norton, 1963).
3 Ellen Malos (ed.), The Politics of Housework, (New York: The New Clarion Press, 1975); Bonnie Fox (ed.), Hidden in the Household: Women's Domestic Labour under Capitalism, (Toronto: The Women's Press, 1980).
4 Rachel Rosen, 'Time, Temporality, and Woman-child Relations,' *Children's Geographies*, 2016, 1–7.
5 Janna Thompson, 'Being in Time: Ethics and Temporal Vulnerability,' in *Vulnerability: New Essays in Ethics and Feminist Philosophy*, ed. Catriona Mackenzie, Wendy Rogers and Susan Dodds (Oxford Scholarship Online, 2013): 3.
6 Thompson, 'Being in Time,' 163.
7 Pia Haudrup Christensen, 'Childhood and the Cultural Constitution of Vulnerable Bodies,' in *The Body, Childhood and Society*, ed. Alan Prout and Jo Campling (London: Macmillan, 2000): 38.
8 Viviana Zelizer, *Pricing the Priceless Child; the Changing Social Value of Children* (New York: Basic Books, 1985).
9 Christensen, 'Childhood and the Cultural Constitution of Vulnerable Bodies', 38.
10 We thank the Young Lives children, families and fieldworkers for generously giving their time and cooperation. Young Lives is core-funded (2001–17) by the UK Department for International Development (DFID). The views expressed are those of the authors. They are not necessarily those of, or endorsed by, Young Lives, the University of Oxford, DFID or other funders.

11 See for example Tronto, *Moral Boundaries*; Selma Sevenhuijsen, *Citizenship and the Ethics of Care. Feminist Considerations on Justice, Morality, and Politics* (London: Routledge, 1998); Fiona Williams, 'In and beyond New Labour: Towards a New Political Ethics of Care,' *Critical Social Policy* 21, no. 4 (2001): 467–93.
12 Glen H. Elder Jr., 'Time, Human Agency, and Social Change: Perspectives on the Life Course,' *Social Psychology Quarterly* 57, no. 1 (1994): 4–15.
13 Tronto, *Moral Boundaries*, 103.
14 Folbre, 'Who Cares?'; Kirstein Rummery and Michael Fine, 'Care: A Critical Review of Theory, Policy and Practice,' *Social Policy & Administration* 46, no. 3 (2012): 321.
15 Virginia Held, 'The Meshing of Care and Justice,' *Hypatia* 10, no. 2 (2017): 128–32.
16 Tom Cockburn, 'Children and the Feminist Ethic of Care,' *Childhood* 12, no. 1 (2005): 71–89; Sevenhuijsen, *Citizenship and the Ethics of Care*; Kittay, *Love's Labor*; Tronto, *Moral Boundaries*; Williams, 'In and beyond New Labour'.
17 Tronto, *Moral Boundaries*, 180.
18 Sevenhuijsen, *Citizenship and the Ethics of Care*; Tronto, *Moral Boundaries*; Williams, 'In and beyond New Labour.'
19 Jenny Morris, 'Care of Empowerment? A Disability Rights Perspective,' *Social Policy & Administration* 31, no. 1 (1997): 54–60.
20 Folbre, 'Who Cares?,' 4; Razavi, 'Political and Social Economy of Care,' 5.
21 Allison James, Chris Jenks and Alan Prout, *Theorizing Childhood* (Cambridge: Polity, 1998).
22 Rachel Bray, 'Who Does the Housework? An Examination of South African Children's Working Roles,' *Social Dynamics* 29, no. 2 (December 2003): 95–131; Berry Mayall, *Towards a Sociology for Childhood: Thinking from Children's Lives* (Buckingham: Open University Press, 2002); Virginia Morrow, 'Rethinking Children's Dependencies,' *The Sociological Review* 44, no. 1 (1996): 58–77.
23 Caroline Day, 'Education and Employment Transitions: The Experiences of Young People with Caring Responsibilities in Zambia,' in *Labouring and Learning. Geographies of Children and Young People*, ed. Tatek Abebe, Johanna Waters, and Tracey Skelton (Singapore: Springer, 2015); Elsbeth Robson, 'Hidden Child Workers: Young Carers in Zimbabwe,' *Antipode* 36, no. 2 (2004): 227–48.
24 Morrow, 'Rethinking Children's Dependencies.'
25 See Olga Nieuwenhuys, *Children's Lifeworlds: Gender, Welfare and Labour in the Developing World* (London and New York: Routledge, 1994); Alula Pankhurst, Michael Bourdillon and Gina Crivello, *Children's Work and Labour in East Africa* (Addis Ababa: OSSREA, 2015).
26 Definition of 'young carer' provided by the UK National Health Service (NHS), 'Being a Young Carer – Your Rights.' http://www.nhs.uk/Conditions/social-care-and-support-guide/Pages/young-carers-rights.aspx.
27 See Saul Becker, 'Global Perspectives on Children's Unpaid Caregiving in the Family: Research and Policy on "Young Carers" in the UK, Australia, the USA and Sub-Saharan Africa,' *Global Social Policy* 7, no. 1 (April 1, 2007): 23–50; Bray, 'Who Does the Housework?; Day, 'Education and Employment Transitions'; Ruth Evans, 'Children's Caring Roles and Responsibilities within the Family in Africa,' *Geography Compass* 4, no. 10 (2010): 1477–96; Ruth Evans and S Becker, *Children Caring for Parents with HIV and AIDS: Global Issues and Policy Responses* (Bristol: The Policy Press, 2009); Robson, 'Hidden Child Workers'; Elsbeth Robson et al., 'Young Caregivers in the Context of the HIV/AIDS Pandemic in Sub-Saharan Africa,' *Population, Space and Place* 12, no. 2 (2006): 93–111; Morten Skovdal, 'Examining the Trajectories of Children Providing Care for Adults in Rural Kenya: Implications for Service Delivery,' *Children and Youth Services Review* 33, no. 7 (July 2011): 1262–9.
28 In the UK, the disability activist Jenny Morris criticised the way children of the disabled are singled out as exceptional, awarded for being 'children of courage', in 'Impairment and Disability: Constructing an Ethics of Care That Promotes Human Rights,' *Hypatia* 16, no. 4 (2001): 1–16.
29 Ruth Evans and Felicity Thomas, 'Emotional Interactions and an Ethics of Care: Caring Relations in Families Affected by HIV and AIDS,' *Emotions, Space and Society* 2 (2009): 111–19.
30 Bray, 2012, cited in Rachel Bray and Andrew Dawes, 'Parenting, Family Care and Adolescence in East and Southern Africa: An Evidence-Focused Literature Review,' *Discussion Paper 2016–02* (Office of Research - Innocenti: UNICEF, 2016).
31 Bray and Dawes, 'Parenting, Family Care and Adolescence,' 35.

32 Find details of research design, sample, research instruments, etc. at http://www.younglives.org.uk.
33 The time-use activities are: sleeping; caring for others; domestic tasks; work on the family farm/business; paid work; at school; studying; and leisure time.
34 Gina Crivello, Virginia Morrow and Emma Wilson, 'Young Lives Longitudinal Qualitative Research. A Guide for Researchers' (Technical Note 26. Oxfod: Young Lives, 2013).
35 Judith Ennew, 'Time for Children or Time for Adults?,' in *Childhood Matters: Social Theory, Practice and Politics*, ed. Jens Qvortrup et al. (Aldershot: Avebury, 1994), p.198.
36 Jo Boyden and Neil Howard, 'Why Does Child Trafficking Policy Need to Be Reformed? The Moral Economy of Children's Movement in Benin and Ethiopia,' *Children's Geographies* 11, no. 3 (2013): 354–68.
37 Gina Crivello, '"There's No Future Here": The Time and Place of Children's Migration Aspirations in Peru,' *Geoforum* 62 (2015): 38–46; Jessaca B. Leinaweaver, 'On Moving Children: The Social Implications of Andean Child Circulation,' *American Ethnologist* 34, no. 1 (2007): 163–80.
38 Tatek Abebe and Sharon Bessell, 'Dominant Discourses, Debates and Silences on Child Labour in Africa and Asia,' *Third World Quarterly* 32, no. 4 (May 2011); Virginia Morrow, 'Rethinking Childhood Dependency: Children's Contribution to the Domestic Economy,' *The Sociological Review* 44, no. 1 (1996): 58–77; Thomas S. Weisner and Ronald Gallimore, 'My Brother's Keeper?: Child and Sibling Caretaking' 18, no. 2 (2017): 169–90
39 Bray, 'Who Does the Housework?,' 119.
40 Renu Singh and Protap Mukherjee, '"Whatever She May Study, She Can't Escape from Washing Dishes": Gender Inequity in Secondary Education – Evidence from a Longitudinal Study in India,' *Compare: A Journal of Comparative and International Education* 7925, no. May (2017): 1–19.
41 Jo Boyden, Birgitta Ling and William Myers, *What Works for Working Children?* (Stockholm: Radda Barnen, 1998); Robson, 'Hidden Child Workers,' 228.
42 Jo Boyden, 'Risk and Capability in the Context of Adversity: Children's Contributions to Household Livelihoods in Ethiopia,' *Children, Youth and Environments* 19, no. 2 (2009): 111–37.
43 Space does not permit inclusion of tests for statistical significance (available from authors).
44 In India (united Andhra Pradesh), 37 per cent of girls from the Young Lives sample had married by age 19, compared to around 2 per cent of boys. In Peru, 20 per cent of girls and 6.7 per cent of boys were married or cohabiting; in Ethiopia, 13 per cent of girls and only 1 per cent of boys; and in Vietnam, 19 per cent of the girls and 5 per cent of the boys were married or living with a partner.
45 Based on Valeria Esquivel's definition of *unpaid care work* which includes caring and household chores and captures *indirect* care undertaken alongside other activities in 'What Is a Transformative Approach to Care, and Why Do We Need It?,' *Gender & Development* 22, no. 3 (October 29, 2014): 423–39.
46 Detailed analysis will be published in a forthcoming paper by Crivello and Espinoza.
47 Naila Kabeer, 'Intergenerational Contracts, Demographic Transitions and the "Quantity-Quality" Trade-off: Children, Parents and Investing in the Future,' *Journal of International Development* 12, no. 4 (2000): 465.
48 Gina Crivello, Vu Thi Thanh Houng and Uma Vennam, 'Gender, Agency and Poverty: Children's Everyday Experiences in Andhra Pradesh and Vietnam,' in *Growing Up in Poverty: Findings from Young Lives*, ed. Michael Bourdilllon and Jo Boyden (New York: Pagrave Macmillan, 2014); Tess Ridge, *Childhood Poverty and Social Exclusion: From a Child's Perspective* (Bristol: Policy Press, 2002).
49 Yisak Tafere and Nardos Chuta, 'Gendered Trajectories of Young People through School, Work and Marriage in Ethiopia' (Oxford: Young Lives, 2016).
50 Judith Butler, Zeynep Gambetti and Leticia Sabsay, *Vulnerability in Resistance* (Durham: Duke University Press, 2016).
51 James, Jenks and Prout, *Theorizing Childhood*; Robson, 'Hidden Child Workers.'
52 Barbara Baird, 'Child Politics, Feminist Analyses,' *Australian Feminist Studies* 23, no. 57 (2008): 291–305; Erica Burman and Jackie Stacey, 'The Child and Childhood in Feminist Theory,' *Feminist Theory* 11, no. 3 (2010): 227–40.

11
International commercial surrogacy
Beyond feminist conundrums and the child as product

Kristen E. Cheney

International commercial surrogacy (ICS) is a growing phenomenon in which the dynamics of global economic inequality between women are often reproduced in the effort to produce children. ICS, in which a commissioning parent(s) goes abroad to hire a surrogate mother to carry a child for them, confounds a number of 'feminist' interpretations and evaluations of the practice: while some believe it provides poor women with an opportunity to use their bodies to increase their wealth while providing a service, others see it as outsourcing reproduction through economic exploitation of surrogate mothers.

ICS thus raises interesting questions not only about the commodification of bodies – women's and children's – but the naturalisation of the woman–child dyad premised on the notion of motherhood. With new assisted reproductive technologies (ART) such as trans-border gestational surrogacy, successful physical reproduction in the form of giving birth to a child is actually a severing link between the surrogate mother who gives birth and the child, who is not genetically linked to the surrogate mother. Surrogacy thus challenges the 'natural' equation of woman/child with mother/child, shifting those relations through financial transaction.

Moreover, 'the best interests of the child' are often invoked in ICS arrangements to defend political positions that tend to reify the 'natural' genetic family – construed as heteronormative and patriarchal. The best-interest principle of children's rights also highlights the lack of consideration for the actual politics of childhood in surrogacy: for example, how children get frozen in time as babies – who are ultimately regarded as 'products' of ICS – and thus their *actual* interests are glossed over. This seldom-considered aspect of ICS may thus help inform feminist debates about the practice. This chapter will therefore attempt to move beyond the feminist conundrum of reproductive labour in ICS to consider the child as more than just a product and/or objective of the practice to thinking about them as persons with their own interests in it – not just in not/being born but in knowing the circumstances around their births and the women who birthed them. Can bringing feminist and childhood scholarship into conversation help to achieve social and economic justice for both women and children involved in surrogacy?

To address this question, after a brief overview of the terms used in surrogacy, I provide an overview of feminist and child-centred analyses of ICS. I then discuss how the phenomenon of ICS speaks to the main questions raised by the editors of this volume, considering how ICS is 'good to think with' in order to disrupt some of the fundamental assumptions about woman–child relationships. This allows me to turn to how a dialogue with childhood studies might help escape some of the quagmires created by feminist analyses of the practice.

A brief history of surrogacy: terminology matters

It is important to note that the words used to describe surrogacy and its various participants have been highly contested, as they tend to reflect the values and ideologies that various speakers – scholars, activists, and policymakers – assign to them.[1] DasGupta and Das Dasgupta point out that the intermediaries of the surrogacy trade have controlled the discourse around it in a way that 'purposefully ignores differentials in global economic and political power and assumes a level playing field'.[2] Bailey further warns that 'extending Western moral frameworks to... surrogacy work raises the specter of discursive colonialism along with concerns about how Western intellectual traditions distort, erase, and misread non-Western subjects' lived experiences'.[3] As in any other field, the words used to describe surrogacy are necessarily political. Moreover, battles over terminology demonstrate how ICS confounds the presumed naturalness of the mother–child dyad.

'Traditional' surrogacy emerged in the 1980s to refer to a scenario in which a woman uses her eggs and womb to bear a child for another woman. However, it was something of a misnomer: '...before the development of third-party reproduction, a woman who gave birth but did not play other maternal roles, as in adoption, was referred to as the "birth mother" or "biological mother", sometimes even with the single but contested word "birthmother". These terms were applied to distinguish her from the "adoptive mother",[4] who is technically a surrogate to the child in place of the birth mother. With advancements in ART, however, it became possible for women to become 'gestational' surrogates: in gestational surrogacy, a fertilised egg is implanted in a surrogate womb and brought to term there. Given the infamous child custody cases that arose from traditional surrogacy in the 1980s and 90s, gestational surrogacy – in which the surrogate mother has no genetic connection to the child, thus precluding any legal challenges over parentage – became a much more desired option and so makes up the bulk of surrogacy arrangements today, including virtually all ICS arrangements. Popular destinations for ICS have included the USA, India and Thailand, but with recent restrictions placed on ICS in India and a ban in Thailand the market is shifting to destinations such as Nepal, Mexico and the Ukraine.[5]

The terminology also obligingly expanded alongside ART to frame the various relationships between mother(s) and child(ren) in surrogacy. These terms either serve to distance or to associate women who act as surrogates and the children to whom they give birth. During the 2014 International Forum on Intercountry Adoption and Global Surrogacy in The Hague, participants noted that those who employ terms that acknowledge the maternity of the surrogate actually incorporated the term 'mother', while terms such as 'gestational carrier' focused more on the task performed by the woman giving birth to children within a surrogacy arrangement, obscuring not only her maternity but also in some cases her humanity.[6] Some examples of the former include 'gestational mother', 'carrying mother', and of course 'surrogate mother', while examples of the latter may employ the same modifiers but in these instances as nouns without the word 'mother': 'gestational host', 'carrier', or simply 'surrogate'. Some terms such as 'contract pregnancy' have also come into usage specifically to further obviate any potential legal claims to motherhood by commercial surrogates.[7]

However, terms used to describe those who wish to become parents in surrogacy arrangements tend to circle around narrow definitions of genetically based biological connection, almost always including the term 'parents'. This is because national and international laws generally privilege genetics in their definitions of relatedness. There is also emphasis on parental aspiration, e.g. 'intended parents'. 'Commissioning parents' or 'contracting parents' have also been commonly used, but many proponents of surrogacy dislike the way these terms index the commercial aspects of the practice. Interestingly, the Hague Conference's 2014 report on surrogacy and parentage contains a footnote explaining that they removed the term 'commercial surrogacy', used in their preliminary report, following criticism from intending parents' groups who found the term offensive.[8] The term must also be distinguished from 'altruistic surrogacy': in commercial surrogacy, the surrogate is paid to carry the pregnancy, while in altruistic surrogacy the intending parents only cover the surrogate's pregnancy-related expenses. It is important to note that the former is currently prohibited in most European countries. At the same time, though, few have placed explicit restrictions on their citizens seeking commercial surrogacy arrangements outside of their home country, both driving the demand for ICS arrangements and complicating international legal parentage and citizenship laws.[9] While several countries – the UK, Netherlands and Spain – do allow altruistic surrogacy, others including Germany, France and Italy have banned *all* forms of surrogacy.

Those lending genetic material (and who may or may not in fact be legally related to the resulting child) are typically referred to as 'donors', ostensibly positioning gamete providers – especially women offering their eggs – as altruistic, even where they may receive payment.[10] Baylis argues that such a term should only be used when someone actually provides gametes altruistically; if they receive payment, however, she advocates using terms that reflect the commercial nature of the transaction, such as 'provider' or 'supplier'.[11]

The resultant child has perhaps ironically received the least attention in debates around terminology, given that desire for a child is the whole point of any type of surrogacy arrangement. Beeson et al. posit that this may be because 'children play a more passive role in the process'.[12] In any case, those born through various forms of ART using gametes other than those of the people raising them tend to refer to themselves as 'donor conceived' – though this is not typically an accurate description of those born through ICS, as they are often conceived using at least one social parent's gametes but are gestated and birthed by a non-genetically related woman. The term 'surrogate-born children' has thus arisen, but even those who have used ART to create their own families agree that there is not yet a satisfactory standard language for describing them.[13]

In sum, even the terminology debates around surrogacy index the contested nature of mother–child relationships in the age of ART. In an attempt to remain as neutral and yet as accurate as possible, I will be using the term *surrogacy* to describe the broader practice and *ICS* to describe the prevalent cross-border gestational surrogacy arrangements that involve payment to the woman who acts as a surrogate – the primary focus here. I will also interchangeably use *intended* and *commissioning* parents to describe those initiating surrogacy arrangements where appropriate. I will also use the terms *surrogate* for the women who carry *surrogate-born children,* with the caveat that we must always keep in mind that children grow up and become adults whose interests must also be considered over the life course.

Feminist analyses of ICS

Feminist analyses of surrogacy tend to centre on the tensions between productive and reproductive labour resulting from the practice. A number of concerns arise in this debate, particularly regarding the marketisation of reproduction and the commodification of women and children. This in turn raises questions about the potential for exploitation, women's labour, and reproductive choice and justice.

Many feminist scholars have shown concern about the marketisation of international surrogacy and its implications for women. Some express objections to the late-capitalist commodification of women's bodies and the outsourcing of sexual and social reproduction from the West to developing countries.[14] When new markets for ICS opened in places like India, Mexico, Thailand and Nepal (largely due to restrictions on commercial surrogacy in Europe and North America), it created competition for the prohibitively priced US commercial surrogacy market. Suddenly, intending parents could access ICS at a fraction of the cost by utilising surrogates in developing countries who would work for less, opening the possibility of new incentives for the potential exploitation of poor women in developing countries by the upper classes who have the financial means to purchase such services.[15] Aside from concerns with the intersections of class and gender, many debates about ICS also invoke the language of 'choice' in sexual and reproductive labour. This debate inevitably elicits comparisons between commercial surrogacy and prostitution.[16] Whereas some feminist scholars invoke the right to bodily autonomy in both instances and draw parallels between the ability to earn through use of one's body in prostitution and in surrogacy, many pragmatists note that such 'choices' and the exercise of agency are often severely constrained by everyday circumstances of poverty such that what appear to be 'choices' might in fact constitute economic coercion.[17] Hewitson therefore concludes that 'Social reproduction is thus "both naturalised and reprivatized" (Allon 2011: 138), and the vast inequalities which characterize these exchanges become reframed as disparate human capital endowments and accumulations within a rhetoric of choice.'[18]

Feminist debates thus end up going around and around in circles concerning the ethical implications of surrogacy for women. At the 2014 International Forum on Intercountry Adoption and Global Surrogacy, participants contested the ethics of the commodification of children's bodies as well, but this hinged on how surrogacy and its resultant offspring were framed in ICS contracts: whether the child is considered a product to be delivered as an indication of the completion of the contract, or surrogacy is considered a contracted 'service'.[19] Darnovsky and Beeson state that, '[i]f surrogacy arrangements are not to be seen as baby selling... payment to gestational mothers must not depend on the success of the pregnancy or the health of the child'.[20] But this again raises questions (similar to those raised by prostitution) about whether surrogacy is to be seen as (re)productive labour: are surrogates labourers who produce a product, or do they provide a service? Many scholars argue that children *cannot* be seen as a product because this would not only reduce the child to a commodity but also 'cheapen' the relational bond between mother and child by subjecting it to marketisation.[21] However one views it, Krawiec claims that commercial surrogacy contracts inevitably have the effect of increasing the role of intermediaries, who in turn stress the 'performance' of surrogates, on whom their own income is dependent. This performance necessarily includes the surrogates' successful delivery of a (healthy) child.[22] Thus, according to Hewitson, 'Consistent with the policy paradigms of the World Bank and the IMF, Indian surrogate mothers are acting as autonomous financialised economic actors maximising their lifetime utility by engaging in market exchanges. Without this sense of self, new reproductive technologies and the privatisation and marketisation of social reproduction in the form of transnational surrogacy could not take place...'[23] She concludes that ICS therefore contributes to global inequalities between women and families rather than challenging them.

Maniere has noted that feminist theorists tend to have a very different take on surrogacy than those who have engaged in empirical studies of the practice. Those who take an abolitionist stance have usually not engaged in fieldwork that examines the actual social practice of surrogacy, while those who have directly observed or interviewed surrogates[24] – though not disagreeing that the practice is highly problematic from a feminist perspective – tend to take a more pragmatic stance, calling for regulation rather than an outright ban. It is interesting that though feminist scholars express concern over the commodification and exploitation of women, few tend to pay much attention to the child produced in surrogacy, beyond the very consideration of the child as 'product'. Yet the surrogate mother and child are still implicated together, experienced together and cannot be separated until birth. In surrogacy, bodily integrity and 'ownership' of 'production' thus take on new meanings. By the same token, childhood studies scholars can also be reluctant to engage with the controversial question of when a foetus/child gains full legal and social personhood.[25] The next section thus considers what a childhood studies approach to ICS might look like.

Formulating a childhood studies approach to ICS?

Unfortunately, childhood studies have yet to engage significantly with the issue of ICS. Scholars of childhood have not done much better than feminist scholarship at humanising the children produced through ICS. Twamley et al. write that theorists of childhood have described feminism as 'adultist', while feminist scholars have accused childhood studies scholars of neglecting the importance of gender relations;[26] this tension may account in some way for the paucity of studies on surrogacy from a childhood studies perspective. Many scholars have suggested that more research is needed on children's actual experiences as surrogate-born people,[27] but few have done such research yet, perhaps also because it is still early days for children born from ICS arrangements. Actual research on children and surrogacy has focused on commercial surrogacy within national boundaries rather than ICS,[28] and there has been broader research in the US around the search for identity by donor-conceived children who have lately come of age.[29] Further, the research has been conducted by scholars who neither identify themselves as childhood scholars nor take explicitly child-centred approaches based in the discipline.

However, quite a number of scholars have considered the parallels and departures between ICS and intercountry adoption studies. On one level, this makes sense, as adoption and surrogacy are two main options people consider when faced with difficulties conceiving children. Intercountry adoption has steadily declined over the past decade while ICS has increased dramatically in recent years.[30] Despite their limitations, such comparisons indicate what adoption studies in particular can contribute to current thought about the status of the child in surrogacy, as well as children's points of view about the circumstances of their births and/or parentage.

Scherman et al. recommend using the adoption triad framework (child, birth mother/family and adoptive mother/family) for studying mother–child relations in surrogacy.[31] However, Rotabi and Bromfield caution that the parallels between adoption and surrogacy are limited and therefore potentially problematic, especially in comparing birth mothers in adoption to surrogates.[32] For starters, birth mothers in adoption do not commence their pregnancies with the intention of giving up the children once they are born. They are also genetically related to the children they relinquish, as opposed to the people to whom they relinquish the child(ren), and birth mothers typically receive no payment for child relinquishment (or at least they are legally prohibited from doing so, or it would be considered child trafficking). Research with birth mothers in adoption typically reveals a continual sense of loss and regret long after relinquishing their children to adoption,[33] whereas surrogates talk somewhat more positively about the experience – even as a selfless act that helps others who are unable to have children.[34] Scherman et al. also point out that 'Unlike their surrogate counterparts, birth mothers do not experience a strong sense of empowerment from their decisions to relinquish. Moreover, there is no evidence indicating that pregnancy or relinquishing children into adoption were ever considered forms of "work".'[35]

The experiences of adoptees and surrogate-born children/adults can also vary widely. Whereas many adoptees may experience difficulties with identity formation due to lack of knowledge of their origins – which can also be true of donor-conceived children – current research as yet shows little indication of such problems for surrogate-born children.[36] Regardless, adoption practices gradually shifted from secrecy to openness, aiding adopted people in understanding their origins and identities through the lens of their adoptions; there is every indication that such openness will be of equal importance to children born through ICS arrangements. Consequently, one thing scholars and activists agree on is that preservation of records is vitally important in both cases;[37] not 'to fetishize the genetic or gestational connection' but 'to acknowledge that these connections are meaningful and resonant to many people born of third-party assisted conception and [are] likely to continue to be so in the future'.[38]

Feminism and the politics of childhood in ICS

While it is true that discussing women and children together runs the risk of reifying their relationship, the reverse is also true: discussing them separately produces a particularly antagonising tension between female and child subjectivities.[39] Given the dimensions described above, surrogacy debates offer a compelling example through which to grapple with the central questions of this volume. Below, I focus on how surrogacy debates speak to three of the central issues raised by the editors.

Ensuring the well-being of children and women

The issue of how to ensure the well-being of both women and children is central to surrogacy debates, as surrogacy itself is a context wherein their interests arguably appear to be at odds – at least in the way various feminists have critiqued it. Feminist scholars have argued that ICS especially is exploitative of poor women of colour in the global South, whose bodies are utilised to produce babies for wealthier white families in the global North. Many bioethicists have taken this stance, arguing that the medical risks taken on by surrogates jeopardise their health in favour of that of the children they carry for commissioning parents.[40] These include hormonal stimulation side effects, heightened medical risks from the non-medically indicated caesarean section births that are routine in surrogacy, lack of follow-up health care, and multiple psychological consequences related to stigmatisation, secrecy and immediate separation from the babies they have carried.[41] Feminist scholars thereby question the ethics of protecting the 'product' at the physical expense of the 'producer'.

Children's best interests in ICS debates tend to be framed within a children's rights discourse. Elsewhere I have argued that such discourses, particularly in international law, are problematic for the ways in which children's 'best interests' are often arbitrarily framed primarily by adults who seldom consult children for their actual views.[42] The Hague Conference on Private International Law, which is responsible for the 1993 Hague Convention on Intercountry Adoption, has been debating the establishment of a separate international convention for the regulation of surrogacy and legal parentage.[43] They claim that while states are not necessarily changing prohibitive policies on allowing domestic surrogacy or travel abroad to avoid national prohibitions on surrogacy arrangements, more and more courts are making decisions regarding legal parentage of children born through surrogacy arrangements 'in the best interests of the child' involved – often to prevent the children from being stateless (a violation of their rights). Yet these decisions constitute *ex post facto* checks once a child already exists as a result of ICS arrangements. Hence, 'this is already too late to be able to exercise any meaningful control'[44] over the ethics or legalities of ICS. This also means that 'the best interests of the child' are effectively being usurped to defend the choices of intended parents. Such examples expose the limits of the 'child's best interest' principle, which sidesteps other issues of human rights and ethics in surrogacy to determine the best interests of a child who may not even have been conceived yet.

The paramountcy of children's best interests is an example of what Baird calls child fundamentalism, 'the ways in which "the child" is so often invoked as a discursive category with which one cannot disagree...'[45] This then gets cited in such a way that policymakers can utilise the 'best interests' of children who do not yet exist to argue for their own political views. Ruddick points out that such legal manoeuvres are often applied in debates about foetal rights, resulting in 'a paradoxical situation where the "fetus" is granted a more authoritative voice in terms of what it "wants" than is the child, whose wishes are perpetually called into question' in legal proceedings.[46] This was also the case in the 2009 New South Wales Surrogacy Bill in Australia. In debates about the bill, politicians invoked 'children's best interests' to make the (heterosexist) argument that allowing gay and lesbian couples to use surrogacy as a means of forming a family deprives children of a 'proper' family environment, which they interpreted as being composed of a heteronormative nuclear family[47] – a topic I return to later in this section.

Challenging the mother–child dyad in ICS

The question of whether women's and children's interests are necessarily opposed or inevitably linked depends on the woman to whom one is referring in an ICS arrangement, as well as the underlying presumptions one makes about the primacy of the mother–child dyad. In the case of an intended mother, proponents evoke the right to motherhood and the cultural/legal primacy of genetic relatedness to justify the commissioning of a surrogate – and since surrogacy in Mexico or India is cheaper than in the United States (and is outlawed in much of Europe), ICS gives women who might not otherwise be able to conceive and/or carry a pregnancy the chance to become mothers. In the case of surrogates, many feminists argue that it exploits their reproductive labour, but in Pande's seminal ethnography of Indian commercial surrogate mothers, *Wombs in Labor*, the surrogates themselves often say that amidst dire poverty, surrogacy offers them their only viable option to help their own families as well as someone else's.[48] In fact, they often invoke their own self-sacrifice as mothers to justify being a commercial surrogate by saying that they decided to do it in order to help provide for their *own* children.

ICS thus both denaturalises and reinforces the mother–child dyad in various ways – and with varying consequences for the relationships between women and children. On the one hand, ICS denaturalises the relations between women and children by offering new ways of understanding mother–child relationality; on the other, many women who cannot carry children themselves are driven by social reproductive imperatives that define womanhood through motherhood to seek alternative means such as surrogacy to have children. Thanks to ART, surrogate-born children can now have up to five 'parents': egg provider, sperm provider, gestational mother, and two intended parents – including up to four mothers.[49] The carrying of a child in the womb loses import as a type of relational, kin work/care – which in turn devalues women's labour (literally) – while still placing primacy on the genetic relatedness of women and children. Moreover, Hewitson has claimed that – partly due to reproduction's marketisation through surrogacy – 'neoliberalism constructs and relies upon the family as a collection of intensely-bonded parents and children while also articulating the family members and surrogate mothers as self-actualizing, risk-managing consumers and entrepreneurs'.[50] Children themselves may no longer be seen (legally or culturally) as 'property' of parents, but they *are* commonly seen as beings that parents are meant to 'invest' in for the 'production' of a future adult who is him/herself a 'productive' person[51] – not to mention the incredible emotional investment with which children have come to be endowed, such that we typically efface the interplay of economy and affect in the commoditisation of children.[52]

Rosen has written about the issue of time and temporality in the construction of woman–child relationships.[53] One of the reasons surrogacy is controversial is because of the transience of surrogate motherhood, which seems to run counter to the notion of a permanent bond created between mother and child through the experience of pregnancy. However, while some surrogates are resigned to the contractual termination of the mother–child link upon delivery (as Rotabi and Bromfield state that many US surrogates are: in fact, they state that the child was never 'theirs to give up' in the first place because it always belonged to the commissioning parents[54]), some surrogates also contest this 'unnatural' temporality of motherhood in their conception of the practice. The surrogates in Pande's study often talked of commercial surrogacy as 'mothering' along the lines of other forms of care work, and as 'kin labour', to counter the ephemerality of the transaction and their own disposability as workers (see Crivello and Espinosa, this volume, for a detailed discussion of care labour and temporal vulnerability). They stated that even though they gave the child to the genetic parents, they have interminable connections by virtue of the pregnancy – and that these in fact (if not in law) override any genetic claim to a maternal bond. As one surrogate told Pande, 'After all, it's my blood even if it's their genes'.[55]

What few studies there are of how surrogacy affects children report that both a surrogate's pre-existing children and surrogate-born children tend to have overwhelmingly positive feelings about the circumstances of their births.[56] Though their sample of surrogate-born children was small, 13 out of the 14 10-year-old children in Jadva et al.'s study who were in contact with their surrogates reported that they liked them.

Meanwhile, donor-conceived offspring are reconfiguring kinship around new ART, using advances in genetics testing and information and communication technologies to establish mechanisms for identification of genetic relations such as the Donor Sibling Registry. Dempsey and Kelly report that 'donor-conceived young people who form relationships with donor siblings often view them as equivalent to "extended family" with all the nuances of meaning that that term entails when applied to family of origin…'[57] It is doubtful that surrogate-born children would feel the same about others born from the same gestational surrogate, however – especially where relationships with surrogates (unlike with gamete donors) fall outside of patriliny and transgress racial, national, and class lines – but this is a crucial area for further study.

In sum, while the practice of ICS itself offers opportunities to denaturalise the mother–child dyad, the ways that the practice is construed and constructed by participants may in fact reinforce the 'natural' links between both surrogate and commissioning women and the children they birth or raise – often as a way to subvert the commercial context of the interaction.

Contesting and reinforcing compulsory heterosexuality?

One of the shortcomings of surrogacy practice is that it does not necessarily challenge patriliny or the compulsory heterosexuality of the nuclear family. Though ICS arrangements themselves are arguably products of neoliberal economic policies that reinforce the heteronormativity of the patriarchal nuclear family,[58] surrogacy also decentres such heteronormativity in that many gay couples are using surrogacy as a means to form genetically related offspring. This confounds the compulsory heterosexism of presumed rights and entitlements to family. However, it is still problematic in that the state has both privatised and reified the imperatives of social reproduction,[59] not just for women but for gay couples. Opening opportunities for gay and lesbian couples to form genetically related families through various ARTs also pulls gay couples into the marketisation of reproduction in ways that expose them to the same classed and gendered criticisms as heterosexual intending parents: of exploitation of poor women, and of reinforcing the patriarchal definitions of family through emphasis on genetic links, particularly to fathers.

Applying a childhood studies lens to ICS: toward a relational approach

Attention to *actual* surrogate-born people's concerns is paramount in emergent ICS debates. The concerns of children born through ICS can help add a vital dimension to the above debates, and may even reconcile some schisms in feminist thinking about ICS. Because of the 'passive' role of children in ICS and the fact that they are yet unborn, childhood studies scholars, who tend to privilege children's 'voices', have as yet done little research on the topic. If adoption studies are any indication, though, surrogate-born children will also want access to information about their origins and/or contact with their surrogate mothers. This opens up an important opportunity not only to advance scholarly debates about surrogacy beyond the conundrums of feminist scholarship but to inform that same scholarship with a more holistic, relational approach. For example, we can expand the discussion of how – though surrogates and intended parents both tend to frame ICS as altruistic – intended parents might see the surrogate as having a more transient relationship with the commissioning parents and child rather than an enduring relationship with the family, as surrogates and surrogate-born children do. Here again, adoption provides an important model for refiguring the relationships between women and children while expanding the notion of family through the 'adoption triad'; we can also start to move toward similar openness in ICS by developing the concept of the 'surrogacy triad' to include children, commissioning parents and surrogate mothers in an ongoing relationship. Studies have shown that this model has been beneficial to all in adoption,[60] and preliminary indications are that openness in surrogacy is also largely positive for all involved.[61]

In order for childhood studies to effectively address issues in ICS around which feminists have continually circled, they will have to go beyond a simple children's rights discourse to consider children's lived experiences. Scholars like Darling and Crawshaw have written extensively about the children's rights implications of commercial surrogacy,[62] making great in-roads especially in regards to challenges of statelessness and citizenship. But they tend to fall into the same quagmire of subjectivity as feminist analyses in that they rely on the highly subjective 'best-interest principle' in international law. Rather than assuming what is best for (imaginary) children in ICS, relying more on empirical evidence centred on the actual viewpoints and experiences of surrogate-born children and the adults they become can more realistically speak to the concerns ICS raises about the relationships between women and children. Further, a relational approach toward examining the connections between surrogate-born children and others in the surrogacy triad – their commissioning *and* surrogate mothers, as well as their relationships with their surrogates' other children – precludes the possibility of neglecting either women or children in the analysis.

It is still early days for ICS, though, and little empirical research has actually been conducted – but this also stems from prevalent assumptions that young children cannot respond to questions about the practice. Childhood studies scholars have developed effective qualitative methods for working with even very young children that could help remove this obstacle; it is not essential to wait until children grow up to see how a phenomenon such as ICS affects them.

On the other hand, it is also important to recognise that children *do* eventually grow up. It is thus important to consider the effects of surrogacy on children without reifying them as individuals or framing childhood as a static state. Early adoption studies as well as policies tended to fall into this trap: freezing adoptees in time as vulnerable children without adequate acknowledgement of the adults they eventually became.[63] Only as a result of adult adoptees lobbying for reform did changes in adoption law and practice occur to start reflecting adoptees' needs over the life course. Scherman et al. note that:

> The field of surrogacy has the unique opportunity to do now what the field of adoption was painfully late in realising: plan for the adults that the children will eventually become. It is critical that the industry does not wait for the children of global surrogacy to grow up before establishing policies and laws that support and protect them not only as children, but also as the autonomous individuals they will become.[64]

Finally, we should embrace the opportunities for more collaborative work afforded by such topics as ICS that necessarily bring women and children into contested contact. In so doing, we should not make undue assumptions of mutual exclusivity; one can be a feminist and a scholar of children and childhood, a scholar of women's studies and a children's advocate, etc. It is not a matter of constantly 'switching lenses' but rather of taking a relational approach that incorporates both feminist and child-centred concerns, working toward the common goals of social and economic justice. Considering the 'surrogacy triad' is one example of how this might be achieved.

NOTES

1. Diane Beeson, Marcy Darnovsky and Abby Lippman, 'What's in a Name? Variations in Terminology of Third-Party Reproduction,' *Reproductive BioMedicine Online* 31 (2015): 807.
2. DasGupta, Sanyantani and Shamita Das Dasgupta, eds., *Globalization and Transnational Surrogacy in India: Outsourcing Life* (Plymouth: Lexington Books, 2014): 191.
3. Alison Bailey, 'Reconceiving Surrogacy: Toward a Reproductive Justice Account of Indian Surrogacy,' in *Globalization and Transnational Surrogacy in India: Outsourcing Life*, ed. Sanyantani DasGupta and Shamita Das Dasgupta (Plymouth: Lexington Books, 2014): 24.
4. Beeson, Darnovsky and Lippman, 'What's in a Name?' 807.
5. While this chapter focuses on ICS, it is important to note that wealthy domestic clients for surrogacy also exist in many countries. With the ban on ICS in India, for example, the market has now shifted back to Indian clients. In either case, ICS has important class implications, with poor women who typically have previously had little reproductive freedom or access to services becoming surrogate mothers for upper-class clients. See Amrita Pande, *Wombs in Labor: Transnational Commercial Surrogacy in India* (New York: Columbia University Press, 2014).
6. Kristen E. Cheney, 'Executive Summary of the International Forum on Intercountry Adoption and Global Surrogacy,' *ISS Working Paper Series/General Series* 40 (The Hague: International Institute of Social Studies of Erasmus University, 2014).
7. Beeson, Darnovsky and Lippman, 'What's in a Name,' 808.
8. The Hague Conference on Private International Law, 'A Study of Legal Parentage and the Issues Arising from International Surrogacy Arrangements,' no. 96 (The Hague: Hague Conference on Private International Law Permanent Bureau, 2014): 17.
9. Hague Conference, 'Study of Legal Parentage'.
10. Beeson, Darnovsky and Lippman, 'What's in a Name'.
11. See for example Francoise Baylis, 'Transnational Commercial Contract Pregnancy in India.' in *Family Making: Contemporary Ethical Challenges*, ed. Francoise Baylis and Carolyn McLeod (Oxford: Oxford University Press, 2014): 278.
12. Beeson, Darnovsky and Lippman, 'What's in a Name,' 811.
13. Beeson, Darnovsky and Lippman, 'What's in a Name,' 811.
14. See Isabella Bakker and Rachel Silvey, eds., *Beyond States and Markets: The Challenges of Social Reproduction* (London: Routledge, 2008), and Gillian Hewitson, 'The Commodified Womb and Neoliberal Families,' *Review of Radical Political Economics* 46, no. 4 (2014).
15. Hewitson, 'The Commodified Womb'.
16. See Kajsa E. Ekman, *Being and Being Bought: Prostitution, Surrogacy, and the Split Self* (North Melbourne, Victoria, Australia: Spinifex Press, 2013); Pande, *Wombs in Labour*; and Kajsa Ekman, Linn Hellerström and The Swedish Women's Lobby, 'Swedish Feminists Against Surrogacy,' in *Babies for Sale? Transnational Surrogacy, Human Rights and the Politics of Reproduction*, ed. Miranda Davies (London: Zed Books, 2017): 298–309.
17. See Cheney, 'Executive Summary,' 29; Emma Maniere, 'Mapping Feminist Views on Surrogacy,' in *Babies for Sale? Transnational Surrogacy, Human Rights and the Politics of Reproduction*, ed. Miranda Davies (London: Zed Books, 2017): 313–27.
18. Hewitson, 'The Commodified Womb,' 492.
19. Cheney, 'Executive Summary,' 13.

20. Marcy Darnovsky and Diane Beeson, 'Global Surrogacy Practices,' in *ISS Working Paper Series / General Series* no. 601 (The Hague, Netherlands: International Institute of Social Studies of Erasmus University, 2014): 26.
21. Maniere, 'Mapping Feminist Views on Surrogacy,' 323.
22. Kimberley D. Krawiec, 'Price and Pretense in the Baby Market,' in *Baby Markets: Money and the New Politics of Creating Families*, ed. Michele B. Goodwin (Cambridge: Cambridge University Press, 2010): 50.
23. Hewitson, 'The Commodified Womb,' 493–4.
24. See Elly Teman, *The Surrogate Body and the Pregnant Self* (Berkeley: University of California Press, 2010); Pande, *Wombs in Labor*; and Karen Smith Rotabi and Nicole F. Bromfield, *From Intercountry Adoption to Global Surrogacy: A Human Rights History and New Fertility Frontiers* (Abingdon: Routledge, 2017).
25. Marc Cornock and Heather Montgomery, 'Children's Rights in and out of the Womb,' *The International Journal of Children's Rights* 19, no. 1 (2011).
26. Katherine Twamley, Rachel Rosen and Berry Mayall, 'The (Im)Possibilities of Dialogue across Feminism and Childhood Scholarship and Activism,' *Children's Geographies* (2016), 3.
27. See Cheney, 'Executive Summary'; Rhoda Scherman et al., 'Global Commercial Surrogacy and International Adoption: Parallels and Differences,' *Adoption & Fostering* 40, no. 1 (2016); Rotabi and Bromfield, *Intercountry Adoption*; Miranda Davies, ed. *Babies for Sale? Transnational Surrogacy, Human Rights and the Politics of Reproduction* (London: Zed Books, 2017).
28. Marilyn Crawshaw, Patricia Fronek, Eric Blyth and Andy Elvin, 'What Are Children's 'Best Interests' in International Surrogacy? A Social Work Perspective from the UK,' in *Babies for Sale? Transnational Surrogacy, Human Rights and the Politics of Reproduction*, ed. Miranda Davies (London: Zed Books, 2017): 163–84.
29. Deborah Dempsey and Fiona Kelly, 'Transnational Third-Party Assisted Conception: Pursuing the Desire for 'Origins' Information in the Internet Era,' in *Babies for Sale? Transnational Surrogacy, Human Rights and the Politics of Reproduction*, ed. Miranda Davies (London: Zed Books, 2017): 204–17.
30. Hague Conference, 'Legal Parentage,' 60; Rotabi and Bromfield, *Intercountry Adoption*.
31. Scherman et al., 'Global Commercial Surrogacy'.
32. Rotabi and Bromfield, *Intercountry Adoption*: 133.
33. Riitta Högbacka, 'Intercountry Adoption, Countries of Origin, and Biological Families,' in *ISS Working Paper Series No. 598* (The Hague: International Institute of Social Studies of Erasmus University, 2014).
34. See Pande, *Wombs in Labor*; Rotabi and Bromfield, *Intercountry Adoption*.
35. Scherman et al., 'Global Commercial Surrogacy,' 26.
36. Crawshaw et al., 'Children's "Best Interests"'.
37. Cheney, 'Executive Summary'.
38. Dempsey and Kelly, 'Transnational Third-Party Assisted Conception,' 216.
39. See Sue Ruddick, 'At the Horizons of the Subject: Neo-Liberalism, Neo-Conservatism and the Rights of the Child Part One: From "Knowing" Fetus to "Confused" Child,' *Gender, Place & Culture* 14, no. 5 (2007); Twamley, Rosen and Mayall, '(Im)Possibilities of Dialogue,' 2.
40. See for example Baylis, 'Transnational Commercial Contract Pregnancy'.
41. See Darnovsky and Beeson, 'Global Surrogacy Practices'.
42. See Kristen E. Cheney, 'Malik and His Three Mothers: AIDS Orphans' Survival Strategies and How Children's Rights Translations Hinder Them,' in *Reconceptualizing Children's Rights in International Development: Living Rights, Social Justice, Translations*, ed. Karl Hanson and Olga Nieuwenhuys (Cambridge: Cambridge University Press, 2013), and Kristen E. Cheney, 'Conflicting Protectionist and Empowerment Models of Children's Rights: Their Consequences for Uganda's Orphans and Vulnerable Children,' in *Children's Lives in an Era of Children's Rights: The Progress of the Convention on the Rights of the Child in Africa*, ed. Afua Twum-Danso Imoh and Nicola Ansell (New York: Routledge, 2014).
43. The Hague Conference on Private International Law, 'The 1993 Hague Convention on Protection of Children and Co-Operation in Respect of Intercountry Adoption' (The Hague, Netherlands: The Hague Conference on Private International Law, 1993).
44. The Hague Conference on Private International Law, 'The Parentage/Surrogacy Project: An Updating Note,' 16. (The Hague, Netherlands: The Hague Conference on Private International Law Permanent Bureau, 2015): 6.

45 Barbara Baird, 'Child Politics, Feminist Analyses,' *Australian Feminist Studies* 23, no. 57 (2008): 291.
46 Ruddick, 'At the Horizons,' 513.
47 Catherine Ruth Collins, Damien W. Riggs and Clemence Due, 'Constructions of the "Best Interests of the Child" in New South Wales Parliamentary Debates on Surrogacy,' in *Reframing Reproduction: Conceiving Gendered Experiences*, ed. Meredith Nash (London: Palgrave Macmillan UK, 2014).
48 Pande, *Wombs in Labor*.
49 Marcy Darnovsky, email communication 28 October 2016. This calculation is notwithstanding new mitochondrial DNA manipulation that could hypothetically involve yet another biological contributor.
50 Hewitson, 'The Commodified Womb', 489.
51 Samantha Brennan, 'The Goods of Childhood and Children's Rights,' in *Family Making: Contemporary Ethical Challenges*, ed. Françoise Baylis and Carolyn McLeod (Oxford: Oxford University Press, 2014).
52 Viviana A. Zelizer, 'Risky Exchanges,' in *Baby Markets: Money and the New Politics of Creating Families*, ed. Michele B. Goodwin (Cambridge: Cambridge University Press, 2010).
53 Rachel Rosen, 'Time, Temporality, and Woman–Child Relations,' *Children's Geographies* (2016). See also Rosen and Newberry, this volume.
54 Rotabi and Bromfield, 'Intercountry Adoption', 138.
55 Pande, *Wombs in Labor*, 148.
56 Vasanti Jadva, Lucy Blake, Polly Casey, and Susan Golombok, 'Surrogacy Families 10 Years On: Relationship with the Surrogate, Decisions over Disclosure and Children's Understanding of Their Surrogacy Origins,' *Human Reproduction* 27, no. 10 (2014).
57 Dempsey and Kelly, 'Transnational Third-Party Assisted Conception,' 214.
58 Hewitson, 'The Commodified Womb,' 491.
59 Kristen E. Cheney, 'Giving Children a 'Better Life'? Reconsidering Social Reproduction and Humanitarianism in Intercountry Adoption.' *European Journal of Development Research* 26, no. 2 (2014).
60 Sarah Richards, 'HCIA Implementation and the Best Interests of the Child,' in *ISS Working Paper Series/General Series* No. 597 (The Hague, Netherlands: International Institute of Social Studies of Erasmus University, 2014).
61 Jadva et al., 'Surrogacy Families 10 Years On'.
62 See Marsha J. Tyson Darling, 'A Welfare Principle Applied to Children Born and Adopted in Surrogacy,' in *Globalization and Transnational Surrogacy in India: Outsourcing Life*, ed. Sanyantani DasGupta and Shamita Das Dasgupta (Plymouth: Lexington Books, 2014); Marsha J. Tyson Darling, 'What About the Children? Citizenship, Nationality and the Perils of Statelessness,' in *Babies for Sale? Transnational Surrogacy, Human Rights and the Politics of Reproduction*, ed. Miranda Davies (London: Zed Books, 2017) 185–203; Crawshaw et al., 'Children's "Best Interests" '.
63 Richards, 'HCIA Implementation'.
64 Scherman et al. 'Global Commercial Surrogacy', 30–1.

12
Stratified maternity in the barrio
Mothers and children in Argentine social programmes[1]

Valeria Llobet and Nara Milanich

Are feminist goals and children's rights necessarily at odds? Diverse fields of academic practice have tended to respond in the affirmative. Scholarship ranging from the gender and development literature to feminist scholarship on carework and reproductive labour emphasises the tension between women and children embedded in social policy design, in which children represent a burden of care for their mothers.[2] As feminists have noted, historical child welfare practices, and more recently the rhetoric of the 'best interests of the child', have often undermined the interests of women.[3] The children's rights literature has paid little attention to women's interests; it renders them invisible or, worse, actively obfuscates them by treating women only as mothers.[4] Feminists have noted how certain children's rights approaches emphasise the practical contradiction between children's care and women's autonomy and how certain child's-rights approaches lead to anti-feminist postures.[5]

Nowhere is this tension more evident than in the antipoverty social policies known as Conditional Cash Transfers, or CCTs. At the turn of the millennium, CCTs became the centrepiece of regimes of social protection in Latin America, which cast aside notions of social rights and labour protection and embraced instead a focus on poverty and 'the poor'. The programmes expanded rapidly, such that by 2011 they covered an estimated 129 million people in the region.[6] Adopted in at least 18 countries in Latin America, they were also exported to Asia and Africa.

CCT programmes do precisely what their name suggests: they pay out monthly cash transfers to poor families who meet certain conditions.

Those conditions involve behaviours related to childrearing, such as ensuring that children are vaccinated and attend school. CCT programmes may also require *contraprestaciones*, or 'workfare' participation, in which recipients contribute labour to community initiatives or attend educational workshops in exchange for benefits. The CCTs' objectives are thus twofold: first, by increasing the poor household's immediate resources, they boost consumption, decrease material insecurity and ameliorate poverty in the moment. Second, in the longer run, they seek to incentivise poor households to invest in 'human capital' through the health and education of their children, thereby attempting to halt the propagation of intergenerational poverty.

The CCTs are an excellent example of what scholars have referred to as the 'maternalisation' of welfare policy. It is mothers who usually receive the cash payments, and it is also mothers who are responsible for ensuring that the programme's conditionalities are met, since it is they who, it is assumed, are in charge of children's medical care and school attendance. Women are also the targeted workforce for the *contraprestaciones*, which tend to involve 'feminine' labours such as working in neighbourhood childcare centres, soup kitchens, clothing drives etc. Finally, they are the intended audience of the educational workshops that CCTs often require recipients to attend: these cover parenting, reproductive rights and other 'female' topics.

CCT programmes have attracted myriad critiques, but none more trenchant than those of feminist social scientists. According to these critics, CCTs treat poor women as the privileged, but subordinated, interlocutors of the state. The emphasis on intergenerational poverty alleviation makes children the privileged targets of policy; women are positioned as mothers, and as mothers, they are narrowly conceived of as the conduits through whom inputs, interventions and resources are channelled to children (themselves narrowly conceived of as citizens-in-the-making).[7] The CCTs are thus a classic example of a maternalist social policy that subordinates women in the name of children's well-being. Not only do they privilege the perceived needs and interests of children as future citizen-workers over and above those of women, but they tend to sacrifice women's immediate well-being, rights, and citizenship, as well as gender equity generally, in the service of their child-focused project.

The sphere of social protection has been a privileged space for debates about women's autonomy insofar as the architecture of welfare programmes powerfully, although usually implicitly, expresses policy makers' ideas about gender. Certainly this is true in the case of CCT programmes. Indeed, they appear to constitute an especially transparent, real-world example of the tensions between the rights and interests of women and children. In this paper, we treat the CCTs as an opportunity to examine these tensions. We take as given the problematic consequences of the maternalisation of anti-poverty policy identified by feminists but then ask two questions: are these tensions intrinsic to the design of these programmes, and do women recipients themselves share this assessment? Given the sheer reach of CCT policies, the numbers of individuals affected by them across Latin America and beyond and their status as the darling of both former leftist 'pink tide' governments in the region and global neoliberal regimes of social protection, it would seem particularly urgent to assess these issues within this particular policy intervention. But the lessons that emerge from our analysis are not necessarily specific to the CCTs and may be relevant to other social policies as well.

Summary of the arguments

This paper explores these questions through data drawn from CCT programs in Argentina in the mid-2000s. We agree with the feminist critique that CCTs fail to reconcile intergenerational mechanisms of social protection with gender equality. However, we posit a more complex relationship between the labour, welfare and rights of poor women and those of their children by examining what might be called the micro-social dynamics at work in the lives, households and communities of CCT recipients. We argue that what critics frame as tensions between women's and children's interests are not necessarily perceived as such by women themselves. This is because certain scenarios and activities that critics have understood to be burdensome or disadvantageous may be understood by the recipients as strategically useful or valuable.

Our analysis looks at the CCTs as they enter the field of neighbourhood social relations and cultural habitus. This perspective reveals the unanticipated and heretofore unacknowledged meanings that certain resources, responsibilities and indeed motherhood itself acquire in this context. These meanings complicate any simple understanding of CCTs as pitting children's welfare against that of their mothers. Motherhood is associated with labour but also potentially with social recognition and status. The maternalised interventions of the CCTs demand the time and labour of poor women but also create a stage for them to perform maternity upon, as a way of obtaining status and resources. Meanwhile, children require work and consume resources, but in the cultural and policy habitus of poor neighbourhoods they may also generate strategic opportunities for their mothers.

We begin by highlighting the sociohistorical density of the contexts in which CCTs are implemented. 'The poor' are not a homogeneous block, contrary to what both the targeting mechanisms of the programmes themselves and the laudatory and critical analyses of the programmes' performance tend to assume. Rather, CCTs are incorporated into complex social landscapes, characterised by relations of hierarchy, solidarity, status and intimacy. As such, there is a need to consider the micro-social or experiential politics of CCTs, that is, the ways these resources are absorbed into the pre-existing hierarchies of gender, class, community and status that the recipients inhabit, and the meanings that they acquire in this context.

In this vein, we suggest that the CCTs' consequences for women – embodied in the required *contraprestaciones* as well as in the cash transfers themselves – cannot be assessed solely in terms of money or time. As recipients incorporate these new forms of work responsibility and income into their lives, they develop meanings that are simultaneously material, social and moral. Taking these meanings into consideration allows us to understand in a more nuanced way both how these policies reproduce gender inequalities and how gender inequalities intersect with other social relations.[8] Our focus, then, is not on the relationship between the state and beneficiary, as in the case of most analyses of the CCTs. Rather we focus on relationships between recipients, their family members and the wider community.

Second, and relatedly, we suggest that CCT recipients must be recognised simultaneously as members of families and of communities. We argue that the traditional emphasis of the policies on women-as-mothers redounds on social relations and networks *outside* the family as well as within. The resources and responsibilities associated with CCTs acquire meaning in the context of quotidian neighbourhood relations, particularly between women. 'Mother' is not merely a private or familial identity; it is expressed or actualised in public spaces and in extra-familial social relations as well. It is a role that provides opportunities for creating networks and affinities, and for ascribing meanings and value to certain relationships and activities. In the context of the community-based *contraprestaciones*, the extra-familial reach of maternity can be experienced as a burden for women but also as a resource through which women build social recognition and social networks for their own benefit, albeit in a restricted or limited manner. As such, the unit of analysis for assessing the gendered implications of these programmes should be broadened to include not just the household –the typical focus of CCT assessments – but the community.

The foregoing analysis prompts a re-evaluation of the role not only of mothers but also of children. First, the presence of children in the household facilitates access to public and state resources for their families. Children may serve as intermediaries or interfaces between their families and the state agencies that are crucial for accessing rights and material goods. Second, and perhaps even more importantly, children represent sources of symbolic and affective capital that their mothers actively mobilise. While we are accustomed to thinking of children as either 'useful' (providing labour) or 'precious' (having sentimental value but representing a drain on others' labour, especially that of their mothers),[9] precious children in this context are also social and cultural assets. That is, 'preciousness' itself may be useful to adults, particularly to their mothers.

This analysis is very much an exploratory exercise, one that aims to be more suggestive than conclusive. It draws on 27 semi-structured interviews with CCT recipients, mostly female but a few male, conducted in three urban locations within Greater Buenos Aires in the years 2006–7. At the time of the interviews, the informants were recipients of the first two CCT programmes in Argentina, the Plan Jefes y Jefas de Hogar Desocupados and, in a few instances, the Plan Familias (described below). The interviews were conducted in six workfare locations, including childcare centres, NGOs, schools and churches.

The data has some notable weaknesses. Besides the modest sample size, the interviews were conducted for other purposes, namely, in conjunction with studies evaluating the impact of the cash transfers and the value of the educational workshops for recipients. Therefore, they did not deliberately or consistently address the themes discussed here. Discussions of childcare strategies, for example, emerged only fortuitously. The fairly long interviews (each about an hour in length) tended to develop somewhat organically and did not always cover the same ground. Moreover, they provide much more insight into women's perceptions of the workfare programs and considerably less about their uses of the cash transfers. Our analysis therefore focuses on workfare, although in the conclusion we review the limited data concerning income and find similar dynamics of meaning-making. An additional concern is the extent to which the nature and purpose of the interviews influenced the women's remarks. Informants may not have felt fully comfortable articulating critiques of social programs of which they were recipients. Moreover, given the extensive presence of child protection authorities in these communities, they may have been careful to talk about their children and childrearing in ways that conformed to the norms propounded by these authorities. Finally, these sources do not allow us to access children's perceptions and perspectives on their practices at all.

Despite these drawbacks, the interviews evinced certain patterns that we believe are worth highlighting, not least because they seemed to complicate some conventional wisdom concerning the CCTs' impact on recipients. Indeed, the recurrence of certain themes in interviews designed for quite different purposes is itself potentially revelatory.

The dynamics we highlight concerning the relationship between women, children and social policy emerge out of a very specific social context, namely the poor, peripheral barrios of greater metropolitan Buenos Aires at the dawn of the twenty-first century. We make no claim for the universality of these dynamics. What we *are* making a claim for is the importance, in assessing the relationship between feminism and the politics of childhood, of attending to local processes of meaning-making and the ways that the immediate material, political and ideological context shapes these processes.

A brief overview of Conditional Cash Transfer programmes in Argentina

In Argentina, the first conditional cash transfer programme was the Plan Jefes y Jefas de Hogar Desocupados (PJJHD), or Programme for Unemployed Male and Female Household Heads. Initiated in 2002 in the wake of the dire political, financial and economic crisis in which the government resigned and half of the population sank into poverty, the programme targeted unemployed heads of households. The PJJHD differed from similar CCT programs in Brazil and Mexico in that it benefited unemployed household heads regardless of sex. Still, approximately 70 per cent of the recipients were women. In exchange for the cash transfer (a monthly payment of Argentinian \$150 (US \$75)), recipients were required to perform 20 hours of community work per week or to participate in educational workshops. They also received economic support in order to finish elementary school. The programme reached an estimated 1.5 to 1.8 million recipients by 2003.

In 2005/6, the PJJHD was replaced by the Seguro de Desempleo y Formación, or Unemployment Insurance, and Plan Familias (PF). This new programme organised recipients according to a highly gendered criterion: those deemed able to work (in practice, mainly men) were given unemployment stipends and reorganised in cooperative work projects, whereas those deemed unemployable (typically women with dependent children) received the PF, which provided mothers with cash transfers dependent on family size. The programme thus incentivised economic inactivity among women, thereby re-inscribing the distinction between male worker and female housewife. In addition, the PF redefined the central problem requiring intervention. Whereas the PJJH had identified the problem as unemployment, the PF defined it as the poverty of female-headed households. Accordingly, the *contraprestación*, which had previously centred on employment training and female community work, now came to focus on the human development of children. In particular, recipients were required to ensure children's school attendance and health visits as a condition of their benefits. The programme also incorporated workshops for mothers on themes related to childcare (nutrition, early childhood development, adolescent challenges, etc.), sexual health and domestic and gender violence. The programme came to cover some two million children before being phased out in 2009,[10] when it was replaced by another CCT programme.

Profile of the recipients: the heterogeneities of poverty

According to data culled from programme evaluations, 57 per cent of PJJH recipients had received only an elementary education (and 20 per cent of those had never completed primary school), 68 per cent had worked in low- or no-skill jobs, and almost a quarter of the women had no work experience outside the home at all. The majority of those with labour experience had worked in domestic service; work in industrial or administrative jobs was also (though to a lesser extent) common.[11] While receiving the PJJH benefits, about a third of women were involved in informal economic activities or petty commerce, including clothing and shoe repair and scavenging for bottles and recyclable cardboard (*cartoneo*), in addition to domestic service.[12] Almost half of the women considered themselves to be 'housewives' (rather than 'heads of household'), meaning the principal household income came from their male partners and the women themselves had not worked in income-generating employment prior to receiving the transfers. In general, the women who had never participated in the labour market were younger and had younger children than women with prior labour market experience.[13]

In terms of educational attainment and labour experience, the recipients in our sample were broadly representative of the general population of CCT recipients: they had little schooling and those who had worked outside the home had primarily done so in domestic service. Yet a generic characterisation of the recipients as poor, uneducated or unskilled tends to obscure certain heterogeneities among them. Specifically, it is possible to distinguish two distinct subsets of households in somewhat different conditions, one more self-sufficient (accounting for roughly three quarters of the women), the other much more vulnerable (about one quarter of the group). The first group consists of those households with ties to the labour market and with more than one member of the household producing income. The second, more vulnerable group had larger numbers of dependent members and little participation in the formal labour market. For them, the financial assistance of the cash transfers constituted the only stable income the households received, although they were living in a monetised economy. The distinction between the two groups rests less on absolute material conditions and more on their distinct social and occupational genealogies, which result in different strategies of household reproduction. As we will see, these differences shape the CCTs and the meanings assigned to them.

The first group was composed of women who tended to self-identify as 'wives' (*esposas*) or 'homemakers' (*amas de casa*). The 'homemakers' were mainly co-resident with male partners, and their strategies of income generation were based primarily on domestic tasks in their own homes or, sporadically, in the homes of others (including sewing, preparing and selling food, etc.), but some of these women had previous experience in industries or the public sector in low-skill jobs. The children of these women participated in household reproductive activities only within their own homes (assisting with cooking and cleaning, caring for siblings, etc.) and contributed their own income to the household only at a much later age.

The second, more vulnerable group was comprised of women on their own with several children, with employment histories linked exclusively to informal and unstable work as domestic help or in scavenging. Many of them were internal migrants; their social networks were restricted, and their formal schooling was even more limited than the general beneficiary population (indeed, some of the women were illiterate). Such women mobilised all of their children in strategies of household survival.

Beyond these broad sociological profiles, myriad emic hierarchies marked the micro-politics of barrio life. Women residents constructed social gradations based on a series of attributes including age, sexual behaviour, maternal practices, domesticity and status as an established resident or a newcomer.

Stratified maternity in barrio life

The heterogeneities of poor women are reflected in distinct practices of maternal carework. Indeed, maternity itself is a criterion of social and moral hierarchy: some mothering behaviours are valorised while others are condemned. Not surprisingly, such judgments issue from the higher-status group, but significantly, they also take the form of self-evaluations on the part of the more vulnerable women. As we will see, the income from the CCTs as well as the *contraprestaciones* are grafted onto these distinctions. The new resources and responsibilities associated with the programmes do not create these hierarchies of maternity, but they do seem to reiterate and perhaps reinscribe them.[14]

Women in the barrio organise carework according to distinct criteria and with distinct goals in mind, according to the resources at their disposal and their strategies of household reproduction. Those with greater resources (educational, social and material) tend to organise care around a central guiding preoccupation: to guarantee the best education possible to their children, and more social capital. For example, these women may send children to more distant or less accessible schools (as does Andrea, who pays for a cab every day to send her three children to a faraway school) under the premise that this will permit the children 'to mix with another kind of people'. In other instances, it may involve paying for private or semi-private schools. This is the case for Mirta and Cristina, who send their children to private schools to ensure educational quality and requisite number of instructional days. As Cristina says: 'here in the barrio many things are missing and if you want children to have all the days of instruction that they need, you have to send them to a private school.'

Meanwhile, more vulnerable women have few opportunities for improving their children's educational opportunities. In these households, children are less subjects of improvement projects than crucial contributors to household survival.[15] As noted above, more vulnerable women must depend on the labour of their children both domestically and in income-generating activities. A migrant of a remote northwest town, Blanca relied on her seven children to assist with scavenging and household labour. Likewise, Nelly, a mother of nine from a small rural town, residing in the home of an uncle, derived her income from scavenging and begging. She would send her oldest son to collect cardboard in the city centre while she stayed in their peripheral neighbourhood with the younger ones.

The women engaged in these activities subtly defended such choices. Nelly asserted that when she brought her children to scavenge for cardboard, she did so because she had nowhere else to leave them: 'I went with the children. Before there was no day care, [where] one can leave the children and go *cartonear* knowing that they are taken care of. We had to bring them with us or leave them at home alone. I brought them with me...It was safer.' In other words, bringing children along reflected not exploitation of their labour or disregard for their well-being, but an expression of maternal responsibility.

Meanwhile, among better-off women, none of the children provided extra income, either as a matter of course or even when the family landed on hard times, although they did perform household tasks. They criticised the strategies of mothers who scavenged for cardboard or participated in street mobilisations (the latter a 'remunerated' activity insofar as protesters sometimes receive gifts or remuneration for their participation) as morally and materially inferior care. Carina notes the risks that children confront when taking part in protests and opines that mothers take advantage of their offspring when they bring them to such events to earn extra money. Andrea, who has observed cardboard scavengers with youngsters in tow late at night out in the streets, asks: 'why do they do that to their children?'

The critique seems to centre on what they perceive as other mothers' instrumental use of their children. In this way, the different roles of children, and associated maternal practices, become a criterion of moral differentiation. As Delia says, there are bad mothers who do not take care of their children; 'being poor is not an excuse'. Better-off women position themselves as devoted mothers and assimilate notions of progress and sacrifice. They may feel they are accountable to middle-class norms of austerity and economic prudence in their approach to material well-being and education, even though they do not have the flexibility (material and social) to perform it.[16]

Such condemnations are issued not only by better-off women but also, significantly, by more vulnerable ones as a form of self-critique. Unable to mobilise an educational project on behalf of their children, these women in a sense see *themselves* as the ones in need of educational intervention. They articulate their own perceived maternal incompetence, as did the cardboard scavenger Nelly, who suggested she required help from the coordinator of the *contraprestación* to stop being 'ignorant'. Such self-critiques were expressed in the course of conversations about the *contraprestaciones*, which publicly showcase relative maternal competency by controlling and critiquing those women considered negligent mothers. It is possible the women experience heightened feelings of incompetence as a result of their incorporation into these new spaces of visibility, or perhaps this is a strategic performance on the part of recipients who believe the co-ordinators of these programs expect such a response. Whatever the reason, as we will see below, the *contraprestaciones* are a new terrain on which maternal stratification plays out.

Ultimately, then, the care of children grants differential moral value to women. The idea of 'taking good care of them' (*tenerlos bien atendidos*) permits women to draw a frontier that they use to establish superiority over others and to mobilise these moral valorisations in the competition for affective and material resources[17] as well as social ones. Women's notion of 'taking good care of them' clearly reflects middle-class cultural repertoires concerning children's care, education and the organisation of domesticity that, in one form or another, have been impressed upon poor women for more than a century.[18] It is noteworthy, however, that while such ideals are disseminated vertically (by agents of the state or other authorities), women express and experience them horizontally, as they compare or are compared to 'other mothers'. Moreover, the meanings of care go beyond its status as unpaid, secondary or contingent labour.

Enter the CCTs: *contraprestaciones* and cash

It is on this social terrain, in which maternal practice is a criterion of moral differentiation, that the CCTs are grafted. For women themselves, these new resources and responsibilities acquired meanings that were not just material but also social and moral. But given the stratified nature of maternity in the barrio, not all women experienced them in the same way. Employment histories, strategies of household sustenance, as well as specific characteristics of the community and neighbourhood shaped their experiences and attitudes towards the *contraprestación*. Meanwhile, their experiences and attitudes did not necessarily square with gendered critiques of the CCTs.

The PJJH provided monthly cash payments in exchange for workfare consisting of 20 hours of weekly labour. Often the work involved service in community childcare centres or soup kitchens as well as in community gardens, street cleaning or other tasks – labours which several women explicitly characterised as 'men's work'. While critics have observed how workfare reinforces gender stereotypes in work assignments, women tended simply to comment on instances in which they were given tasks they considered 'men's work': a fact some found curious or noteworthy, and others disliked.

Another critique is that workfare represents an undue burden on already struggling poor people and is a source of cheap labour for the state. Again, women's experiences did not quite square with this assessment. For many of the 'housewives', the PJJH *contraprestaciones* constituted the first time they had systematically left the home to work and generated the first stable income of their own. Rather than resent these obligations as an additional burden on their time, they tended to talk about why they were preferable to the alternative of paid employment. Specifically, the programmes permitted them to reconcile work outside the household with the care of their children and in this sense gave them a (minimal) margin of choice in terms of the conditions they could demand of employment 'outside the *barrio*'. In this sense, while *contraprestaciones* may well have been an additional burden, women understood them as a favourable alternative to other, even less desirable forms of remunerated work.

Miriam, for example, had always been a housewife. When her husband no longer earned sufficient income from his appliance repair shop, she entered the PJJH. In this context, she considered the *contraprestación* her best option because it was compatible with what she considered to be her primary labour, namely caring for her six children. The *contraprestación* was located in her neighbourhood, which saved her the time and expense of reaching a more distant job; it allowed for flexibility in terms of adapting to her carework; it permitted her to share her carework with other women participants, and to use the resources (food, clothing, etc.) of the social service organisation where she worked. Meanwhile, for many women, the costs – symbolic, social and material – of working in informal jobs and leaving children in the care of elder siblings (usually girls) were higher than accepting the conditionalities associated with the cash transfers.

But some women regarded *contraprestaciones* as more than simply the lesser of two possible burdens. Notably, the conditionalities themselves had certain positive associations. For one, the requirement introduced housewives, whose labours previously occurred in the isolation of their own homes, into a network of neighbourhood women. When asked on whom they relied when in need, most women said their family members, noting that their neighbours were strangers. 'Not to nose around in others' business' and 'being a woman of her house' are common ways of referring to the normative ideal that confines a woman to her own home and family relations. In this very conservative environment, women needed an 'excuse' to get out of their homes. In this context many women appreciated the opportunity afforded by the *contraprestación* for social connections for which they had previously had neither time nor opportunity. 'Women also need to get out a bit...People like to be in company', noted Monica of the isolation of working alone in one's household.

Indeed, many women talked about the *contraprestacion* as an opportunity for a certain form of gendered sociability. 'We get together to talk' was the most usual way of describing the exchanges that occurred in community centres. 'I met a lot of people...I made many girlfriends', noted Marcela of her labour cleaning streets in work gangs. Such sociability was hardly 'idle chatter' but provided women with certain resources and opportunities, psychological and economic. Imelda noted that the *contraprestación* provided the 'companionship' and mutual aid of other women that allowed her to separate from her abusive husband. In some instances, sociability became 'networking' as women parlayed new social relationships into joint economic activities. This was the case for Gladys, a widow who sold weavings made in the *contraprestaciones* in collaboration with her 'new friends'. Others invested in petty commerce (although unstable and short term) with women they had met through workfare. It is a deep irony of this consummately neoliberal contrivance that workfare was experienced by some women as an opportunity for communal exchange and social and affective solidarity.

Meanwhile, the performance of the *contraprestaciones* constituted a means by which to gain social recognition for activities that mobilised and 'improved' their skills as caretakers and mothers. Carina, mother of three, noted that what she learned helped her better care for her children, which earned her new respect from her offspring: 'we sit together and we do homework. Now I can explain to them what they do not understand.' For Nelly, the *contraprestación* 'is my second home', the place where she learned to be a more educated person. 'I changed my personality for good,' she noted.

At the same time, the intimacies and sociabilities associated with *contraprestaciones* could form the basis not just for support, solidarity or self-improvement but also for stratification and control. Recall that the self-critiques of maternal incompetence on the part of more vulnerable women were expressed in the context of *contraprestación* activities. The very act of bringing children into public workfare spaces to care for them generated critiques on the part of more 'experienced' mothers. Children's behaviour was evaluated as a function of the mother's identity, insofar as younger mothers, women on their own, and those who came from the most vulnerable households became objects of critique by others who criticised their childrearing abilities. The *contraprestación* was absorbed into the micro-hierarchies of barrio life.

In 2005/6, with the transition from the PJJH to the Plan Familias, the *contraprestación* was replaced by private carework: recipients were no longer required to work in community projects and henceforth received the cash transfer in exchange for ensuring their children's school attendance and attendance at medical check-ups. But this change, rather than being welcomed as easing their labour burden, acquired for these women a double negative valence. First, it reprivatised work after the experience of communal labour. And second, it created the moral dilemma of receiving pay for something that women considered to be their responsibility as mothers. Lidia, a separated mother of five, found the idea of being told to perform her maternal duties condescending: 'no one has to obligate me to do anything, I already know what I have to do.' In this sense, while removing the workfare requirement decreased women's work load, attending only to this consequence misses the positive valences the old labour requirements had acquired for some women, as well as the negative meanings that accrued to the new, seemingly less burdensome conditionalities.

While the foregoing discussion has focused on the CCTs' workfare conditionalities, it is worth briefly mentioning the touchstone of these programmes, namely, the cash payments themselves. While our data is limited, the evidence suggests that income use, like workfare, reflected the stratified nature of the barrio, acquiring different uses and meanings for the two groups of women. Those with greater access to social and material resources mobilised caretaking ideals as a way to establish a degree of independent license over the transfers, and sometimes even over income generated by men, because women are understood (by themselves as well as by men) as 'naturally understanding the needs of the children'. At the same time, their choices in spending the money were constrained by the dynamics discussed above, in which women judged one another for their choices.

For higher-status women, certain 'middle-class' ideals of child-rearing shaped convictions about what constituted appropriate and inappropriate expenditures on children. For instance, Carina expressed the view that CCT money should be used for the goods and supplies required for children to be 'decent' at school – expenditures like shoes, snacks and school uniforms. In this view, spending the payments on superfluous material goods, such as expensive sneakers, was considered morally condemnable. This use of the money, as part of a strategy of investing in and 'improving' children, distinguished this group from the more vulnerable one. For women in a more precarious situation, meanwhile, the transfers were often the principal or even the only source of household income, and the money tended to be spent on basic consumption needs. This was the case for Estela, who worked as a domestic worker and used the money to feed the family since her husband's income from *changas* (odd jobs) did not suffice for their four children.

Conclusion

Critiques of CCTs identify troubling patriarchal assumptions built into the structure of these programmes, and by extension into the state's relationship to poor women. As the critiques suggest, these policies contribute to gender subordination and inequality by positioning women as mothers and naturalising their work as care providers. By making mothers subordinated 'bearers of policy'[19] directed at children, the CCTs both reflect and reinforce the tensions between women's rights and children's rights that the literatures on carework, reproductive labour and children's rights have brought to the fore. We accept these critiques but argue that interviews with CCT recipients from poor Argentine barrios suggest additional dynamics that these assessments do not address or account for. The dynamics we highlight are embedded in the lived experience of social programmes (as opposed to their policy design) and in the social life of maternalism (as opposed to its abstract expression).

While there are most certainly tensions in barrio households and communities, the most salient ones from the perspective of women themselves are not those between mothers and children. Maternal carework is certainly labour, but it is not just labour. Mothers do not experience it exclusively as a burden on their time and autonomy; rather, they mobilise carework for certain strategic ends in accordance with dominant maternal ideologies. Meanwhile, the interviews make clear that we cannot reduce *contraprestaciones* to labour performed or cash transfers to income received. Even when they were required to perform as many as 20 hours of community work weekly, some women – depending on their prior labour biography, household organisation, and specific aspects of the expected work – regarded workfare as a way out of hyper-exploitive informal jobs and even as a way to access social recognition.

As women incorporate these responsibilities and resources into lives situated in heterogeneous contexts of family and community, they acquire meanings and create strategic opportunities. Motherhood is a public identity as well as a familial one, with consequences outside the family as well as within it. Women mobilise motherhood to create status, form or strengthen social networks, garner recognition, and validate and consolidate (frequently conservative) approaches to women's needs and rights. If CCTs position women as mothers, women use this maternalisation instrumentally. If the policy design of the CCTs treats women as passive conduits for children's well-being, recipients themselves do not *act* simply as conduits. The material and ideological resources invested in children-as-citizens may create opportunities for their mothers.[20] In strategically mobilising the state's maternalism for their own ends, barrio women may indeed forgo certain possibilities for autonomy. But they do so in the service of other goals, such as making ends meet and constructing a respectable social position.

Of course, not all women benefit, or benefit to the same degree, from these strategic mobilisations. Maternalisation creates opportunities for assigning moral worth but also for condemning moral shortcomings. For example, the way that women participate in workfare evinces implicit divisions that need to be explored further. But clearly hierarchies between women are based on a complex interplay in which age, sexual behaviour, maternal practices and domesticity come into play.

Such observations suggest the importance of attending to horizontal as well as vertical relations of power. Feminist analyses of welfare policy, including the CCTs, tend to privilege vertical interactions between women and the state. Indeed, the CCT programs are hardly the only state interlocutors with which poor barrio women interact: systems of child rights protection are also omnipresent, giving mothers access to certain institutional resources even as they expose them to additional forms of state regulation. At the same time, our evidence suggests that for recipients, the meanings of the CCTs also derive from horizontal linkages. Women's interactions with partners, children, other family members, community members, and each other ultimately shape the experiences and meanings associated with resources and responsibilities conferred by the state.

What, then, is the analytic takeaway of the preceding discussion? First, we stress what it is *not*. It is not a claim about the relationship between women's and children's interests *tout court*. We do not propose that there are no tensions between these interests, that maternalism is actually 'good', or that in point of fact CCTs are benign policies that empower their female recipients. Rather, the assessments, choices and bargains we highlight pertain to a specific group of women in a specific time and place. Ours is a local case study, and the choices these mothers make, and the meanings they assign to certain resources and responsibilities, have no necessary applicability beyond this particular setting. But embedded in this very limitation is an analytic lesson of broader scope: the lesson that context matters. Social policy in general, and state-sponsored maternalism in particular, can have no meaning in abstraction from the social context in which it is applied.

In the Argentine barrios, children are not only a constraint on women's autonomy, but also a substantive resource. The opposition between the two, which recurs in feminist critiques of the CCTs, is much more a consequence of material and symbolic restrictions that reduce legitimate social roles for lower classes women to the 'good mother' than of any intrinsic opposition.[21] Examining women and children's roles in their immediate social context may help us better understand the many ways in which the social construction of gender and childhood are mutually constitutive, and the ways in which, for better or for worse, the social protection of women is tied to ideologies of childhood.

From the foregoing we may also infer a political lesson. Once again, we stress what the lesson is *not*. The fact that CCT recipients in certain situations express enthusiasm for workfare or actively engage the policy's maternalist design should not be interpreted as vindication of conditional transfers or their gendered, neoliberal logic. Rather, the choices of poor Argentine mothers should be understood to reflect the formidable material constraints, ideological frameworks and disciplinary structures that circumscribe their lives, ranging from limited employment options to scarce opportunities for social recognition. Their choices thus speak not to some intrinsic merit of these programmes but to a strategic calculus based on the conditions of possibility in a manifestly unequal, patriarchal context. Gender equality and children's rights, as decontextualised and abstract discourses, may make invisible certain idiosyncratic patriarchal bargains.[22] We need not accept neoliberalism's romance with self-reliance and co-responsibility to recognise how barrio women may instrumentally mobilise neoliberal maternalism to their own benefit, however limited that benefit may be.

The CCTs and the dynamics they engender reinforce the dominant ideal that treats mothers as responsible for children's well-being. And of course, assigning differential social value to women based on their maternal behaviours is deeply problematic. In these ways, the maternalisation of the CCTs reinforces patriarchy. But while CCTs maternalise welfare, the effects of these policies cannot be read as simply creating or reinforcing a tension between mothers and their children. Rather, the relationship of women's and children's interests must be evaluated on the actual social field – political, material, cultural – on which it plays out.

NOTES

1. We are grateful for the comments of Susana Borda Carulla, Erica Burman, Kristen E. Cheney and the editors.
2. Ruth Lister, 'Investing in the Citizen-Workers of the Future: Transformations in Citizenship and the State under New Labour,' *Social Policy and Administration* 37 no. 5 (2003): 427–8; Maxine Molyneux, 'Mothers at the Service of the New Poverty Agenda: Progresa/Oportunidades, Mexico's Conditional Transfer Programme,' *Social Policy and Administration* 40, no. 4 (2006): 425; Karina Batthyani Dighicro, *Las políticas y el cuidado en América Latina. Una mirada a las experiencias regionales* (CEPAL: Serie Asuntos de Género 124, 2015).
3. Linda Gordon, 'The Perils of Innocence, Or What's Wrong With Putting Children First,' *Journal of the History of Childhood and Youth* 1, no. 3 (2008): 331.
4. Emilio García-Mendez, 'De las relaciones públicas al neomenorismo: 20 años de Convención Internacional de los Derechos del Niño en América Latina (1989–2009),' *Revista Criminología, de Cuadernos de Doctrina y Jurisprudencia Penal* 7, no. 2 (2010): 587; Ligia Ortiz, 'La Convención de los Derechos del Niño veinte años después,' *Revista Latinoamericana de Ciencias Sociales, Niñez y Juventud* 7, no. 2 (2009): 587.
5. Carla Villalta and Valeria Llobet, 'Resignificando la protección. Los sistemas de protección de derechos de niños y niñas en Argentina,' *Revista Latinoamericana de Ciencias Sociales, Niñez y Juventud* 13 (2015): 167; Pamela Reynolds, Olga Nieuwenhuys and Karl Hanson, 'Refractions of Children's Rights in Development Practice. A View from Anthropology,' *Childhood* 13 (2006): 291; Erica Burman, 'Beyond "Women vs. Children" or "Womenandchildren": Engendering Childhood and Reformulating Motherhood,' *International Journal of Children's Rights* 16 (2008): 177.
6. Marco Stampini and Leopoldo Tornarolli, 'The Growth of Conditional Cash Transfers in Latin America and the Caribbean: Did They Go Too Far?' *Inter-American Development Bank Social Sector Social Protection and Health Division Policy Brief* No. Idb-Pb-185 http://idbdocs.iadb.org/wsdocs/getdocument.aspx?docnum=37306295 (2012).
7. Lister, 'Investing in the Citizen-Workers'; Ruth Lister, 'Children (But Not Women) First: New Labour, Child Welfare and Gender,' *Critical Social Policy* 26, no. 2 (2006): 315.
8. See Burman and Cheney, this volume.
9. Viviana Zelizer, *Pricing the Priceless Child. The Changing Social Value of Children* (New York: Basic Books, 1985).
10. Ministerio de Economía, 'Asignación Universal por Hijo.' Nota Técnica Num. 23 Perteneciente al Informe Económico Num. 70, cuarto trimestre. Secretaría de Política Económica, 2009.
11. Laura Pautassi, *Beneficios y beneficiarias: análisis del Programa Jefes y Jefas de Hogar Desocupados de Argentina Proyecto Género, Pobreza y Empleo (GPE-OIT) y el Proyecto Enfrentando los Retos del Trabajo Decente en la Crisis Argentina* (Proyecto de Cooperación Técnica OIT-Gobierno de Argentina), (Buenos Aires: OIT, 2003).
12. Ministerio de Trabajo, Empleo y Seguridad Social, S. de P. T. y E. L. 'Segunda evaluación del Programa Jefes de Hogar. Resultados de la encuesta a beneficiarios,' 2004.
13. The women in the sample ranged in age from 25 to 66, with an average age of 42. Their households ranged in size from 1 to 10 children, with the average being 4.5. Twelve lived with various family members, 14 lived with children and male partner, three had unknown arrangements.
14. See Cheney in this volume, who makes a similar point about new reproductive technologies.
15. See Rosen and Newberry, this volume, for a discussion on the role of children in family arrangements.
16. Cameron Macdonald, 'What's Culture Got to Do with It? Mothering Ideologies as Barriers to Gender Equity.' In *Gender Equality: Transforming Family Divisions of Labour*, ed. Janet Gornick and Marcia Meyers (London: Verso, 2009): 411.
17. Andrea Cornwall, 'Myths to Live By? Female Solidarity and Female Autonomy Reconsidered,' *Development and Change* 38, no. 1 (2007): 149.
18. Maxine Molyneux, 'Mothers at the Service of the New Poverty Agenda'; Marcela Nari, *Políticas de Maternidad y Maternalismo Político* (Buenos Aires: Biblos, 2002).
19. Maxine Molyneux, 'The "Neoliberal Turn" and the New Social Policy in Latin America: How Neoliberal, How New?' *Development and Change* 39, no. 5 (2008): 775.

20 Kristen E. Cheney, 'Global Rights Discourse, National Developments, and Local Childhoods: Dilemmas of Childhood and Nationhood in Uganda, East Africa,' in *Histoires d'enfant, histoires d'enfance, Tome I: Civilisation (GRAAT No. 36, June 2007) Histoire de l' Education*, ed. Rosie Findlay and Sébastien Salbayre (Tours, France: Presses Universitaires François Rabelais, 2007).
21 See similar points by Burman, Rosen and Newberry, this volume.
22 Deniz Kandiyoti, 'Bargaining with Patriarchy,' *Gender and Society* 2, no. 3 (1988): 274–90.

13
Decolonising childrearing and challenging the patriarchal nuclear family through Indigenous knowledges
An Opokaa'sin project

Tanya Pace-Crosschild

Indigenous peoples have a long and tumultuous history in Canada. Since first contact in the late fifteenth century, the ultimate goal of the settler-colonists was to rid themselves of the Indigenous peoples to facilitate the acquisition of resources. Violence has been, and continues to be, imposed on Indigenous peoples, families and communities through various forms of oppression and marginalisation. Settler colonialism is an ongoing reality of intersecting structures through which Indigenous peoples have been displaced from their land, cultures and each other. As Canada developed as a nation these structures of violence became internalised within Indigenous communities. Shifts began to occur within the fabric of Indigenous society, including family structures.

Family and complex kinship structures have always been at the heart of Blackfoot wellness and Blackfoot ability to function as a self-determining nation.[1] The Euro-Western nuclear family model is in contradiction to that of Indigenous families, where women and children weren't seen as one and the same. In traditional societies, men and women held mutually respectful positions. Children played an integral role in the tribe, with extended family playing a large and crucial role in the raising of children. Grandparents, aunts, uncles and extended family surrounded the children in a network of support with responsibility shared amongst this network.

Residential schools instituted a system of forced removal of Indigenous children from their communities for colonial socialisation in church or state boarding schools. When they were introduced, the preceding Indigenous networks were disrupted. Although the stated intent of the residential schools was education, the outcome was the loss of language, culture and identity for many Indigenous people.

Recently, the numbers of Indigenous children in foster care have sky-rocketed. Decisions about children's custody are made predominantly according to the *mother's* ability to care for them. Many kinship relations have been displaced and/or disregarded as a result of colonisation. Indigenous children are frequently placed in non-Indigenous foster homes based on an erroneous set of colonial assumptions that fail to see Indigenous family and kinship models or see them as incapable of fulfilling childcare needs. The result is that thousands of Indigenous children are being raised away from their traditions, culture and community, which is a clear indication of the ongoing forms of colonisation that continue today. The current child welfare approach provides a clear example of the impact that colonialism has had on women–child relations in Indigenous communities.

One thing is clear: the history of settler colonialism is not a matter of a single event, but of a set of policies designed for assimilation. When we look to the past and examine the displacement of our traditional value systems and social structures, it is evident that the patriarchal values that were imposed on Indigenous people resulted in the imbalances we have experienced between settlers and Indigenous people and in the position of women and children. These values, perpetuated by both church and state, have further dispossessed women and children.

The process of decolonisation requires reassertion of Indigenous knowledge systems and the restoration of salient relationships within family and kinship models. In order to move towards a transformational shift in the Indigenous–settler relationship, we must engage in a framework for regenerating a vital source of strength, namely connections to culture and language. Settler colonialism is about maintaining the narrative of Indigenous inferiority and justifying continued forms of violence and dispossession. Therefore, embodying tradition through cultural practice is a central tactic for engaging in a paradigm of decolonial knowledge production and repelling the harmful narratives surrounding colonial misrepresentations.

Centring Indigenous knowledge in childhood development is the foundation of Opokaa'sin, an Indigenous child and family centre located in the heart of traditional Blackfoot territory. Situated at the base of the great Rocky Mountains of present-day western Canada, Opokaa'sin is dedicated to 'decolonising' approaches to early childhood and to strengthening cultural identity amongst Indigenous families and youth. Rebuilding Indigenous nations requires us to rebuild our childrearing practices. Prior to colonisation, many Indigenous communities viewed children as sacred beings. They were held in the highest regard because they were seen to be extremely close to the spirit world. Their location in society required the collective efforts of the community in childrearing, not just the sole responsibility of the mother. Opokaa'sin is working with families to address the insidious acts of violence that settler colonialism has placed on our family structures and childrearing practices. This is a large project as it requires decolonising our mindsets and rejecting the imposed colonial values of patriarchy, women's labour, the nuclear family and capitalist ideas about children. Through the incorporation of our traditional teachings, stories and language, we are reorienting ourselves back to our traditions.

Opokaa'sin, which means 'all our children' in Blackfoot, believes that cultural reconnection is one of the means through which true reconciliation and healing can take place. Our Headstart and kindergarten programmes are focused through a Blackfoot lens. Children access traditional Blackfoot language instruction, storytelling, music and elders' teachings. The centre uses a holistic approach to learning, incorporating extended family into the education of our children. Parents and grandparents are encouraged to participate and much of our programming

Fig. 13.1 Blackfoot girl playing by the Old Man River that borders the Blood Indian Reserve and city of Lethbridge. (Photograph by Bill Healy)

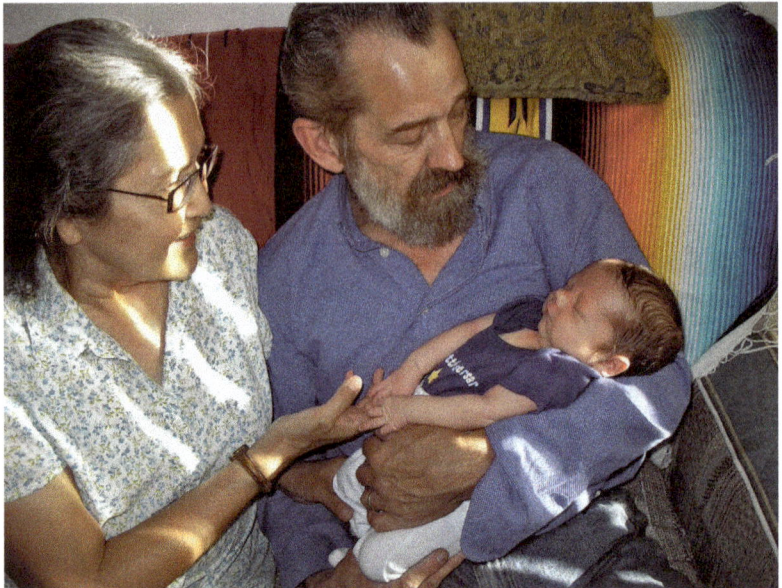

Fig. 13.2 Grandparents talking with their new grandson. (Photograph by Jessica Goodrider-Loewen)

focusses on the whole family, and not just on mainstream society's definition of the nuclear family.

Self-recognition of what's best for our children lies at the heart of our approaches in programmes and services. Our Blackfoot ways of knowing are dependent on relationship: relationship to each other but also to the land and the environment. Our interdependence in our modern world within urban centres also makes us cognizant that we must have relationships with mainstream society and the greater community. We have developed partnerships with other community agencies and post-secondary institutions.

One particular partnership, Raising Spirit, is a research project with Dr. Jan Newberry (associate professor of anthropology) from the local university, the University of Lethbridge. The project began when we started to examine programmes and service models that could potentially assist the families and children we work with. We noticed that may of the models did not 'fit' the Blackfoot worldview. Upon discussion with various stakeholders, we were advised that we might need to examine the traditional parenting and childrearing value systems of the Blackfoot. Articulating our traditional value systems would help assist us in decolonising our mindset about childrearing. Our goal was ultimately to restore our Indigenous approach to childrearing practices, particularly from the Blackfoot perspective.

Fig. 13.3 Blackfoot cousins playing. (Photograph by Chantilly Prairie Chicken)

Although this undertaking was seemingly simple, we faced a multitude of challenges. How do we articulate something so implicit in our being as a value system? Are our traditional value systems still practiced and followed? How do we get people to articulate the values that are important to Blackfoot culture, specific to childrearing? Are these value systems still applicable and realistic?

We used photo-elicitation as a method to provoke a response from members of the Blackfoot community. This approach was based on the idea that these values exist but are not articulated formally. Instead, they are implicit and exist as everyday, mundane knowledge shared informally and anecdotally.[2]

We recruited Indigenous families to photograph everyday moments of childrearing and then asked why the photographers chose those things to photograph. Next, a subset of photographs (chosen by staff members and Indigenous researchers) were chosen and displayed around the community. We hoped to elicit responses from the broader community about Blackfoot childrearing values and practices. Short interviews were also conducted to hear people's reflections on their own values and experiences.

The next step of the research was to share these photographs with our Wisdom Committee of Elders. The elders discussed the childrearing value systems in the Blackfoot language and then translated these into English. The results of our project are still being analysed. So far, they are demonstrating that nuclear family models where women alone are held responsible for the care and conditions of our children are something that has been imposed through the violence of colonialism. Part of 'Indigenising' childrearing is a formal articulation of the traditional value systems which place childrearing and care for the world as a collective responsibility.

It is our belief that traditional childrearing practices of the Blackfoot people will guide us to develop more effective programming for parent education and support, family reunification and early childhood education.

Fig. 13.4 Father connecting with his son. (Photograph by Alison Crop Eared Wolf)

NOTES

1 Blackfoot is the collective name of three Indigenous tribes in Canada and the United States. Blackfoot people were nomadic bison hunters who lived on the Great Plains of western North America. Many Blackfoot people still live in this region today.
2 Kristine Alexander et al., 'Translating Encounters: How a Transmedia Project Connects University Education with Early Childhood Education,' *Journal of Community Engagement and Higher Education* (in review).

Section 3
Political Projects and Movement Building

14
'Too young to wed'
Envisioning a 'generous encounter' between feminism and the politics of childhood

Virginia Caputo

Introduction[1]

Children, as Sharon Stephens noted in her groundbreaking work *Children and the Politics of Culture* (1995), live their lives at the intersection of local and global processes. These processes intensify interactions and movements of people, ideas, images and things. Stephens's insightful analysis focused specifically on considering children's lives in view of global neoliberalism by troubling the notion of culture as part of this context for understanding childhood. In arguing that children's lives are entwined with, and affected by, global forces, Stephens pointed to the circulation of Eurocentric ideas of childhood within the realm of internationally circulating signs, goods, labour and capital. Childhood becomes a symbol of nature and an object of protection through this circulation, an ideal held up against the realities of children's lives in changing conditions and in diverse world regions and social contexts. One of Stephens's concerns was that through this circulation, the category 'child' – like the category 'woman' – risks becoming essentialised and homogenised, thereby obscuring the diversity that constitutes it in local contexts. [2]

Stephens's work to link globalisation and childhood was timely and significant. Her expansive thinking brought together insights from anthropology, feminism and childhood studies to explore global political, cultural and social transformations and how they articulate with substantive changes in children's lives. Importantly, her view of 'culture' as a theoretically and politically contested term was set alongside a dynamic concept of childhood in a time of far-reaching local and global change and uncertainty.[3]

Following Stephens, childhood scholars have continued to expand their analyses of children's lives in global political-economic contexts. Anthropologists Nancy Scheper-Hughes and Carolyn Sargent (1999), for instance, suggest that children are both affected by global political-economic conditions and, in turn, affect everyday practices embedded in local-level interactions. Their work considers a cultural politics of childhood and its articulation with local instances of violence. Implicit in the arguments put forward by all three of these scholars are several shared concerns of feminist and childhood studies:[4] to view power through a matrix of gender and other social lines of difference; to understand the intersection of global political-economic systems with systematic disadvantage and oppression in actual people's lives; to account for the social and cultural characteristics of inequalities that give rise to gendered harmful practices, including discrimination and violence, that affect both women and children; and to acknowledge that through globalising forces, once-localised representations of the 'child', like that of 'woman', circulate on a global landscape where they are made meaningful and deployed in diverse contexts.

In this chapter, I use a feminist childhood studies lens through which to view the issue of the early and forced marriage of girls.[5] Over the past decade, this issue has emerged as one of concern and urgency on the global stage.[6] I take up this inquiry with a particular interest in the representation and rhetoric that accompanies circulating images of children and childhood from the global South. For this analysis, the photo exhibit Too Young to Wed serves as a focal point. The exhibit debuted at the first United Nations International Day of the Girl in New York in 2012. It was sponsored by the United Nations Population Fund[7] as part of a globally launched initiative to end the early and forced marriage of girls worldwide.[8,9] Audiences in places around the world, as well as virtually, have viewed the images.[10] By using a feminist childhood studies lens, I explore the contours of the politics of visibility and invisibility arising from this circulation and the implications this has for social change.

Specifically, I advance three arguments. First, that forced marriage, situated at the nexus of feminism and childhood studies, is an embodied practice that, as Lila Abu-Lughod notes,[11] encodes local social and cultural dynamics in broader contexts of politics, poverty, patriarchy and culture. Regardless of their age, women and children are positioned through forced marriage as victims, as property or commodities in a system that devalues and dehumanises children and infantilises women. This treatment marks the conceptual connection between children and women in forced marriage as less than fully human. Images of the forced marriage of girls in the Too Young to Wed photo exhibit extend this connection through representations that guarantee children's dependency, passivity and silence, and secure their victimhood through a paternalistic rhetoric that focuses primarily on rescue and protection.

The rhetoric of rescue and protection is key to the second argument advanced in this chapter. Too Young to Wed circulates images of girls of the global South to receptive audiences in the industrialised North in a play of distant viewers and visual objects. The rhetoric that accompanies the exhibit frames the relationship between viewers and subjects in the images; namely, girls in a forced marriage are to be pitied and protected from cultural contexts that are viewed as backward, ignorant and 'barbaric'. This framing all but negates the agency of those images to powerfully engage viewers in questioning what is being expressed and makes inaudible the voices and lived experiences of the girls themselves. It is a situation reminiscent of Gayatri Spivak's question: 'Can the subaltern speak?'[12] Spivak points to the power-laden process of *giving* silenced 'others' a voice with which to express their own lives and experiences. She argues that global power relations erase the lived experiences of those living in the global South by replacing them with knowledge about the global South. This knowledge is generated and rearranged so that it is made palpable and intelligible. In effect, this process makes it impossible for the 'subaltern' to speak. Moreover, it unproductively detaches knowledge from its context and produces it without accounting for the experiences of people themselves. Knowledge that emerges in this way, Spivak argues, merely reproduces narratives that reinforce Western dominance and authority.[13] This process of 'speaking for' those in positions of powerlessness occurs in the Too Young to Wed exhibit where images and rhetoric further reinforce the cultural divide between viewers and the exhibit's visual objects. The division between girls of the industrialised North and girls living in the global South is clear. What emerges in this paternalistic process is an 'Us/Them' binary that assigns benevolent agency to the dominant 'Us' of the West, and victimisation and passivity to the subordinate 'Them' of the global South, who are imagined as oppressed and in need of rescue and protection.[14]

In writing on the politics of visuality and interpreting images in the 1970s, Susan Sontag points to a similar situation in the images of victims of war. She questions whether or how photographs connect to truth or reality, arguing that 'photographs of the victims of war are themselves species of rhetoric. They reiterate. They simplify. They agitate. They create the illusion of consensus.'[15] Sontag's insightful comments regarding images as rhetoric that flatten complexity bring me to the third argument that I advance in this chapter. I query whether Too Young to Wed fulfills its goal to galvanise political action to end early and forced marriage or whether the images fuel the rhetoric of rescue and protection and obscure truths about people's lives only to reveal 'partial truths'. What are the consequences of circulating these images? Do the images foster understanding and solidarity with those experiencing early and forced marriage or do they serve to bolster imperialist rhetoric that may exacerbate rather than alleviate problems of forced marriage, moving no closer to ending the practice?

In examining these arguments, I echo Sara Ahmed's call for a 'generous encounter',[16] one that unravels and complicates the mutual interests, conceptual dependencies and theoretical conflicts and tensions between women and children. Considering a 'generous encounter' between feminism and the politics of childhood for exploring early and forced marriage is not, as Ahmed argues, a plea for commonalities and equivalencies. Rather, as she acknowledges, while there is incommensurability at some level, it does not necessarily mean that they cannot co-exist in relation to each other.[17] Further, Ahmed notes that the effort is not to move beyond oppositions that totalise and refuse the 'other';[18] rather it is to argue for 'an economy' which includes conflicting and competing co-existence. This seems to be a particularly appropriate strategy for exploring forced marriage given that feminist interest in children and childhood in the past has often positioned children as adversaries rather than women's contemporaries, with more differences than commonalities.[19] Forced marriage provides an opportunity to highlight these commonalities and explore tensions and mutual interests that arise. Thus, I invoke Ahmed's notion of a 'generous encounter' to contemplate the resemblances between the lives of children and women without hierarchy. In doing so, forced marriage becomes a context within which childhood and womanhood emerge as categories of experience. This formulation is far from the one that might be proposed by Firestone, who might call for the obliteration of childhood altogether (see Zehavi, this volume). Rather, for feminism and the politics of childhood, envisioning this 'generous encounter' appears to offer a productive approach that enriches understanding of lived experiences, interrupts adult-centricity, and reflects the challenges of theorising and practice in contemporary dynamic contexts. It seems to me that an invigorated position emerges from which to conceptually move across, through and around, rather than beyond, the barriers of binaries including child/adult and girl/woman. At a broader level still, forced marriage may offer the possibility to produce what Jacqui Alexander and Chandra Mohanty argue, is a shared sense of 'engagement based on empathy and on a vision of justice for everyone'.[20]

When I first encountered the practice of the early and forced marriage of girls, I felt frustrated by the tendency to treat it as a problem of vulnerable, helpless and silent girls. It reminded me of portrayals of women similarly imaged as passive and victimised.[21] My concern was heightened by an opportunity to work closely with the Too Young to Wed exhibit in 2013.[22] I began to more fully understand and question the scope of the exhibit's reach to both live and virtual audiences around the world.[23] Drawing on feminist and post-colonial critiques, I queried the relations of 'knowing' offered by the set of circulating images of children and childhoods and questioned how political action can be constituted through visuality. Of particular concern was the repeated deployment of the notion of 'barbarity', which was linked to particular societies by those hoping to raise awareness of the scope and consequences of the practice. The phrase was used, for example, at the UN General Assembly in 2013 during the introduction of the first ever stand-alone resolution condemning early and forced child marriage: proponents called for an end to the 'barbaric' practice.[24]

The child protection, legal and non-governmental communities rose to the challenge to find ways to end the practice. They explored legislative, activist and protectionist avenues alongside political attempts.[25] Notably, what marks many of the efforts directed at ending early and forced marriage is a focus on saving and protecting girls that, when cast within a global neoliberal framing (as Stephens suggests), relies on individual rather than communal and structural solutions to ending such a practice. These solutions sometimes neglect to consider the contexts in which girls live amid adults. They also fail to attend to the cultural politics of childhood and how ideologies of girlhood, childhood and womanhood intersect in locales that naturalise what it means to be a girl or a child. This occurs in part because of the tenacity of dominant Eurocentric notions of childhood and girlhood that rest firmly on vulnerability, innocence and a lack of agency. By emptying out the significance of the contexts of early and forced marriage, and obscuring what gives rise to the inequalities that fuel this practice, such efforts render girls as failing: failing to be resilient, or to stay in school, or to manage their own reproductive health. This casting back to individuals works hand in hand with a rhetoric that positions those in the industrialised North as authority figures who are able to guide those located in the global South in overcoming their problems and to help them to 'acquire the characteristics of civilized peoples, and take their place alongside them in the world'.[26]

Early and forced child marriage at the nexus of feminism and a politics of childhood[27]

Scholarly research reveals that some of the challenges of early and forced marriage are due, in part, to complex definitional issues. Forced marriage, for example, becomes early marriage when we pay attention to cultural understandings of age and capacity. Concepts of consent and coercion come to the foreground as well, marking the definition of early and forced marriage as complicated terrain.[28]

In addition to definitional challenges, early and forced marriage has garnered attention from legal and human rights scholars. In analyzing the practice they appeal to human rights instruments including the Universal Declaration of Human Rights 1948, the Convention on the Elimination of All Forms of Discrimination Against Women 1979, and the UN Convention on the Rights of the Child 1989. A 2006 UN study on all forms of violence against women highlights in its definition of forced marriage a lack of meaningful consent. Further, the Convention Against Slavery considers forced marriage a 'slavery-like' practice[29] and the Convention on the Rights of the Child, applying to all people under the age of 18 years, states that this practice is a violation of children's rights.

Scope and context of early and forced marriage

According to the United Nations Children's Fund, over 700 million women today were married before they reached the age of 18.[30] Ideology, power, legal responses and language are some of the factors that fuel the practice of forced marriage, coupled with contexts characterised by oppressive patriarchal social structures, gender discrimination, poverty and inequality. When enmeshed with cultural attitudes and religious practices, these factors help to sustain the practice in diverse local contexts. In contexts affected by war and conflict, the conditions for early and forced marriage are further exacerbated.

To consider these factors in turn, let us look first at how ideological aspects drive and sustain the practice of the forced marriage of girls. Feminist and childhood scholars argue that one of the conditions that makes girls and women vulnerable and susceptible to forced marriage is a process of devaluation that rests on the notion of girls and women as less than fully human. That is, not only are girls viewed as 'on their way to becoming' fully human, their full humanity remains precarious even when they reach adulthood. The slippage between childhood, girlhood and womanhood locates girls on unstable conceptual terrain. Moreover, dehumanisation as a process acts to guarantee their dependency by enforcing passivity and restricting agency.[31] Situated in positions of relative powerlessness and ensconced in families that are in turn embedded in communities, for girls in these contexts, control is at the heart of the practice of forced and early marriage. The practice is linked too with sexuality and gender relations, as well as culturally situated ideas about girlhood, womanhood, family obligations and honour.

Within these local contexts, legal responses to early and forced marriage are complicated as well. For example, while the practice may be prohibited in civil or common law, customary laws and practices may condone it. This means that decisions regarding early and forced marriage may be made in terms of securing a daughter's future by 'marrying' her with an older male, while other decisions are concerned with the larger family unit by using 'marriage' as an opportunity to connect families and create alliances through reciprocity systems, or to enable access to resources such as land. These decisions may have tremendous personal consequences for individual girls' physical and emotional health: the well-being of the family or community is effectively allowed to supersede that of the girl.[32] As Carolyn Archambault notes with regard to early and forced marriage in the life of a Maasai girl named Esther,[33]

> In light of the circumstances in which Esther's father's decision was made and his intentions, he shifts from a symbol of patriarchal oppression to a persona of a concerned father. No longer simply a violator of his daughter's rights to an education, he can be understood as a victim himself of economic, ecological, and political forces beyond his control that render the path that would attain security for Esther (and other young women like her) more uncertain.

'Barbarism' and rescuing and protecting girls

The connection between barbarism and early and forced marriage plays a powerful role in sustaining the practice. The term 'barbaric' captures a constellation of meanings from notions of cruelty and brutality to backwardness and uncivilised ignorance.[34] Moreover, labelling a practice such as early and forced marriage as 'barbaric' has strategic and powerful consequences. It encodes a paternalistic stance and reinforces geographic and cultural distances that set up a dichotomy of locales where the practice does or supposedly does not occur.[35] Indeed, deploying the term 'barbaric' firmly attaches the practice to persons living in particular localities; in turn, this aids in justifying interventions in their lives. As Dana Cloud argues with regard to circulating images of Afghan women, they serve to 'establish the barbarity of a society in which women are profoundly oppressed'.[36] Cloud analyses the ways images of Afghan women circulate alongside a 'clash of civilizations' rhetoric that reproduces the narrative of a 'white man's burden'.[37] Stabile and Kumar go a step further to argue that the visibility of Afghan women in the post-9/11 context was used to sell the war to the US public by constructing the West as 'a beacon of civilization with an obligation to tame the Islamic world and liberate its women'.[38] In the example of Too Young to Wed, the discourse of barbarism legitimises calls for an end to the practice in the lives of those living in the global South.

Too Young to Wed as political photography

Too Young to Wed circulates images to audiences in the industrialised North in both live and virtual spaces. Some viewers will see in the images an unmediated and authentic replica of reality, while others will recognise the photographer's influence in constructing these images for particular effect. Lutz and Collins describe the politics of what viewers 'see' as 'political photography',[39] where images are used to educate and motivate viewers who wish to see social change. They argue that rhetorical strategies combined with images expose audiences to human suffering and 'often operate by encouraging an empathic involvement with the photographed subject – a desire to intervene directly with the frame of the photograph in order to ease the depicted pain or comfort a hungry child'.[40] Lutz and Collins posit that by portraying people living in the global South as exotic, idealised and natural, viewers in the industrialised North are situated both in opposition and authoritatively.[41]

It is hardly a coincidence that the Too Young to Wed photo exhibit distances early and forced marriage from any association with those living in industrialised Northern countries; none of the girls in the images are located in a North American or European context. This omission is significant for it accomplishes a number of things: first, it displaces the practice of early and forced marriage elsewhere, creating an insularity and providing the comfort of distance to the viewers of the images. Second, by framing the practice as an issue for girls located in the global South, this focus diverts attention away from equally oppressive and patriarchal practices that affect the lives of girls in the industrialised North.[42] Further, framing this practice through a discourse situated firmly within Eurocentric ideas of childhood and girlhood makes the problem appear as though located in places both geographically and culturally distant from the industrialised North. The rhetoric obscures many reasons for this practice: the poverty experienced by families who cannot afford to provide for their daughters; security for girls and their well-being as future adult women; devaluation of daughters in comparison with sons; debts and/or conflicts that can be settled through early and forced marriage in order to address threats to family relationships. In this culturally and politically charged landscape, girls are portrayed as a problem to be remedied.[43] In the Too Young to Wed example, governments appear to deliver solutions that may or may not have any resonance in the contexts and circumstances in which girls live: that is, by keeping girls in school, assisting them in choosing to delay marriage, offering information about reproductive health and training in life skills to make them better wives and mothers at a later time in their lives. These 'solutions' may or may not bring early and forced marriage to an end.[44]

Moreover, paternalism emerges when the issue of early and forced marriage is displaced to people living in the global South. What remain hidden are the social and political-economic dimensions of this global issue. Attention is diverted away from government policies, international trade agreements and other political arrangements that tie the very governments that are championing the campaign to end early and forced marriage to the local contexts in which the practice continues to flourish.

The photo exhibit appears to mimic this strategy of deflection and individualisation through the very composition of the images. For instance, in many of the exhibit's images, girls are depicted alone, pictured outside of familiar contexts of family and community, placed against gloomy backdrops or in open and vast unpopulated landscapes. If not alone they are with a child or husband, further reinforcing their roles as wives and mothers. The imaging engenders a sense of isolation, quiet desperation and powerlessness and, by extension, reinforces the practice as if it takes place in isolation from other relationships, which is hardly the case. The solution to the problem of early and forced marriage appears in equally simplistic terms: to halt the practice.

This strategy of individualisation and decontextualisation is a powerful one, yet it is hardly surprising that it occurs in a neoliberal globalised era. As Xiaobei Chen has argued, the twenty-first century has produced the birth of 'the new child-victim citizen'.[45] Moreover, at a broader political level, it also reflects, among other things, a shift to a renewed political interest in children, and in this example, girls. The increased attention to girls as a concern for foreign policy is remarkable given the lack of political will that has been a much more common occurrence in relation to girls.[46]

An economy of visibility and invisibility

Too Young to Wed is both compelling and contradictory. On one hand, the photographs are aesthetically beautiful; on the other, the images offer viewers meanings that may be understood in unintended ways. The power of the photographs compels viewers to consider the multiple meanings of girls and girlhood, including girls as children who experience a loss of childhood, girls as 'becoming women', girls as brides, girls as victims of violence and girls as mothers. The process of determining which meanings become 'real' to viewers and which ones remain invisible is part of the sense-making that viewers undertake, selecting some elements and leaving others aside. Feminist communications scholar Sarah Banet-Weiser calls this process 'an economy of visibility'[47] to describe the relationship between viewers and those who are imaged. This economy consists of an interplay between visibility and invisibility whereby something appears, circulates and becomes exchanged. In Too Young to Wed, the girls and their suffering are circulated, exchanged and become 'real'. Banet-Weiser explores this process for the possibilities it holds in transforming oneself into a commodity in social media as a space of visibility for girls. If Banet-Weiser's argument is extended to the Too Young to Wed images, given the viewership of this exhibit worldwide and the many different audiences it has reached, we must consider the implications of turning girls into commodities or what Claudia Aradau argues are 'spectral presences on the scene of politics'[48].

Related questions emerge. Who assesses the value of what is circulated in such an exchange, for whom and with what consequences? Too Young to Wed offers viewers an instance to suppress and replace details of girls' lives and experiences with meanings that are consistent with dominant Eurocentric notions of girlhood and ideal childhood. In its quest to raise awareness and end early and forced marriage, does Too Young to Wed clear a space of visibility for *actual* girls so that the practice might end, as the UNFPA initiative suggests? Or does the exhibit merely provide another space of *invisibility* for girls' lives, wherein securing their human rights remains outside of their grasp? As the photo exhibit circulates, it engages viewers with girls' suffering framed within an ethos of compassion. Compassion enables viewers to 'suffer' with the girls, yet at a distance. Viewers of the images become 'witnesses' to the suffering of girls. Following Hannah Arendt,[49] if compassion is actualised in situations in which those who do not suffer meet and come face to face with those who do, distance becomes a political dimension that has the effect of unifying across spatial and temporal locations. This interaction comprises what has been called a 'politics of pity',[50] one that does not attach itself in a localised way yet cannot completely free itself from the local and particular either.

In Too Young to Wed, we see this dimension unfold when audiences view the images of girls through a lens of compassion. Compassion grounds these elements that create both an intimacy with viewers as well as a comfortable distance from the subjects of the images. By masking the diversity of those experiencing early and forced marriage, the images appear to exacerbate this distance. Devoid of contextual details, they homogenise girls' lives into a unified representation of girlhood so that early and forced marriage appears as a singular, integrated issue. Postcolonial childhood and feminist scholars including Sarada Balagopalan,[51] Olga Nieuwenhuys,[52] and Erica Burman[53] have argued that this compression and glossing-over of the intricacies of how local and global forces intertwine is partly an effect of the circulation of liberal categories like freedom, rights and equality. They argue that their repetition in postcolonial contexts produces children's lives in limited ways, against a Eurocentric, bourgeois notion of childhood as a global ideal.[54]

The politics of pity is not only apparent in the photo exhibit: it is used too in interventions orchestrated in international politics. As we see in high-level political gatherings at the UN, discussions of early and forced child marriage are framed by unifying notions of 'poor victims' and 'barbaric' practices. These discussions feature tokenistic participation by articulate young women on high-level panels who are asked to speak on behalf of all girls who have experienced early and forced marriage. These appeals to emotion in turn create superficial solidarities that employ a politics of pity combined with a rhetoric of rescue and protection. Activism through these solidarities manifests as a real possibility linking pity with praxis. Claudia Aradau has written extensively about the way this works in the lives of trafficked women. She argues that 'a politics of pity tackles the "disordered situation"... These emotions drive political interventions and strategies of governance.'[55] As Aradau notes, 'from the war on terror to interventions in crisis situations (e.g., famine and natural catastrophes), political actions depend on and are limited by emotions'.[56] For girls who are, as Aradau says, placed among categories of individuals who are 'non-dangerous', this is a particularly salient point. Indeed, like the figure of the 'child', the figure of the 'girl' enables a 'safe' intervention for those who engage with it because girls are situated in relative positions of powerlessness vis-à-vis adults. Aradau argues that for trafficked women, 'if human rights have become the rights of those who are too weak or too oppressed to actualize and enact them, they are not "their" rights. They are deprived of political agency; the only rights are our rights to practice pity and humanitarian interventions. Victims are therefore divorced from the very possibility of political agency...'.[57] Consider how for girls imaged in the Too Young to Wed photo exhibit, it appears the exclusion of their political agency is guaranteed.

It behooves us, therefore, to carefully contemplate whose interests are served by silent, decontextualised images of girls in the global South, circulated to audiences in the industrialised North. It befits questioning interventions to end the practice of early and forced marriage framed by rights discourses and governmental efforts to attend to, and uphold, girls' rights. While these efforts no doubt bring attention to the matter as well as positioning girls on political agendas from which they, like women, might otherwise continue to be excluded, I would argue that they also extend and ignite foreign policy relations in problematic ways. To be clear, the problem is not that governments have a stake in reducing violence in girls' and women's lives, whether because it has implications on the stability of their own countries, for health costs or other reasons. Instead, and what may be less apparent, the issue is the connection between eliminating girls' suffering – in this case by ending the practice of early and forced marriage – and the *kind* of political attention it garners, for whom and for which purposes. Again, Aradau makes a similar point in the case of trafficked women, arguing that 'the elimination or alleviation of suffering is part of a process of governing, of social re-ordering, in which the causes of suffering are eradicated, dealt with or transformed. In governmental terms such an intervention has not only to represent and constitute a particular situation, but also to confer particular identities upon subjects.'[58]

Too Young to Wed confers identities to girls that are both complex and political. As it circulates specific sets of meanings and discourses regarding their lives, framed by compassion and pity as well as rescue and protection, Too Young to Wed has the potential to exacerbate the challenges for actual girls rather than improve them. By visually encoding ideas about girlhood, womanhood, motherhood, culture, consent and coercion, it helps to shape connections, conceptually and substantively, in an economy of visibility that both facilitates and impedes the goal of ending early and forced marriage. It impedes by engaging audiences in a politics that *may not* translate into an active force within the political arena and that may oppose some children against others by deeming some lives (i.e. those of children living in the industrialised North) more valuable than others. It is political in that it captures viewers' emotional responses but keeps the girls in a state of what scholar Luc Boltanski has called 'distant suffering',[59] a divide that may ultimately work against active engagement and social change for the *actual* empowerment of girls as called for by the international community.

To conclude

I opened this chapter recalling Sharon Stephens' words on the importance of highlighting the politics of childhood, and of troubling the notion of culture in contexts framed by global neoliberalism and marked by poverty and rising inequality. Women's and children's lives and interests emerge as intertwined and demonstrates how they can be productively considered in dynamic socio-political and globalised contexts. Stephens compels us to pay attention to children in relational ways with adults and to account for the conditions of their lives within a broader global political-economic and sociocultural framing. She views children not only as 'on their way to becoming' full members of society but as fully present among adults and important to what matters politically, economically, socially and culturally in the world. Her words remind us to understand children's experiences, like those of women, in their locally unique and relational situations, combined with the external forces that drive and affect their lives and, in turn, affect and intertwine with the lives of women. I would argue that this conceptual and political intertwining emerges through a generous encounter between feminism and a politics of childhood. Using the example of Too Young to Wed, I have pointed out what an increased visibility has to do with conceptualising the figure of the child as a powerful symbol of the future, as well as a locus for the present interplay of local and global forces that challenges childhood, girlhood and womanhood in contemporary contexts. Thus the contribution of this chapter has been to theorise childhood in a way that reimagines the mutual interests, conceptual dependencies and tensions between women and children through the example of forced marriage. Forced marriage provides an opportunity to contemplate the resemblances and tensions between the lives of children and women without hierarchy when envisaged as a context within which both childhood and womanhood are constituted and emerge as viable categories of experience.

NOTES

1 I wish to thank the editors and reviewers for their insightful comments on an earlier draft: these greatly assisted in the writing of this chapter. I am also grateful to Taylor and Francis for permission to revise and reprint a portion of the article 'Children's Participation and Protection in a Globalized World: Reimagining "Too Young to Wed" Through a Cultural Politics of Childhood', which appears in the *International Journal of Human Rights* 21, no. 1 (2017): 76–88.
2 Representations of Afghan women and girls have been deployed and have circulated in similar ways, including, for instance, the image 'Afghan Girl' on *National Geographic*'s June 1985 cover. For more on the ways images of Afghan women circulate, see Rae Lynn Schwartz-DuPre, 'Portraying the Political: National Geographic's 1985 Afghan Girl and a US Alibi for Aid,' *Critical Studies in Media Communication* 27, no. 4 (2010): 336–56; Vera Mackie, 'The "Afghan Girls": Media Representations and Frames of War,' *Continuum: Journal of Media & Cultural Studies* 26 (2012): 115–31.
3 Sharon Stephens, *Children and the Politics of Culture* (New Jersey: Princeton University Press, 1995), 4.
4 For more on diverse traditions of 'childhood studies' in the United States, Britain and Scandinavia, see entries for 'anthropology of childhood' and 'sociology of childhood' in Oxford Bibliographies, available at http://www.oxfordbibliographies.com/.
5 I use the term 'early and forced marriage of girls' in this chapter to mean a formal marriage or informal union before the age of 18. This phrase is sometimes used interchangeably in the literature as 'forced, early marriage' and 'child marriage'. The term 'early marriage' is also used in the literature to refer to an individual's level of physical, emotional, sexual and psychosocial development, in addition to age, which could complicate their ability to consent to marriage. The term 'forced marriage' can refer to women at any age and connotes any marriage without the full and free consent of one or both of the parties involved, or when one or both parties is prevented from ending or leaving the marriage. For more, see Office of the High Commission, 'Preventing and Eliminating Child, Early and Forced Marriage,' Report of the Office of the United Nations High Commissioner for Human Rights. April 2014. A/HRC/26/22, http://www.girlsnotbrides.org/new-ohchr-report-child-early-forced-marriage/; and UNICEF, 'Child Marriage,' https://www.unicef.org/protection/57929_58008.html.
6 For examples of early and forced child marriage initiatives, see the United Nations Population Fund website at http://www.unfpa.org/child-marriage.
7 UNFPA is a UN agency dedicated to addressing issues such as sexual and reproductive health, matters concerning young people including child marriage, human rights and gender equality, and population matters. For more, see their website at http://www.unfpa.org.
8 The initiative was championed by ministers of foreign affairs from Canada, Ghana and the Netherlands.
9 Too Young to Wed is the name of an initiative organised through a partnership between the United Nations Population Fund and US-based VII Photo Agency to raise awareness and end early and forced child marriage. The exhibit features the documentary photography work of VII's photographer Stephanie Sinclair and videos by cinematographer Jessica Dimmock.
10 Too Young to Wed's images are of girls who have been forced into early marriage living in Afghanistan, Ethiopia, India, Nepal and Yemen. After the photo exhibit's debut in New York, where it was also featured on billboards in Times Square, it arrived in Ottawa, Canada in the spring of 2013 as a first stop on a tour that over the rest of the year took in Washington, Montreal, Copenhagen, Morocco and The Hague. In early 2014, the photo exhibit appeared in Tangiers, Oslo and in March at the UN's Palais des Nations in Geneva. Later in the year it was displayed in Stockholm, Helsinki, Lisbon, Madrid, Vienna, the UK, Beirut, Amman and Argentina. The exhibit returned to New York at the end of 2014 and in early 2015 was seen in Khartoum, Sudan; Bihar and Mumbai, India; Dhaka, Bangladesh and Ankara, Turkey.
11 Lila Abu-Lughod, 'Do Muslim Women Really Need Saving? Anthropological Reflections on Cultural Relativism and Its Others,' *American Anthropologist* 3, no. 104 (2002): 783–90.
12 Gayatri Chakravorty Spivak, 'Can the Subaltern Speak?' in *Marxism and the Interpretation of Culture*, ed. Cary Nelson and Lawrence Grossberg (Urbana, IL: University of Illinois Press, 1988), 271–313.
13 Spivak, 'Can the Subaltern Speak?'

14 Spivak, 'Can the Subaltern Speak?'
15 Susan Sontag, *On Photography* (London: Penguin, 1973), 6.
16 Sara Ahmed, *Strange Encounters: Embodied Others in Post-Coloniality* (London: Routledge, 2000); Sara Ahmed, 'Identifications, Gender and Racial Difference: Moving Beyond a Psychoanalytical Account of Subjectivity,' in *Representations of Gender, Democracy and Identity Politics in Relation*, ed. Kumar Renuka (New Delhi, India: Sri Satguru Publications, 1996), 288–302.
17 Ahmed, 'Identifications, Gender and Racial Difference,' 288–9.
18 Ahmed, 'Identifications, Gender and Racial Difference,' 288–9.
19 Erica Burman, 'Beyond "Women Vs. Children" or "Womenandchildren": Engendering Childhood and Reformulating Motherhood,' *International Journal of Children's Rights* 16, no. 2 (2008): 177–94.
20 M. Jacqui Alexander and Chandra Talpade Mohanty, *Feminist Genealogies, Colonial Legacies, Democratic Futures* (xiii) (New York: Routledge, 1997).
21 Rae Lynn Schwartz-DuPre, "Portraying the Political: National Geographic's 1985 Afghan Girl and a US Alibi for Aid." *Critical Studies in Media Communication* 27, no. 4 (2010): 336–56.
22 Too Young to Wed was installed at the Carleton University Art Gallery in Ottawa, Canada in May and June 2013. My involvement came at the invitation of my university to co-organise a speakers' panel for the exhibit.
23 According to a 6 January 2014 post by Stephanie Sinclair on the Too Young to Wed blog, the photo exhibit has had a vigorous online presence as well: 'Since we started, images from the campaign flooded the mainstream media, appearing in more than 100 online and print media outlets including CNN, The New York Times and National Geographic…Too Young to Wed raised awareness about child marriage around the world…Thanks to you, our voice through social media was powerful and we had an amazing Instagram campaign that brought 500,000+ likes to our images and stories of children who bravely refused their marriages in India.' Some of the images in the Too Young to Wed photo exhibit are available at http://tooyoungtowed.org/#/video .
24 For the full text of John Baird's speech to the UN General Assembly see *Huffpost Politics* (blog), 'John Baird's Speech To The United Nations: Full Text Of Speech Delivered At The UN October 1st, 2012,' *Huffington Post*, 1 October 2012, http://www.huffingtonpost.ca/2012/10/01/john-bairds-speech-united-nations-text_n_1928907.html.
25 Cécile Aptel, 'Child Slaves and Child Brides,' *Journal of International Criminal Justice* 14 (2016): 305–25; Alexia Sabbe, Marleen Temmerman, Eva Brems and Els Leye, 'Forced Marriage: An Analysis of Legislation and Political Measures in Europe,' *Crime, Law and Social Change* 62 (2014): 171–89; Girls Not Brides; Alphaxard Chabari and Eva Palmqvist, 'Violence against Children in Southern Sudan: A Participatory Study on PHP, Sexual Abuse and Early and Forced Marriage,' *Save the Children Sweden*, 1997. http://resourcecentre.savethechildren.se/sites/default/files/documents/1403.pdf; Neha Jain, 'Forced Marriage as a Crime against Humanity,' *Journal of International Criminal Justice* 6 (2008): 1013–32; Joar Svanemyr, Venkatraman Chandra-Mouli, Charlotte Sigurdson Christiansen and Michael Mbizvo. 'Preventing Child Marriages: First International Day of the Girl Child, 'My Life, My Right, End Child Marriage,' *Reproductive Health* 9 (2012): 31. Published online. Doi 10.1186/1742-4755-9-31.
26 Catherine A. Lutz and Jane L. Collins, *Reading National Geographic* (Chicago: University of Chicago Press, 1993), 164.
27 'Girls Not Brides' is a global partnership directed at ending early and forced marriage. It includes 400 civil society organisations from over 60 countries. For more information see http://www.girlsnotbrides.org/.
28 See Women Living Under Muslim Laws, *Child, Early and Forced Marriage: A Multi-Country Study. A Submission to the UN Office of the High Commissioner on Human Rights (OCHCR)*. December 2013, http://www.wluml.org/sites/wluml.org/files/UN%20report%20final.pdf
29 Forced marriage is not commonly defined as slavery despite increasing attention to this argument. See the UN General Assembly, 'Resolution 66/140, Calls for an End to Forced Marriage as a "Harmful Traditional Practice",' 2006. http://www.un.org/en/ga/search/view_doc.asp?symbol=%20A/RES/66/140. See also United Nations General Assembly, 'Report of the Special Rapporteur on Contemporary Forms of Slavery, Including its Causes and Consequences, Gulnara Shahinian: Thematic Report on Servile Marriage,' 10 July 2012, http://www.ohchr.org/Documents/HRBodies/HRCouncil/RegularSession/Session21/A-HRC-21-41_en.pdf.

30. See UNICEF, 'Ending Child Marriage: Progress and Prospects' (Geneva: UNICEF, 2014), https://www.unicef.org/media/files/Child_Marriage_Report_7_17_LR..pdf. See also UNICEF, 'Committing to Child Survival: A Promise Renewed, Progress Report' (Geneva: UNICEF, 2012), http://www.unicef.org/lac/Committing_to_Child_Survival_APR_9_Sept_2013.pdf; UNFPA, 'Motherhood in Childhood: Facing the challenge of adolescent pregnancy' (Geneva: UNFPA, 2013), https://www.unfpa.org/sites/default/files/pub-pdf/EN-SWOP2013-final.pdf
31. See Fiddian-Qasmiyeh (this volume) for a discussion of how Sahrawi refugee women and girls are marginalised on the basis of gender and generation.
32. See Office of the High Commissioner for Human Rights, 'Preventing and Eliminating Child, Early and Forced Marriage,' Report of the Office of the United Nations High Commissioner for Human Rights, April 2014, A/HRC/26/22 (Geneva: United Nations, 2014), on the wide-ranging impact of child forced marriage on girls who face physical, psychological, economic and other violences resulting from the practice.
33. Carolyn Archambault, 'Ethnographic Empathy and the Social Context of Rights. Rescuing Maasai Girls from Early Marriage,' *American Anthropologist* 113, no. 4 (2011): 638.
34. Merryl Wynn Davies, Ashis Nandy and Ziauddin Sardar. *Barbaric Others: A Manifesto on Western Racism* (London: Pluto Press, 1993).
35. For more, see Julia Alanen, 'Crafting a Competent Framework to Combat Forced Marriage,' *American Journal of Family Law* 30, no. 2 (2016): 1–14; Julia Alanen, 'Shattering the Silence Surrounding Forced and Early Marriage in the United States,' *Children's Legal Rights Journal* 32, no. 2 (Summer 2012): 1–37, both on the situation in the United States.
36. Dana L. Cloud, 'To Veil the Threat of Terror: Afghan Women and the <Clash of Civilizations> in the Imagery of the US War on Terrorism,' *Quarterly Journal of Speech* 90, no. 3 (2004): 287.
37. 'White man's burden' is a phrase used to justify European imperialism in the nineteenth and early twentieth centuries. *New Dictionary of Cultural Literacy*, s.v. 'White man's burden.' Eric Donald Hirsch, Joseph F. Kett and James S. Trefil. New York: Houghton Mifflin Harcourt, 2002.
38. Carol A. Stabile and Deepa Kumar, 'Unveiling Imperialism: Media, Gender and the War on Afghanistan,' *Media Culture & Society* 27, no. 5 (2005): 766.
39. Lutz and Collins, *Reading National Geographic*.
40. Lutz and Collins, *Reading National Geographic*, 271.
41. Lutz and Collins, *Reading National Geographic*, 271.
42. Thanks to Ohad Zehavi for pointing out this dialectical omission.
43. Leti Volpp, 'Blaming Culture for Bad Behavior,' *Yale Journal of Law and the Humanities* 12, no. 1 (2000): 89–116.
44. To read more on the links between early and forced marriage and education, see the Girls Not Brides website at http://www.girlsnotbrides.org/themes/education/
45. Xiaobei Chen argues that for children who had historically remained non-citizens, a reconfiguration of citizenship has occurred vis-à-vis the child and childhood, and that this emerges in discourse in cultural, legal and political settings. Chen describes this figure as the 'new child-victim citizen'. Xiaobei Chen, 'The Birth of the Child-victim Citizen,' in *Reinventing Canada: Politics of the 21ˢᵗ century*, ed. Janine Brodie and Linda Trimble (Toronto: Prentice-Hall, 2003): 162–87.
46. Advocate Cindy Blackstock, executive director of the First Nations Child and Family Caring Society, filed a complaint against the Canadian government with the Canadian Human Rights Commission in February 2007. The complaint alleges that Canada fails to provide equitable and culturally based child welfare services to First Nations children and that this treatment amounts to racialised discrimination. She won the decision of the Human Rights Tribunal in 2016. For more, see First Nations Child and Family Caring Society, 'I Am a Witness,' https://fncaringsociety.com/i-am-witness
47. Sarah Banet-Weiser, 'Am I Pretty or Ugly: Girl, Digital Media and the Economy of Visibility.' Paper presented at the Girlhood Studies and the Politics of Place: New Paradigms of Research Symposium, McGill Institute for Gender, Sexuality and Feminist Studies, Montreal, QC, 10–12 October 2012.
48. Claudia Aradau, 'The Perverse Politics of Four-Letter Words: Risk and Pity in the Securitisation of Human Trafficking,' *Millennium: Journal of International Studies* 33, no. 2 (2004): 276.
49. Hannah Arendt, *On Revolution* (Harmondsworth: Penguin, 1990).
50. Arendt, *On Revolution*.

51 Sarada Balagopalan, 'Constructing Indigenous Childhoods: Colonialism, Vocational Education and the Working Child,' *Childhood* 9 (2002): 19–34.
52 Olga Nieuwenhuys, 'Keep Asking: Why Childhood? Why Children? Why Global?' *Childhood* 17, no. 3 (2010): 291–6.
53 Erica Burman, 'Innocents Abroad: Western Fantasies of Childhood and the Iconography of Emergencies,' *Disasters* 18, no. 3 (1994): 238–53; Erica Burman, 'Local, Global or Globalized? Child Development and International Child Rights Legislation,' *Childhood* 3 (1996): 45–66.
54 Jo Boyden, 'Childhood and the Policy Makers: A Comparative Perspective on the Globalisation of Childhood,' in *Constructing and Reconstructing Childhood: Contemporary Issues in the Sociological Study of Childhood*, ed. Allison James and Alan Prout (London: The Falmer Press, 1997): 187–226.
55 Aradau, 'Perverse Politics,' 257.
56 Aradau, 'Perverse Politics,' 255.
57 Aradau, 'Perverse Politics,' 276.
58 Aradau, 'Perverse Politics,' 259.
59 Luc Boltanski, *Distant Suffering: Morality, Media and Politics* (Cambridge: Cambridge University Press, 1999).

15
Feminists' strategic role in early childhood education

Sri Marpinjun, Nindyah Rengganis, Yudha Andri Riyanto, and Fransisca Yuni Dhamayanti

The Early Childhood Care and Development Resource Centre (ECCD RC) was co-founded by Lembaga Studi dan Pengembangan Perempuan dan Anak (Institute for Women's and Children's Studies and Development; LSPPA), an organisation formed in 1991 in Yogyakarta, Indonesia, to introduce women's and children's rights to the people. The founders of LSPPA were university students whose research indicated that most citizens did not know about gender issues, gender equality perspectives and analysis, and the laws which support women's rights. While the National Constitution (UUD 45) and some Acts of Parliament were progressive in that they followed UN conventions on human rights, women's rights and children's rights, in practice women and children were still in trouble. For instance, child marriage and maternal mortality remained issues in the country. Many Indonesians did not understand the concept of 'rights', and the problems facing women and children were not viewed as abuses of the rights of women and children.

As a result, LSPPA's main programme in the 1990s was to disseminate information and stimulate discussions about gender inequality in the Indonesian context. The organisation hosted public discussions and seminars, published scholarly books and engaged in economic empowerment activities with poor women in rural areas. It also joined the local and national chapters of the Alliance in Gender Equality to support policy and regulation changes.

After seven years spent focusing on gender inequality issues with citizens, we found that our strategies were not very effective. We expected positive responses from the audiences in every forum we organised. What we got was resistance. We understood that adults would not change the attitudes, ideas and practices that they had believed in since they were young. They thought that gender and feminism were alien to our culture and should be rejected. They argued that our culture was fine in terms of gender equality. The rejections also included threatening phone calls: callers said they would kill LSPPA's leaders and burn our office. We were exhausted mentally, and we felt that we were not achieving our goals because the resistance of those whom we were targetting for change was too strong. Also, other women's organisations were offering similar programmes, so we thought that as feminist activists we could combine our efforts towards achieving social justice.

These factors led us to develop new strategies. In 1998, we launched our programme to influence the early childhood education system. Our focus did not actually move away from women's issues; we remained committed to promoting gender equality in and through early childhood education. This change in our activities was based on our analysis that people learn to become a woman or man, and about gender roles, when they are very young. Early childhood care and development became LSPPA's new brand.

Why early childhood?

Fig. 15.1 Early Childhood Care and Development Resource Centre (Yogyakarta, Indonesia). (Source: ECCDRC Yogyakarta)

Children start learning about identities in the early years of their life and begin to form their gender identities by the time they are two to three years old. This is an opportunity for feminists! Through our early childhood work, we want to show the strategic role of women/feminists in ensuring girls and boys can develop identities that are equal with others and that they can feel proud about themselves, not inferior or superior to others.

Child caring is not a new job for women; however many women have not utilised this job to contribute to achieving social justice. Many women are still acting as agents of injustice in a culture that marginalises women and minority groups. Some women choose to focus on their careers and ignore children. In contrast, the ECCD RC invites women (and men) to join together to improve the quality of early childhood education through feminist principles such as equality, inclusion, diversity and freedom from all violence. We mean to harness 'education' to transform patriarchal culture.

ECCD RC programmes

The ECCD RC runs a number of initiatives:

1. We offer teacher training on gender equity in early childhood education (ECE) and support teachers to:
   a. Reflect on their own understanding about who they are, what they know about being women and men, what sort of person they want to be and what they want for the girls and boys they teach.
   b. Engage with women's rights as well as children's rights and the importance of children's voice.
   c. Identify gender/culture bias in ECE and provide an inclusive education for young children.
   d. Set up an equal learning environment for girls and boys.
2. We run an inclusive ECE centre for two- to seven-year-old girls and boys which celebrates diversity, ensures equality and supports the development of healthy self-esteem through:
   a. Facilitating high-quality interactions between children.
   b. Ensuring girls and boys can access any learning materials.
   c. Specialised curriculum.
   d. Provision of an equal learning environment. Teachers ensure that all girls and boys are able to learn about equality in terms of access and control and that all children feel safe, invited, involved and treated equally.

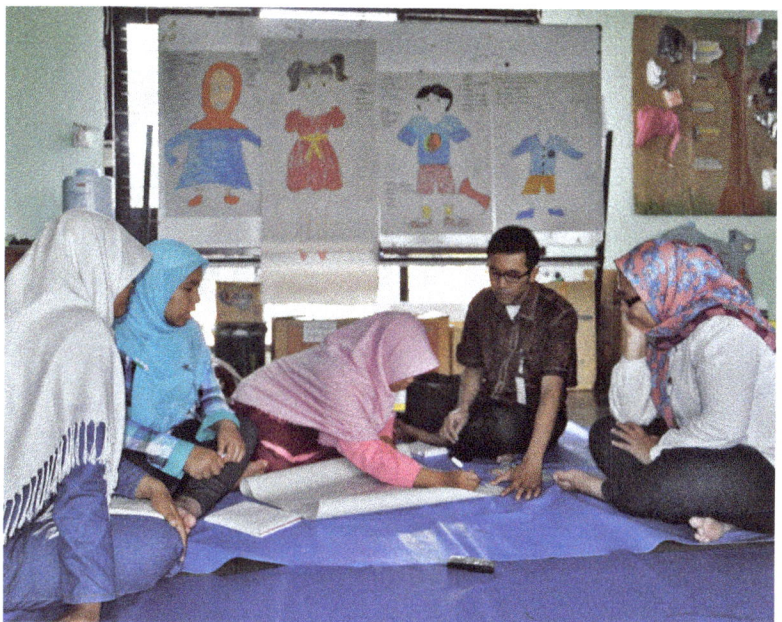

Fig. 15.2 Teachers reflect upon what it means to be men and women. (Source: ECCDRC Yogyakarta)

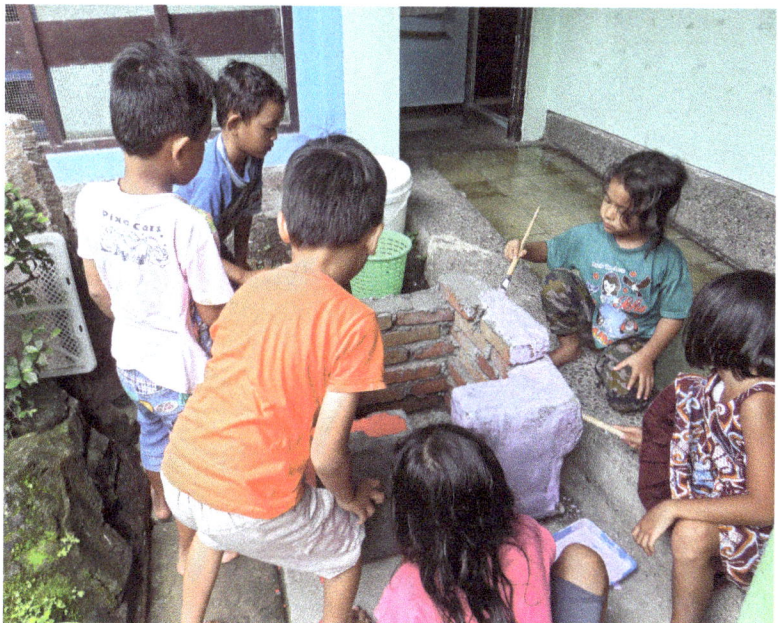

Fig. 15.3 Girls and boys have equal access to learning materials. (Source: ECCDRC Yogyakarta)

Fig. 15.4 Children learn to work together and respect others. (Source: ECCDRC Yogyakarta)

3. We collaborate with parents and the community to promote social justice for all.
4. We make policies to ensure that we are an inclusive centre. These include:
   a. A women's leadership policy, which states that the director of ECCD RC must be a woman.
   b. A staffing policy which encourages men and people from minority groups to become learning facilitators for children and ensures fair recruitment of staff regardless of the minority group they come from or their sexual orientation.
   c. An enrollment policy designed to ensure girls and boys are enrolled regardless of ability, race and social class, and allocates spaces for poor children.
   d. A class policy which ensures that each class has two facilitators of different genders (if possible) so that children can experience learning with female and male facilitators and so children see that men can become educators for young children.
   e. A fatherhood policy which provides one month's leave for male staff with a newborn child (as the government only gives one week of fatherhood leave).

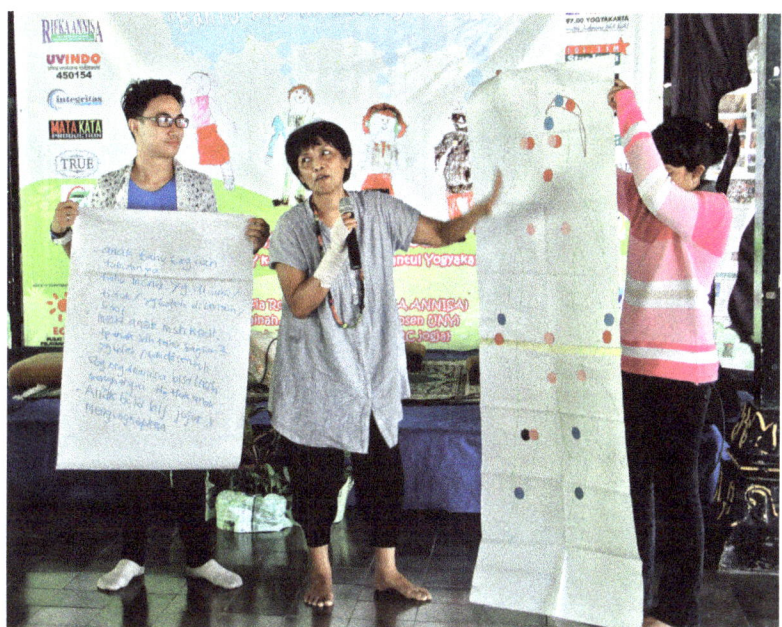

Fig. 15.5 Mapping parents' and teachers' experiences of violence.
(Source: ECCDRC Yogyakarta)

Fig. 15.6 Involving fathers and mothers in an outing.
(Source: ECCDRC Yogyakarta)

To be a feminist is to be a fighter for social justice. It is through our struggle, and analysis of our experiences, that we can develop a vision for achieving social justice. This may mean changing our strategies based on changing contexts. Our work demonstrates that early childhood is one of the arenas where feminists can challenge patriarchy. Focusing on early childhood involves redefining the role of women (and men) in rearing children, as well as ensuring all girls and boys feel good about themselves and equal with others.

16
'Gimme shelter'?
Complicating responses to family violence

Sevasti-Melissa Nolas, Erin Sanders-McDonagh and Lucy Neville

Responses to domestic violence, such as those codified in state and voluntary sector service provision, have historically provided both 'common ground' and 'contested' territory for thinking about the intersections between feminism and the politics of childhood.[1] Drawing on the evaluation of a voluntary sector programme, the Community Group Programme for children and their mothers in London, England,[2] the chapter explores 'the (im)possibilities of dialogue'[3] across feminism and childhood for those children and women/mothers who have experienced family violence. We argue that drawing children, as active meaning makers, into the analysis of and responses to domestic violence offers a way of extending the possibilities of social support systems in ways that can further strengthen women's recovery experiences, as well as benefitting children and young people themselves. At the same time, we argue that the focus on the mother–child couple does not take us far enough in complicating responses to domestic violence. Our intention in the analysis presented here is to imagine more complex and contextualised responses to domestic violence. An analysis that focuses on the messy actualities of practice responses[4] has the potential to recruit further interlocutors into the fold and move the practice conversation beyond its currently exclusive focus on women as heterosexual mother-victims and children as genderless witnesses (and sometimes victims) to predominantly male-perpetrated violence. Troubling these categories can help to complicate responses to *family* violence that are sensitive to a diversity of genders, ages, sexualities and cultures, extending service provision to young men and to heterosexual and homosexual fathers who may have experienced violence (from female or male partners, respectively), as well as lesbian mothers and parents of both or either gender who experience violence from their children and mothers/fathers.[5]

Thinking through case studies

The Community Group Programme (CGP) is a psychoeducational 12-week programme designed for children 'exposed to woman abuse'.[6] The programme developed in London, Ontario (Canada) in the late 1980s and early 1990s and focused on working with children and their mothers who had left a violent family relationship. The programme aims to strengthen child–mother relationships and to support children in processing their experiences of witnessing or experiencing woman abuse. Children are encouraged to recognise, name and explore the multiplicity of feelings surrounding incidences of their mother's abuse and are given opportunities to respond to these feelings using creative methods (e.g. arts and crafts) in a safe space facilitated by professionals, and in the company of peers who have had similar experiences. A parallel series of groups with mothers assists women in supporting their children with coming to terms with their experiences.

The programme emerged out of research and clinical practice (in family therapy), following observations by clinicians that no local provisions existed for supporting children and youth affected by domestic violence.[7] The original programme was firmly located within a discourse of 'woman abuse', a feminist perspective that casts domestic violence as a gendered crime committed by men against women. At the same time the programme was also rooted in a deep concern for children's experiences and their needs, which the programme originators saw as largely unmet. The idea of working with, and strengthening the relationship between, children and their mothers is a key theoretical component of the CGP.

In many ways, the programme is typical of framings of domestic violence which rely on particular feminist interpretations of gender-based violence – situating men as violent/perpetrators and women as oppressed/victims. For example, Women's Aid, one of the leading domestic violence charities in the UK, defines domestic violence as a form of patriarchal violence that disproportionately impacts women: 'Domestic abuse perpetrated by men against women is a quantitatively and qualitatively distinct phenomenon rooted in women's unequal status in society and oppressive social constructions of gender and family'.[8] The idea that it is predominantly women who are victims of domestic violence is certainly not unwarranted. In the UK, statistics suggest that women are overwhelmingly present in reported incidents of domestic violence,[9] men are four times more likely to perpetrate violence than women,[10] and the violence perpetrated against women by men is often more severe in nature.[11] As such, many programmes that seek to provide help and support for those experiencing domestic violence focus on women as victims of domestic violence.

At the same time, the CGP was innovative in creating a child-focused *and* relational space, that was concerned with both individual (children or women) and shared (children-and-women) needs and experiences. In this respect, CGP is a good example of a turn towards more complex practices of intervening to support those who have experienced family violence – in this case children and their mothers. Through the CGP case study we highlight the various necessary relational struggles in contemporary responses to family violence. The analysis builds on an understanding of practice responses to social injustice as necessarily pluralistic and complex, and enmeshed in theories, methods, values and practices.[12] By following these complexities and enmeshments new conceptualisations of family violence can emerge that are better able to engage with the multifarious experiences and needs of all involved.

The (im)possibilities of dialogues?

Historically UK domestic violence services have drawn on particular feminist framings of gender-based violence, and focused efforts on ensuring the safety of women who have experienced domestic abuse. The impact of domestic violence on women's psychological health, well-being and social positioning has long been recognised, and the reality of domestic violence, and creating socially supportive responses to it, has played a pivotal role in the shaping of the women's movement.

However, it was not until the 1980s, with the collision between the categories of childhood, youth and risk in policy and practice and the institutionalisation of the children's rights movement, that children started to become a topic of public concern in relation to incidences of domestic violence. At the same time a new legal concept of parental responsibility emerged that saw parents and parenting increasingly scrutinised by the state.[13] This historical shift has disrupted the well-established refuge practices that previously focused primarily on women, and new practices of support have begun to emerge that take mothers *and their children* into account.

With children coming to the fore, the tensions highlighted between women/mothers-and-children become salient.[14] Burman argues that formulations such as 'womenandchildren' or 'women vs. children' are conceptually, politically and practically inadequate: the first because it perpetuates inequalities by essentialising both children and women's positions, and the second because it creates competitive and unhelpful divisions, maintaining a status quo that misses the needs of both parties. As such, Burman offers the useful conceptual framing of children and women being in 'a necessary struggle-in-relation'.[15] This is a struggle that is encoded into the history of women's fights to bring child abuse to the attention of the state, as well as in the coining of the term 'battered woman syndrome' as a response and reaction to the 'battered child syndrome', which implicated mothers without acknowledging how complex maternal practices of protection can be.[16] In the CGP training, for example, trainers often used the example of one former participant who reported smacking her child because she knew she could minimise the level of violence and hurt inflicted on her child if she intervened between her husband and their child and undertook the smacking action herself instead of leaving it to her partner.

In the UK, AVA, the charity which rolled out the CGP in London, did not use the term 'woman abuse'. Instead, the CGP was described as a programme 'to support children and women affected by domestic violence'. While the 'children and women' phrasing carries echoes of essentialism, the reversal of the order to 'childrenandwomen', we argue, has the potential for thinking through what Lisa Baraitser calls 'the ethics of interruption', those interruptions created by bringing children into the adult fold, which Baraitser argues have the potential to provide both children and their mothers 'new "raw materials" for experiencing [them]selves, others and our worlds' differently.[17] Furthermore, the longer description leaves open the possibility to explore what Burman calls the 'complex relationalities and mutualities between [mothers'] mental and physical states and those of [their] children',[18] and what Haaken has described as the common ground between women and children in calling on the state (or civil society in this case) to intervene on family violence.[19]

An ethics of interruption?

Children's experiences of domestic violence, and the consequences of violence for them, have come to the fore in the last 25 years in Anglo-American contexts, on account of the introduction and ratification of the United

Nations Convenion on the Rights of the Child (UNCRC; 1989), which has precipitated policy and practice changes towards more child-centred service provision.[20] In England, for example (which is the main focus of this chapter), we have witnessed an increase in the commissioning of national evidence reviews to better understand and support children's experiences of domestic violence from a range of professional perspectives, including public health, social work and clinical psychology.[21] A shift in focus to children's concerns with regards to family violence provides a number of creative junctures to rethink support for women and children. In this section, we re-read our evaluation report[22] with a view to picking out three key ways in which bringing children and young people into the fold, and listening to the 'interruptions of the child',[23] may contribute towards complicating responses to family violence.

Guilt and blame

Guilt and blame have been identified as key discourses in women's and children's accounts of experiencing domestic violence.[24] However, such knowledge is based on mothers' and/or clinicians' perspectives and not on children's own experiences. These discourses have in turn fed into practice responses, including the CGP, where professionals delivering the programme repeatedly emphasised that children should not blame themselves for what happened. Our evaluation found that only a minority of the children made reference to the theme of self-blame in the qualitative research ($n=3$),[25] and that the majority of children we surveyed identified that children are not to blame for parents' fighting both before *and* after taking part in the programme (with no significant shift taking place). This was surprising given how much emphasis both the programme manual and professionals placed on absolving children from blame, and the findings from previous programme evaluations that suggest that groups reduce self-blame.[26] Instead the theme of blame was more prominent in mothers' accounts, with many mothers appearing to experience their children's anger and withdrawal as their punishment for what had happened. Yet in the questionnaire data (pre-groups) none of the children blamed their mothers for what happened. Neither did children blame themselves for their parents' fighting. More recent research on children's views of domestic violence suggests that children know whom to hold responsible for violence/abuse – this tends not to be themselves and is instead usually the abuser or both the parents.[27] Taking children's and young people's perspectives into account can help develop a more nuanced analysis of emotional experiences of family violence that takes us beyond dichotomies of perpetrators and victims, guilt and blame.

Cycles of violence

A further challenge to established discourses used to frame experiences of family violence comes from the intersections of age and gender in childhood. In thinking about either women-and-children or women vs. children, children appear as genderless subjects to be subsumed under the gendered, female and largely heterosexual mother. The CGP, for example, which was designed to run with children and young people from the ages of 4 to 16, was explicit about gender not being an important consideration in convening a primary-school-aged group. In the Canadian manual, it was argued that mixed sex groups for adolescents could be productive for addressing gender-related issues. In England, the advice given to London practitioners was to run same-sex groups for older children where possible. This disaggregation was seen as especially important for girls as it helped 'to create a safe environment for disclosing personal information' but left young men (over 16s) occupying an especially precarious position with regards to the possibilities and limits of support.

Younger and adolescent boys presented a source of anxiety for mothers. From those mothers we interviewed, some were concerned with the 'cycle of violence' theory, and their anxieties for their children unfolded along gender lines – with some women expressing concern that their sons would grow up to be violent (like their fathers). Some mothers hoped that the CGP might alter their sons' destinies without challenging the idea of 'violence as destiny':

> ...it was like my son was getting very, like, really arrogant behaviour, he was turning out just like his dad so I think, in a way, the groups really helped him. It's calmed him down a bit – but not as much as, you know, you'd expect (Beth, mother, lines 248–51).
>
> They've started mimicking the partners' behaviours and, you know, you're just not wanting that, you don't want the future to be a repeat of the past... (Doris, mother, line 260).

Findings from interviews with coordinators highlighted their difficulties in breaking from popular yet contentious theories of domestic violence such as the 'cycle of violence' theory. 'Cycle of violence' theories are problematic and are not espoused by the programme.[28] However, even where coordinators were aware of such problems they found it hard to deviate from the core metaphors provided by these theories:

> ...because I know that violence isn't automatically inter-generational...I see enough of it to know there's a greater propensity for children that have lived in violent homes...You knew the parents, and now the children are in the same service...Some of them you'd know as grandparents...So the cycle has to stop somewhere, doesn't it? (Coordinator, Area 16).

Such discourses, particularly if they invoke convenient and easily grasped – as well as evocative – images of a problem, such as the image of a cycle that needs to be broken, are hard to shift even when the nuances of experience are understood. This suggests that a new metaphor is necessary in order to re-imagine historical discourses on domestic violence that would allow a safe environment for adolescent boys in particular to address their anxieties, as well as their mothers' concerns for them.

Reinstating the everyday

A final creative junction to established discourses for thinking about domestic violence emerged in considering children's experiences of the programme. These experiences largely focused on the space the programme had given children to rehabilitate their 'everyday' lives. In recounting what they enjoyed the most about the programme, children and young people reported valuing their time on the programme because it provided a fun space and fun food.

Jenny: We hide from the parents.
MJ: Yeah, that was the best thing about it.
Cherry: We was 'hiii' [sic], at the end, yeah, when the parents came to get us we used to make all these hiding places and always hid in them.
Bugatti: We played hide and seek.
MJ: We should do that again! We should all hide from the parents! (lines 381–98)

Children placed much more importance on the experience of fun and being together than they did on the learning derived from the programme.[29] For us this was a reminder to be mindful of the multiple identities that children and their mothers occupy, which can be easily overlooked in simplistic, binary analyses of family violence. While seemingly banal observations, these reports can be read as an assertion of the value of everyday experiences themselves as important in providing sources of creativity and renewal.[30] Hiding (previous quotation), which for many children would have previously been a practice of protection (to hide from violence in the home), is rehabilitated to a more pleasurable and thrilling experience of childhood hide-and-seek and the mischievous teasing of mothers. Our findings are echoed in research by Nicky Stanley and colleagues on young people's experiences and perceptions of specialist domestic violence services, with those young people who took part in the NSPCC research reporting that youth spaces 'gave us a break, it let us be children... we never had a chance to be children'.[31] Children's experiences of the programme are an important reminder of the limitations of single identities (victim or witness, in this case) and the need for provisions that address children and women's multiple needs and identities.

Separate and connected

Historically the women's movement has been instrumental in creating the foundations for a responsive infrastructure to domestic violence and child abuse. Much of that early infrastructure revolved around the creation of refuges, or shelters, for 'battered women' – temporary accommodation that women could access in order to physically remove themselves from a violent relationship. Shelters were an important feminist intervention, and later institution, and remain an important physical and symbolic space of refuge for women leaving violent relationships. More recently, however, with the joining up of academic research and good practice, international bodies such as the Council of Europe[32] have advocated the need for a range of services in responding to domestic violence. These include helplines and shelters which offer immediate services, with 24-hour access to counselling and safe accommodation for women and children; early proactive services; short-term counselling and advocacy; trauma care and long-term support; and outreach work and mobile services.[33]

The CGP is, we believe, an example of a transitional moment in traditions of responding to domestic violence; a shift from responses that focused on an individual, liberal subject (the woman) to approaches that start to embrace what 'the maternal' means, namely a lifelong intersubjective and relational need to care and to be cared for.[34] By bringing children into the fold the opportunity arises to rethink a number of foundational assumptions underpinning support practices.

Our own evaluation, and large mixed-methods studies on children's experiences of domestic violence,[35] suggest that taking children's views seriously can open up new understandings of the emotional landscapes of family violence. The idea that guilt and blame, and the responsibilities those imply, may be the predominant emotional responses to violence experienced simplifies the affective assemblages of violence.[36] It also places specific demands on women to assume a status of victimhood and children to reflect vulnerability in order to be worthy of collective concern, intervention and support services.[37] Children and young people's responses to violence bring a family perspective to the fore, in that violence is perceived as an interaction between adults with varied consequences for children.

The persistent theory that violence is transmitted from fathers to sons, and a generalised anxiety about all men being perpetrators of violence, puts young men in an uncertain position, and can make access to support difficult. Boys' and young men's complex and nuanced understanding of themselves and their positions in the social world can be undermined by essentialised and binary understandings of gender.[38] Research evidence also suggests that the pathways for inter-generational transmission of violence are far from direct, often requiring the co-existence of neglect as well as multiple forms of abuse in a person's life history.[39] Persistent metaphors of the dynamics of violence can contribute to young men's precarity. In recognition of this AVA extended the provision of the programme up to 21 years of age, and developed an educational programme to address violence and abuse in teenage relationships. However, we are not sure to what extent this programme provides young men with the tools required to explore their own biographies and relationship patterns without being positioned as potential perpetrators.

Finally, listening to children's experiences of participating in social support provides an avenue for reframing the dominant identities ascribed and enacted to those affected by domestic violence. The children in both our evaluation and similar evaluations[40] interrupted dominant responses that focus on safety and protection, reminding us through their narratives of their agency and participation. The shift from women-only to 'the necessary struggle-in-relation' opens a space for theory and practice in family violence to go beyond the woman/mother-and-(genderless)-child couple relationship. In the final section of this chapter, we sketch out ways in which responses to family violence can be further complicated in the journey from individual and couple to family and community responses to violence.

Imagining complexity

The focus on children in violent homes/families has coincided with an international and national triptych of trends characteristic of knowledge-based economies in late modernity: the institutionalisation of the evidence-based (medicine) movement,[41] the rise in parenting cultures,[42] and the systematic dismantling of the welfare state under neoliberalism and austerity policies.[43] As such, we are at a point of witnessing a shift in the policy and practice landscape, from a framing of domestic violence and intimate partner violence as a 'woman-only' issue to a public child mental health issue.[44] At the same time calls have been made in the literature for a more meaningful integration between feminist, sociological and childhood studies approaches,[45] and a reimagining of the dynamics of, and responses to, experiences of domestic violence in order to generate new practices.

Given the shifting frameworks it is perhaps unsurprising that evaluation research finds that attempts for more holistic responses to domestic violence, both in terms of prevention and provision/intervention, are currently fragmented on the ground.[46] In the CGP the relational message given in the training was often at odds with the programme commitment to a 'gender-based analysis' of violence. At the same time, the practitioners' responses[47] suggest that the transitional moment that we are arguing the programme represents was well recognised. Practitioners identified the programme as providing children *and* mothers a start to recovery; the child-centred nature of the programme was well understood and in their accounts of the programme a number of the guiding principles, such as respecting and listening to children, were well articulated. Professionals also identified the programme as neither a parenting programme nor a woman abuse group, but, rather, something in between. Professionals varied in the extent to which they found the feminist theoretical underpinning of the programme useful for practice, and often drew on other bodies of knowledge (theoretical and policy) to make aspects of the programme theory more meaningful to them.

It is our argument in this chapter that the well-being of children *and* women can be improved when an attempt is made to work through the necessary tensions embodied in their relationship. Children and women are inevitably connected at the same time as also having separate cares and concerns. The next generation of responses to family violence needs to build on these emergent understandings of responses to domestic violence as a 'struggle-in-relation' in order to think about the broader contexts and ecologies in which violence takes place. In thinking about the plurality of relationships that are implicated and explicated in thinking about family violence, consideration also needs to be given to relationships beyond the heterosexual couple/family (partners; parent–child).

The need for such consideration is important for the well-being of all involved, but is most starkly illustrated in family relationships that do not conform to the normative conceptions that were embedded in the CGP model. Women's decisions to leave a violent relationship are multi-faceted (especially where a woman has children) and often involve multiple and complex considerations about her own and her children's safety, housing, finances, immigration status and access to legal information.[48] The most internationally comprehensive reviews of the research evidence on identifying and responding to domestic violence[49] suggest that advocacy, outreach and information services can play an important role in mediating a woman's decision to leave a violent relationship.

The CGP grappled with the tensions that many women experience between their rights and their society's cultural values.[50] For instance, the specific gender-based analysis of the CGP meant that, in a diverse city like London, which is home to a number of different communities, some women who were unable to leave the family home were not able to take part in the CGP. Children and women from Orthodox Jewish families, for example, often continued to live in the same home with the perpetrator even after they had officially split up. This is likely to be true for a number of women and children from cultural or religious backgrounds where multiple generations may live together in one house, or where perpetrators had modified their behaviours through perpetrator programmes.[51] Decisions to leave a family home are also dependent on structural constraints and possibilities. For example, in the UK, refuge spaces are under threat, and UKROL data suggests the England's refuge provision requires nearly 2,000 more spaces to meet Council of Europe Taskforce recommendations.[52] This means that while some women fleeing violence will be able to secure safe accommodation in a shelter, others will have to seek out alternatives (e.g. friends or family members) if possible, or continue living with violence until other options become available.

Burman argues that services for children are often good on provision and protection but not on participation.[53] While practices of children's participation have become more widespread in children's service provision across sectors in England, there has been a narrow focus on Article 12 of the UNCRC – and the elicitation of children's views in decisions that affect them – but less of a focus on trying to understand what matters to children beyond the confines of an institutional moment.[54] More programmes like the CGP need to be offered to children and young people, and the needs of young people who witness or experience domestic violence should be prioritised and listened to.

Analyses of violence need to move beyond the current models that rest on essentialised ideas about men and women, and that ignore the multiplicity of experiences and factors that might lead someone to experience violence. Support needs to go beyond the reification of the idea that being violent (for men) and experiencing violence (for women) are ontological realities. Instead, analyses need to consider the contextual elements of violence that are situated in relation to power dynamics that include but are not limited to gender. Perpetrator and victim are not ontological positions, and should not be imagined as such. There are fathers who have experienced violence at the hands of female or male partners, and mothers who have experienced violence in the context of a lesbian partnership. While these people may only represent a minority of those in violent relationships, they are not unimportant. Equally, recent research in perpetrator programmes[55] make clear that established interventions with violent men can lead to dramatic changes within relationships.

At the same time, further responses need to consider the complexities and challenges of 'intimate autonomy' and the complex dynamics of relating and separating.[56] A US survey on women who had experienced domestic violence showed that while respondents from the 90 DV programmes surveyed reported their primary needs as being largely met by existing provision, they nevertheless had some key unmet needs, namely economic support and help for perpetrators of domestic violence.[57] Women's concern for perpetrators is unsurprising given the complexities of intimate relationships, yet these concerns are rarely represented in research or practice. It has been suggested that the theoretical dominance of feminist and cognitive behavioural theories in framing research on domestic violence is partly responsible for such concerns being overlooked.[58] In the CGP there was some recognition of the complexity of intimate family relationships. A repeated relational message in the training was that violence was a *response* to a situation and not a personal attribute ('dad is not a violent person, he reacted violently'). Such a message allows for the possibility of change and transformation to apply to all, including potentially the perpetrator of violence, and needs to be further embraced in the provision of services.

Responding to family violence emerged as a political project built on women's communities.[59] We have argued that the CGP, and programmes like it, are emblematic of a crossroads in responses to domestic violence, an indication that the original political project is changing in response to social and cultural changes in how gender is understood and experienced. One of the analytical and practical challenges of carving up social problems in terms of demographic categories (young/old; male/female) and binary oppositions (victims/perpetrators) is that any gestalt between parts and wholes become severed. Haaken's analysis of the narratives that have framed the women's movement and the struggle to support women who have experienced domestic violence suggests a meaningful way of reintegrating parts and wholes. In her book, *Hard Knocks,* Haaken develops her arguments by engaging with the myths and counter-myths that have been historically employed to mobilise awareness and action against domestic violence. 'It takes two to tango' vs. 'men initiate ninety-five percent of incidents of couple violence' have for a long time framed knowledge of domestic violence. Original framings of women's experiences of domestic violence also largely ignored children.

Drawing on object-relations psychoanalytic thinking, Haaken argues that 'battered women have been valorized within feminism because they do bear – literally and symbolically – the collective injuries of women'.[60] She goes on to explain that, while completely understandable, such idealisation results in denying women the 'full range of [their] humanity'.[61] In other words, a 'battered woman' is not only positioned as a victim, but specific demands are placed on her victimhood in order for her to be a symbol that can mobilise collective action: she must, above all, be 'good' in order to be worthy of collective concern. A woman who feels anger, rage or violence herself is a challenging candidate for a symbol of collective mobilisation.

Haaken argues for the cultivation of a more 'depressive position' in response to domestic violence, a term that comes from a Kleinian object-relations school of thought and 'represents a movement beyond all-good and all-bad categories'. At the same time, recent feminist analyses of violence in other contexts have begun to reconceptualise violence as 'a dynamic relational process that produces docile bodies *and* complex intersectional subjectivities'.[62] Such analyses of violence and intervention as the one presented in this chapter have the capacity to instigate a movement towards more integrated and inclusive ethical responses to social problems that cut across age, gender, sexuality, class, and culture. Such analyses would enable a more dynamic and fluid model of family violence – and responses to it – to emerge, one that would place oppression and hierarchy at the centre of an analysis of *contexts* that produce violence,[63] moving past ontologically determined positions that rely on essentialist notions of age and gender alone.

NOTES

1. Janice Haaken, *Hard Knocks: Domestic Violence and the Psychology of Storytelling* (London: Routledge, 2010).
2. Sevasti-Melissa Nolas, Lucy Neville and Erin Sanders-McDonagh, *Evaluation of the Community Group Programme for Children & Young People: Final Report* (London: AVA, 2012), https://core.ac.uk/download/pdf/9551653.pdf.
3. Katherine Twamley, Rachel Rosen, and Berry Mayall, 'The (Im)possibilities of Dialogue across Feminism and Childhood Scholarship and Activism,' *Children's Geographies* (2016): 1–7, doi: 10.1080/14733285.2016.1227611.
4. Sevasti-Melissa Nolas, 'Towards a New Theory of Practice for Community Health Psychology,' *Journal of Health Psychology* 19, no. 1 (2014): 126–36.
5. The chapter deals exclusively with the issue of family violence as it affects heterosexual women who are mothers and their children. The issue of family violence towards children, such as child abuse, raises equally important questions about responses and social support; it is however beyond the scope of this chapter.
6. The term 'woman abuse' is frequently used in a North American service context to refer to violence perpetrated by a man against their female partner. It is often used interchangeably with the terms domestic violence and/or intimate partner violence. It usually signals a radical feminist analysis of patterns of violence. Susan Loosley et al., *Groupwork with Children Exposed to Woman Abuse: A Concurrent Group Program for Children and their Mothers. Children's Program Manual* (London, Ontario: The Community Group Program for Children Exposed to Woman Abuse, 2006). This manual is available from the Children's Aid Society of London and Middlesex, PO Box 7010, London, Ontario, Canada N5Y 5R8.
7. Loosley et al., *Groupwork with Children Exposed to Woman Abuse;* Peter G. Jaffe, David A. Wolfe and Susan Kaye Wilson, *Children of Battered Women* (Thousand Oaks, CA: Sage Publications, Inc., 1990); Audrey Mullender, 'Groups for Child Witnesses of Woman Abuse: Learning from North America', in *Children Living With Domestic Violence: Putting Men's Abuse of Women on the Child Care Agenda*, eds. Audrey Mullender and Rebecca Morley (London: Whiting & Birch Ltd., 1994), 187–212.
8. Women's Aid, *Domestic Abuse is a Gendered Crime* (Bristol, UK: Women's Aid, 2016), https://www.womensaid.org.uk/information-support/what-is-domestic-abuse/domestic-abuse-is-a-gendered-crime/.
9. Crime Survey for England and Wales, *Domestic Violence in England and Wales* (2016), http://researchbriefings.parliament.uk/ResearchBriefing/Summary/SN06337; Home Office, *Crime in England and Wales 2008/09: Volume 1, Findings from The British Crime Survey and Police Recorded Crime* (London: Home Office, 2009).
10. Michael S. Kimmel, '"Gender Symmetry" in Domestic Violence: A Substantive and Methodological Research Review,' *Violence Against Women* 8, no. 11 (2002): 1332–63.
11. Russell P. Dobash and R. Emerson Dobash, 'Women's Violence to Men in Intimate Relationships: Working on a Puzzle,' *British Journal of Criminology* 44, no. 3 (2004): 324–49.
12. Nolas, 'Towards a New Theory of Practice for Community Health Psychology'.
13. Amanda Holt, *Adolescent-to-Parent Violence: Current Understandings in Research, Policy and Practice* (Bristol: Policy Press, 2013).
14. Erica Burman, 'Beyond 'Women vs. Children' or 'Womenandchildren': Engendering Childhood and Reformulating Motherhood,' *The International Journal of Children's Rights* 16, no. 2 (2008): 177–94; Llobet and Milanich, this volume.
15. Burman, this volume.
16. Haaken, *Hard Knocks.*
17. Lisa Baraitser, *Maternal Encounters: An Ethic of Interruption,* (London: Routledge, 2009), 3.
18. Burman, this volume.
19. Haaken, *Hard Knocks.*
20. Sevasti-Melissa Nolas, 'Children's Participation, Childhood Publics and Social Change: A Review,' *Children & Society* 29, no. 2 (2015): 157–67.
21. Christopher M. Adams, 'The Consequences of Witnessing Family Violence on Children and Implications for Family Counselors,' *The Family Journal* 14, no. 4 (2006): 334–41; Hedy Cleaver, Ira Unell and Jane Aldgate. 'Child Abuse: Parental Mental Illness, Learning Disability, Substance Misuse and Domestic Violence.' Children's Needs-Parenting Capacity Series, 2nd

ed. (London: TSO, 2011); Holt, *Adolescent-to-Parent Violence;* Audrey Mullender and Rebecca Morley, eds, *Children Living With Domestic Violence: Putting Men's Abuse of Women on the Child Care Agenda* (London: Whiting & Birch, 1994); NICE, *Review of Interventions to Identify, Prevent, Reduce, and Respond to Domestic Violence* (London: NICE, 2013), https://www.nice.org.uk/guidance/ph50/resources/review-of-interventions-to-identify-prevent-reduce-and-respond-to-domestic-violence2; NICE, *Domestic Violence and Abuse [QA116],* (London: NICE, 2016), https://www.nice.org.uk/guidance/qs116; Nicky Stanley, *Children Experiencing Domestic Violence: A Research Review* (Totnes: RIP, 2011), https://www.safeguardingchildrenbarnsley.com/media/15486/domestic_violence_signposts_research_in_practice_-_july_2012.pdf.

22 Nolas, Neville and Sanders-McDonagh, *Evaluation of the Community Group Programme.*
23 Baraitser, *Maternal Encounters.*
24 Hilary Abrahams, *Supporting Women After Domestic Violence: Loss, Trauma and Recovery* (London: Jessica Kingsley Publishers, 2007); Jaffe, Wolfe and Wilson, *Children of Battered Women;* Loosley et al., 'Groupwork with Children Exposed to Woman Abuse'.
25 The evaluation used a mixed-methods research design using pre- and post-questionnaire measures and interviews with women-mothers and focus groups with children. Further details can be found in Nolas, Neville and Sanders-McDonagh, *Evaluation of the Community Group Programme.*
26 Marlies Sudermann, Larry Marshall and Susan Loosely, 'Evaluation of the London (Ontario) Community Group Treatment Programme for Children who have Witnessed Woman Abuse,' *Journal of Aggression, Maltreatment & Trauma* 3, no. 1 (2000): 127–46; Michael Sullivan, Marcia Egan and Michael Gooch, 'Conjoint Interventions for Adult Victims and Children of Domestic Violence: A Program Evaluation,' *Research on Social Work Practice* 14, no. 3 (2004): 163–70.
27 Audrey Mullender et al., *Children's Perspectives on Domestic Violence* (Thousand Oaks, CA: Sage, 2002), 149, 167.
28 Mullender and Morley, 'Children Living With Domestic Violence'.
29 Nolas, Neville and Sanders-McDonagh, *Evaluation of the Community Group Programme.*
30 Baraitser, *Maternal Encounters.*
31 Nicky Stanley et al., *Children and Families Experiencing Domestic Violence: Police and Children's Social Services' Responses* (London: NSPCC, 2010), https://www.nspcc.org.uk/globalassets/documents/research-reports/children-families-experiencing-domestic-violence-report.pdf: 65.
32 Elina Ruuskanen and Kauko Aromaa, *Administrative Data Collection on Domestic Violence in Council of Europe Member States* (Strasbourg: Council of Europe, 2008), https://www.coe.int/t/dg2/equality/domesticviolencecampaign/Source/EG-VAW-DC(2008)Study_en.pdf.
33 NICE, *Review of Interventions.*
34 Polona Curk, 'Maternal Studies: Beyond the Mother and the Child,' *Studies in the Maternal* 1, no. 1 (2009): 1–5, DOI: http://doi.org/10.16995/sim.163.
35 See e.g. Mullender et al., *Children's Perspectives on Domestic Violence.*
36 Rachelle Chadwick, 'Ambiguous Subjects: Obstetric Violence, Assemblage and South African Birth Narratives,' *Feminism & Psychology,* Online First 1 January 2017, DOI: https://doi.org/10.1177/0959353517692607
37 Haaken, *Hard Knocks.*
38 Stephen Frosh, Ann Phoenix and Rob Pattman, *Young Masculinities: Understanding Boys in Contemporary Society* (London: Palgrave Macmillan, 2001).
39 Vered Ben-David et al., 'The Association between Childhood Maltreatment Experiences and the Onset of Maltreatment Perpetration in Young Adulthood Controlling for Proximal and Distal Risk Factors,' *Child Abuse & Neglect* 46 (2015): 132–41; Richard Thompson, 'Exploring the Link between Maternal History of Childhood Victimization and Child Risk of Maltreatment,' *Journal of Trauma Practice* 5, no. 2 (2006): 57–72; Cathy Spatz Widom, Sally J. Czaja and Kimberly A. DuMont, 'Intergenerational Transmission of Child Abuse and Neglect: Real or Detection Bias?', *Science* 347, no. 6229 (2015): 1480–5; With thanks to Robbie Duschinsky (Cambridge) for the careful explanation and relevant references regarding the intergenerational transmission of violence and abuse (personal communication, 26 October 2015).
40 See e.g. Stanley et al., *Children and Families.*

41   Michael Little, *Proof Positive: 'Improving Children's Outcomes Depends on Systemizing Evidence-based Practice...'*, (London: Demos, 2010), http://www.demos.co.uk/files/Proof_positive_-_web.pdf?1288258385
42   Ellie Lee et al., *Parenting Culture Studies* (New York, NY: Springer, 2014).
43   Jill Rubery, 'Austerity and the Future for Gender Equality in Europe', *ILR Review* (2015), DOI: 0019793915588892.
44   Department of Health, *Improving Safety, Reducing Harm: Children, Young People and Domestic Violence – A Practical Toolkit for Front-line Practitioners* (London: Department of Health, 2009). http://webarchive.nationalarchives.gov.uk/20130107105354/http:/www.dh.gov.uk/prod_consum_dh/groups/dh_digitalassets/@dh/@en/@ps/documents/digitalasset/dh_116914.pdf; NICE, *Domestic Violence and Abuse [QA116]*; NICE, *Review of Interventions*; Panos Vostanis et al., 'Mental Health Problems and Social Supports among Homeless Mothers and Children Victims of Domestic and Community Violence,' *The International Journal of Social Psychiatry* 47, no. 4 (2000): 30–40.
45   Kristin L. Anderson, 'Gender, Status, and Domestic Violence: An Integration of Feminist and Family Violence Approaches,' *Journal of Marriage and the Family* 59, no. 3 (1997): 655–69.
46   Stanley, *Children Experiencing Domestic Violence*.
47   Nolas, Neville, and Sanders-McDonagh, *Evaluation of the Community Group Programme*.
48   NICE, *Review of Interventions*; Masemetse Baholo et al., Nicola Christofides, Anne Wright, Yandisa Sikweyiya, and Nwabisa Jama Shai, 'Women's Experiences Leaving Abusive Relationships: A Shelter-based Qualitative Study', *Culture, Health & Sexuality* 17, no. 5 (2015): 638–49; Abrahams, *Supporting Women After Domestic Violence*; Burman, 'Beyond "women vs. children" or "womenandchildren"'; Lorraine Radford and Marianne Hester, *Mothering Through Domestic Violence* (London: Jessica Kingsley Publishers, 2006).
49   NICE, *Review of Interventions*; Michaeljon Alexander-Scott, Emma Bell, and Jenny Holden, *Shifting Social Norms to Tackle Violence against Women and Girls (VAWG)* (London: DFID, 2016), https://www.gov.uk/government/uploads/system/uploads/attachment_data/file/507845/Shifting-Social-Norms-tackle-Violence-against-Women-Girls3.pdf.
50   Amy Borovoy and Kristen Ghodsee, 'Decentering Agency in Feminist Theory: Recuperating the Family as a Social Project,' *Women's Studies International Forum* 35, no. 3 (2012): 153–65.
51   For more on perpetrator programme efficacy see Liz Kelly and Nicole Westmarland, *Domestic Violence Perpetrator Programmes: Steps Towards Change*, Project Mirabal Final Report (2016), http://www.nr-foundation.org.uk/downloads/Project_Mirabal-Final_report.pdf.
52   In Women's Aid, *SOS: Save Refuges, Save Lives* (Bristol, UK: Women's Aid, 2015), accessed September 22, 2016, https://1q7dqy2unor827bqjls0c4rn-wpengine.netdna-ssl.com/wp-content/uploads/2015/11/SOS_Data_Report.pdf
53   Burman, 'Beyond "women vs. children" or "womenandchildren"'.
54   Nolas, 'Children's Participation, Childhood Publics and Social Change'.
55   Kelly and Westmarland, *Domestic Violence Perpetrator Programmes*.
56   Curk, 'Maternal Studies'.
57   Eleanor Lyon, Jill Bradshaw and Anne Menard, *Meeting Survivors' Needs through Non-residential Domestic Violence Services and Supports: Results of a Multi-state Study* (Washington, DC: National Institute of Justice, 2011, https://www.ncjrs.gov/pdffiles1/nij/grants/237328.pdf
58   NICE, *Review of Interventions*, 30.
59   Haaken, *Hard Knocks*.
60   Haaken, *Hard Knocks*, 58.
61   Haaken, *Hard Knocks*, 58.
62   Rachelle Chadwick, 'Ambiguous Subjects'.
63   Erin Sanders-McDonagh, Lucy Neville, and Sevasti-Melissa Nolas, 'From Pillar to Post: Understanding the Victimisation of Women and Children who Experience Domestic Violence in an Age of Austerity,' *Feminist Review* 112, no. 1 (2016): 60–76; Clegg, this volume.

17
Becoming-woman, becoming-child
A joint political programme

Ohad Zehavi

Solidarity

What better way to take up the issue at stake – the politics of women and children – than with Shulamith Firestone's 1970 *The Dialectic of Sex*? Not only is it a groundbreaking work of feminist thinking, it should also be regarded as a true milestone in the history of the politics of childhood, if only for its fourth chapter, 'Down with Childhood', which is dedicated exclusively to this cause. In this remarkable chapter Firestone juxtaposes and interrelates, unflinchingly and unapologetically, the political predicaments of both women *and* children, and lays out a joint revolutionary manifesto, famously proclaiming that 'we must include the oppression of children in any program for feminist revolution'.[1] Although Firestone is a common footnote in many essays concerned with the woman-and-child issue, her bold thought on the matter has generally not been thoroughly attended to, and insofar as it has been addressed it seems to have elicited rather negative responses.[2] Laura Purdy, for instance, who does look into the details of Firestone's argument in her 1988 essay 'Does Women's Liberation Imply Children's Liberation?', bluntly concludes that 'Firestone's thesis is wrong'.[3]

I beg to differ. In fact, I think that in dismissing Firestone's claims and proving them 'wrong', Purdy completely misconstrues the nature of Firestone's argument. For while Purdy's reflections are all couched in a liberal rights discourse (as illustrated, for instance, by the title of another paper in which she rejects Firestone's stance, 'Why Children Shouldn't Have Equal Rights'),[4] Firestone presents an incommensurably radical political view based on revolutionary Marxist thought, which undermines the very foundations of the common reflections on the proper way to treat children. It is therefore worthwhile to trace some of the basic tenets of Firestone's argument, and to appreciate its rhetorical force and vigour, before attending to her more discrete observations.

The polemical tone is set from the very start: 'Sex class is so deep as to be invisible.'[5] Sex is not merely a biological phenomenon; it is rooted in class conflict and calls for a class analysis. The division according to sex under patriarchy serves an oppressive regime, in which men dominate, exploit and subjugate women, just as under capitalism the bourgeoisie have dominated, exploited and subjugated the proletariat.[6] Indeed, for this purpose Firestone draws on Marx and Engels, mobilising their dialectical materialism and revolutionary drive into the sexual sphere. The aim of this analysis, and of this political programme, is not mere reforms that would ameliorate some superficial inequality (in fact, Firestone suggests that traditional categories of political thought would not apply to such an agenda, and could not be part of the solution for they are themselves part of the problem), but eradicating the class system – all class systems – altogether.[7] This, for her, is the task of a revolutionary feminism:

> [...] just as the end goal of socialist revolution was not only the elimination of the economic class *privilege* but of the economic class *distinction* itself, so the end goal of feminist revolution must be [...] not just the elimination of male *privilege* but of the sex *distinction* itself: genital differences between human beings would no longer matter culturally.[8]

Firestone's class analysis goes further than that. For, according to her, in contemporary society not only *sex* forms a class division, but so does *age*. This is a crucial link Firestone draws between femininity and childhood, one that must not be overlooked. Children, according to Firestone,[9] are an oppressed group just like women: 'children of every class *are* lower-class, just as women have always been'.[10] This oppression is brought about not only by the vast segregation of children, primarily (but not exclusively) by means of the education system, but also by children's economic dependency, by their constant subjection to external authority and by their overall disenfranchisement. And, according to Firestone, just as mere reforms would not suffice in the sexual sphere, they would not do so in the realm of age either, for 'our final step must be the elimination of the very conditions of femininity and childhood themselves'.[11] Firestone, who to a large extent bases her observations on childhood on Philippe Ariès's then recent and by now canonical account, draws from this historical analysis the crucial philosophical conclusion: that if 'childhood' is a mere contingency[12] – a historical, social construct – then we can, in principle, do away with it.[13] In other words, for Firestone both femininity and childhood are fabricated, constructed myths,[14] and since both myths serve as bases for oppressive social regimes they both should – and could – be eradicated. As a result we would no longer recognise a person as man or woman, adult or child, thus 'clearing the way for a fully "human" condition'.[15]

This is the gist of Firestone's polemics: she asks us to harness the radical thinking about the politics of femininity for the sake of thinking radically about the politics of childhood. However, Firestone's work does not only propose a theoretical thesis, but in this very process performs a political act in its own right. By including in a pioneering book concerned with the political status of women a long and detailed chapter devoted to the analysis of the political status of children, Firestone performs, in what should be regarded as a veritable speech act,[16] a keen performative gesture of solidarity with children.[17] This is no accident. 'Few men', she says, 'show any interest in children. And certainly not enough to include them in any books on revolution'.[18] It is up to feminist revolutionaries to do so, she says, so they would not miss an important substratum of oppression merely because it didn't directly concern them.[19] If women are to eradicate the class system into which they are thrust, they must also eradicate all class systems, starting with the prevailing yet somewhat unapparent class system subjugating the young.

Unschooling

Childhood is a myth. It is a contrived notion, historically produced and then 'naturalised' through various cultural practices and social institutions. And it is a class-forming myth, entailing daily acts of repression exerted on young people. Firestone wonders if the original myth, born in previous centuries, had not lost its force by the twentieth century, but concludes that on the contrary, its force had consistently grown and magnified.[20] But hasn't this tendency seen a radical shift in recent decades, with the growing attention given to children and the advent of potentially liberating technologies? Perhaps the most convincing testament to the fact that it has not, and that what we have witnessed is just more of the 'pseudo-emancipation' Firestone already acknowledged almost fifty years ago, is the persistent reality of the school, an institution whose hold on the lives of young human beings seems to be stronger than ever.

The modern school is, in essence, a place of incarceration. Although it is clearly less violent and brutal than the prison, it could be seen as much harsher and much less legitimate, for two main reasons. First, because of the scale of imprisonment involved: compulsory education *is* 'the great confinement' *par excellence*, to paraphrase Foucault,[21] who referred to the institutionalisation of the mad and other outcasts starting in the seventeenth century; it is a relentless and perpetual mass segregation and expulsion of the young from the rest of society. The second reason is that whereas the convicted criminal could be seen to have merited his or her imprisonment, the child is subject to a bitter physical detainment without any intrinsic justification: he or she is institutionalised due to the mere fact of being young of age, 'childness' being their only fault.

In Ivan Illich's seminal tract on deschooling he gives a phenomenological account of the school intended to unmask and uncover its true operations, and one of the main phenomena he scrutinises is the school's requirement of full-time attendance.[22] The school, Illich reminds us, is an institution that physically restricts the young for long hours, day after day, for many successive years, to a territory in which most of the rules of ordinary reality are suspended.[23] As a result, 'their chronological age disqualifies children from safeguards which are routine for adults in a modern asylum – madhouse, monastery, or jail'.[24] As Firestone observes, children are *forced* to go to school – in fact they spend most of their waking hours in the coercive structure of the school or doing homework for it.[25] The modern school, she reminds us, in its structural definition, exists to implement repression, the result of which is docility and servitude.[26] 'Young teachers entering the system idealistic about their jobs', Firestone says, 'suddenly are up against it: many give up in despair. If they had forgotten what a jail school was for them, it all comes back now. And they are soon forced to see that though there are liberal jails and not-so-liberal jails, by definition they are jails.'[27]

The benevolence of the school system and beatitude of the school years is just one childhood myth that needs to be deconstructed. Another one is that school is the exclusive site in which learning takes place. Again, Illich claims the complete opposite: the right to learn of most people, he says, 'is curtailed by the obligation to attend school'.[28] This is caused by the widely accepted but ultimately erroneous conflation of learning with teaching. As a matter of fact, he says, learning takes place everywhere and at any time, most of it casually and regardless of any authoritative attempt to dictate it.[29] Jacques Rancière reminds us that children learn from cradle without any teaching involved: they learn to walk and to talk without any set of rules or mandatory instructions.[30] But at some point this innate capacity to learn from the various encounters with the social and physical world seems to curiously disappear, at least in the eyes of adult society, and the young are told that they now must attend a special institution for the sake of learning.

This second myth, which Rancière calls 'the myth of pedagogy',[31] serves to legitimise, and further entrench, the subordination of the young. If learning is only the result of teaching and explication, as the myth goes, then compulsory education is warranted, and the school is vindicated. However, Rancière contends that any effort to conduct and instruct the unruly will of the child diminishes the child's powers, leading to what he calls 'enforced stultification'.[32] According to Firestone, the main result of compulsory education is 'retardation'.[33] The alternative is, in Rancière's view, emancipation: in order to achieve it, all that needs to be done is to ignite in the child the dormant will, and the rest will take care of itself. Firestone's programme is even simpler, and arguably even more emancipatory: 'The best way to raise a child', she says, 'is to LAY OFF'.[34]

But perhaps the ultimate and most harmful myth the school propagates is the very myth of childhood. 'If childhood was only an abstract concept', says Firestone, 'then the modern school was the institution that built it into reality'.[35] Illich seems to agree: 'If there were no age-specific and obligatory learning institution, "childhood" would go out of production', he says.[36] When the school groups people according to age, when it segregates the young from the rest of society, it produces childhood as such. The man-made distinction between adults and children – implying a difference not just in age, but in kind[37] – is produced by the man-made institution that designates a secluded space for the so-called child.

The school is not the sole producer of childhood, but it is definitely a major one. And not only does it contribute to the contrived construction of the child as such, it endows it with particular traits and attributes, which ultimately render the so-called child as an inferior being, justifying constant manipulation. When the young are routinely segregated within the boundaries of the school they are subjected to what Gilles Deleuze deems a process of 'infantilization',[38] which produces them as 'children', and the imposition of teaching and education within the confines of the school belittles them, producing them as weak and inferior. Education, under the auspices of the school, paints the young human being in the shades of incompetence. The severe initiation process embedded in the practice of schooling results in a systematic disrespect for and underestimation of the abilities of the young.[39] Even if we do not accept Firestone's claim that under such conditions 'childhood is hell',[40] one can reasonably claim, as Illich does, that many children are 'not at all happy playing the child's role',[41] in other words they do not enjoy the invention of childhood.

For children may find themselves in a constant conflict between, on the one hand, their sense of themselves and of their abilities, and on the other hand, the constrained role imposed on them by society.[42]

John Berger, in his poignant account of the gradual disappearance of animals from human life, has described the public zoo as a sad and ironic monument to the impossibility of encountering real animals.[43] In a similar vein one could argue that the school is a monument to the impossibility of encountering real young people, for all we see now is 'children', or rather 'schoolchildren',[44] which is a completely different species – a much more subdued, disciplined, domesticated creature than what young people can and should be.

Anti-Oedipus

In the third chapter of *The Dialectic of Sex*, titled 'Freudianism: The Misguided Feminism', Firestone turns Freud's theory on its head. She accepts the Oedipal structure that Freud evokes, according to which, crudely stated, the boy desires his mother and wishes to kill his father, but rather than seeing this as the mythological structure of the psyche, which each concrete child has to resolve individually, Firestone sees this structure as valid only in terms of power[45] – that is, as a political affair. According to her, the child's passions and drives are not innate, mythological dispositions of the mind; rather, they are engendered by the political structure – the power relations – the child encounters within the nuclear (heterosexual) family. The child (who in Freud is predominantly male) is not attracted to his mother as a consequence of an inescapable stage in the mythic Oedipal complex: his heart goes out to her out of sheer sympathy, in view of her stark powerlessness, which echoes his own. For the same reason he dislikes his father, who exhibits and exerts his dominating might. The child grows up in an oppressive climate. He is not oblivious to the hierarchy of power and authority, in which he occupies the lowest of ranks, but he can also sense other profound antagonisms and possible affinities:

> He knows that in every way, physically, economically, emotionally, he is completely dependent on, thus at the mercy of, his two parents, whoever they may be. Between the two of them, though, he will certainly prefer his mother. He has a bond with her in oppression: while he is oppressed by both parents, she, at least, is oppressed by one. The father, so far as the child can see, is in total control.[46]

Firestone observes that for the child, the nuclear family is not necessarily a haven of kinship and care as ideology has it, but could be a very polarised, aggressive and abusive realm. Freud, so the argument goes, recognised this fact, but relegated all the familial tumult and commotion to the unconscious, which allegedly functions within the boundaries of a mythological psychic structure. In doing so, Freud has unfortunately depoliticised the real workings of the family and relegitimised the established order, of which the nuclear family is a key functionary.

This is also the crux of Gilles Deleuze and Félix Guattari's argument in their provocative 1972 book *Anti-Oedipus*.[47] Firestone's and Deleuze and Guattari's combined reflections on the political role of the family in children's lives, against the backdrop of psychoanalytical theory, can perhaps be condensed into three main contentions. First, within the family the child is subordinated to his parents. This is performed by the most benign of gestures, starting with the very designation of certain individuals as 'father' and 'mother', or 'mom' and 'dad', a reiterated speech act that marginalises all other individuals and gives the crowned ones privilege and authority over the child, who is territorialised in his 'home' and made to revere his parents and obey their commands. Second, within the confines of his nuclear family home, the child is compelled to accept and internalise the oppressive dialectic of sex which he or she will one day 'naturally' come to embody and perpetuate. Third, the family is not only a place of unequal power relations (adult/child, man/woman), it is the place where power relations are forged and structured in the first place, as an alleged essence of human nature. In the family the child learns to accept and obey notions such as hierarchy, authority and domination. In this sense it is the initiating place of politics – the conflictual and contentious politics of dialectics. The best way to undermine these functions of the family must therefore be an anti-dialectical, anti-Oedipal way.

The girl

Jo Freeman recounts a telling tale from the late 1960s:

> At the August 1967 National Conference for New Politics a women's caucus met for days, but was told its resolution wasn't significant enough to merit a floor discussion. By threatening to tie up the convention with procedural motions the women succeeded in having their statement tacked to the end of the agenda. It was

never discussed. The chair refused to recognize any of the many women standing by the microphone, their hands straining upward. When he instead called on someone else to speak on 'the forgotten American, the American Indian,' five women rushed the podium to demand an explanation. But the chairman just patted one of them on the head (literally) and told her, 'Cool down, little girl. We have more important things to talk about than women's problems.'[48]

'The "little girl,"' Freeman goes on to say, 'was Shulamith Firestone, future author of *The Dialectic of Sex* [...], and she didn't cool down'.[49]

When Firestone sets the task for feminist revolutionaries to speak up for children as well, she designates those revolutionaries in parentheses as 'ex-child and still oppressed child-women'.[50] 'Little girls', as it turns out, are the living link between the subordination of women and the subordination of children. A pure coalescence of woman and child, they are the quintessential person to be undergoing both repressions. The patting on the head is indicative of this strong link and of this cunning oppression. In patriarchal, adult society both women and children are supposed to be 'cute', and this inherent 'cuteness' warrants a physical attitude towards the woman and the child that is both degrading ('Imagine this man's own consternation were some stranger to approach him on the street in a similar fashion – patting, gurgling, muttering baby talk')[51] and offensive, making resistance much more difficult than in the face of open and blunt oppression.[52]

But the 'little girl' is key to the link between feminism and the politics of childhood in another important sense. If femininity is a myth, then the person on whom this myth is first exercised, the person in whom it is engrained, is the (so-called) girl. Judith Butler explains that femininity is 'not the product of a choice, but the forcible citation of a norm, one whose complex historicity is indissociable from relations of discipline, regulation, punishment'.[53] The polymorphous child acquires a feminine subjectivity through various ideological interpellations,[54] starting with 'the initiatory performative, "It's a girl!"',[55] which is then followed by an infinite set of speech acts and material practices, from the room that awaits her through the toys and clothes she is offered to the multitude of instructions and prohibitions she is required to obey along the way. According to Gilles Deleuze and Félix Guattari, our body is stolen from us early on:

> This body is stolen first from the girl: Stop behaving like that, you're not a little girl anymore, you're not a tomboy, etc. The girl's becoming is stolen first, in order to impose a history, or prehistory,

upon her. The boy's turn comes next, but it is by using the girl as an example, by pointing to the girl as the object of his desire, that an opposed organism, a dominant history is fabricated for him too.[56]

The young girl is the site on which femininity is insistently constructed, until she can no longer deny it.[57] She is called on and taught to perform femininity, in order to become a proper woman – to facilitate her own submission to her impending lower-class status. In fact, children of both sexes are forced into a dualism machine, in which they are compelled to assume a subjectivity that is decisively either this or that. Moreover, according to Deleuze and Guattari, 'when the child sees itself reduced to one of the two sexes, masculine *or* feminine, it has already lost everything; man or woman already designates beings from whom *n* sexes have been stolen'.[58] Thus children of both sexes undergo a constant interpellation into their designated gender, having to forsake their polymorphous bodies, but out of this arbitrary dualism machine comes a well-defined class system, in which one gender dominates the other. So if the very condition of femininity is to be undone, as Firestone demanded, in order to do away with the class system which it perpetuates, then the girl must lead the way.

But note that the girl is subject to two simultaneous interpellations – at the same time as she is turned into a future woman, she is also turned into a present child. Childhood is a myth just like femininity, and the ideology of adulthood constantly interpellates the young, in a similar fashion to the workings of the patriarchal ideology – through speech acts (baby talk, quizzing, etc.), designated heterotopias (the school, of course, but also the playground, the toy store, and so on), and exclusive attitudes and gestures (like the patting on the head) specifically designed for the young. For one is not born a child, but becomes one.

The girl is the site on which both femininity *and* childhood are built. She should therefore play a pivotal role in any true revolutionary movement concerning women and children.[59]

Becoming

While feminism has been carried out in several successive waves, and has undeniably had a substantial (if not sufficient) impact, 'childism' is still awaiting its *first* wave.[60] While the feminist revolution is well underway, the corresponding revolution concerning children is yet to erupt. Perhaps this is because women have been more and more able to speak in their own voice, while children have had greater difficulty in gaining access to the public sphere. Firestone's concluding remark in her chapter on childhood is this: 'There are no children yet able to write their own books, tell their own story. We will have to, one last time, do it for them.'[61] This clearly sets the task for the revolutionary politician of childhood to theoretically and practically construct the means for children to speak out for themselves, in their own name, and be properly heard. It also asks us to be extremely cautious and self-critical in our political reflections on children: we should treat with immense suspicion the concepts that we habitually use whenever we regard children, as well as the concepts figuring in our conventional political vocabulary. This is not only in order to refrain from inflicting 'epistemic violence'[62] on the young, who are regarded through concepts that have not issued from them, but also in order to be aware of the position from which we are speaking – are we merely reproducing the established order and serving the powers that be, or are we enabling and enhancing revolutionary forces challenging the dominant and dominating norms?

Whose business is the business of feminism? And whose is the politics of childhood? In the material dialectics advocated by Firestone it might *appear* to be the business of women and the business of children respectively, each out to overthrow the class system dominating them: women of the world, unite! Children of the world, unite! But this crude and schematic dialectics seems to be both impractical – how would the children of the world be able to unite within such an elaborate social machine that effectively binds them both materially and ideologically to their inferior rank? – and conceptually dubious, for it collaborates with the very ideology (adult-man ideology?) that fabricates essences and paints everything in the bleak colours of antagonism and conflict. Does feminism, for instance, appeal to women alone? Or should it appeal to humans of both (or rather all) sexes, who are appalled by the power regimes in which they participate and reluctant to continue playing along with them?[63]

This is where the minoritarian politics of 'becoming' proposed by Deleuze and Guattari may come in handy. What is a minoritarian politics? It is a politics that intends to cater not for the ruling classes, but for minorities. What is a minority that a minoritarian politics should cater for? According to Deleuze and Guattari, 'when we say majority, we are referring not to a greater relative quantity but to the determination of a state or standard in relation to which larger quantities, as well as the smallest, can be said to be minoritarian: white-man, adult-male, etc. Majority implies a state of domination [...].'[64] Women and children, they say, are clearly minorities, deserving the minoritarian politics of becoming-woman, becoming-child;[65] and women first: 'It is perhaps the special situation of women in relation to the man-standard that accounts for the fact that becomings, being minoritarian, always pass through a becoming-woman.'[66] So the very first act of a minoritarian politics is 'becoming-woman', which is a rather vague notion, thought of in 'molecular' terms as the process of 'emitting particles [...] of a microfemininity, in other words, that produce in us a molecular woman'.[67] This microfemininity is constantly produced by those identified as women, but the political agent that is called on to become-woman is the so-called man: '[...] the subject in a becoming is always "man", but only when he enters a becoming-minoritarian that rends him from his major identity.'[68] The majority-oriented politics of women, fighting to win their own subjectivity within the macropolitics of conflict and contention, should be complemented by a minoritarian politics of (those identified as) men, who are asked to perform a metaphysical and political act of becoming that would not only dispossess them of their patriarchal privileges, but would also dismantle the very distinction between man and woman – the distinction on which patriarchy is constructed. For what is the act of becoming? It is a movement, but not from one clearly identified and stable point to another – say, from masculine to feminine – but rather a swift movement that 'passes *between* points, [...] comes up through the middle, [...] runs perpendicular to the points first perceived [...]',[69] and that sweeps both points along with it until they are no longer distinguishable, as they enter a zone of immense proximity and copresence.[70] It is a movement which is tangent to the dialectic, dissolving ostensible oppositions altogether. And just as the man is called on to become-woman, so is the adult – male or female – called on to become-child, a movement in which '"a" child coexists with us, in a zone of proximity or a block of becoming, on a line of deterritorialization that carries us both off'.[71] This minoritarian, anti-dialectical movement, creating such an intense contiguity between apparently separated entities that they become indistinguishable, should lead to a great affinity between groups of people and to intimate kinship between individuals – but one that does not derive from predetermined classifications and is free from power relations.

The body is stolen from both male and female children, resulting in two seemingly distinct sexes and the ensuing class system. It is a metaphysical theft, with political repercussions. The most profound way to politically overcome this dialectics is to metaphysically undo its basic tenets – it is for the (so-called) man to become-woman and disintegrate the concocted distinction on which privilege feeds. In the very same manner a presumed 'adult' must 'become-child' – forget that he or she is an 'adult', and forget that the young person is a 'child',[72] in order to stop performing or playing the role of the adult (the father, the teacher, etc.). In so doing, the adult relinquishes the fabricated authority that he or she has over other human beings just because they happen to be younger.

The notion of *becoming* is an ambiguous one, and Deleuze and Guattari's specific use of it is a rather peculiar one, and should be elucidated – particularly in its *becoming-child* conjunction.[73] First it should be noted that, while in common academic discourse regarding children, 'becoming' is usually contrasted with 'being' in designating the child as developing towards adulthood rather than a living presence,[74] for Deleuze and Guattari it is almost the other way around: 'becoming' denotes an individual's instantaneous ability to metamorphose into something that is radically different from their gradually evolving, well-determined 'being'. In fact, Deleuze and Guattari maintain that children are particularly prolific in becoming (attesting to every human's potentially immense ability to become, a capacity that is increasingly curbed and therefore tends to diminish): 'it is as though, independent of the evolution carrying them toward adulthood, there were room in the child for other becomings, "other contemporaneous possibilities" that are not regressions but creative involutions',[75] such as becoming-animal of all sorts. But note – and this is another important caveat – that in the political action of becoming-child advocated here it is not the child, but rather the adult, who is becoming (just as becoming-woman must be practiced, politically, by men). Becoming-child does not mean regressing to a childlike state or conjuring up your own childhood, and certainly not turning miraculously into a child. It means shedding off your contrived adult skin, so to speak – a productive forgetfulness allowing one to lose oneself, if only momentarily – so that a child can do away with its fabricated child skin. It is a political movement of an adult towards a child that wrests the latter from its child-being, and simultaneously the adult from its adult-being, so that the two can be, if only for a while, on truly equal terms.[76]

Becoming-child, if performed *en masse*, would unquestionably have substantial macropolitical consequences, such as disestablishing the school and reconfiguring society so as to accommodate the young more fairly. But becoming-child is essentially a micropolitical affair, taking place whenever an adult encountering a child becomes-child and does away with his or her prerogatives and presuppositions in order to let the youngster be – or rather become. This adult can be a teacher, a salesperson, a neighbour, a researcher, but perhaps most prominently a parent, who is set on de-Oedipalising familial relations and doing away, in an anti-dialectical fashion, with the dialectics of sex and age. Becoming is a concrete micropolitical action concerning concrete dominated individuals and taken by concrete cultural agents who habitually, and perhaps inadvertently, exercise class division and domination. And in a political programme concerned with women and children, girls – real, concrete girls – should be the focus. Girls are turned into women and into children, and thus are doubly subordinated, by real, material measures – by everyday utterances, gestures and rituals. To become-woman and to become-child – to become-girl, if you like – is to persistently fight off these old habits and refrain from exercising these measures. According to Deleuze and Guattari, 'Girls do not belong to an age group, sex, order, or kingdom; they slip in everywhere, between orders, acts, ages, sexes',[77] crossing right through the dualism machines out to grind them. To become-girl is therefore to set girls free from their culturally and perpetually determined roles, to let them keep slipping in between (and to let boys follow suit). It is to dissipate the presuppositions of femininity and childhood governing the encounter with another human being that only *appears* to be a girl.

The result of these minoritarian acts of becoming would not be a homogeneous society, where there is no apparent difference between individuals. On the contrary, the elimination of these exclusive differences should bring out an infinite abundance of differences, not subject to a priori transcendent categories such as male and female, adult and child, but liberated to form a multitude of contingent, dynamic, intensive relations between humans of all ages and all sexes.

NOTES

1. Shulamith Firestone, *The Dialectic of Sex: The Case for Feminist Revolution* (London: Jonathan Cape, 1971), 118.
2. These two features are clearly manifested, for example, in Barrie Thorne, 'Re-Visioning Women and Social Change: Where are the Children?' *Gender & Society* 1, no. 1 (1987): 105 (endnote 4).
3. Laura M. Purdy, 'Does Women's Liberation Imply Children's Liberation?' *Hypatia* 3, no. 2 (1988): 60.
4. Laura M. Purdy, 'Why Children Shouldn't Have Equal Rights,' *The International Journal of Children's Rights* 2 (1994): 223.
5. Firestone, *Dialectic of Sex*, 1.
6. This analogy, which is quite common in certain strands of feminist thinking, is of course rather crude. It has been contested both analytically and pragmatically (see e.g. Anna Pollert, 'Gender and Class Revisited: The Poverty of "Patriarchy",' *Sociology* 30, no. 4 [1996]: 639–59), and definitely deserves a more nuanced account, which cannot be given here. I do, however, wish to harness here its *programmatic* force.

7   Firestone, *Dialectic of Sex*, 12–3.
8   Firestone, *Dialectic of Sex*, 11–2.
9   Firestone, *Dialectic of Sex*, 81.
10 Firestone, *Dialectic of Sex*, 102.
11 Firestone, *Dialectic of Sex*, 118.
12 See Priscilla Alderson, *Young Children's Rights: Exploring Beliefs, Principles and Practice*, 2nd ed. (London and Philadelphia: Jessica Kingsley Publishers, 2008), 117.
13 Note that this conclusion does not depend on the veracity of Ariès's historical account, which has been contested since – see e.g. Stevi Jackson, 'Questioning the Foundations of Heterosexual Families: Firestone on Childhood, Love, and Romance,' in *Further Adventures of* The Dialectic of Sex: *Critical Essays on Shulamith Firestone*, ed. Mandy Merck and Stella Sandford (New York: Palgrave MacMillan, 2010), 115–6.
14 See e.g. Firestone, *Dialectic of Sex*, 99.
15 Firestone, *Dialectic of Sex*, 118.
16 J. L. Austin, *How to Do Things with Words* (London: Oxford University Press, 1962).
17 In this sense, I would argue, Firestone's book is much better read as a political manifesto (Gillian Howie, 'Sexing the State of Nature: Firestone's Materialist Manifesto,' in *Further Adventures of* The Dialectic of Sex: *Critical Essays on Shulamith Firestone*, ed. Mandy Merck and Stella Sandford [New York: Palgrave MacMillan, 2010], 216) – 'a fierce, funny, and outrageous exhortation to political change' (Mandy Merck and Stella Sandford, introduction to *Further Adventures of* The Dialectic of Sex: *Critical Essays on Shulamith Firestone*, ed. Mandy Merck and Stella Sandford [New York: Palgrave MacMillan, 2010], 2) that forges a world-changing fiction (Howie, 'Sexing the State of Nature,' 231) and exerts a poetic revolutionary force – than as an academic study inviting a hair-splitting critique of every single proposition (such as it undergoes in Jackson, 'Questioning the Foundations of Heterosexual Families'); all the more so with regards to its audacious attention to the politics of childhood.
18 Firestone, *Dialectic of Sex*, 118.
19 Firestone, *Dialectic of Sex*, 118.
20 Firestone, *Dialectic of Sex*, 103.
21 Michel Foucault, *Madness and Civilization: A History of Insanity in the Age of Reason*, trans. Richard Howard (London: Routledge, 2001).
22 Ivan Illich, *Deschooling Society* (New York: Harper & Row, 1972), 38.
23 Illich, *Deschooling Society*, 47.
24 Illich, *Deschooling Society*, 47.
25 Firestone, *Dialectic of Sex*, 112–3.
26 This, it should be stressed, is the overarching structural function of the school. This does not mean that there are no pertinent differences between various types of schools; and, more importantly, this of course does not take into account the myriad of ways (such as those described by Rachel Rosen in her conversation with Jan Newberry in this volume: 'through screams, silences, hiding, and more') in which children constantly resist, play with and thrive within school practices (and, obviously, beyond the school's premises), as all oppressed people do.
27 Firestone, *Dialectic of Sex*, 112. Following David Oldman ('Childhood as a Mode of Production,' in *Children's Childhoods Observed and Experienced*, ed. Berry Mayall [London: The Falmer Press, 1994], 164) one could argue further that the school does not only perform a crude subjugation of children: in the generational mode of production, which is interwoven into the complementary capitalistic and patriarchal modes, it is also a site of exploitation (in Marxist terms) of children's labour, manifested in their schoolwork (a manifestation of labour that is also analysed as such by Rachel Rosen and Jan Newberry in this volume). This occurs for the benefit of adults, such as teachers, who gain income from working with children – an economic abuse which ultimately serves the dominant classes in the other two modes, i.e. men.
28 Illich, *Deschooling Society*, iv.
29 Illich, *Deschooling Society*, 18.
30 Jacques Rancière, *The Ignorant Schoolmaster*, trans. Gregory Elliott (Stanford, CA: Stanford University Press, 1991), 5–6.
31 Rancière, *The Ignorant Schoolmaster*, 6.
32 Rancière, *The Ignorant Schoolmaster*, 7.
33 Firestone, *Dialectic of Sex*, 96, 102–3.
34 Firestone, *Dialectic of Sex* , 103.

35 Firestone, *Dialectic of Sex*, 92.
36 Illich, *Deschooling Society*, 41.
37 Firestone, *Dialectic of Sex*, 97.
38 Gilles Deleuze and Michel Foucault, 'Intellectuals and Power,' in Gilles Deleuze, *Desert Islands and Other Texts, 1953–1974*, ed. David Lapoujade, trans. Michael Taormina (New York: Semiotext(e), 2004), 209.
39 Firestone, *Dialectic of Sex*, 94.
40 Firestone, *Dialectic of Sex*, 117.
41 Illich, *Deschooling Society*, 40–1.
42 Illich, *Deschooling Society*, 41. And see Berry Mayall, 'Children in Action at Home and School,' in *Children's Childhoods Observed and Experienced*, ed. Berry Mayall (London: The Falmer Press, 1994), 123–4.
43 John Berger, 'Why Look at Animals?' in John Berger, *About Looking* (New York: Vintage Books, 1980), 21.
44 See Mayall, 'Children in Action,' 118.
45 Firestone, *Dialectic of Sex*, 53.
46 Firestone, *Dialectic of Sex*, 54–5. And see Ann Oakley, 'Women and Children First and Last: Parallels and Differences between Children's and Women's Studies,' in *Children's Childhoods Observed and Experienced*, ed. Berry Mayall (London: The Falmer Press, 1994), 19.
47 Gilles Deleuze and Félix Guattari, *Anti-Oedipus: Capitalism and Schizophrenia*, trans. Robert Hurley, Mark Seem and Helen R. Lane (Minneapolis: University of Minnesota Press, 1983).
48 Jo Freeman, 'On the Origins of Social Movement,' in *Waves of Protest: Social Movements Since the Sixties*, ed. Jo Freeman and Victoria Johnson (Lanham, MD: Rowman and Littlefield, 1999), 18–9.
49 Freeman, 'On the Origins of Social Movement,' 19.
50 Firestone, *Dialectic of Sex*, 118.
51 Firestone, *Dialectic of Sex*, 102.
52 Firestone, *Dialectic of Sex*, 101.
53 Judith Butler, 'Critically Queer,' *GLQ* 1 (1993): 23.
54 Louis Althusser, *Lenin and Philosophy, and Other Essays*, trans. Ben Brewster (New York: Monthly Review Press, 1971), 170.
55 Butler, 'Critically Queer,' 22.
56 Gilles Deleuze and Félix Guattari, *A Thousand Plateaus: Capitalism and Schizophrenia*, trans. Brian Massumi (Minneapolis: University of Minnesota Press, 2000), 276. For detailed accounts of Deleuze's notion of 'the girl' see e.g. Catherine Driscoll, 'The Little Girl,' in *Deleuze and Guattari: Critical Assessments of Leading Philosophers*, vol. 3, ed. Gary Genosko (New York: Routledge, 2001); Alicia Youngblood Jackson, 'Deleuze and the Girl,' *International Journal of Qualitative Studies in Education* 23, no.5 (2010).
57 Firestone, *Dialectic of Sex*, 60.
58 Gilles Deleuze et al., 'The Interpretation of Utterances,' in Gilles Deleuze, *Two Regimes of Madness: Texts and Interviews 1975-1995*, ed. David Lapoujade, trans. Ames Hodges and Mike Taormina (New York: Semiotext(e), 2006), 94.
59 The notion of 'the girl' figures prominently in a series of intellectual endeavours of the twentieth century, from Simone de Beauvoir's famous 1949 *The Second Sex* (trans. and ed. H.M. Parshley [London: Jonathan Cape, 1953], Part IV, Chapter II) to the more notorious 1999 *Preliminary Materials For a Theory of the Young-Girl* by Tiqqun (trans. Ariana Reines [Los Angeles: Semiotext(e), 2012]); for comprehensive accounts of this diverse and multifaceted trend see Catherine Driscoll, 'The Mystique of the Young Girl,' *Feminist Theory* 14, no. 3 (2013): 285–94; Jen Kennedy, 'The Young-Girl in Theory,' *Women & Performance: A Journal of Feminist Theory* 25, no. 2 (2015): 175–94. It is worth emphasising that in employing this notion here I draw on the more constructive and empowering versions of it, seeing the girl as the essential object of sexual division, leading eventually to sexual oppression, and therefore as the ultimate subject of potential defiance of and resistance to this very division and its ensuing oppression. It is also worth noting that I see the girl as simultaneously playing a similar part in relation to the generational division and to the consequent subordination of the young. Finally, 'the girl' for me is no mere abstraction: in fact, the micropolitics that I propose in the last section of this chapter calls on us to attend politically and ethically to the *concrete* human beings compelled to assume the role of 'the girl' but yet to fully comply with this demand.

60 On "childism" see John Wall, *Ethics in Light of Childhood* (Washington, DC: Georgetown University Press, 2010), 3.
61 Firestone, *Dialectic of Sex*, 118.
62 Gayatri Chakravorty Spivak, 'Can the Subaltern Speak?' in *Marxism and the Interpretation of Culture*, ed. Cary Nelson and Lawrence Grossberg (Urbana, IL: University of Illinois Press, 1988), 280ff.
63 It is worth noting that the female authors of the 1969 'Redstockings Manifesto', Firestone amongst them, 'call on all men to give up their male privilege and support women's liberation in the interest of our humanity and their own' (Robin Morgan, ed., *Sisterhood is Powerful: An Anthology of Writings from the Women's Liberation Movement* [New York: Vintage Books, 1970], 535).
64 Deleuze and Guattari, *Thousand Plateaus*, 291.
65 Although Deleuze and Guattari refer to a wide range of minorities that call for a minoritarian politics, women and children always seem to figure first (see e.g. Deleuze and Guattari, *Thousand Plateaus*, 291–4), suggesting that the sexual and generational divides are in their view somehow more fundamental. And while on a metaphysical level the ultimate aim of becoming is becoming-imperceptible (Deleuze and Guattari, *Thousand Plateaus*, 277), this process almost always starts with becoming-woman and becoming-child (see e.g. Deleuze and Guattari, *Thousand Plateaus*, 272–7), reaffirming women's and children's primacy in the philosophy of becoming.
66 Deleuze and Guattari, *Thousand Plateaus*, 291. While there is much debate among feminist scholars about the use of Deleuze and Guattari's politics for feminism, Pegalia Goulimari ('A Minoritarian Feminism? Things to do with Deleuze and Guattari,' in *Deleuze and Guattari: Critical Assessments of Leading Philosophers*, vol. 3, ed. Gary Genosko [New York: Routledge, 2001], 1486) has notably suggested that in placing becoming-woman at the forefront of their minoritarian politics, Deleuze and Guattari invite feminism to pave the way for other minoritarian movements, within and without the female realm.
67 Deleuze and Guattari, *Thousand Plateaus*, 275.
68 Deleuze and Guattari, *Thousand Plateaus*, 291.
69 Deleuze and Guattari, *Thousand Plateaus*, 293.
70 Deleuze and Guattari, *Thousand Plateaus*, 273.
71 Deleuze and Guattari, *Thousand Plateaus*, 294.
72 Deleuze and Guattari, *Thousand Plateaus*, 294.
73 For an elaborate explication of Deleuze and Guattari's notion of *becoming* see Ohad Zehavi, 'Minoracy,' trans. Nick John and Natalie Melzer, *Mafte'akh: Lexical Review of Political Thought*, 1st ed. (2010): 37–49.
74 See e.g. Oakley, 'Women and Children First and Last,' 23; Oldman, 'Childhood as a Mode of Production,' 155; Emma Uprichard, 'Children as "Being and Becomings": Children, Childhood and Temporality,' *Children & Society* 22 (2008): 303–13.
75 Deleuze and Guattari, *Thousand Plateaus*, 273. This might correspond with the notion of 'growing sideways' taken up in this volume by Erica Burman and by Rachel Thomson and Lisa Baraitser.
76 This rendering of becoming-child resonates with Rachel Thomson and Lisa Baraitser's wonderful reflections, in this volume, on maternity as a challenge to conventional thought that invites us to contemplate the possibility 'that a "person" could [...] potentially become two' and a 'child' can be thought of as 'potentially multiple, interdependent, a "fleshy continuity" emergent at the intersection of self and other'. This seems to me like an exemplary case of becoming-child, which Deleuze and Guattari allude to themselves, seeing mother and child as contemporaries, almost conjoined twins, contesting the notion of individual selves (see e.g. Deleuze and Guattari, *Anti-Oedipus*, 158; *Thousand Plateaus*, 164). However, rather than thinking of it as the potential of a person to become two I would suggest that we think of it as the potential of the alleged two to become one – an undifferentiated, shared entity that is patently manifested in pregnancy and nursing but that can emerge out of any becoming.
77 Deleuze and Guattari, *Thousand Plateaus*, 277.

18
Feminist intuitions in Peru's Movement of Working Children
A dialogue between Alejandro Cussianovich Villaran and Jessica Taft

> *Founded in 1976, Peru's movement of working children has for decades been organising for the well-being, rights, dignity and full social, political and economic inclusion of working children. Made up of several different organisations, including MANTHOC (Movimiento de Adolescentes y Niños Trabajadores Hijos de Obreros Cristianos) and MNNATSOP (Movimiento Nacional de Niños y Adolescentes Trabajadores Organizados del Perú), the movement involves around 10,000 working children and adolescents (NATs) and several hundred adult supporters (colaboradores). In addition to advocating for working children in local, national and international policy circles, the movement articulates and practices a model of intergenerational collaboration that challenges age-based hierarchies and seeks to create more egalitarian relationships between children and adults. In this dialogue, we consider the connections and disconnections between the movement of working children and feminism.*

Jessica: From my point of view, there appears to be a strong feminist influence within the movement's theories. The inclusion of household labour in the category of 'work' and the movement's pedagogical approach, which emphasises the political significance of building caring personal relationships, engaging with emotions as a site of critical knowledge, and practicing tenderness as a political act, all seem to me to have intellectual debts to feminist economic and political theory. But feminism, as a named concept or term, doesn't seem to come up very often in movement discussions. Do you (and others) see the movement as part of a feminist tradition? Why do you think the term 'feminism' is absent?

Alejandro: We have not had a systematic reflection on this topic, nor a sustained discussion of feminism in the movement. But there has also been an instinct and an orientation against gender discrimination, even when the children did not use that word, although they do use it more now. They and we would always say everyone is equal, everyone deserves respect, and both girls and boys have been and can be delegates and leaders in the movement. And there are certainly points of convergence with feminism that have come from the lived experiences of the women and girls who have been part of this movement.

Thinking back to the meetings of the Juventud Obrera Cristiana in Lima, during the period when MANTHOC was being formed, there were two sets of young people active in the movement. One was the workers, young men and young women, who had been recently fired because of their union organising and other political activity, and who were now unemployed. The other was organised domestic workers. The unemployed women had a view of themselves as active and equal parts in the union struggles. The women in the domestic workers group had many insights about how their work lives included experiences of discrimination and mistreatment as women.

Jessica: It seems to me that one of the points of convergence then, probably comes from these domestic workers, in terms of thinking about household labour, both paid and unpaid, as work. Is that right?

Alejandro: Yes, I remember one meeting, in the early 1970s, where a union leader told the domestic workers that they should all leave that employment and go work in the factories because domestic labour wasn't really work. One of the young women, an Afro-Peruvian, stood up and said: 'How can you say I don't work!?' The union leader responded with the line that it doesn't produce surplus value, and various things about labour and capital, etcetera. She responded that they produce time: time for others to do other labour, to produce other things, and so they produce surplus value indirectly. This didn't come from feminist theory, but it came from her experiences and her analysis of her experiences.

Jessica: And now, in the movement, children who work in their own households also see themselves as workers. They identify that labour, which produces time, as labour. Paid or unpaid, it is labour. I've had several young people say to me that they used to think of what they did as just 'helping out' but now they understand it as work.

Alejandro: The economists never count this labour; they don't think of it. It is invisible. So, one of the things the movement does encourage is for children to see their 'helping out' as labour, as work that is valuable, and as work that should be valued and respected. The form of their work may be helping out at home, caring for siblings and so on, but it is work.

Jessica: This is, for me, very clearly in line with feminist theories, as is the movement's attempt to bring children and children's issues into the public sphere, rather than treat them as private or domestic matters.

Alejandro: That also is a point of connection. There are elements of the history of women's movements and the pursuit of women's rights that are also reflected in the history of our movements and the pursuit of children's rights. But in our own history, while we have had moments of talking more directly about gender and about the particular experiences of women and girls, we have never really taken the time to think through these connections, to write out the history of these moments, or to name some of this knowledge as feminist or even as rooted in the perspectives of women and girls. I think about the young women from the movement who presented in 1979 at a conference in Mexico about women and liberation theology, who emphasised their subjectivity and agency not just as youth but as young women. And I think about the conversations we had about gender quotas in the 1990s, when many political groups and the government were all discussing these things, and when some girls in the movement initiated a big debate about whether or not we should also have quotas or if we should pursue gender equity in our leadership without forcing it in this manner. And the example I gave about producing time. But these stories of women and girls taking up these kinds of issues are not linked together in any of our reflections. So, there is a loss here, in having not written this story, not thought more systematically about these issues. It is unfortunate. Your questions make me wonder: how might our movement be different if we had done so? What might we have learned? How might we better understand our own dynamics and practices? What might our work look like today with this perspective?

There have not been very many people who participate in the movement who have identified themselves as feminists, or who have come to us with this particular lens. We have had lots of other direct influences and engagements with other sets of ideas, including decolonial theory, Indigenous politics, critiques of neoliberalism, class and labour politics, children's rights and human rights, but not so much with feminism. There have been indirect connections, certainly, but not as many direct relationships. And maybe that is because feminism here in Peru has been more associated with an elite, or maybe because feminist and women's groups, including the more popular, working-class ones, have concerns about engaging with working children in the way that we do, with a critical appreciation for their work – because the topic is so polemical, and it can seem risky or controversial for them to support this version of childhood, to say they support children's right to work. There have not been any conflicts or anything like that, but whatever the reasons, this has been a gap in our relationships.

Jessica: It seems to me, though, that in just the past two years the movement has become much more engaged in issues of gender and sexuality, participating in campaigns with Amnesty International around adolescents' sexual rights, and the #niunamenos march against violence against women and girls.

Alejandro: Yes, recently, some of this has begun to change. More of the girls in the movement are coming with a perspective of women's rights. We have also become much more involved with several new campaigns related to gender discrimination, violence against women and girls, and sexual rights. This has come from the NATs wanting to talk more about these issues, especially issues of relationships, sexual diversity and reproductive health, and from the *colaboradores* acknowledging that these things are an important part of the lives of the NATs in the movement. And also from people involved in these campaigns reaching out to us as they seek to build more relationships with organised children and adolescents. But there is much more work for us to do along these lines, places for us to grow and to continue to learn.

Bibliography

Abbott, Andrew. 'What Do Cases Do?' In *Time Matters: On Theory and Method.* Chicago: University of Chicago Press, 1992: 63–4.
Abebe, Tatek and Sharon Bessell. 'Dominant Discourses, Debates and Silences on Child Labour in Africa and Asia.' *Third World Quarterly* 32, no. 4 (May 2011): 765–86.
Abebe, Tatek. 'The Ethiopian 'Family Collective' and Child Agency.' *Barn*, no. 3 (2008): 89–108.
Abrahams, Hilary. *Supporting Women After Domestic Violence: Loss, Trauma and Recovery.* London: Jessica Kingsley Publishers, 2007.
Abu-Lughod, Lila. 'Do Muslim Women Really Need Saving? Anthropological Reflections on Cultural Relativism and Its Others.' *American Anthropologist* 3, no. 104 (2002): 783–90.
Adams, Christopher M. 'The Consequences of Witnessing Family Violence on Children and Implications for Family Counselors.' *The Family Journal* 14, no. 4 (2006): 334–41.
Ahmed, Sara. 'Identifications, Gender and Racial Difference: Moving Beyond a Psychoanalytical Account of Subjectivity.' In *Representations of Gender, Democracy and Identity Politics in Relation*, edited by Kumar Renuka, 288–302. New Delhi, India: Sri Satguru Publications, 1996.
Ahmed, Sara. *Strange Encounters: Embodied Others in Post-Coloniality.* London: Routledge, 2000.
Alanen, Julia. 'Shattering the Silence Surrounding Forced and Early Marriage in the United States.' *Children's Legal Rights Journal* 32, no. 2 (Summer 2012): 1–37. Available at: http://papers.ssrn.com/sol3/papers.cfm?abstract_id=2143910.
Alanen, Julia. 'Crafting a Competent Framework to Combat Forced Marriage.' *American Journal of Family Law* 30, no. 2 (2016): 1–14. Available at: http://papers.ssrn.com/sol3/papers.cfm?abstract_id=2752017.
Alanen, Leena. 'Explorations in Generational Analysis.' In *Conceptualising Adult-Child Relations*, edited by Leena Alanen and Berry Mayall, 11–22. London: RoutledgeFalmer, 2001.
Alanen, Leena. 'Generational Order.' In *The Palgrave Handbook of Childhood Studies*, edited by Jens Qvortrup, William Corsaro and Michael-Sebastian Honig, 159–74. Basingstoke: Palgrave MacMillan, 2011.
Alanen, Leena and Berry Mayall (eds). *Conceptualizing Child–Adult Relations*, London and New York: Routledge Falmer, 2001.
Alanen, Leena. 'Gender and Generation: Feminism and the "Child Question".' In *Childhood Matters*, edited by Jens Qvortrup, Marjatta Bardy, Giovanni Sgritta and Helmut Wintersberger, 27–42. Aldershot: Avebury, 1994.
Alasuutari, Maarit. 'Voicing the Child? A Case Study in Finnish Early Childhood Education.' *Childhood* 21, no. 2 (2014): 242–39.
Alderson, Priscilla. *Young Children's Rights: Exploring Beliefs, Principles and Practice.* Second Edition. London and Philadelphia: Jessica Kingsley Publishers, 2008.
Alexander, Kristine, Hudson Eagle Bear, Tesla Heavy Runner, Ashley Henrickson, Taylor Little Mustache, Amy Mack, Jan Newberry, et al. 'Translating Encounters: How a Transmedia Project Connects University Education with Early Childhood Education.' *Journal of Community Engagement and Higher Education* (in review).
Alexander, M. Jacqui and Chandra Talpade Mohanty. *Feminist Genealogies, Colonial Legacies, Democratic Futures.* Routledge: London and New York, 1997.
Alexander-Scott, Michaeljon, Emma Bell and Jenny Holden. *Shifting Social Norms to Tackle Violence against Women and Girls (VAWG).* London: DFID, 2016. https://www.gov.uk/government/uploads/system/uploads/attachment_data/file/507845/Shifting-Social-Norms-tackle-Violence-against-Women-Girls3.pdf

Alldred, Pam and Val Gillies. 'Eliciting Research Accounts: Re/producing Modern Subjects.' In *Ethics in Qualitative Research*, edited by Tina Miller, Maxine Birch, Melanie Mauthner and Julie Jessop, 146–65. London: Sage, 2002.

Althusser, Louis. *Lenin and Philosophy, and Other Essays*. Translated by Ben Brewster. New York: Monthly Review Press, 1971.

Amot, Ingvild and Borgunn Ytterhus. '"Talking Bodies": Power and Counter-power Between Children and Adults in Day Care.' *Childhood* 21, no. 2 (2014): 260–74.

Anderson, Bridget. 'Against Fantasy Citizenship: The Politics of Migration and Austerity.' *Renewal: a Journal of Labour Politics* 24, no. 1 (2016): 53–62.

Anderson, Kristin L. 'Gender, Status, and Domestic Violence: An Integration of Feminist and Family Violence Approaches.' *Journal of Marriage and the Family* 59, no. 3 (1997): 655–69.

Angulo-González, María Victoria and Mike Núñez Lozano. *Diagnóstico, políticas y acciones en relación con el desplazamiento forzado hacia Bogotá*. Bogotá: Secretaría de Hacienda Distrital, 2004.

Anzaldúa, Gloria E. *Borderlands/ La Frontera: The New Mestiza*. San Franscisco: Aunt Lute Books, 1987.

Aptel, Cécile. 'Child Slaves and Child Brides.' *Journal of International Criminal Justice* 14 (2016): 305–25.

Aradau, Claudia. 'The Perverse Politics of Four-Letter Words: Risk and Pity in the Securitisation of Human Trafficking.' *Millennium: Journal of International Studies* 33, no. 2 (2004): 251–77.

Archambault, Carolyn. 'Ethnographic Empathy and the Social Context of Rights. Rescuing Maasai Girls from Early Marriage.' *American Anthropologist* 113, no. 4 (2011): 632–43.

Arendt, Hannah. *On Revolution*. Harmondsworth: Penguin, 1990.

Austin, John. L. *How to Do Things with Words*. London: Oxford University Press, 1962.

Baholo, Masemetse, Nicola Christofides, Anne Wright, Yandisa Sikweyiya and Nwabisa Jama Shai. 'Women's Experiences Leaving Abusive Relationships: A Shelter-based Qualitative Study.' *Culture, Health & Sexuality* 17, no. 5 (2015): 638–49.

Bailey, Alison. 'Reconceiving Surrogacy: Toward a Reproductive Justice Account of Indian Surrogacy.' In *Globalization and Transnational Surrogacy in India: Outsourcing Life*, edited by Sanyantani DasGupta and Shamita Das Dasgupta, 23–44. Plymouth: Lexington Books, 2014.

Baird, Barbara. 'Child Politics, Feminist Analyses.' *Australian Feminist Studies* 23, no. 57 (2008): 291–305.

Bakker, Isabella and Rachel Silvey, eds. *Beyond States and Markets: The Challenges of Social Reproduction*. London: Routledge, 2008.

Balagopalan, Sarada. 'Constructing Indigenous Childhoods: Colonialism, Vocational Education and the Working Child.' *Childhood* 9 (2002): 19–34.

Balagopalan, Sarada. *Inhabiting 'Childhood': Children, Labour and Schooling in Postcolonial India*. London: Palgrave Macmillan, 2014.

Banerjee, Sumanta. *Dangerous Outcaste: The Prostitute in Nineteenth Century Bengal*. Kolkata: Seagull Books, 2000.

Banet-Weiser, Sarah. 'Am I Pretty or Ugly: Girl, Digital Media and the Economy of Visibility.' Paper presented at the Girlhood Studies and the Politics of Place: New Paradigms of Research Symposium, McGill Institute for Gender, Sexuality and Feminist Studies, Montreal, QC, 10–12 October 2012.

Baraitser, Lisa. 'Maternal Publics: Time, Relationality and the Public Sphere.' In *Critical Explorations through Psychoanalysis*, edited by Ayden Gulerce, 221–40. Basingstoke: Palgrave, 2011.

Baraitser, Lisa. *Maternal Encounters: The Ethics of Interruption*, London: Routledge, 2009.

Battersby, Christine. *The Phenomenal Woman: Feminist Metaphysics and the Patterns of Identity*. London: Polity Press, 1998.

Batthyani Dighiero, Karina. *Las políticas y el cuidado en América Latina. Una mirada a las experiencias regionales*. CEPAL: Serie Asuntos de Género 124, 2015.

Baylis, Françoise. 'Transnational Commercial Contract Pregnancy in India.' In *Family Making: Contemporary Ethical Challenges*, edited by Francois Baylis and Carolyn McLeod, 265–86. Oxford: Oxford University Press, 2014.

Beauvoir, Simone de. *The Second Sex*. Translated and edited by H.M. Parshley. London: Jonathan Cape, 1953.

Becker, Saul. 'Global Perspectives on Children's Unpaid Caregiving in the Family: Research and Policy on 'Young Carers' in the UK, Australia, the USA and Sub-Saharan Africa.' *Global Social Policy* 7, no. 1 (1 April, 2007): 23–50.

Beeson, Diane, Marcy Darnovsky and Abby Lippman. 'What's in a Name? Variations in Terminology of Third-Party Reproduction.' *Reproductive BioMedicine Online* 31 (2015): 805–14.
Ben-David, Vered, Melissa Jonson-Reid, Brett Drake and Patricia L. Kohl. 'The Association between Childhood Maltreatment Experiences and the Onset of Maltreatment Perpetration in Young Adulthood Controlling for Proximal and Distal Risk Factors.' *Child Abuse & Neglect* 46 (2015): 132–41.
Benhabib, Seyla. *Situating the Self*. Cambridge: Polity Press, 1992.
Benítez-Tobón, Jaime. *Por los niños de Colombia*. Medellín: Martín Vieco, 1995.
Benjamin, Jessica. *Like Subjects, Love Objects*. Princeton: Yale University Press, 1998.
Berger, John. 'Why Look at Animals?' In John Berger, *About Looking*. New York: Vintage Books, 1980.
Bhambra, Gurminder K. *Connected Sociologies*. London: Bloomsbury, 2014.
Bittman, Michael and Wajcman Judy. 'The Rush Hour: The Character of Leisure Time and Gender Equity.' *Social Forces* 79, no. 1 (2000): 165–89.
Blackman, Lisa, John Cromby, Derek Hook, Dimitris Papadopoulos and Valerie Walkerdine. 'Creating Subjectivities.' *Subjectivity* 22, no. 1 (2008): 1–27.
Boltanski, Luc. *Distant Suffering: Morality, Media and Politics*, Cambridge: Cambridge University Press, 1999.
Borda Carulla, Susana. 'L'enfant comme levier du développement: régulation sociale par les politiques sur l'enfance en Colombie'. *Autrepart* 4, no. 72 (2015): 23–40.
Borovoy, Amy and Kristen Ghodsee. 'Decentering Agency in Feminist Theory: Recuperating the Family as a Social Project.' *Women's Studies International Forum* 35, no. 3 (2012): 153–65.
Boyden, Jo. 'Childhood and the Policy Makers: A Comparative Perspective on the Globalisation of Childhood.' In *Constructing and Reconstructing Childhood: Contemporary Issues in the Sociological Study of Childhood*, edited by Allison James A. and Alan Prout, 187–226. London: The Falmer Press, 1997.
Boyden, Jo. 'Risk and Capability in the Context of Adversity: Children's Contributions to Household Livelihoods in Ethiopia.' *Children, Youth and Environments* 19, no. 2 (2009): 111–37.
Boyden, Jo and Neil Howard. 'Why Does Child Trafficking Policy Need to Be Reformed? The Moral Economy of Children's Movement in Benin and Ethiopia.' *Children's Geographies* 11, no. 3 (2013): 354–68.
Boyden, Jo, Birgitta Ling and William Myers. *What Works for Working Children?* Stockholm: Radda Barnen, 1998.
Bragg, Joanna, Erica Burman, Anat Greenstein, Terry Hanley, Afroditi Kalambouka, Ruth Lupton, Lauren McCoy, Kate Sapin and Laura Winter. *The Impacts of the 'Bedroom Tax' on Children and Their Education: A Study in the City of Manchester*. Manchester: Manchester Institute of Education, University of Manchester, 2015. http://www.seed.manchester.ac.uk/research/poverty-and-social-justice/bedroom-tax/
Bray, Rachel, and Andrew Dawes. 'Parenting, Family Care and Adolescence in East and Southern Africa: An Evidence-Focused Literature Review.' *Discussion Paper 2016-02*. Office of Research – Innocenti: UNICEF, 2016.
Bray, Rachel. 'Who Does the Housework? An Examination of South African Children's Working Roles.' *Social Dynamics* 29, no. 2 (December 2003): 95–131.
Brazier, Chris. 'Special Edition: War and Peace in Western Sahara.' *The New Internationalist*, no. 297 (1997).
Brennan, Samantha. 'The Goods of Childhood and Children's Rights.' In *Family Making: Contemporary Ethical Challenges*, edited by Françoise Baylis and Carolyn McLeod, 26–46. Oxford: Oxford University Press, 2014.
Brisenden, Simon. 'A Charter for Personal Care.' *Progress* 16 (1989).
Brisky, Zana and Ross Kaufmann, dirs. *Born into Brothels*. 2004; New York: THINKFilm.
Burawoy, Michael. 'For Public Sociology.' *American Sociological Review* 70 (2005): 4–28.
Burman, Erica. 'Beyond "Women Vs. Children" or "Womenandchildren": Engendering Childhood and Reformulating Motherhood.' *International Journal of Children's Rights* 16, no. 2 (2008): 177–94.
Burman, Erica. 'Conceptual Resources for Questioning Child as Educator.' *Studies in Philosophy and Education* 32, no. 3 (2013): 229–43.
Burman, Erica. *Developments: Child, Image, Nation*. London: Routledge, 2008.
Burman, Erica. 'From Subjectification To Subjectivity In Educational Policy Research Relationships'. In *Discursive Perspectives on Education Policy and Implementation*, edited by Jessica Nina Lester, Chad R. Lochmiller and Rachael E. Gabriel. New York: Palgrave, in press.

Burman, Erica. 'Innocents Abroad: Western Fantasies of Childhood and the Iconography of Emergencies.' *Disasters* 18, no. 3 (1994): 238–53.
Burman, Erica. 'Local, Global or Globalized? Child Development and International Child Rights Legislation.' *Childhood* 3 (1996): 45–66.
Burman, Erica, Anat Greenstein, Afroditi Kalambouka and Kate Sapin. 'Subjects of, or Subject to, Policy Reform? A Foucauldian Discourse Analysis of Regulation and Resistance in UK Narratives of Educational Impacts of Welfare Cuts – The Case of the "Bedroom Tax"'. *Education Policy Analysis Archives* (in press).
Burman, Erica and Jackie Stacey. 'The Child and Childhood in Feminist Theory.' *Feminist Theory* 11, no. 3 (2010): 227–40.
Butler, Judith. 'Critically Queer.' *GLQ* 1 (1993): 17–32.
Butler, Judith, Zeynep Gambetti and Leticia Sabsay. *Vulnerability in Resistance*. Durham: Duke University Press, 2016.
Cantwell, Nigel. 'Are Children's Rights Still Human?'. In *The Human Rights of Children: From Visions to Implementation*, edited by Jane Williams and Antonella Invernizzi. Farnham: Ashgate, 2011.
Caputo, Virginia. 'Children's Participation and Protection in a Globalized World: Reimagining "Too Young to Wed" Through a Cultural Politics of Childhood.' *International Journal of Human Rights* 21, no. 1 (2017): 76–88.
Carbin, Maria and Sara Edenheim. 'The Intersectional Turn in Feminist Theory: A Dream of a Common Language?' *European Journal of Women's Studies* 20 no. 3 (2013): 233–48.
Castañeda, Claudia. 'The Child as a Feminist Figuration: The Case for a Politics of Privilege.' *Feminist Theory* 2, no. 1(2010): 29–53.
Castillo-Cardona, Carlos, Nelson Ortiz-Pinilla and Alejandra Gonzalez-Rossetti. *Los hogares comunitarios de bienestar y los derechos del niño: el caso colombiano*. Innocenti Occasional Papers, Child Rights Series 3. Florence: Unicef, 1993.
Chabari, Alphaxard and Eva Palmqvist. 'Violence against Children in Southern Sudan: A Participatory Study on PHP, Sexual Abuse and Early and Forced Marriage.' *Save the Children Sweden*, 1997. Available at: http://resourcecentre.savethechildren.se/sites/default/files/documents/1403.pdf
Chadwick, Rachelle. 'Ambiguous Subjects: Obstetric Violence, Assemblage and South African Birth Narratives.' *Feminism & Psychology,* Online First, 1 January 2017. DOI: https://doi.org/10.1177/0959353517692607
Chase, Elaine and Robert Walker. 'The Co-construction of Shame in the Context of Poverty: Beyond a Threat to the Social Bond.' *Sociology* 47, no. 4 (2012): 739–54.
Chen, Xiaobei. 'The Birth of the Child-victim Citizen.' In *Reinventing Canada: Politics of the 21st century,* edited by Janine Brodie and Linda Trimble, 189–202. Toronto: Prentice-Hall, 2003.
Cheney, Kristen E. 'Conflicting Protectionist and Empowerment Models of Children's Rights: Their Consequences for Uganda's Orphans and Vulnerable Children.' In *Children's Lives in an Era of Children's Rights: The Progress of the Convention on the Rights of the Child in Africa*, edited by Afua Twum-Danso Imoh and Nicola Ansell, 17–33. New York: Routledge, 2014b.
Cheney, Kristen E. 'Executive Summary of the International Forum on Intercountry Adoption and Global Surrogacy.' In *ISS Working Paper Series* No. 596. The Hague, Netherlands: International Institute of Social Studies of Erasmus University, 2014c.
Cheney, Kristen E. 'Giving Children a "Better Life"? Reconsidering Social Reproduction and Humanitarianism in Intercountry Adoption.' *European Journal of Development Research* 26, no. 2 (2014): 247–63.
Cheney, Kristen E. 'Global Rights Discourse, National Developments, and Local Childhoods: Dilemmas of Childhood and Nationhood in Uganda, East Africa.' In *Histoires d'enfant, histoires d'enfance, Tome I: Civilisation (GRAAT No. 36, June 2007) Histoire de l' Education*, edited by Rosie Findlay and Sébastien Salbayre. Tours, France: Presses Universitaires François Rabelais, 2007.
Cheney, Kristen E. 'Malik and His Three Mothers: Aids Orphans' Survival Strategies and How Children's Rights Translations Hinder Them.' In *Reconceptualizing Children's Rights in International Development: Living Rights, Social Justice, Translations*, edited by Karl Hanson and Olga Nieuwenhuys, 152–72. Cambridge: Cambridge University Press, 2013.
Cheney, Kristen E. *Pillars of the Nation: Child Citizens and Ugandan National Development*. Chicago: University of Chicago Press, 2007.
Cho, Sumi, Kimberlé Williams Crenshaw and Leslie McCall. 'Towards a Field of Intersectionality Studies: Theory, Applications, Praxis.' *Signs* 38, no. 4 (2013): 785–810.

Christensen, Pia Haudrup. 'Childhood and the Cultural Constitution of Vulnerable Bodies.' In *The Body, Childhood and Society*, edited by Alan Prout and Jo Campling. London: Macmillan, 2000.

Cleaver, Hedy, Ira Unell and Jane Aldgate. 'Child Abuse: Parental Mental Illness, Learning Disability, Substance Misuse and Domestic Violence.' Children's Needs-Parenting Capacity Series. 2nd ed. London: TSO, 2011.

Cloud, Dana L. 'To Veil the Threat of Terror: Afghan Women and the <Clash of Civilizations> in the Imagery of the US War on Terrorism.' *Quarterly Journal of Speech* 90, no. 3 (2004): 285–306.

Cockburn, Tom. 'Children and the Feminist Ethic of Care.' *Childhood* 12, no. 1 (2005): 71–89.

Colen, Shellee. '"Like a Mother to Them": Stratified Reproduction and West Indian Childcare Workers and Employers in New York.' In *Conceiving the New World Order: The Global Politics of Reproduction*, edited by Faye D. Ginsburg and Rayna Rapp. Berkeley: University of California Press, 1995.

Collard, David. 'Generational Transfers and the Generational Bargain.' *Journal of International Development* 12, no. 4 (2000): 453–62.

Colley, Helen. 'Learning to Labour with Feeling: Class, Gender and Emotion in Childcare Education and Training.' *Contemporary Issues in Early Childhood* 7, no. 1 (2006): 15–29.

Collins, Catherine Ruth, Damien W. Riggs and Clemence Due. 'Constructions of the "Best Interests of the Child" in New South Wales Parliamentary Debates on Surrogacy.' In *Reframing Reproduction: Conceiving Gendered Experiences*, edited by Meredith Nash, 39–53. London: Palgrave Macmillan UK, 2014.

Committee on Economic, Social and Cultural Rights. *Consideration of reports submitted by States parties under article 16 and 17 of the Convenant: Concluding observations of the Committee on Economic, Social and Cultural Rights: Colombia*, E/C.12/115/12, 1995.

Cornock, Marc and Heather Montgomery. 'Children's Rights in and out of the Womb.' *The International Journal of Children's Rights* 19, no. 1 (2011): 3–19.

Cornwall, Andrea. 'Myths to Live By? Female Solidarity and Female Autonomy Reconsidered.' *Development and Change* 38, no. 1 (2007): 149–68.

Crafter, Sarah, Lindsay O'Dell, Guida de Abreu and Tony Cline. 'Young Peoples' Representations of "Atypical" Work in English Society.' *Children & Society* 23, no. 3 (2009): 176–88.

Crawshaw, Marilyn, Patricia Fronek, Eric Blyth and Andy Elvin. 'What Are Children's "Best Interests" in International Surrogacy? A Social Work Perspective from the UK.' In *Babies for Sale? Transnational Surrogacy, Human Rights and the Politics of Reproduction*, edited by Miranda Davies, 163–84. London: Zed Books, 2017.

Crenshaw, Kimberlé. Williams. 'Mapping the Margins: Intersectionality, Identity Politics, and Violence against Women of Color.' *Stanford Law Review* (1991), 1241–99.

Cresswell, Mark and Helen Spandler. 'The Engaged Academic: Academic Intellectuals and the Psychiatric Survivor Movement.' *Social Movement Studies* 12, no. 2 (2013): 138–54.

Crime Survey for England and Wales. *Domestic Violence in England and Wales* (2016). http://researchbriefings.parliament.uk/ResearchBriefing/Summary/SN06337

Crivello, Gina. '"There's No Future Here": The Time and Place of Children's Migration Aspirations in Peru.' *Geoforum* 62 (2015): 38–46.

Crivello, Gina and Elena Fiddian-Qasmiyeh. 'The Ties that Bind: Sahrawi Children and the Mediation of Aid in Exile.' In *Deterritorialized Youth: Sahrawi and Afghan Refugees at the Margins of the Middle East*, edited by Dawn Chatty, 85–118. Oxford: Berghahn Books, 2010.

Crivello, Gina, Virginia Morrow and Emma Wilson. 'Young Lives Longitudinal Qualitative Research. A Guide for Researchers.' Technical Note 26. Oxford: Young Lives, 2013.

Crivello, Gina, Vu Thi Thanh Houng and Uma Vennam. 'Gender, Agency and Poverty: Children's Everyday Experiences in Andhra Pradesh and Vietnam.' In *Growing Up in Poverty: Findings from Young Lives*, edited by Michael Bourdilllon and Jo Boyden. New York: Palgrave Macmillan, 2014.

Curk, Polona. 'Maternal Studies: Beyond the Mother and the Child.' *Studies in the Maternal* 1, no. 1 (2009): 1–5. DOI: http://doi.org/10.16995/sim.163

Darling, Marsha J. Tyson. 'A Welfare Principle Applied to Children Born and Adopted in Surrogacy.' In *Globalization and Transnational Surrogacy in India: Outsourcing Life*, edited by Sanyantani DasGupta and Shamita Das Dasgupta, 157–78. Plymouth: Lexington Books, 2014.

Darling, Marsha Tyson. 'What About the Children? Citizenship, Nationality and the Perils of Statelessness.' In *Babies for Sale? Transnational Surrogacy, Human Rights and the Politics of Reproduction*, edited by Miranda Davies, 185–203. London: Zed Books, 2017.

Darnovsky, Marcy and Diane Beeson. 'Global Surrogacy Practices.' In *ISS Working Paper Series* No. 601. The Hague, Netherlands: International Institute of Social Studies of Erasmus University, 2014.

DasGupta, Sanyantani and Shamita Das Dasgupta, eds. *Globalization and Transnational Surrogacy in India: Outsourcing Life*. Plymouth: Lexington Books, 2014.

Davies, Miranda, ed. *Babies for Sale? Transnational Surrogacy, Human Rights and the Politics of Reproduction*. London: Zed Books, 2017.

Day, Caroline. 'Education and Employment Transitions: The Experiences of Young People with Caring Responsibilities in Zambia.' In *Labouring and Learning. Geographies of Children and Young People*, edited by Tatek Abebe, Johanna Waters and Tracey Skelton. Singapore: Springer, 2015.

de Beauvoir, Simone. *The Second Sex* (Trans. H. M. Parshley). Harmondsworth: Penguin, 1972.

Delannoy, Pierre. 'Le Cauchemar des Mariages Forcés.' *Paris Match International*, 1 (September 2012). Available at http://www.parismatch.com/Actu/International/Le-cauchemar-des-mariages-forces-160402

Deleuze, Gilles and Michel Foucault. 'Intellectuals and Power.' In Gilles Deleuze, *Desert Islands and Other Texts, 1953–1974*, edited by David Lapoujade and translated by Michael Taormina, 206–13. New York: Semiotext(e), 2004.

Deleuze, Gilles and Félix Guattari. *A Thousand Plateaus: Capitalism and Schizophrenia*. Translated by Brian Massumi. Minneapolis: University of Minnesota Press, 2000.

Deleuze, Gilles and Félix Guattari. *Anti-Oedipus: Capitalism and Schizophrenia*. Translated by Robert Hurley, Mark Seem and Helen R. Lane. Minneapolis: University of Minnesota Press, 1983.

Deleuze, Gilles, Félix Guattari, Claire Parnet and André Scala. 'The Interpretation of Utterances.' In Gilles Deleuze, *Two Regimes of Madness: Texts and Interviews 1975–1995*, edited by David Lapoujade and translated by Ames Hodges and Mike Taormina, 89–112. New York: Semiotext(e), 2006.

Dempsey, Deborah and Fiona Kelly. 'Transnational Third-Party Assisted Conception: Pursuing the Desire for "Origins" Information in the Internet Era.' In *Babies for Sale? Transnational Surrogacy, Human Rights and the Politics of Reproduction*, edited by Miranda Davies, 204–17. London: Zed Books, 2017.

Department of Health. *Improving Safety, Reducing Harm: Children, Young People and Domestic Violence – A Practical Toolkit for Front-line Practitioners*. London: Department of Health (2009). http://webarchive.nationalarchives.gov.uk/20130107105354/http:/www.dh.gov.uk/prod_consum_dh/groups/dh_digitalassets/@dh/@en/@ps/documents/digitalasset/dh_116914.pdf

Dobash, Russell P. and R. Emerson Dobash. 'Women's Violence to Men in Intimate Relationships: Working on a Puzzle.' *British Journal of Criminology* 44, no. 3 (2004): 324–49.

Doezema, Jo. *Sex Slaves and Discourse Masters: The Construction of Trafficking*. London: Zed Books, 2010.

Dresser, Ian. 'Psychological Homelessness: A Clinical Example.' *Journal of Social Work Practice* 1, no. 4 (1985): 67–76.

Driscoll, Catherine. 'The Little Girl.' In *Deleuze and Guattari: Critical Assessments of Leading Philosophers*, vol. 3, edited by Gary Genosko, 1464–79. New York: Routledge, 2001.

Driscoll, Catherine. 'The Mystique of the Young Girl.' *Feminist Theory* 14, no. 3 (2013): 285–94.

Dutta, Debolina and Oishik Sircar, dirs. *We Are Foot Soldiers*. 2011; New Delhi: Public Service Broadcasting Trust.

Edelman, Lee. *No Future: Queer Theory and the Death Drive*. Duke University Press: Durham and London, 2004.

Edwards, Adrian. 'Global Forced Displacement Hits Record High.' UNHCR News and Stories, 20 June 2016. http://www.unhcr.org/uk/news/latest/2016/6/5763b65a4/global-forced-displacement-hits-record-high.html

Edwards, Rosalind, Val Gillies and Nicola Horsley. 'Brain Science and Early Years Policy: Hopeful Ethos or "Cruel Optimism"?' *Critical Social Policy* 35, no. 2 (2015), 167–87.

Ekman, Kajsa Ekis. *Being and Being Bought: Prostitution, Surrogacy, and the Split Self*. North Melbourne, Victoria, Australia: Spinifex Press, 2013.

Ekman, Kajsa, Linn Hellerström and The Swedish Women's Lobby. 'Swedish Feminists Against Surrogacy.' In *Babies for Sale? Transnational Surrogacy, Human Rights and the Politics of Reproduction*, edited by Miranda Davies, 298–309. London: Zed Books, 2017.

Elder Jr., Glen H. 'Time, Human Agency, and Social Change: Perspectives on the Life Course.' *Social Psychology Quarterly* 57, no. 1 (1994): 4–15.

Enloe, Cynthia. 'Womenandchildren: Propaganda Tools of Patriarchy.' In *Mobilizing Democracy: Changing the U.S. Role in the Middle East*, edited by Greg Bates, 29–32. Monroe, ME: Common Courage Press, 1991.

Ennew, Judith. 'Time for Children or Time for Adults?' In *Childhood Matters: Social Theory, Practice and Politics*, edited by Jens Qvortrup, Marjatta Bardy, Giovanni Sgritta and Helmut Wintersberger. Aldershot: Avebury, 1994.

Erel, Umut, Jin Haritaworn, Encarnación Gutiérrez Rodríguez and Christian Klesse. 'On the Depoliticisation of Intersectionality Talk: Conceptualising Multiple Oppressions in Critical Sexuality Studies.' In *Theorizing Intersectionality and Sexuality,* edited by Yvette Taylor, Sally Hines and Mark E. Casey, 56–77. Basingstoke: Palgrave Macmillan, 2010.

Es-Sweyih, Mohamed-Fadel. *El Primer Estado del Sahara Occidental*. Translated by Nathanaël Raballand and Carmen Astiaso. Tindouf: Sahrawi Arab Democratic Republic, 2001.

Esquivel, Valeria. 'What Is a Transformative Approach to Care, and Why Do We Need It?' *Gender & Development* 22, no. 3 (October 29, 2014): 423–39.

Ettinger, Bracha L. *The Matrixial Borderspace*, Minneapolis and London: University of Minnesota Press, 2006.

Evans, Ruth. 'Children's Caring Roles and Responsibilities within the Family in Africa.' *Geography Compass* 4, no. 10 (2010): 1477–96.

Evans, Ruth and Saul Becker. *Children Caring for Parents with HIV and AIDS: Global Issues and Policy Responses*. Bristol: The Policy Press, 2009.

Evans, Ruth and Felicity Thomas. 'Emotional Interactions and an Ethics of Care: Caring Relations in Families Affected by HIV and AIDS.' *Emotions, Space and Society* 2 (2009): 111–19.

Everingham, Christine. 'Engendering Time: Gender Equity and Discourses of Workplace Flexibility.' *Time & Society* 11, no. 2/3 (2002): 335–51.

Ferguson, James. *The Anti-Politics Machine: Development, Depoliticization and Bureaucratic Power in Lesotho* (Cambridge: Cambridge University Press, 1990).

Fiddian-Qasmiyeh, Elena. 'Gender and Forced Migration.' In *The Oxford Handbook of Refugee and Forced Migration Studies*, edited by Elena Fiddian-Qasmiyeh, Gil Loescher, Katy Long and Nando Sigona. Oxford: Oxford University Press, 2014.

Fiddian-Qasmiyeh, Elena. 'Histories of Displacement: Intersections between Ethnicity, Gender and Class.' *Journal of North African Studies* 16, no. 1 (2011): 31–48.

Fiddian-Qasmiyeh, Elena. 'Representing Sahrawi Refugee's 'Educational Displacement' to Cuba: Self-sufficient Agents or Manipulated Victims in Conflict?' *Journal of Refugee Studies* 22, no. 3 (2009): 323–50.

Fiddian-Qasmiyeh, Elena. *South-South Educational Migration, Humanitarianism and Development: Views from the Caribbean, North Africa and the Middle East*. Oxford: Routledge, 2015.

Fiddian-Qasmiyeh, Elena. *The Ideal Refugees: Gender, Islam and the Sahrawi Politics of Survival*. New York: Syracuse University Press, 2014.

Fiddian-Qasmiyeh, Elena. 'Transnational Abductions and Transnational Jurisdictions? The Politics of "Protecting" Female Muslim Refugees in Spain.' *Gender, Place and Culture* 21, no. 2 (2014): 174–94.

Firestone, Shulamith. *The Dialectic of Sex: The Case for Feminist Revolution*. London: Jonathan Cape, 1971.

First Nations Child and Family Caring Society. 'I Am a Witness.' https://fncaringsociety.com/i-am-witness

Fisk, Robert. 'Remaining Issues.' *London Review of Books* (23 February 1995): 13–16.

Folbre, Nancy. 'Who Cares? A Feminist Critique of the Care Economy.' New York: Rosa Luxemburg Stiftung, 2014.

Folbre, Nancy. 'The Care Economy in Africa: Subsistence Production and Unpaid Care.' *Journal of African Economies* 23, no. supp. 1 (6 February 2014): i128–56.

Ford Foundation. '2011 Annual Report on Child Marriage.' Available at: http://www.fordfoundation.org/2011-annual/youth-sexuality-and rights/map/#/married-by-18/Afghanistan

Forum on Marriage and the Rights of Women and Girls. 'Early Marriage: Whose Right to Choose?' 2000. Available at: www.crin.org/docs/resources/publications/ WhoseRighttoChoose.pdf

Foucault, Michel. *Madness and Civilization: A History of Insanity in the Age of Reason*. Translated by Richard Howard. London: Routledge, 2001.

Foucault, Michel. 'The Political Technology of Individuals'. In *Technologies of the Self: A Seminar with Michel Foucault Technologies of the Self*, edited by Luther H. Martin, Huck Gutman and Patrick H. Hutton, 145–62. London: Tavistock, 1988.

Fraser, Nancy. 'Struggle over Needs: Outline of a Socialist-Feminist Critical Theory of Late-Capitalist Political Culture.' In *Women, the State, and Welfare*, edited by Linda Gordon, 199–225. Madison: University of Wisconsin Press, 1990.

Freeman, Elizabeth. *Time Binds: Queer Temporalities, Queer Histories*. Durham and London: Duke University Press, 2010.

Freeman, Jo. 'On the Origins of Social Movement.' In *Waves of Protest: Social Movements Since the Sixties*, edited by Jo Freeman and Victoria Johnson, 7–24. Lanham, MD: Rowman and Littlefield, 1999.

Frosh, Stephen and Lisa Baraitser. 'Psychoanalysis and Psychosocial Studies.' *Psychoanalysis, Culture & Society* 13, no. 4 (2008): 346–65.

Frosh, Stephen, Ann Phoenix and Rob Pattman. *Young Masculinities: Understanding Boys in Contemporary Society*. London: Palgrave Macmillan, 2001.

García-Mendez, Emilio. 'De las relaciones públicas al neomenorismo: 20 años de Convención Internacional de los Derechos del Niño en América Latina (1989–2009).' *Revista Criminología, de Cuadernos de Doctrina y Jurisprudencia Penal* 7, no. 2 (2010): 587–619.

Gayen, Swapna. 'Nightmares on Celluloid.' *The Telegraph*, 15 March 2005. Available at https://www.telegraphindia.com/1050315/asp/opinion/story_4491793.asp.

Geinger, Freya, Michel Vandenbroeck and Griet Roets. 'Parenting as a Performance: Parents as Consumers and (De)constructors of Mythic Parenting and Childhood Ideals.' *Childhood* 21, no. 4 (2014): 488–501.

Gershuny, Jonathan. *Changing Times: Work and Leisure in Postindustrial Society*. Oxford: Oxford University Press, 2000.

Ghosh, Shohini, dir. *Tales of the Night Fairies*. 2002; New Delhi: Mediastorm Collective.

Gibb, Kenneth. 'The Multiple Policy Failures of the UK Bedroom Tax.' *International Journal of Housing Policy* 15, no. 2 (2015): 148–66.

Gillies, David. 'Agile Bodies: A New Imperative in Neoliberal Governance.' *Journal of Education Policy* 26, no. 2 (2011): 207–23.

Gilligan, Carol. *In a Different Voice: Psychological Theory and Women's Development*. Cambridge, MA: Harvard University Press, 1982.

Gillis, John. 'Transitions to Modernity.' In *The Palgrave Handbook of Childhood Studies*, edited by Jens Qvortrup, William Corsaro and Michael-Sebastian Honig. Basingstoke: Palgrave MacMillan, 2011.

Gilman, Charlotte Perkins. *Herland*. New York: Pantheon Books, 1915.

Gilman, Charlotte Perkins. *Concerning Children*. Walnut Creek, CA: AltaMira Press, 2003 (first published 1900).

Girls Not Brides Campaign. 'What Is the Impact?' http://www.girlsnotbrides.org/what-is-the-impact.

González Ramírez, J.-.L. and I. M. Durán. 'Evaluar para mejorar: el caso del programa Hogares Comunitarios de Bienestar del ICBF.' *Desarrollo y Sociedad*, no. 69 (2012): 187–234.

Goodman, Lisa A., Leonard Saxe and Mary Harvey. 'Homelessness as Psychological Trauma: Broadening Perspectives.' *American Psychologist* 46, no. 11 (1991): 1219–25.

Gordon, Linda. 'The Perils Of Innocence, Or What's Wrong With Putting Children First.' *Journal of the History of Childhood and Youth* 1, no. 3 (2008): 331–50.

Goulimari, Pegalia. 'A Minoritarian Feminism? Things to do with Deleuze and Guattari.' In *Deleuze and Guattari: Critical Assessments of Leading Philosophers*, vol. 3, edited by Gary Genosko, 1480–503. New York: Routledge, 2001.

Greenstein, Anat. *Radical Inclusive Education: Disability, Teaching and Struggles for Liberation*. Hove: Routledge, 2016.

Greenstein, Anat, Erica Burman, Afroditi Kalambouka and Kate Sapin. 'Construction and Deconstruction of "'Family" by the "Bedroom Tax"', *British Politics* 11, no. 4 (2016): 508–25.

Gupta, Ruchira, dir. *Selling of Innocents*. 1996; Toronto: Associated Producers Ltd.

Haaken, Janice. *Hard Knocks: Domestic Violence and the Psychology of Storytelling*. London: Routledge, 2010.

Hague Conference on Private International Law, 'A Study of Legal Parentage and the Issues Arising from International Surrogacy Arrangements.' 96. The Hague, Netherlands: Hague Conference on Private International Law Permanent Bureau, 2014.

Hague Conference on Private International Law. 'The 1993 Hague Convention on Protection of Children and Co-Operation in Respect of Intercountry Adoption.' The Hague, Netherlands: Hague Conference on Private International Law, 1993.

Hague Conference on Private International Law, 'The Parentage/Surrogacy Project: An Updating Note.' 16. The Hague, Netherlands: Hague Conference on Private International Law Permanent Bureau, 2015.

Harrell-Bond, Barbara E. *Imposing Aid: Emergency Assistance to Refugees*. Oxford: Oxford University Press, 1986.

Harrell-Bond, Barbara E. 'The Experience of Refugees as Recipients of Aid'. In *Refugees: Perspectives on the Experience of Forced Migration*, edited by Alastair Ager, 136–68. London: Pinter, 1999.

Harrell-Bond, Barbara E. *The Struggle for the Western Sahara*. Hanover: American Universities Field Staff, 1981.

Held, Jacob M. 'Marx Via Feuerbach: Species-Being Revisited.' *Idealistic Studies* 39, no. 1/3 (2009): 137–48.

Held, Virginia. 'The Meshing of Care and Justice.' *Hypatia* 10, no. 2 (2017): 128–32.

Helleiner, Jane. 'Toward a Feminist Anthropology of Childhood.' *Atlantis* 24, no. 1 (1999): 27–38.

Help Refugees. 'Latest Calais Census,' 24 August 2016. http://www.helprefugees.org.uk/2016/08/24/latest-calais-census/

Hennessy, Rosemary. *Profit and Pleasure: Sexual Identities in Late Capitalism*. New York: Routledge, 2000.

Herreño-Hernández, Ángel Libardo. *No hay derecho... Las madres comunitarias y jardineras frente al derecho laboral*. Bogotá: ILSA, 1999.

Hewitson, Gillian. 'The Commodified Womb and Neoliberal Families.' *Review of Radical Political Economics* 46, no. 4 (2014): 489–95.

Hirsch, Eric D. Jr. *New Dictionary of Cultural Heritage*. 4th ed. Boston, MA: Houghton Mifflin Harcourt, 2005.

Hodges, Tony. *The Western Saharans*. London: Minority Rights Group, 1984.

Hodges, Tony. *Western Sahara: The Roots of a Desert War*. Westport: Lawrence Hill, 1983.

Högbacka, Riitta. 'Intercountry Adoption, Countries of Origin, and Biological Families.' In ISS Working Paper Series No. 598. The Hague, Netherlands: International Institute of Social Studies of Erasmus University, 2014.

Höijer, Birgitta. 'The Discourse of Global Compassion: The Audience and Media Reporting of Human Suffering.' *Media Culture and Society* 26, no. 4 (2004): 513–31.

Holt, Amanda. *Adolescent-to-Parent Violence: Current Understandings in Research, Policy and Practice*. Bristol: Policy Press, 2013.

Home Office. *Crime in England and Wales 2008/09: Volume 1, Findings from The British Crime Survey and Police Recorded Crime*. London: Home Office, 2009.

Hood-Williams, John. 'Patriarchy for Children: On the Stability of Power Relations in Children's Lives.' In *Childhood, Youth, and Social Change. A Comparative Perspective*, edited by Lynne Chisholm, Peter Brüchner, Heinz-Hermann Krüger and Phillip Browne, 155–71. New York: The Falmer Press, 1990.

Howie, Gillian. 'Sexing the State of Nature: Firestone's Materialist Manifesto.' In *Further Adventures of* The Dialectic of Sex: *Critical Essays on Shulamith Firestone*, edited by Mandy Merck and Stella Sandford, 215–34. New York: Palgrave MacMillan, 2010.

Huffpost Politics (blog). 'John Baird's Speech To The United Nations: Full Text Of Speech Delivered At The UN October 1st, 2012.' *Huffington Post*, 1 October 2012, http://www.huffingtonpost.ca/2012/10/01/john-bairds-speech-united-nations-text_n_1928907.html

Illich, Ivan. *Deschooling Society*. New York: Harper & Row, 1972.

Jackson, Alicia Youngblood. 'Deleuze and the Girl.' *International Journal of Qualitative Studies in Education* 23, no. 5 (2010): 579–87.

Jackson, Stevi. 'Questioning the Foundations of Heterosexual Families: Firestone on Childhood, Love, and Romance.' In *Further Adventures of* The Dialectic of Sex: *Critical Essays on Shulamith Firestone*, edited by Mandy Merck and Stella Sandford, 113–41. New York: Palgrave MacMillan, 2010.

Jacobs, Jerry A. and Kathleen Gerson. *The Time Divide: Work, Family, and Gender Inequality*. Cambridge, MA: Harvard University Press, 2004.

Jadva, Vasanti, Lucy Blake, Polly Casey and Susan Golombok. 'Surrogacy Families 10 Years On: Relationship with the Surrogate, Decisions over Disclosure and Children's Understanding of Their Surrogacy Origins.' *Human Reproduction* 27, no. 10 (2014): 3008–14.

Jaffe, Peter, Susan Wilson, and David A. Wolfe. 'Promoting changes in attitudes and understanding of conflict resolution among child witnesses of family violence.' *Canadian Journal of Behavioural Science* 18, no. 4 (1986): 356–66.

Jaffe, Peter G., David A. Wolfe and Susan Kaye Wilson. *Children of Battered Women*. Thousand Oaks, CA: Sage Publications, Inc, 1990.

Jain, Neha. 'Forced Marriage as a Crime against Humanity.' *Journal of International Criminal Justice* 6 (2008): 1013–32.

James, Allison, Chris Jenks and Alan Prout. *Theorizing Childhood*. Cambridge: Polity, 1998.

James, Allison and Alan Prout. *Constructing and Reconstructing Childhood*. London and New York: Routledge, 1990, 1997, 2015.

Kabeer, Naila. 'Intergenerational Contracts, Demographic Transitions and the "Quantity-Quality" Trade-off: Children, Parents and Investing in the Future.' *Journal of International Development* 12, no. 4 (2000): 463–82.

Kallio, Kirsi Pauliina and Jouni Häkli. 'Are There Politics in Childhood?'. *Space and Polity* 15, no. 1 (2011): 21–34.

Kandiyoti, Deniz. 'Political Fiction Meets Gender Myth: Post-conflict Reconstruction, "Democratisation" and Women's Rights.' *IDS Bulletin* 35, no. 4 (2004): 134–6.

Kandiyoti, Deniz. 'Bargaining with Patriarchy.' *Gender and Society* 2, no. 3 (1988): 274–90.

Kapur, Ratna. *Erotic Justice: Law and the New Politics of Postcolonialism*. Ranikhet: Permanent Black, 2005.

Katz, Cindi. 'Cultural Geographies Lecture: Childhood as Spectacle: Relays of Anxiety and the Reconfiguration of the Child.' *Cultural Geographies* 15, no. 1 (2008): 5–17.

Katz, Cindi. 'On the Grounds of Globalization: A Topography for Feminist Political Engagement.' *Signs: Journal of Women in Culture and Society* 26, no. 4 (2001): 1213–34.

Katz, Cindi. 'Towards Minor Theory', *Environment and Planning D: Society and Space* 14 (1996): 487–99.

Katz, Cindi. 'Vagabond Capitalism and the Necessity of Social Reproduction.' *Antipode* 33, no. 4 (2001): 709–28.

Kelly, Liz and Nicole Westmarland. *Domestic Violence Perpetrator Programmes: Steps Towards Change*. Project Mirabal Final Report (2016). http://www.nr-foundation.org.uk/downloads/Project_Mirabal-Final_report.pdf

Kelsh, Deborah P. 'The Pedagogy of Excess.' *Cultural Logic: Marxist Theory & Practice* (2013): 137–56.

Kennedy, Jen. 'The Young-Girl in Theory.' *Women & Performance: A Journal of Feminist Theory* 25, no. 2 (2015): 175–94.

Kilkey, Majella and Diane Perrons. 'Gendered Divisions in Domestic-Work Time. The Rise of the (Migrant) Handyman Phenomenon.' *Time and Society* 19, no. 2 (2010): 239–64.

Kimmel, Michael S. '"Gender Symmetry" in Domestic Violence: A Substantive and Methodological Research Review.' *Violence Against Women* 8, no. 11 (2002): 1332–63.

Kittay, Eva Feder. *Love's Labor: Essays on Women, Equality, and Dependency*. New York: Routledge, 1999.

Koffman, Ofra and Ros Gill. '"The Revolution Will Be Led by a 12-year-old Girl": Girl Power and Global Biopolitics.' *Feminist Review* 105, no. 1 (2013): 83–102.

Kofman, Eleonore. 'Gendered Migrations, Social Reproduction and the Household in Europe.' *Dialectical Anthropology* 38, no. 1 (2014): 79–94.

Krawiec, Kimberley D. 'Price and Pretense in the Baby Market.' In *Baby Markets: Money and the New Politics of Creating Families*, edited by Michele B. Goodwin, 41–55. Cambridge: Cambridge University Press, 2010.

Kristeva, Julia. 'Women's Time'. *Signs* 7, no. 1 (1981): 13–35.

Kumar, Manasi. 'The Poverty in Psychoanalysis: "Poverty" of Psychoanalysis?' *Psychology & Developing Societies* 24, no. 1 (2012): 1–34.

Lee, Ellie, Jennie Bristow, Charlotte Faircloth and Jan Macvarish. *Parenting Culture Studies*. New York, NY: Springer, 2014.

Leinaweaver, Jessaca B. 'On Moving Children: The Social Implications of Andean Child Circulation.' *American Ethnologist* 34, no. 1 (2007): 163–80.

Lesnik-Oberstein, Karin, ed. *Rethinking Disability Theory and Practice: Challenging Essentialism*. Basingstoke: Palgrave Macmillan, 2015.

Lippert, Anne. 'The Sahrawi Refugees: Origins and Organization, 1975–1985'. In *War and Refugees: The Western Sahara Conflict*, edited by Richard Lawless and Laila Monahan. London: Pinter, 1987.

Lister, Ruth. 'Children (But Not Women) First: New Labour, Child Welfare and Gender.' *Critical Social Policy* 26, no. 2 (2006): 315–35.

Lister, Ruth. 'Investing in the Citizen-Workers of the Future: Transformations in Citizenship and the State under New Labour.' *Social Policy and Administration* 37(5) (2003): 427–43.

Little, Michael. *Proof Positive: 'Improving Children's Outcomes Depends on Systemizing Evidence-based Practice...'*. London: Demos (2010). http://www.demos.co.uk/files/Proof_positive_-_web.pdf?1288258385

Loosley, Susan, Derrick Drouillard, Darlene Ritchie and Susan Abercromby. *Groupwork with Children Exposed to Woman Abuse: A Concurrent Group Program for Children and their Mothers. Children's Program Manual*. London, Ontario: The Community Group Program for Children Exposed to Woman Abuse, 2006.

Lopez, Nina. *The Perspective of Caring: Why Mothers and All Carers Should Get a Living Wage for their Caring Work*. London: Global Women's Strike, 2016.

Lupton, Deborah. 'Infant Embodiment and Interembodiment: A Review of Sociocultural Perspectives.' *Childhood* 20, no. 1 (2013): 37–50.

Lutz, Catherine A. and Jane L. Collins. *Reading National Geographic*. Chicago: University of Chicago Press, 1993.

Lykke, Nina. 'Intersectional Analysis: Black Box or Useful Critical Feminist Thinking Technology?' In *Framing Intersectionality: Debates on a Multi-faceted Concept in Gender Studies*, edited by Helma Lutz, Maria Teresa Herrera Vivar and Linda Supik, 207–20 (Farnham: Ashgate, 2011).

Lyon, Eleanor, Jill Bradshaw and Anne Menard. *Meeting Survivors' Needs through Non-residential Domestic Violence Services and Supports: Results of a Multi-state Study*. Washington, DC: National Institute of Justice (2011). https://www.ncjrs.gov/pdffiles1/nij/grants/237328.pdf

Macdonald, Cameron. 'What's Culture Got to Do with It? Mothering Ideologies as Barriers to Gender Equity.' In *Gender Equality: Transforming Family Divisions of Labor*, edited by Janet Gornick and Marcia Meyers, 411–34. London: Verso, 2009.

Mackie, Vera. 'The "Afghan Girls": Media Representations and Frames of War.' *Continuum: Journal of Media & Cultural Studies* 26 (2012): 115–31.

Malaver, Florentino and Jorge Serrano. 'El Instituto Colombiano de Bienestar Familiar, ICBF: un caso de gestión pública. Las paradojas de una evolución incomprendida.' *Revista Innovar Journal*, no. 7 (1996): 27–49.

Malkki, Liisa H. *Purity and Exile: Violence, Memory and National Cosmology Among Hutu Refugees in Tanzania*. London: University of Chicago Press, 1995.

Malkki, Liisa. 'National Geographic: The Rooting of Peoples and the Territorialization of National Identity among Scholars and Refugees'. *Cultural Anthropology* 7, no. 1 (1992): 24–44.

Malkki, Liisa. 'Refugees and Exile: From "Refugee Studies" to the National Order of Things.' *Annual Review of Anthropology*, 24 (1995): 495–523.

Malkki, Liisa. 'Speechless Emissaries: Refugees, Humanitarianism, and Dehistoricization.' *Cultural Anthropology* 11, no. 3 (1996): 377–404.

Maniere, Emma. 'Mapping Feminist Views on Surrogacy.' In *Babies for Sale? Transnational Surrogacy, Human Rights and the Politics of Reproduction*, edited by Miranda Davies, 313–27. London: Zed Books, 2017.

Mayall, Berry. 'Children in Action at Home and School.' In *Children's Childhoods Observed and Experienced*, edited by Berry Mayall, 114–27. London: The Falmer Press, 1994.

Mayall, Berry. *Towards a Sociology for Childhood: Thinking from Children's Lives*. Buckingham: Open University Press, 2002.

Mayall, Berry. *Visionary Women and Visible Children, England 1900-1920: Childhood and the Women's Movement*. London: Palgrave Macmillan, 2017.

McCarthy, Jane Ribbens, Carol-Ann Hooper, and Val Gillies, eds. *Family Troubles: Exploring Changes and Challenges in the Family Lives of Children and Young People*. Bristol: Policy Press, 2013.

McDowell, Linda. 'Debates and Reports: Beyond Patriarchy: A Class Based Explanation of Women's Subordination.' *Antipode* 18, no. 3 (1986): 311–21.

McKeown, Mick, Fiona Jones and Helen Spandler. 'Challenging Austerity Policies: Democratic Alliances Between Survivor Groups and Trade Unions.' *Mental Health Nursing* 33, no. 6 (2013): 26–9.

McNally, David. *Global Slump: The Economics and Politics of Crisis and Resistance*. Oakland, CA: PM Press/Spectre, 2010.

McRobbie, Angela. 'Top Girls: Young Women and the Post-feminist Sexual Contract.' *Journal of Cultural Studies* 41, no. 4–5 (2007): 718–37.

Meekosha, Helen and Russell Shuttleworth. 'What's So "Critical" About Critical Disability Studies?' *Australian Journal of Human Rights* 15, no. 1 (2009): 47–75.

Merck, Mandy and Stella Sanford. Introduction to *Further Adventures of* The Dialectic of Sex: *Critical Essays on Shulamith Firestone*, edited by Mandy Merck and Stella Sandford, 1–8. New York: Palgrave MacMillan, 2010.

Ministerio de Economía. 'Asignación Universal por Hijo.' Nota Técnica Num. 23 Perteneciente al Informe Económico Num. 70, cuarto trimestre. Secretaría de Política Económica, 2009.

Ministerio de Trabajo, Empleo y Seguridad Social, S. de P. T. y E. L. 'Segunda evaluación del Programa Jefes de Hogar. Resultados de la encuesta a beneficiarios'. 2004.

Mizen, Phillip and Yaw Ofosu-Kusi. 'Agency as Vulnerability: Accounting for Children's Movement to the Streets of Accra.' *The Sociological Review* 61, no. 2 (2013): 363–82.

Molyneux, Maxine. 'Mothers at the Service of the New Poverty Agenda: Progresa/Oportunidades Mexico's Conditional Transfer Programme.' *Social Policy & Administration* 40, no. 4 (2006): 425–49.

Molyneux, Maxine. 'The "Neoliberal Turn" and the New Social Policy in Latin America: How Neoliberal, How New?' *Development and Change* 39, no. 5 (2008): 775–97.

Moore, Henrietta L. 'Global Anxieties: Concept-Metaphors and Pre-Theoretical Commitments in Anthropology.' *Anthropological Theory* 4, no. 1 (2004): 71–88.

Morgan, Robin, ed. *Sisterhood is Powerful: An Anthology of Writings from the Women's Liberation Movement*. New York: Vintage Books, 1970.

Morris, Jenny. 'Impairment and Disability: Constructing an Ethics of Care That Promotes Human Rights.' *Hypatia* 16, no. 4 (2001): 1–16.

Morris, Jenny. 'Care of Empowerment? A Disability Rights Perspective.' *Social Policy & Administration* 31, no. 1 (1997): 54–60.

Morrow, Virginia. 'Rethinking Childhood Dependency: Children's Contribution to the Domestic Economy.' *The Sociological Review* 44, no. 1 (1996): 58–77.

Mowles, Chris. *Desk Officer's Report on Trip to the Sahrawi Refugee Camps near Tindouf, Southern Algeria, June 16-21, 1986*. Oxfam. Refugee Studies Centre Grey Literature Collection, University of Oxford, 1986.

Mullender, Audrey. 'Groups for Child Witnesses of Woman Abuse: Learning from North America.' In *Children Living With Domestic Violence: Putting Men's Abuse of Women on the Child Care Agenda*, edited by Audrey Mullender and Rebecca Morley, 187–212. London: Whiting & Birch Ltd., 1994.

Mullender, Audrey, Gill Hague, Umme F. Imam, Liz Kelly, Ellen Malos and Linda Regan. *Children's Perspectives on Domestic Violence*. Thousand Oaks, CA: Sage, 2002.

Mullender, Audrey and Rebecca Morley, eds. *Children Living With Domestic Violence: Putting Men's Abuse of Women on the Child Care Agenda*. London: Whiting & Birch, 1994.

Muncy, Robyn. *Creating a Female Dominion in American Reform 1890-1935*. New York: Oxford University Press, 1991.

Nari, Marcela. *Políticas de Maternidad y Maternalismo Político*. Buenos Aires: Biblos, 2002.

Nash, Jennifer C. 'Re-thinking Intersectionality.' *Feminist Review* 89, no. 1 (2008): 1–15.

Neale, Anne and Nina Lopez. 'Suffer the Little Children and Their Mothers: A Dossier on the Unjust Separation of Children from Their Mothers.' London: Legal Action for Women, Crossroads Women's Centre, 2017.

Newberry, Jan. '"Anything Can Be Used to Stimulate Child Development": Early Childhood Education and Development in Indonesia as a Durable Assemblage.' *Journal of Asian Studies* (in press).

Newberry, Jan. 'Women against Children: Early Childhood Education and the Domestic Community in Post-Suharto Indonesia.' *TRaNS: Trans-Regional and -National Studies of Southeast Asia* 2 (2014): 271–91.

NICE. *Domestic Violence and Abuse [QA116]*. London: NICE (2016). Accessed 21 September 2016. https://www.nice.org.uk/guidance/qs116

NICE. *Review of Interventions to Identify, Prevent, Reduce, and Respond to Domestic Violence*. London: NICE (2013). Accessed 21 September 2016. https://www.nice.org.uk/guidance/ph50/resources/review-of-interventions-to-identify-prevent-reduce-and-respond-to-domestic-violence2

Nieuwenhuys, Olga. *Children's Lifeworlds: Gender, Welfare and Labour in the Developing World*. London and New York: Routledge, 1994.

Nieuwenhuys, Olga. 'Embedding the Global Womb: Global Child Labour and the New Policy Agenda.' *Children's Geographies* 5, no. 1–2 (2007): 149–63.

Niewenhuys, Olga. 'Keep Asking: Why Childhood? Why Children? Why Global?' *Childhood* 17, no. 3 (2010): 291–6.

Nolas, Sevasti-Melissa. 'Towards a New Theory of Practice for Community Health Psychology.' *Journal of Health Psychology* 19, no. 1 (2014): 126–36.

Nolas, Sevasti-Melissa. 'Children's Participation, Childhood Publics and Social Change: A Review.' *Children & Society* 29, no. 2 (2015): 157–67.

Nolas, Sevasti-Melissa, Lucy Neville and Erin Sanders-McDonagh. *Evaluation of the Community Group Programme for Children & Young People: Final Report*. London: AVA (2012). https://core.ac.uk/download/pdf/9551653.pdf

Nordstrom, Carolyn. 'Girls and War Zones: Troubling Questions.' In *Engendering Forced Migration: Theory and Practice*, edited by Doreen Indra, 63–82. New York: Berghahn Books, 1999.

Norwegian Refugee Council. *NRC Reports: Western Sahara. Occupied Country, Displaced People*. Norwegian Refugee Council, 2008.

Oakley, Ann. *From Warfare to Welfare: A Forgotten History of Women Reformers*. Bristol: Policy Press, forthcoming.

Oakley, Ann. 'Women and Children First and Last: Parallels and Differences between Children's and Women's Studies.' In *Children's Childhoods Observed and Experienced*, edited by Berry Mayall, 13–32. London: The Falmer Press, 1994.

Office of the High Commissioner for Human Rights. 'Preventing and Eliminating Child, Early and Forced Marriage.' Report of the Office of the United Nations High Commissioner for Human Rights. April 2014. A/HRC/26/22

Office of the Special Representative of the Secretary on Violence against Children. 2012. 'Protecting Children from Harmful Practices in Plural Legal Systems.' Available at: http://srsg.violenceagainstchildren.org/sites/default/files/publications_final/SRSG_Plan_harmful_practices_report_final.pdf

Oldman, David. 'Childhood as a Mode of Production.' In *Children's Childhoods Observed and Experienced*, edited by Berry Mayall, 153–66. London: The Falmer Press, 1994.

Ortiz, Ligia. 'La Convención de los Derechos del Niño veinte años después.' *Revista Latinoamericana de Ciencias Sociales, Niñez y Juventud* 7, no. 2 (2009): 587–619.

Palacios, Marco. *Entre la legitimidad y la violencia. Colombia, 1875-1994*. Bogotá: Grupo Editorial Norma, 2003.

Pande, Amrita. *Wombs in Labor: Transnational Commercial Surrogacy in India*. New York: Columbia University Press, 2014.

Pankhurst, Alula, Michael Bourdillon, and Gina Crivello. *Children's Work and Labour in East Africa*. Addis Ababa: OSSREA, 2015.

Parrenas, Rhacel Salazar. 'The Reproductive Labour of Migrant Workers.' *Global Networks* 12, no. 2 (2012): 269–75.

Pautassi, Laura. *Beneficios y beneficiarias: análisis del Programa Jefes y Jefas de Hogar Desocupados de Argentina Proyecto Género, Pobreza y Empleo (GPE-OIT) y el Proyecto Enfrentando los Retos del Trabajo Decente en la Crisis Argentina* (Proyecto de Cooperación Técnica OIT-Gobierno de Argentina), Buenos Aires: OIT, 2003.

Perregaux, Christiane. *Femmes sahraouies, femmes du désert*. Paris: L'Harmattan, 1990.

Pollert, Anna. 'Gender and Class Revisited: The Poverty of 'Patriarchy''.' *Sociology* 30, no. 4 (1996), 639–59.

Presidencia de la República de Colombia. *Por nuestros niños. Programas para su protección y desarrollo en Colombia*. Bogotá: Benjamín Villegas, 1990.

Puar, Jasbir K. '"I Would Rather Be a Cyborg Than a Goddess": Becoming-Intersectional in Assemblage Theory.' *PhiloSOPHIA* 2, no. 1 (2012): 49–66.

Punch, Samantha. 'The Generationing of Power: A Comparison of Child-parent and Sibling Relationships in Scotland', in *Sociological Studies of Children and Youth* 10, edited by Loretta Bass (2005): 169–88.

Pupavac, Vanessa. 'Punishing Childhoods: Contradictions in Children's Rights and Global Governance.' *Journal of Intervention and Statebuilding* 5, no. 3 (2011), 285–312.

Purdy, Laura M. 'Does Women's Liberation Imply Children's Liberation?' *Hypatia* 3, no. 2 (1988): 49–62.

Purdy, Laura M. 'Why Children Shouldn't Have Equal Rights.' *The International Journal of Children's Rights* 2 (1994): 223–41.

Puwar, Nirmal and Sanjay Sharma. 'Curating Sociology.' *The Sociological Review* 60, no. 1 suppl (2012): 40–63.

Quinche-Ramírez, Manuel Fernando. *Derecho constitucional colombiano. De la Carta de 1991 y sus reformas*. Bogotá: Ediciones Doctrina y Ley Lta., 2010.

Qvortrup, Jens. 'From Useful to Useful: The Historical Continuity of Children's Constructive Participation.' In *Sociological Studies of Children*, edited by Nancy Mandell and Anne-Marie Ambert, 49–76. Greenwich, CT: JAI Press, 1995.

Radford, Lorraine and Marianne Hester. *Mothering Through Domestic Violence*. London: Jessica Kingsley Publishers, 2006.

Rancière, Jacques. *The Ignorant Schoolmaster*. Translated by Gregory Elliott. Stanford, CA: Stanford University Press, 1991.

Razavi, Shahra. 'The Political and Social Economy of Care in a Development Context. Conceptual Issues, Research Questions, and Policy Options.' *Gender and Development Programme*. Paper Number 3. Geneva: UNRISD, 2007.

Reynolds, Pamela, Olga Nieuwenhuys and Karl Hanson. 'Refractions on Children's Rights in Development Practice. A View from Anthropology.' *Childhood* 13 (2006): 291–302.

Rich, Adrienne. *Of Woman Born: Motherhood as Experience and Institution*. New York: Norton, 1976.

Richards, Sarah. 'HCIA Implementation and the Best Interests of the Child.' In *ISS Working Paper Series* No. 597. The Hague, Netherlands: International Institute of Social Studies of Erasmus University, 2014.

Ridge, Tess. *Childhood Poverty and Social Exclusion: From a Child's Perspective*. Bristol: Policy Press, 2002.

Rikowski, Glenn. 'Alien Life: Marx and the Future of the Human.' *Historical Materialism* 11, no. 2 (2003): 121–64.

Riley, Denise. *War in the Nursery: Theories of the Child and Mother*. London: Virago, 1983.

Roberts, Adrienne. 'Gender, Financial Deepening and the Production of Embodied Finance: Towards a Critical Feminist Analysis.' *Global Society* 29, no. 1 (2015): 107–27.

Robson, Elsbeth, Nicola Ansell, Ulli S. Huber, William T. S. Gould and Lorraine van Blerk. 'Young Caregivers in the Context of the HIV/AIDS Pandemic in Sub-Saharan Africa.' *Population, Space and Place* 12, no. 2 (2006): 93–111.

Robson, Elsbeth. 'Hidden Child Workers: Young Carers in Zimbabwe.' *Antipode* 36, no. 2 (2004): 227–48.

Roelvink, Gerda. 'Rethinking Species-Being in the Anthropocene.' *Rethinking Marxism* 25, no. 1 (2013): 52–69.

Rosen, Rachel. '"The Scream": Meanings and Excesses in Early Childhood Settings.' *Childhood* 22, no. 1 (2015): 39–52.

Rosen, Rachel. 'The Use of the Death Trope in Peer Culture Play: Grounds for Rethinking Children and Childhood?' *International Journal of Play* 4, no. 2 (2015): 163–74.

Rosen, Rachel. 'Time, Temporality, and Woman–Child Relations.' *Children's Geographies* (2016): 1–7.

Rosen, Rachel, Suzanne Baustad and Merryn Edwards. 'The Crisis of Social Reproduction under Global Capitalism: Working Class Women and Children in the Struggle for Universal Childcare.' In *Caring for Children: Social Movements and Public Policy in Canada*, edited by Rachel Langford, Susan Prentice and Patrizia Albanese. Vancouver: UBC Press, 2017.

Roseneil, Sasha and Kaisa Ketokivi. 'Relational Persons and Relational Processes: Developing the Notion of Relationality for the Sociology of Personal Life.' *Sociology* 50, no. 1 (2016): 143–59.

Rotabi, Karen Smith and Nicole F. Bromfield. *From Intercountry Adoption to Global Surrogacy: A Human Rights History and New Fertility Frontiers*. Abingdon: Routledge, 2017.

Rubery, Jill. 'Austerity and the Future for Gender Equality in Europe.' *ILR Review* (2015): DOI 0019793915588892.

Ruddick, Sara. 'Care as Labour and Relationship.' In *Norms and Values: Essays on the Work of Virginia Held*, edited by Joram G. Haber and Mark S. Halfon, 3–25. Oxford: Rowman & Littlefield Publishers, 1998.

Ruddick, Sue. 'At the Horizons of the Subject: Neo-Liberalism, Neo-Conservatism and the Rights of the Child Part One: From 'Knowing' Fetus to 'Confused' Child.' *Gender, Place & Culture* 14, no. 5 (2007): 513–26.

Rummery, Kirstein and Michael Fine. 'Care: A Critical Review of Theory, Policy and Practice.' *Social Policy & Administration* 46, no. 3 (2012): 321–43.

Ruuskanen, Elina and Kauko Aromaa. *Administrative Data Collection on Domestic Violence in Council of Europe Member States*. Strasbourg: Council of Europe (2008). https://www.coe.int/t/dg2/equality/domesticviolencecampaign/Source/EG-VAW-DC(2008)Study_en.pdf

Ryan, Sara and Katherine Runswick-Cole. 'Repositioning Mothers: Mothers, Disabled Children and Disability Studies.' *Disability & Society* 23, no. 3 (2008): 199–210.

Sabbe, Alexia, Marleen Temmerman, Eva Brems and Els Leye. 'Forced Marriage: An Analysis of Legislation and Political Measures in Europe.' *Crime, Law and Social Change* 62 (2014): 171–89.

Sanders-McDonagh, Erin, Lucy Neville and Sevasti-Melissa Nolas. 'From Pillar to Post: Understanding the Victimisation of Women and Children who Experience Domestic Violence in an Age of Austerity.' *Feminist Review* 112, no. 1 (2016): 60–76.

Sayer, Andrew. *Why Things Matter to People: Social Science, Values and Ethical Life*. Cambridge: Cambridge University Press, 2011.

Scheper-Hughes, Nancy. 'Maternal Thinking and the Politics of War'. In *The Women and War Reader*, edited by L. A. Lorentzen and J. Turpin, 227–33. New York: New York University Press, 1998.

Scheper-Hughes, Nancy and Carolyn Sargent. *Small Wars: The Cultural Politics of Childhood*. University of California Press, 1999.

Scherman, Rhoda, Gabriela Misca, Karen Rotabi and Peter Selman. 'Global Commercial Surrogacy and International Adoption: Parallels and Differences.' *Adoption & Fostering* 40, no. 1 (2016): 20–35.

Schwartz-DuPre, Rae Lynn. 'Portraying the Political: National Geographic's 1985 Afghan Girl and a US Alibi for Aid.' *Critical Studies in Media Communication* 27, no. 4 (2010): 336–56.

Segal, Lynne. *Making Trouble: Life and Politics*. London: Serpent's Tail, 2007.

Sevenhuijsen, Selma. *Citizenship and the Ethics of Care. Feminist Considerations on Justice, Morality, and Politics*. London: Routledge, 1998.

Shami, Seteney. 'Transnationalism and Refugee Studies: Rethinking Forced Migration and Identity in the Middle East.' *Journal of Refugee Studies* 9, no. 1 (1996): 3–26.

Shildrick, Tracy and Robert MacDonald. 'Poverty Talk: How People Experiencing Poverty Deny Their Poverty and Why They Blame "the Poor".' *The Sociological Review* 61, no. 2 (2013): 285–303.

Sierra-Pardo, Claudia Patricia. *La organización gremial de las madres comunitarias: un proceso de participación y movilización popular*. Bogotá: Universidad Nacional de Colombia, 1992.

Singh, Renu and Protap Mukherjee. '"Whatever She May Study, She Can't Escape from Washing Dishes": Gender Inequity in Secondary Education – Evidence from a Longitudinal Study in India.' *Compare: A Journal of Comparative and International Education* 7925, no. May (2017): 1–19.

Sircar, Oishik and Debolina Dutta. 'Beyond Compassion: Children of Sex Workers in Kolkata's Sonagachi.' *Childhood* 18, no. 3 (2011): 333–49.

Skott-Myhre, Hans, Veronica Pacini-Ketchabaw and Kathleen Skott-Myhre, eds. *Youth Work, Early Education and Psychology: Liminal Encounters*. Basingstoke: PalgraveMacmillan, 2015.

Skovdal, Morten. 'Examining the Trajectories of Children Providing Care for Adults in Rural Kenya: Implications for Service Delivery.' *Children and Youth Services Review* 33, no. 7 (July 2011): 1262–9.

Smart, Carol. *Regulating Womanhood: Historical Essays on Marriage, Motherhood and Sexuality*. London: Routledge, 1992.

Sontag, Susan. *On Photography*. London: Penguin Books, 1973.

Spivak, Gayatri Chakravorty. 'Can the Subaltern Speak?' In *Marxism and the Interpretation of Culture*, edited by Cary Nelson and Lawrence Grossberg, 271–313. Urbana, IL: University of Illinois Press, 1988.

Stabile, Carol A. and Deepa Kumar. 'Unveiling Imperialism: Media, Gender and the War on Afghanistan.' *Media Culture & Society* 27, no. 5 (2005): 765–82.

Stampini, Marco and Leopoldi Tornarolli. 'The Growth of Conditional Cash Transfers in Latin America and the Caribbean: Did They Go Too Far?' *Inter-American Development Bank Social Sector Social Protection and Health Division Policy Brief* No. Idb-Pb-185 http://idbdocs.iadb.org/wsdocs/getdocument.aspx?docnum=37306295. 2012.

Stanley, Nicky. *Children Experiencing Domestic Violence: A Research Review*. Totnes: RIP (2011). https://www.safeguardingchildrenbarnsley.com/media/15486/domestic_violence_signposts_research_in_practice_-_july_2012.pdf

Stanley, Nicky, Pam Miller, Helen Richardson Foster and Gill Thomson. *Children and Families Experiencing Domestic Violence: Police and Children's Social Services' Responses*. London: NSPCC (2010). https://www.nspcc.org.uk/globalassets/documents/research-reports/children-families-experiencing-domestic-violence-report.pdf

Stephens, Sharon. *Children and the Politics of Culture*. New Jersey: Princeton University Press, 1995.

Stockton, Katherine Bond. *The Queer Child, Or Growing Up Sideways in the Twentieth Century.* Durham and London: Duke University Press, 2010.

Stockton, Kathryn Bond. *Growing Sideways.* Durham: Duke University Press, 2009.

Sudermann, Marlies, Larry Marshall and Susan Loosely. 'Evaluation of the London (Ontario) Community Group Treatment Programme for Children who have Witnessed Woman Abuse.' *Journal of Aggression, Maltreatment & Trauma* 3, no. 1 (2000): 127–46.

Sullivan, Michael, Marcia Egan and Michael Gooch. 'Conjoint Interventions for Adult Victims and Children of Domestic Violence: A Program Evaluation.' *Research on Social Work Practice* 14, no. 3 (2004): 163–70.

Sullivan, Oriel. 'Changing Gender Relations Within the Household: A Theoretical Perspective.' *Gender & Society* 18, no. 2 (2004): 207–23.

Sullivan, Oriel. 'The division of domestic labour: Twenty years of change?' *Sociology* 34, no. 3 (2000): 437–456.

Svanemyr, Joar, Venkatraman Chandra-Mouli, Charlotte Sigurdson Christiansen and Michael Mbizvo. 'Preventing Child Marriages: First International Day of the Girl Child, 'My Life, My right, End Child Marriage.' *Reproductive Health* 9 (2012): 31. Published online. Doi 10.1186/1742-4755-9-31

Switzer, Heather. '(Post) Feminist Development Fables: The Girl Effect and the Production of Sexual Subjects.' *Feminist Theory* 14, no. 3 (2013), 345–60.

Sylvester, Christine. 'Homeless in International Relations? Women's Place in Canonical Texts and Feminist Re-imaginings.' In *Feminism & Politics,* edited by Anne Phillips, 67–92. Oxford & New York: Oxford University Press, 1998.

Tafere, Yisak and Nardos Chuta. 'Gendered Trajectories of Young People through School, Work and Marriage in Ethiopia.' Working Paper No. 155. Oxford: Young Lives, 2016.

Taylor, Affrica. *Reconfiguring the Natures of Childhood.* London: Routledge, 2013.

Teman, Elly. *The Surrogate Body and the Pregnant Self.* Berkeley: University of California Press, 2010.

The British Crime Survey and Police Recorded Crime. London: Home Office (2009). http://webarchive.nationalarchives.gov.uk/20110220105210/rds.homeoffice.gov.uk/rds/pdfs09/hosb1109vol1.pdf

Thompson, Janna. 'Being in Time: Ethics and Temporal Vulnerability.' In *Vulnerability: New Essays in Ethics and Feminist Philosophy,* edited by Catriona Mackenzie, Wendy Rogers and Susan Dodds. Oxford Scholarship Online, 2013.

Thompson, Richard. 'Exploring the Link between Maternal History of Childhood Victimization and Child Risk of Maltreatment.' *Journal of Trauma Practice* 5, no. 2 (2006): 57–72.

Thomson, Rachel, Liam Berriman and Sara Bragg. *Researching Everyday Childhoods: Time, Technology and Documentation.* London: Bloomsbury, forthcoming.

Thomson, Rachel, Mary Jane Kehily, Lucy Hadfield and Sue Sharpe. *Making Modern Mothers.* Bristol: Polity Press, 2011.

Thorne, Barrie. 'Re-Visioning Women and Social Change: Where are the Children?' *Gender & Society* 1, no. 1 (1987): 85–109.

Thornton, Davi Johnson. 'Neuroscience, Affect and the Entrepreneurialization of Motherhood.' *Communication and Critical/Cultural Studies* 8, no. 4 (2011): 399–424.

Tiqqun. *Preliminary Materials for a Theory of the Young-Girl.* Translated by Ariana Reines. Los Angeles: Semiotext(e), 2012.

Tronto, Joan. *Moral Boundaries. A Political Argument for an Ethic of Care.* New York, London: Routledge, 1993.

Twamley, Katherine, Rachel Rosen and Berry Mayall. 'The (Im)Possibilities of Dialogue across Feminism and Childhood Scholarship and Activism.' *Children's Geographies* 15, no. 2 (2017): 249–55.

UK National Health Service (NHS). 'Being a Young Carer – Your Rights.' http://www.nhs.uk/Conditions/social-care-and-support-guide/Pages/young-carers-rights.aspx.

United Nations General Assembly. 'Report of the Special Rapporteur on Contemporary Forms of Slavery, Including its Causes and Consequences, Gulnara Shahinian: Thematic Report on Servile Marriage.' 10 July 2012. http://www.ohchr.org/Documents/HRBodies/HRCouncil/RegularSession/Session21/A-HRC-21-41_en.pdf.

UN Women. 'Prevention of forced and child marriages.' EGM/PVAWG/2012/BP.1 September 2012. http://www.unwomen.org/~/media/Headquarters/Attachments/Sections/CSW/57/EGM/cs557-EGM-prevention-background-paper%20pdf.pdf.

UNFPA. 'Motherhood in Childhood: Facing the challenge of adolescent pregnancy.' UNFPA (2013). https://www.unfpa.org/sites/default/files/pub-pdf/EN-SWOP2013-final.pdf.
UNHCR Operational Portal. 'Refugee Situations. Mediterranean Situation.' http://data.unhcr.org/mediterranean/country.php?id=83
UNHCR Refugee Women and Gender Equality Unit. *A Practical Guide to Empowerment: UNHCR Good Practices on Gender Equality Mainstreaming*, Geneva: UNHCR, 2001.
UNICEF. 'Early Marriage: A Harmful Traditional Practice.' 2005. http://www.unicef.org/publications/files/Early_Marriage_12.lo.pdf
UNICEF. *State of the World's Children Report*. Geneva: UNICEF, 1995.
UNICEF. 'Committing to Child Survival: A Promise Renewed, Progress Report.' Geneva: UNICEF, 2012. http://www.unicef.org/lac/Committing_to_Child_Survival_APR_9_Sept_2013.pdf.
UN General Assembly. 'Resolution 66/140, Calls for an End to Forced Marriage as a "Harmful Traditional Practice".' 2006. http://www.un.org/en/ga/search/view_doc.asp?symbol=%20A/RES/66/140.
Uprichard, Emma. 'Children as "Being and Becomings": Children, Childhood and Temporality.' *Children & Society* 22 (2008): 303–13.
Vidal, D. 'Apre, doux, suave'. *Révolution*, 22 March 1986.
Villalta, Carla and Valeria Llobet. 'Resignificando la protección. Los sistemas de protección de derechos de niños y niñas en Argentina.' *Revista Latinoamericana de Ciencias Sociales, Niñez y Juventud* 13 (2015): 167–80.
Vogel, Lise. 'Domestic Labor Revisited.' *Science & Society* 64, no. 2 (2000): 151–70.
Vogel, Lise. *Marxism and the Oppression of Women: Toward a Unitary Theory*. New Brunswick: Rutgers University Press, 1983.
Volpp, Leti. 'Blaming Culture for Bad Behavior.' *Yale Journal of Law and the Humanities* 12, no. 1 (2000): 89–116.
Vostanis, Panos, V. Tischler, Stuart Cumella and Tina Bellerby. 'Mental Health Problems and Social Supports among Homeless Mothers and Children Victims of Domestic and Community Violence.' *The International Journal of Social Psychiatry* 47, no. 4 (2000): 30–40.
Voutira, Eftihia and Barbara E. Harrell-Bond. '"Successful" Refugee Settlement: Are Past Examples Relevant?' In *Risks and Reconstruction: Experiences of Resettlers and Refugees*, edited by Michael M. Cernea and Chris McDowell, 56–76. Washington, DC: World Bank, 2000.
Wajcman, Judy. 'Life in the Fast Lane? Towards a Sociology of Technology and Time.' *British Journal of Sociology* 50, no. 1 (2008): 59–77.
Walkerdine, Valerie and Helen Lucey. *Democracy in the Kitchen: Regulating Mothers and Socialising Daughters*. London: Virago, 1989.
Wall, John. 'Childism: The Challenge of Childhood to Ethics and the Humanities.' In *The Children's Table: Childhood Studies and the New Humanities*, edited by Anna Mae Duane, 68–84. Athens, GA: University of Georgia Press, 2013.
Wall, John. *Ethics in Light of Childhood*. Washington, DC: Georgetown University Press, 2010.
Weisner, Thomas S. and Ronald Gallimore. 'My Brother's Keeper: Child and Sibling Caretaking.' *Current Anthropology* 18, no. 2 (1977): 169–90
WFP. *Protracted Relief and Recovery Operation – Algeria 6234.00*. World Food Programme, 2000.
WFP. *Protracted Relief and Recovery Operation - Algeria 10172.0*. World Food Programme, 2002.
WFP. *Protracted Relief and Recovery Operation - Algeria 10172.1*. World Food Programme, 2004.
Widom, Cathy Spatz, Sally J. Czaja and Kimberly A. DuMont. 'Intergenerational Transmission of Child Abuse and Neglect: Real or Detection Bias?' *Science* 347, no. 6229 (2015): 1480–5.
Wilcox, Steve. *Housing Benefit Size Criteria: Impacts for Social Sector Tenants and Options for Reform*. York: Joseph Rowntree Foundation, 2014.
Williams, Fiona. 'In and beyond New Labour: Towards a New Political Ethics of Care.' *Critical Social Policy* 21, no. 4 (2001): 467–93.
Winnicott, Donald Woods. 'The Theory of the Parenting Relationship.' In *The Maturational Processes and the Facilitating Environment: Studies in the Theory of Emotional Development*, 37–55. London: Hogarth Press, 1965.
Winter, Laura, Erica Burman, Terry Hanley, Afroditi Kalambouka and Lauren McCoy. 'Education, Welfare Reform and Psychological Well-being: A Critical Psychology Perspective.' *British Journal of Educational Studies*, **DOI:** 10.1080/00071005.2016.1171823 (2016).

Women Living Under Muslim Laws. *Child, Early and Forced Marriage: A Multi-Country Study. A Submission to the UN Office of the High Commissioner on Human Rights (OCHCR)*. December 2013. http://www.wluml.org/sites/wluml.org/files/UN%20report%20final.pdf

Women's Aid. *Domestic Abuse is a Gendered Crime*. Bristol, UK: Women's Aid (2016). https://www.womensaid.org.uk/information-support/what-is-domestic-abuse/domestic-abuse-is-a-gendered-crime/

Women's Aid. *SOS: Save Refuges, Save Lives*. Bristol, UK: Women's Aid (2015). https://1q7dqy2unor827bqjls0c4rn-wpengine.netdna-ssl.com/wp-content/uploads/2015/11/SOS_Data_Report.pdf

Woodhead, Martin. 'Psychology and the Cultural Construction of Children's Needs.' In *Constructing and Reconstructing Childhood: Contemporary Issues in the Sociological Study of Childhood*, edited by Allison James and Alan Prout, 63–84. London: Falmer, 1997.

Wynn Davies, Merryl, Ashis Nandy and Ziauddin Sardar. *Barbaric Others: A Manifesto on Western Racism*. London: Pluto Press, 1993.

Yuval-Davis, Nira. *Gender and Nation*, London: Sage, 1997.

Zehavi, Ohad. 'Minoracy.' Translated by Nick John and Natalie Melzer. *Mafte'akh: Lexical Review of Political Thought*, 1st ed. (2010): 37–49.

Zelizer, Viviana. *Pricing the Priceless Child. The Changing Social Value of Children*. New York: Basic Books, 1985.

Zelizer, Viviana A. 'Risky Exchanges.' In *Baby Markets: Money and the New Politics of Creating Families*, edited by Michele B. Goodwin, 267–77. Cambridge: Cambridge University Press, 2010.

Index

accumulation, 8, 68, 124, 127, 133, 160
activism, arts and culture-based, 83–9, 193
adoption, 157, 160–2, 163, 167, 168
adulting, 79
adultism or adultist, 4, 14, 133, 161
advocacy, 54, 56–7, 87, 232, 235
age
   ages and stages, 4, 143, 246
   and gender, 230, 253
   and vulnerability, 149
   chronological, 35, 140
   hierarchies, 151, 179, 187, 237, 242–5, 257
   social, 146, 206, 147–9, 214
agency
   and childhood, 142, 143, 233
   and constraints, 151, 159, 212
   and gender, 259
   and inequalities, 151, 203, 205, 207
   and vulnerability, 146, 150, 151
Ahmed, Sara, 3, 204
Algeria, 8, 91
Amnesty International, 260
Amra Padatik, 5, 85
anti-categorical, 13
anxiety, 31, 230, 233
Argentina, 7–8, 176, 177–8
armed conflict, *see* violence; war
attachment, 35, 67, 78
austerity, 12, 32, 47, 109, 181, 234
autonomy
   and liberal/individualist ideal, 9, 10, 16, 28, 69
   and maternalist welfare policy, 173, 187
   and parenting, 31–2
   and surrogacy, 159
   children as a constraint, 172, 186, 188
   intimate, 236
   see also conceptual autonomy

Balagopalan, Sarada 211
becoming
   becoming-child, 251–2
   becoming-girl, 14, 253
   becoming-woman, 251
   children as development becomings, 69, 206, 210, 213, 249–50, 252
   minoritarian politics of, 14, 250–3
   and deleuze, 74
bedroom tax, 24, 29, 32, 35–6
binaries, 152, 237
   academic-activist, 5
   and psychosocial studies, 26

child-adult, 204
feminism-childhood studies, 4, 24
gender, 71, 233
good-bad mother, 32
in analysis of domestic violence, 232
West-global South, 203
woman-child, 12–13, 14, 36
birth, 68, 123, 125–6, 137
   and reproductive technologies, 155–6, 157, 161, 163
   children's views, 161, 166
Blackfoot, 191–7
body, 26, 123, 247
   and care, 141
   and decolonisation, 192
   docile, 237
   polymorphous, 249
   children's, 28, 140, 159, 248, 51
   commodification of, 155, 159–60, 163
   women's, 76, 155
Boltanski, Luc, 213
boy child, 101, 146–9, 154, 220, 230–1, 233, 246, 249
Burman, Erica, 1, 3, 7, 11, 211, 228, 235
Butler, Judith, 248

Calais, *see* refugee camps
campaigns, political, 135–7, 209, 215, 260
Canada, 40, 124–5, 129, 191–2, 197, 214–6, 226, 238
care
   across life course, 127–8, 133, 140–1, 149–51, 232
   and gendered responsibilities, 1, 29, 32, 50, 58, 129, 135, 139, 173, 186, 192, 220
   as basis of movement building, 47, 49, 135–6, 138, 257
   as burden, 17, 43, 136, 139, 172
   as unacknowledged labour, 135
   by 'child carers', 120–1, 143–4, 146–9, 179, 259
   children as objects of, 2, 4, 53–4, 120, 136, 142
   circulations, 145
   class and, 29–30, 40, 47, 123, 126–7, 179–82
   for the world, 196
   labour, 15, 48, 119, 120, 122–3, 128, 165, 183, 186–65, 183, 186
   privatisation, 120, 185
   see also ethics of care

child as trope/symbol of
  child first, 51–2
  deserving, 10, 47
  for the future, 68, 127
  futurity, 68, 71–2, 120
  innocence, 3, 31, 84, 118, 126
  victim, 3, 10, 13, 98
child carer, *see* care, by 'child carers'
child marriage, *see* forced marriage
child–mother relationship, 15, 17, 33, 66, 69, 79–80, 125, 128, 130, 146, 149, 174, 188, 218
  Reproductive technology and, 155, 157, 158, 160, 165
child protection, 51–4, 64, 126, 137, 176, 187
childcare, *see* early childhood education and care
childhood studies, 3–4, 16, 25, 28, 66–7, 70, 76, 122, 126, 151–2, 161, 167–8
childing, 79
childism, 4, 16, 18
  'waves', 249
children/childhood,
  as analytic category, 69–70, 237, 253
  as citizens, *see* citizenship
  as dependent, 1, 10, 15, 67, 98, 126, 130, 203, 207
  as political actors, 18, 47, 85, 86, 258
  embodied experience, 27, 66, 119, 122–3, 202
  investing in, 24, 125, 127, 173 *see also* child as trope/symbol of the future
  naturalisation of, 133, 155, 166, 205, 243
  'non-normative', 120
  norms, 27, 28, 68, 106, 123, 126, 146
  regulation of, 8, 26, 67
children's contribution to household labour/survival/finances, 61, 119, 120–1, 127, 128, 133, 143, 145, 148–50
'children's rights', *see* rights
citizenship, 35, 86, 158, 168, 173, 216
class, *see* social class
coercion, 32, 86, 206, 212
  economic, 159
Colombia, 8, 51
colonialism
  and personhood, 67
  colonial assumptions, 27
  discursive, 156
  impact on communities 192
  occupation, 94–5
  settler colonialism, 191–3
  violence and, 196
community, 35, 207
  involvement in childrearing, 193
  organising, 17, 19, 40, 54
conceptual autonomy, 14–15, 67, 69, 71, 80, 132
consent, 74, 206, 214
constructions of childhood, femininity, *see* representations
crisis
  children's care work as response to, 143
  for refugees, 94, 109
  financial, 52, 109, 177
  humanitarian, 211
  political, 53
critical disability studies, 28, 33–4

day-care, *see* early childhood education and care
De beauvoir, Simone, 100, 255
decolonisation, 7, 94, 192–3
decontextualisation, 209, 212
Deleuze, Gilles, 14, 27, 245, 247–53
democracy, 93, 95, 99, 106, 117
dependency
  and care ethics, 69, 141–2
  children's economic, 242
  conceptual, 204, 213
  generational, 149, 150, 151, 180
  see also vulnerability
  on aid, 96
  on state welfare, 29, 57, 130
  women constructed as dependent, 98
  see also interdependency
development,
  gender and development, 172
  child, 28, 67, 77, 125, 143, 178, 192, 214, 218–9, 220
  of the nation, 50
dialogue,
  across feminism and childhood, 2–3, 8, 11, 89, 156, 227
  between childhood and maternal studies, 66–7
  between academic and public, 4–5, 18
  between state and civil society, 54
dichotomies, *see* binaries
disability, 33, 34, 143, 153
  see also critical disability studies
division of labour
  gendered, 121, 125–6, 139
  generational, 120, 126
  global, 125, 130
domestic abuse, *see* violence
domestic violence, *see* violence
domestic work/domestic workers, 40, 117–8, 120, 122, 129, 130
  see also global care chains
domination
  male, 98, 242, 249, 251
  colonial *see* colonialism

early childhood education and care (ecec), 8, 15, 41, 43, 47–9, 51–2, 120, 124–8, 131, 132, 182
  campaigns for publicly funded, 2, 41, 43–7
Edelman, Lee, 68
education,
  achievement, 119
  anti-sexist, 8, 218–9
  further education, 104
  higher education, 148
  schooling, 13, 127, 131, 133, 148, 245
  system as oppressive, 242–3
  transnational, 100
  unschooling, 243–6
  see also early childhood education and care
emergence, *see* becoming
emotions
  and violence, 229, 233
  as critical knowledge, 257
  emotional health, 207
  political action and, 211

empowerment, 91, 92, 97, 105, 112, 162, 213, 218
Engels, Friedrich, 242
Enloe, Cynthia, 1
essentialisation of
　the self, 10
　woman/child, 35, 98, 201, 228, 233
essentialism, challenging, 28, 142, 236
ethics of care, 141–2
Ethiopia, 144, 145, 146, 148, 154, 214
eurocentrism
　and notions of childhood, 4, 201, 205, 208, 210, 211
　and social theory, 6
exploitation
　children of sex workers and, 84
　intersectionality and, 15
　Marx and, 120, 134
　of women's and children's labour, 25, 43, 48, 119, 120, 143, 181, 186
　of working-class, 47, 48
　patriarchy and, 242
　surrogacy and, 155, 159, 160, 163, 164, 167
　women-child relations and, 10

family
　as site of oppression, 1
　dynamic, 30
　extended, 35, 61, 76, 100, 104, 143, 166, 191, 193
　nuclear, 56, 164, 166, 191, 193–4, 196, 246–7
　siblings, 33, 35, 74, 104, 128, 130, 145–46, 149, 166, 179, 183, 259
fathers, fatherhood
　Reproductive technology and, 167
　child custody and, 136–7
　'cycle of violence' and, 230, 233
　engaging, 196, 222, 223
　forced marriage and, 207
　Freud and, 246–7
　housing policies and, 39
feminism
　abolitionist, 84
　as elite, 16
　black feminism, 25
　Marxist, 25, 120, 131
　post-colonial, 19, 67, 86
　pro-sex work, 84, 88–9
　second-wave, 67, 69
foetus, 11, 125, 161, 164
financial
　insecurity, 35, 56, 82, 173
　stability, 179, 183
　crisis, 52, 177
Firestone, Shulamith, 204, 241–9, 254, 256
food
　and nutrition, 52, 60
　deprivation, 32–3, 150
　provision, 59, 109
　regulations, 61, 63
forced marriage, definition of, 214
foster care, 192
Foucault, Michel, 27, 132, 244
France, 109, 158
Freud, Sigmund, 246–7

gender
　-blind, 101
　gendered childhoods, 4, 25, 106, 146, 230
　mainstreaming, 91, 97
　quotas, 259
　studies, 16, 19 *see also* women's studies
generational
　inequalities, 1, 106, 254
　positions, 1, 27, 67
　relations, 27, 34, 67, 72–3, 124, 129, 140–1, 145, 149–51, 257
generationing, 4
　see childing, adulting
girl
　differential treatment, 25, 103–4
　girlhood, 4, 104, 205, 206–7, 208, 210, 211–3
　invisible, 91, 100, 103, 105, 210–13
　see also visibility
　refugee, 8, 91–2
global care chains, 125, 130
global inequalities, 155, 160, 202, 205, 213
Global Women's Strike, 136, 138
grandparent care, 191, 194
Guattari, Felix, 247–53, 256

heteronormativity, 166, 225, 235
heterosexism, 164, 166
homelessness, 35
honour, 207
housing benefits, *see* welfare, benefits
human capital development, *see* children, investing in
human rights *see* rights
humanitarian aid, 91–2, 99, 105–6, 112, 212

identities,
　binaries, 32
　fixing, inscribing, 35, 212, 233
　indigenous, 192–3
　learning, 220
　multiple, 231–2
　politics of, 25–6
　public, 186
　relational, 69
　social, 25–6, 78, 81, 162
Illich, Ivan, 244–5
IMF (International Monetary Fund), 160
imperialism, 42, 204, 216
India, 144, 146, 148, 154, 157, 159, 160, 164, 169, 214, 215
indigenous
　knowledge, 192
　people, 7, 40, 191–2, 193
　politics, 260
　practices, 194
individualisation, 10, 13, 31, 151, 209
Indonesia, 117–9, 218
infantilisation, 203, 245
interdependency, 28, 33, 50, 64, 67, 123, 129, 142, 194
intersubjectivity, 80
intergenerational contract, 149
interpellation, 10, 33, 38, 248, 249
intersectionality, 3, 15, 24, 25–6, 30–1, 34, 151, 237

justice
  childcare and, 220
  ethic of, 142
  means to achieve, 15–8

Katz, Cindi, 7, 120
Kittay, Eva Feder, 142
knowledge
  emancipatory/world-changing, 6, 19
  indigenous, 192
  knowing/not-knowing, 205
  stratification, 6, 7

labour
  care, *see* care labour
  emotional, 31–2, 36, 165
  low-paid, 2, 43, 55, 57, 58, 76, 131
  power, 120, 127, 128, 131, 134–5
  rights, 56, 64
  voluntary, 2, 15, 55, 56, 117, 118, 120, 128, 131
  see also Wages for Housework Campaign; wages
labour power, 120, 127–31, 134–5
Latin America, 52, 58, 172, 174
liberal rights discourse, *see* rights
life course
  of individuals, 12, 140, 141, 144, 146–9, 151, 159, 168
  of policy, 24
love, 10, 35, 119, 122, 129, 138, 145

Malkki, Liisa, 98, 100
marginalisation
  common to women and children, 23
  of children, 105–6, 142, 247
  of women, 106
marriage, 148, 150
  see also forced marriage
Marxism, 25, 120, 121–2, 124, 134, 241–2, 254
masculinism, 27
material culture, 74, 78
maternal mortality, 218
maternal studies, 15, 66–7, 70–2, 79–80
maternal/ism, 8, 71, 80, 126
  and welfare policy, 173–4, 187–8
men
  absent, 96–7
  and children dyad, 1
  anti-sexist education and, 220–2
  domestic/care work and, 134, 135, 142, 191, 220
  emancipation of children and, 243
  experiencing domestic violence, 225–6, 236
  relinquishing privilege, 14
  see also cycle of violence; becoming
mental health, 33, 143, 149, 234
methodology
  case study, 51, 72–3, 76, 93, 187, 226
  community-based research, 117
  ethnography, 51, 58, 73, 92, 164
  evaluation, 229, 233
  longitudinal, 77, 140, 144
  participatory, 86
  survey, 144, 229
Mexico, 157, 159, 164, 177, 259
migration

  internal, 78
  international, 17, 109, 112, 118, 235
  see also global care chains, refugee camps
minoritarian politics, *see* becoming
Mohanty, Chandra, 205
Mother's Day, 41, 44, 46, 48
motherhood, 73–4, 136, 138
  and 'good enough' mother, 32
  and class, 117, 169, 182
  and entrepreneurial mothering, 32
  and exploitation, 119, 128
  and intensive mother, 31
  and mother-child relations, 11, 15, 17, 27, 30–1, 34, 36, 42, 68–70, 72–3, 79–80, 89, 111, 130, 137, 160, 162, 164–6, 225, 228, 256
  and national development, 68
  and social policy, 51–2, 55–6, 172–5, 187–8
  as site of resistance, 30, 32, 43, 85, 186–7
  biological, 157
  naturalisation of, 125–6, 142, 155, 185, 192–3, 209
  regulation of, 30, 31–2, 47, 117, 136–7, 182–4, 228
  status of, 30, 174
  stigma/judgement of, 29, 102–5, 180–2, 185–6, 188, 229
  surrogate, 156–8, 161, 167–8
movements, social and political, 4–6, 9, 18, 19, 252
  and solidarity, 13
  anti-colonial, 94–5
  anti-imperialist, 47
  anti-poverty, 41
  children's, 16–7, 19, 227, 257–60
  minoritarian, 249, 256
  of community mothers, 56–8
  of sex workers, 84–5
  socialist, 94, 134
  women's, 16–17, 47, 135, 137–8, 227, 232, 237, 259
  see also campaigns, political

naturalisation, *see* children/childhood, motherhood
needs
  and adoption, 168
  as familised, 12
  as site of tension in woman-child relations, 72–3, 91, 103–4, 119, 128, 129–30
  as unequally distributed, 11, 78, 100, 127, 129, 236
  'children's', 15, 67, 105, 123, 126, 173, 185, 226, 236
  differentiated, 123, 227
  embodied, 11, 111, 120, 122, 122–4, 136, 145, 183, 232
  for childcare, 47, 118, 125, 192
  outlawed, 124–5
neoliberal
  critiques, 260
  regimes, 35, 47, 166, 174, 184
  responsibility, 31, 188
  restructuring, 120, 131, 234
  subjects, 34, 165, 205
Nepal, 157, 159, 214
Nieuwenhuys, Olga, 25, 211

norms
    and normalisation, 26, 35, 121
    and refugees, 98–9, 105, 106
    challenges to, 250
    developmental, 2, 27, 28, 68, 123, 126
    gender, 8, 106, 146, 183, 248
    heteronormative, 155, 164, 166
    legal, 54
    religious, cultural and social, 8, 12, 13, 19, 31, 102, 105, 176–7, 181
North America, 159, 208, 238
nursery care, *see* early childhood education and care

objectification of children, 15
Oedipal Complex, 246–7, 253
oppression, 1, 25, 202, 237
    of children, 2, 16, 241–3, 248
    of indigenous people, 191
    of women and children, 47–8
    of women, 17, 68, 120, 139, 141, 248, 255
    struggles against, 10
othering, 26, 66, 69

parenting culture, 234
parenting skills, 31, 184, 209
paternalism, 203, 207, 209
patriarchal bargain, 188
patriarchal culture, 242, 248–9, 251
    and state policies, 130, 186, 188
    and the family, 155, 166, 167
    and violence, 226
    as grounds for relations between women and children, 11, 14
    colonial impositions of, 7, 192–3
    indigenous variations of, 8, 83, 208
    transforming, 220
peace and reconciliation, 53
pedagogy, myth of, 245
performativity, 31, 32, 38, 174, 181–2, 184, 243, 247–9, 251–2
perpetrator programmes, 235, 236, 240
Peru, 16, 144, 145, 148, 149, 154, 257, 260
Polisario Front, 94–5, 99, 105, 107
politics of pity, 8, 211–12
political organising, 15, 17, 19, 40, 47, 56, 137, 257
    see also campaigns, political
poverty
    'child', 47, 53, 140, 222
    and 'choice', 159, 164, 188
    and disability, 33–4
    and early marriage, 209
    and geographic segregation, 52
    and policy, 33, 172–4, 177–8
    and shame, 32
    feminisation of, 23
    impacts of, 36, 129–30, 141, 145, 149, 151, 155, 159, 163, 169, 173, 182, 183
power relations
    and 'giving' voice, 203
    and the family, 247
    as asymmetric and intersectional, 1, 89, 122, 135, 137, 202, 207, 209, 236
    as more than difference, 25
    as repressive, 136
    between adults and children, 3, 15, 138, 245, 246
    between women, 187
    global, 203
    political and institutional, 27, 98, 102, 156
    transforming, 14, 19, 137, 250–1
precarity, 11, 17, 185, 122–3, 206, 230, 233
pregnancy, 69, 76, 104
    surrogacy and, 157–8, 160, 162, 165–6, 256
private/public divide, 1–3, 120, 159–60, 166–7, 175–6, 185–6, 259
prostitution, 84, 89, 159–60 *see also* sex work
psychoanalytic theory, 11, 12, 26–7, 32–3, 69, 71, 79–80, 237, 247
publics, 3, 4–6, 18, 19, 80, 83, 227

queer theory, 28, 68

racialisation and racism, 37, 38, 67, 81, 130, 216
recognition, social, 15, 56, 135, 142, 174, 175, 184, 186, 188
Redstockings Manifesto, 256
refuge, 13, 227, 232, 235
refugee camps
    Calais refugee camp, 17, 109–12
    Sahrawi refugee camps, 8, 13, 95–7, 105–6
reification, of social categories, 17–18, 20, 26, 236
relationality
    and audience-subject relations, 203, 210
        see also representations
    and capitalist social relations, 128, 129, 134–5, 253
    and care, 136, 140–1, 145
    and commitments to others, 32–3, 36, 118–9, 143–4
    and constitution of subject positions, 30, 35, 67, 69, 72
    and dependency, 142
    and domestic violence, 227–8, 233, 234–7
    and human-non-human relations, 194
    and indigenous–settler relations, 192
    and labour relations, 121–2
    and marketisation, 155, 160
    and need, 123
    and political projects, 16–17, 36, 257
    and selfhood, 69
    and surrogacy, 167–9
    and temporality, 129, 140, 165
    and vulnerability, 149
    and women-child relations, 125–6, 131, 133, 162, 165, 187–8, 226–7
    as a conceptual lens, 9–12
    as stratified, 174–5
    concept-metaphors of, 14–15, 80
    of entities, 72–3, 79–80, 204
    see also power relations; generational relations; family
relatives, *see* family
representations,
    and affect, 26, 211
    of 'woman and child', 1
    politics of, 26, 105–6, 202, 203, 211–13
    strategies of, 91–2, 99–100, 203–4, 214
    see also 'speaking for' other; social construction; subjects
reproductive labour, *see* social reproduction
reproductive technologies, assisted, 125, 155, 160, 189 *see also* pregnancy; surrogacy

rescue rhetoric, 83, 203–4, 211, 212
residential schools, 192
responsibility
  and men, 135
  collective, 43, 48–9, 125, 191, 196
  gendered, 1, 10, 17, 34, 39, 50, 95, 104–5, 108, 126, 129, 135, 181, 185, 193
  neoliberal, 31, 36, 188
  socio-political, 28, 126, 149, 175, 180, 187, 227
  to others, 13, 36, 118, 142, 233
rights
  children's, 23, 51, 52, 54, 63–4, 70, 84–6, 138, 155, 163–4, 167–8, 172, 206, 218, 227, 257, 260
  human, 54–5, 65, 83–4, 112, 172, 211–12, 216, 244
  liberal, 14, 24, 69, 142, 241
  tensions between women's and children's rights, 8, 141, 151–2, 174, 186–7
  to self-determination, 92
  women's, 24, 41, 51, 55–6, 57, 58, 63–4, 95, 106, 159, 206, 218, 235, 259–60

Scheper-Hughes, Nancy, 202
school as incarceration, 244–5 *see also* education
separability, 11, 35–6, 72
sex work/ers, 5, 83–6, 89, 137
  see also prostitution
sexuality, 15, 125, 166, 207, 222, 225, 230, 235, 246, 260
shelter, *see* refuge
siblings, *see* family
slavery, 7, 67, 206, 215
social class
  'class' analysis of gender and generation, 242, 249, 254
  class privilege, 67, 129–30, 242
  class relations, 126–7, 132, 135, 159
  classed ideologies, 4, 29, 67, 123, 181, 182, 185, 188
  dominant classes, 126–7
  impacts of class system, 38, 40, 123, 130, 169
  working class, 36, 40, 47, 135, 260
  see also solidarity
social construction
  of childhood, 70, 140, 143, 188, 249, 260
  of gender, 188, 226, 249
social and economic justice
  and feminist activism, 219–20, 224
  and interdependency/relationality, 64, 141, 169
  and school achievement, 119
  as a political project, 8, 11, 18, 137
social investment state, 24, 125
social reproduction
  and men, 132
  and outsourcing, 159
  and surrogacy, 159–60
  and the division of domestic responsibilities, 108, 144
  and time, 130–1
  and voluntary labour, 118
  and women-child relations, 12–3, 120–1, 124–8

feminist analysis of, 3, 43, 47, 156, 172
stratified, 129
social services, 48, 117 *see also* welfare, benefits
socially necessary labour, 120–1, 125–6
solidarity
  and state policy, 53, 184
  class and gender, 33, 36
  conditional, 8, 105–6, 204
  with 'refugee women', 97, 99–100, 109, 112
  generational, 6, 242–3
  liberal, 13
'speaking for' others, 29, 203
species-being, 50, 121–4, 129, 132, 141
Spivak, Gayatri, 81, 203
strategic essentialism, 68, 81
struggle-in-relation, 36, 228, 233–4
subject position
  agentic, 84 *see also* agency
  and commonalities across 'woman' and 'child' positions, 3, 4, 17, 23, 67–8, 202, 237, 251
  and masculine subject as violent perpetrator, 226, 233
  and the good parent/good mother, 1, 31, 33
  child, 1, 10, 67, 69, 123, 180, 230, 245, 249
  dismantling, 14, 204, 251–3
  liberal, 9, 11, 33, 69, 121, 232
  maternal, 67, 78
  non-western, 156
  privileged subjects, 14, 127, 173
  relational, 77, 79
  representations of, 83–4, 86–8, 203, 208, 211–12
  women as mothers, 143
  see also neoliberal; victim status
subordination
  and links between women and children, 15, 130, 248
  as idealised position, 26
  of children, 3, 245, 247
  of girls, 253, 255
  of global south, 203
  of women, 57, 64, 119, 120, 173, 186
surrogacy
  and commissioning parents, 159
  and global inequities, 15, 163, 164–5
  and heterosexuality, 166–7
  and marketisation, 159, 165
  and surrogate-born children, 158, 161, 165, 166–8
  ethical implications of, 160–1, 163
  gestational surrogacy, 157
  international commercial (ics), 155, 157–8
  traditional, 156
  see also pregnancy
surveillance
  of parents, 34
  of red light district in Kolkata, 89

teacher training, 220
temporality
  and accumulation, 15, 126–9, 131
  and maternity, 68, 80, 165
  and norms, 68
  and relationships, 15

and space, 132
and temporal lag, 15, 127, 130
and vulnerabilities, 12, 140, 151–2
see also child as trope/symbol of
Thailand, 157, 159
Thorne, Barrie, 23, 67, 69, 253
Tronto, Joan, 141, 142
truth and reconciliation, 193

UN Convention on the Rights of the Child (CRC), 50, 64, 70, 206, 229, 235
union
 labour, 56, 258
 National Union of Sahrawi women, 94, 96, 99, 106, 108
United Kingdom, 29, 70, 109, 139, 143, 153, 158, 214, 226, 227, 228, 235
United Nations (UN), 57, 64, 202, 206, 214
United States, 53, 139, 157, 164, 214, 216
unschooling/deschooling, 243–4

value
 of representations, 210
 sentimental, 176
 surplus value, 15, 122, 124, 127–31, 133, 258
 unrecognised, 135, 137, 143, 165, 259
values
 moral and social, 54, 83, 99, 135, 141–2, 156, 175, 180–2, 187, 192, 194–6, 235
 normative, 15, 118
 political, 53
victim status
 inscription of children and women with, 3, 13, 202–3
 and refugees, 98–9, 105
 critiques of, 10

and the child, 209, 216
and early marriage, 211–12
and domestic violence, 225, 227, 232, 236–7
Vietnam, 144, 148, 149, 154
violence, 223
 against sex workers, 86
 colonial, 191–3
 domestic, 13, 136, 225–6
 epistemic, 250
 family violence programmes, 226–8, 232–3
 gender-based, 92, 178, 202, 206, 210, 216, 226, 236, 260
 political, 53, 58, 94–5
 rape and sexual assault, 111, 123
visibility, 91, 93, 100–1, 103, 105–106, 135, 172, 182, 202, 208, 210–3, 242, 259
Vogel, Lise, 124
volunteers, 2, 15, 55–6, 110, 117–8, 120, 128, 225
vulnerability, 10–2, 15, 105, 118, 123, 126, 140, 142–3, 149, 151, 233

wages, 2, 43, 48, 112, 118, 120, 124, 126, 130–1, 137, 139, 143, 145, 183, 258
Wages for Housework Campaign, 135–6
war, 41, 48, 96, 97–8, 109, 135, 137, 203, 206, 208, 211
weaning, 15, 72, 79–80
welfare, benefits, 24, 29, 34, 118, 120, 173, 187–8, 234
women 'versus' children, 1, 8, 64, 119, 102, 139, 173, 228, 204, 230
women's movement, *see* movements, social and political
women's studies, 3–4, 16, 19, 20, 70, 169
women and children, 1–2, 8, 13, 17, 98, 228
working children, 16, 257–60
World Bank, 53, 119, 160

www.ingramcontent.com/pod-product-compliance
Lightning Source LLC
LaVergne TN
LVHW050007140426
836100LV00010B/52